DAVE PELZER

The complete texts of

A MAN NAMED DAVE

and

HELP YOURSELF

A PLUME BOOK

PLUME
Published by the Penguin Group
Penguin Group (USA) Inc., 375 Hudson Street, New York,
New York 10014, U.S.A.
Penguin Group (Canada), 90 Eglinton Avenue East, Suite 700, Toronto,
Ontario, Canada M4P 2Y3 (a division of Pearson Penguin Canada Inc.)
Penguin Books Ltd., 80 Strand, London WCR2 0RL, England
Penguin Ireland, 25 St. Stephen's Green, Dublin 2, Ireland
(a division of Penguin Books Ltd.)
Penguin Books Australia Ltd., 250 Camberwell Road, Camberwell,
Victoria 3124, Australia (a division of Pearson Australia Group Pty Ltd.)
Penguin Books India Pvt Ltd., 11 Community Centre,
Panchsheel Park, New Delhi – 110 017, India
Penguin Group (NZ), Cnr Airborne and Rosedale Roads, Albany,
Auckland 1310, New Zealand (a division of Pearson New Zealand Ltd)
Penguin Books (South Africa) (Pty) Ltd., 24 Sturdee Avenue,
Rosebank, Johannesburg 2196, South Africa

Penguin Books Ltd., Registered Offices:
80 Strand, London WC2R 0RL, England

Published by Plume, a member of Penguin Group (USA) Inc.
Previously published as Dutton editions.

Previously published as *A Man Named Dave*,
copyright © 1999 by Dave Pelzer and *Help Yourself*,
copyright © 2000 by Dave Pelzer
All rights reserved.

 REGISTERED TRADEMARK—MARCA REGISTRADA

Library of Congress Cataloging-in-Publication Data available

Special Markets ISBN 0-452-28827-4

Printed in the United States of America

1   3   5   7   9   10   8   6   4   2

BOOKS ARE AVAILABLE AT QUANTITY DISCOUNTS WHEN USED TO PROMOTE PRODUCTS
OR SERVICES. FOR MORE INFORMATION PLEASE WRITE TO PREMIUM MARKETING DIVISION,
PENGUIN GROUP (USA) INC., 375 HUDSON STREET, NEW YORK, NEW YORK, 10014.

CONTENTS

A MAN NAMED DAVE

ACKNOWLEDGMENTS		xi
AUTHOR'S NOTE		xiii
1.	The End	1
2.	Fly Away	24
3.	Letter from Home	38
4.	Wishful Thinking	54
5.	Slip Away	69
6.	Regroup	99
7.	Foolish Crusade	114
8.	Changes	134
9.	Heaven Sent	163
10.	The Source	174
11.	A Personal Matter	189
12.	The Long Farewell	199
13.	The Last Dance	214
14.	Resolve	229
15.	All Good Things	253
EPILOGUE		265

PERSPECTIVES   Dave   269

                       Claire   272

                       Stephen   276

                       Marsha   277

HELP YOURSELF

ACKNOWLEDGMENTS   287

THE STANDARD   289

Part One   Get Rid of the Garbage in Your Life

1. The Need to Free Yourself   299

2. Surviving a Negative Environment   321

3. Learning to Forgive   345

Part Two   Know What You Want out of Your Life

4. The One Thing   371

5. The Price You Pay   401

Part Three   Celebrate Who You Are and What You Have

6. If It All Ended Tomorrow   431

7. What Do You Say When
   You Talk to Yourself?   457

8. Creating Your Own
   Positive Environment   489

EPILOGUE   505

ABOUT THE AUTHOR   511

KEYNOTES   513

A MAN NAMED DAVE

A STORY OF TRIUMPH AND FORGIVENESS

To the lady who gave her all to make me the man I am today, my lovely bride, my best friend, Mrs. Marsha Pelzer. You make me whole and will forever be my Princess.

To my son, Stephen, I can never tell you how precious you are and how much you have changed my life for the better. Everything I do, I do for you.

Acknowledgments

Since this has been my most arduous project, it is only prudent I pay respect to those who made this book possible:

With all respect, I bid adieu to my former publisher. I wish to convey my deepest thanks to Irene Xanthos, Lori Golden, Ronnie O'Brien, Jane Barone, Joy Fauver, Doreen Hess, and the small band of others who truly believed in my works before their commercial success.

Also, to Peter, Terri, Kim, and Bob: against all odds, thank you for allowing me to become a *New York Times* best-selling author.

To my dear friend Youngsuk Chi, "The Book Expert," for his excitability, mentoring, and for believing, just as I do, in maintaining the uncompromising standard of excellence. With dignity and honor!

A special thank-you to the owners and staff of Sonoma County's finest coffee establishment, Coffee Bazaar, for again allowing me and Marsha to plug in, take over, and wreak havoc at all hours, while maintaining the maximum level of mocha-ness that is still keeping us up at nights.

To Cathy Lewis and Nancy Graves of Carmel's Carriage House Inn—my home away from home—taking me in from the cold and putting me up in "my room."

A special thank-you to the institution formerly known as The Hogs Breath Inn of Carmel, where Law, Order, and Ice Cream still prevail. My gratitude to Tim, Joyce, Lana, and the entire crew for granting me space so to slave away at all hours among the beauty of your serene town.

To the musician Pat Metheny, who unknowingly provided haunting yet soul-stirring theme music to all three tomes. With *A Child Called "It"* it was "Farmer's Trust," for *The Lost*

Boy, "If I Could," and now with *A Man Named Dave,* the incredibly moving music of "The Bat, Part II." Spending endless hours listening to these tracks made me draw from the recesses of my soul.

To Marsha, editor extraordinaire, of Donohoe Publishing Projects for her absolute devotion to every word of every page. This is only one of the many reasons why I love you. For Marsha, it was a matter of . . . "The Bat, Part II."

To the staff of Dutton Plume for their overwhelming professionalism and sincere kindness, as well as believing that I was indeed worthy of being a hardcover author. To Brian Tart, editor-in-chief, for his trust, genuine sincerity, and meticulous attention to detail as well as for his patience when it counted the most. I also wish to thank Mary Ellen O'Boyle for an inspiring and majestic cover to the book. To everyone at Dutton Plume, thank you for making me a member of your family.

Finally, to the millions of readers who took *A Child Called "It"* and *The Lost Boy* into their hearts: I am forever grateful. You may not realize, but your actions have made the world a better place.

Author's Note

Some of the names in this book have been changed in order to protect the dignity and privacy of others.

As with the first two installments of the trilogy, this third part depicts the language and wisdom that was solely developed from my viewpoint as well as that particular time period.

This book is not under any circumstances meant to be used as a reprisal or an opportunity to be vindictive, but rather to serve a purpose of what transpires in my life and the valuable lessons learned.

CHAPTER 1

THE END

MARCH 4, 1973
DALY CITY, CALIFORNIA

I'm scared. My feet are cold and my stomach cries for food. From the darkness of the garage I strain my ears to pick up the slightest sound of Mother's bed creaking as she rolls over in the bedroom upstairs. I can also tell by the range of Mother's hacking cough if she's still asleep or about to get up. I pray Mother doesn't cough herself awake. I pray I still have more time. Just a few more minutes before another day in hell begins. I close my eyes as tightly as I can and mumble a quick prayer, even though I know God hates me.

Because I am not worthy enough to be a member of "The Family," I lie on top of an old, worn-out army cot without a blanket. I curl up into a tight ball to keep as warm as possible. I use the top of my shirt as a tent to cover my head, imagining my exhaled air will somehow keep my face and ears warm. I bury my hands either between my legs or into my armpits. Whenever I feel brave enough, and only after I'm certain that Mother has passed out, I steal a rag from the top of a dirty pile and wrap it tightly around my feet. I'll do anything to stay warm.

To stay warm is to stay alive.

I'm mentally and physically exhausted. It's been months

since I've been able to escape through my dreams. As hard as I try, I cannot go back to sleep. I'm too cold. I cannot stop my knees from shaking. I cautiously rub my feet together because I somehow feel if I make any quick movements, "The Mother" will hear me. I am not allowed to do anything without The Mother's direct authority. Even though I know she has returned to sleep in the bottom bunk bed of my brother's bedroom, I sense that she still has control over me.

The Mother always has.

My mind begins to spin as I fight to remember my past. I know that to somehow survive, my answers are in my past. Besides food, heat, and staying alive, learning why Mother treats me the way she does dominates my life.

My first memories of Mother were caution and fear. As a four-year-old child, I knew by the sound of Mother's voice what type of day was in store for me. Whenever Mother was patient and kind, she was my "Mommy." But whenever Mother became crossed and snapped at everything, "Mommy" transformed into "The Mother"—a cold, evil person capable of unexpected violent attacks. I soon became so scared of setting The Mother off, I didn't even go to the bathroom without first asking permission.

As a small child, I also realized that the more she drank, the more my mommy slipped away, and the more The Mother's personality took over. One Sunday afternoon before I was five years old, during one of The Mother's drunken attacks, she accidentally pulled my arm out of its socket. The moment it happened, Mother's eyes became as big as silver dollars. Mother knew she had crossed the line. She knew she was out of control. This went far beyond her usual treatment of face slapping, body punching, or being thrown down the stairs.

But even back then Mother developed a plan to cover her tracks. The next morning, after driving me to the hospital, she cried to the doctor that I had fallen out of my bunk bed during the night. Mother went on to say how she had desperately tried to catch me as I fell, and how she could never forgive herself for reacting so slowly. The doctor didn't even bat an eye. Back at home, Father, a fireman with medical training, didn't question Mother's strange tale.

Afterward, as Mother cuddled me to her chest, I knew to never, ever expose the secret. Even then I somehow thought that things would return to the good times I had with Mommy. I truly believed that she would somehow wake up from her drunken slumber and banish The Mother forever. As a four-year-old child, rocking in Mother's arms, I thought the worst was over and that Mother would change.

The only thing that had changed was the intensity of Mother's rage and the privacy of my secret relationship with her. By the time I was eight, my name was no longer allowed to be spoken. She had replaced "David" with "The Boy." Soon The Boy seemed too personal, so she decided to call me "It." Because I was no longer a member of "The Family," I was banished to live and sleep in the garage. When not sitting on top of my hands at the bottom of the staircase, my function was to perform slave-like chores. If I did not meet one of Mother's time requirements for my task, not only was I beaten, but I was not allowed to receive any food. More than once Mother refused to feed me for over a week. Of all of Mother's "games" of control, she enjoyed using food as her ultimate weapon.

The more bizarre things The Mother did to me, the more she seemed to know she could get away with any of her Games. When she held my arm over a gas stove, she told horrified teachers that I had played with a match and burned myself. And when Mother stabbed me in the chest, she told my frightened brothers that I had attacked her.

For years I did all that I could do to think ahead, to somehow outwit her. Before Mother hit me, I would tighten up parts of my body. If Mother didn't feed me, I would steal scraps of food anywhere I could. When she filled my mouth with pink dish washing soap, I'd hold the liquid in my mouth until I could spit it in the garage garbage can when she wasn't looking. Defeating The Mother in any way meant the world to me. Small victories kept me alive.

My only form of escape had been my dreams. As I sat at the bottom of the staircase with my head tilted backward, I saw myself flying through the air like my hero, Superman. Like Superman, I believed I had two identities. My Clark Kent personality was the child called "It"—an outcast who ate out of garbage cans, was ridiculed, and did not fit in. At times as I lay sprawled out on the kitchen floor unable to crawl away, I *knew* I was Superman. I knew I had an inner strength, a secret identity that no one else realized. I came to believe if Mother shot me, the bullets would bounce off my chest. No matter what "Game" Mother invented, no matter how badly she attacked me, I was going to win; I was going to live. At times when I couldn't block out the pain or the loneliness, all I had to do was close my eyes and fly away.

Just weeks after my twelfth birthday, Mother and Father separated. Superman disappeared. All my inner strength shriveled up. That day I knew Mother was going to kill me—if not that Saturday, then someday soon. With Father out of the way, nothing could stop The Mother. Even though for years Father had at times watched in dismay while he sipped his evening drink when Mother had me swallow tablespoons of ammonia or shrug his shoulders while she'd beat me senseless, I had always felt safer whenever he was in the house. But after Mother dropped off Father's meager belongings and drove away, I clasped my hands together as tightly as I could and whispered, ". . . and may He deliver me from evil. Amen."

That was almost two months ago, and God never answered my prayers. Now, as I continue to shiver in the darkness of the garage, I know the end is near. I cry for not having the courage or the strength to fight back. I'm too tired. The eight years of constant torture have sucked my life force out of me. I clasp my hands together and pray that when The Mother kills me, she will have mercy to kill me quickly.

I begin to feel light-headed. The harder I pray, the more I

feel myself drift off to sleep. My knees stop quivering. My fingers loosen from digging into my bony knuckles. Before I pass out, I say to myself, "God . . . if you can hear me, can you somehow take me away? Please take me. Take me today."

My upper body snaps upright. I can hear the floorboards strain upstairs from Mother's weight. Her gagging cough follows a moment later. I can almost visualize her bent over as she nearly coughs up her lungs from the years of heavy smoking and her destructive lifestyle. *God, how I hate her cough.*

The darkness of my sleep quickly fades away. A chill fills my body. I so badly want to remain asleep, forever. The more I wake from my slumber, the more I curse God for not taking me in my sleep. He never answers my prayers. I so badly wish I were dead. I don't have the energy to live another day in "The House." I can't imagine another day with The Mother and her sinister games. I break down and cry. A waterfall of tears runs down my face. I used to be so strong. I just can't take it anymore.

Mother's stumbling brings me back to my dismal reality. I wipe my runny nose and my tears away. I must never, *ever* expose a sign of weakness. I take a deep breath and gaze upward. I lock my hands together before retreating inside my shell that will protect me for another day. *Why?* I sigh. *If you are God, what is your reason? I just . . . I so badly want to know, Why? Why am I still alive?*

Mother staggers out of her bedroom. *Move!* my brain screams. *Move it!* I only have a few seconds before . . . I was supposed to be up an hour ago to begin my chores.

I stand up and fumble through the darkness, trying to find the light switch to the garage. I trip over one of the legs to the army cot. By reflex, I reach out to the floor to soften the impact, but I'm too slow. A moment later the side of my face smashes against the cold cement. Bright silver dots fill my view. I smack the palms of my hands on the floor. I so badly want to pass out. I never want to regain consciousness ever again.

I push myself up off the cement as I hear Mother's footsteps leading to the bathroom. After flicking on the light switch, I snatch the broom before racing up the staircase. If I can finish sweeping the stairs before Mother catches me, she will never know I'm behind. *I can win.* I smile as I tell myself, *Come on, man, go! Move it!* I seem so out of breath. My mind races at supersonic speed, but my body responds in slow motion. My feet feel like blocks of cement. The tips of my fingers are so cold. I don't understand why I'm so slow. I used to be lightning fast.

Without thinking I reach my left hand out to the wooden rail that I use to pull myself up the stairs. *I'm going to win,* I say to myself, *I'm actually going to make it!* I can hear the gurgling sound of the toilet flushing from above. I quicken my pace. I extend my arm toward the rail. I smile inside. *I'm going to beat her.* A split second later my heart skips a beat as my hand misses the rail and grabs air. My body begins to wobble. *The rail! Grab the stupid rail!* As hard as I fight to concentrate, my fingers refuse to obey.

My world turns black.

A blinding glare pierces my eyes. My head seems as if it is stuck in a fog. I can make out a figure standing above me in front of a bright white light. "... aht ime is it?"

I try to shake my head clear. For a moment I thought I was staring at an angel sent to take me to heaven.

But Mother's sickening cough soon erases my fantasy. "*I* said, 'What time is it?' " The sound of her voice nearly makes me pee my pants. Mother uses a soft, evil tone so not to wake up her precious babies. "Let's see how fast . . . you can move that sorry little behind of yours up here . . . now!" Mother demands with a snap of her fingers. My body shudders as I place the broom against the base of the stairs.

"Oh, no!" Mother beams. "Bring your friend with you." I'm not sure what she means. I spin around, then look back up at Mother. "The broom, you moron. Bring it with you."

With every step I take, my mind begins to plot a defense for whatever Game Mother has in store for the crime of not completing my chore on time. I warn myself to stay focused. I know she plans on using the broom as a weapon, either against my chest or face. Sometimes when we're alone, Mother likes to smash the end of the broom directly behind my knees. If she has me follow her into the kitchen, I'm dead. I won't be able to walk to school, let alone run. But if Mother keeps me on the stairs, I know she'll only hit me in my upper body.

Upon reaching the top of the stairs, I automatically assume "the position of address": my body stands perfectly straight, with my head bent down and my hands glued to my sides. I am not allowed to move a muscle, blink, look at her or even breathe without Mother's direct permission.

"Tell me, tell me *I'm stupid,*" Mother whispers as she leans over. I cringe as I imagine her taking a bite from my ear. It's part of the Game. She's testing me to see if I'll flinch. I dare not look up or back away. My heels hang over the edge of the stair. I pray Mother doesn't push me . . . today.

"Go ahead, tell me. Please," Mother begs. The tone of her voice changes. Mother's voice seems calm, nonthreatening. My mind spins. I don't understand. Did Mother just give me permission to speak? I have no idea what she expects of me. Either way, I'm trapped. I focus my energy on the front of my shoes. The more I stare, the more my body begins to sway.

Without warning Mother thrusts a finger under my chin, lifting my face to hers. Her rancid breath makes my stomach coil. I fight not to pass out from her stench. Even though she does not allow me to wear my glasses at home, I glance at Mother's puffy, reddened face. Her once gleaming hair is now oily and matted against the sides of her face. "Just how stupid do you think I am? Tell me, exactly: How stupid am I?"

I sheepishly look up and reply, "Ma'am?"

A raging fire stings the side of my face. "Just who in the hell gave you permission to speak, let alone look!" Mother hisses.

I snap my head back down as I quickly bury the pain inside. *My God,* I say to myself, *I didn't see it coming. What's happening to me?* I'm always able to see her arm swing back before she strikes me. I cannot figure out why I am so slow. *Dammit, David, stay focused! Think!*

"When is *It* going to begin *Its* chores?" Mother bellows. "What is it with you? I bet you think I'm stupid! You think you can get away with whatever you damn well please! Don't you?" Mother shakes her head. "I'm not the one hurting you. You are. You choose your actions. You know who— what—you are and what your purpose is in this household.

"If *It* wants to be fed, then it's simple: *It* does exactly as *It's* told. If It doesn't want to be punished, then It stays out of trouble. It knows the rules. I don't treat you any different from anybody else. It simply refuses to obey." Mother stops to take a deep breath. Her chest begins to wheeze. It's time for her fix. I know what's coming next. I wish she'd go ahead and hit me. "And what about me?" Her voice rises. "I should be asleep, but no, I have to be here with It. You pathetic piece of filth! You little bastard! You know your function. You're not a *person,* but . . . a *thing* to do with as *I* please. Do you understand? Am I making myself clear, or perhaps It needs another lesson?" Mother thunders.

Mother's words echo inside my soul. For years I've heard the same thing over and over again. For years I've been her human robot to do with as she pleases, like some toy that she can turn on and off whenever she wishes.

I break down inside. My body begins to shake. I can't take it anymore. *Go ahead,* I say to myself. *Do it! Just kill me! Come on!* Suddenly, my vision sharpens. My insides stop shaking. Rage slowly begins to fill me. I no longer feel ice cold. I shift my head from side to side as my eyes creep up Mother's robed body. The fingers to my right hand tighten around the wooden broom handle. As I slowly let out a deep breath, my eyes stare directly into Mother's. *"Leave me alone . . . you bitch!"* I hiss.

Mother becomes paralyzed. I focus every fiber of my being on piercing through her silver-framed glasses and reddened eyes. I will myself to somehow transfer every moment I had to carry for the last eight years of pain and loneliness into Mother.

Mother's face turns ash white. She knows. Mother knows exactly what I'm feeling. *It's working,* I tell myself. Mother tries to break away from my stare. She moves her head slightly to the left. I match Mother's movement. She can't escape. Mother looks down and away. I tilt my head up and sharpen my stare. I smile. From the bottom of my soul I feel so warm. Now *I'm* the one in control.

From the back of my mind I hear a chuckle. For a moment I think it's me laughing at Mother. I lower my eyes and see Mother's crocodile smile. Her putrid breath breaks my concentration. The more Mother smiles, the more my body becomes tense. She tilts her head toward the light. *Now,* I tell myself, *now I can see it coming. Go ahead, give it to me! Come on, do it! Show me what you got!* I see the blur a split second before I feel her hand collide against my face. A moment later, warm blood seeps from my nose. I let it drip on the black-matted stairs. I refuse to give Mother the pleasure of watching me cry or reacting in any way whatsoever. I defy her by remaining numb inside and out.

"Showing a little guts, are you? Well, you're a few years too late!" Mother sneers. "You don't have what it takes. You never have and you never will. You're such a pathetic little worm. I can kill you anytime I please. Just like *that,*" Mother says with a snap of her fingers. "You are only alive because it pleases me. You are nothing more than . . ."

I block out Mother's words as a cold fear creeps back inside my soul. I bow my head, resuming the position of address.

Dark red blood spatters the toes of my shoes. *For a fleeting moment I felt so alive.*

She's in control now.

The more that Mother babbles, the more I nod my head, acknowledging Mother is indeed almighty and God-like for allowing me to live another day in her household. "You don't know how lucky you are. When I was your age, you wouldn't believe what *I* was put through. . . ."

I let out a deep sigh and close my eyes in a vain attempt to block out the sound of her voice. How I wish she would pass out and drop dead. In my mind I fantasize Mother sprawled on the hallway floor. I would give anything to be there as she quivered helplessly on her back before taking her last breath.

Mother's voice changes in pitch. Suddenly my throat feels as if it is on fire as Mother tightens her grip around my neck. My eyes want to pop out of my head. I did not focus on Mother's attack before it came. By reflex I wrap my hands around Mother's fingers. As much as I try, I cannot pry her hands off. The more I struggle, the more Mother tightens her death grip. I try to scream, but only a gurgling sound leaks out. My head slumps forward. As my eyes roll backward, I concentrate on Mother's face. *Do it!* I shout to myself. *Come on, do it! You're so bad, you're so tough, come on! Show me, show me what you got! Kill me, you bitch!*

Mother's cheeks twitch from her intense hatred. Her nostrils flare from her rapid breathing. I want Mother to kill me. I begin to feel myself drift away. My hearing seems as if I am in the middle of a long tunnel. My arms fall to my side. For the first time in years, my body relaxes. I'm no longer cold inside. I'm no longer frightened. I'm ready to . . .

A hard slap makes my head shake from side to side. "Oh no, wake up! Wake up, you miserable piece of trash! I'm not through with you yet! I know exactly what you want!" Mother hisses. "So, you think you're so smart? How about . . . instead of sending you to your Uncle Dan's this weekend, maybe I should have the boys go instead, so you and I can spend some *private time* together? Bet you didn't think of that one, did you?"

I know by the sound of her voice that I am supposed to respond, but I can't.

"Oh, what's the matter? Does the little insect have a sore throat? Oh well, that's just too bad!" Mother smiles. I can see her lips moving, but I can barely make out what she's saying. After another quick squeeze, Mother lets go of her hold. Without permission, I rub my neck, gasping for air. Somehow I know she's not done with me—not yet. A second later I nearly lose my balance as Mother snatches the broom from beside me. I automatically tighten my upper body. "This," she says, "this is for cheating on your chores. I've told you a hundred times that you are to get that miserable butt of yours up and working before I get up. *Do I make myself perfectly clear?*"

I hesitate, not knowing how or if I should respond.

"I said, *is that clear?*"

"Yes . . . ah, yes, ma'am," I stutter in a hoarse voice.

"Tell me, what is your name?" Mother asks as she tilts her head upward in a show of supremacy.

" 'It,' " I answer in a sheepish tone.

"And what is *'Its'* function?"

"Ta . . . ta . . . ta do . . . do as you command and stay outta . . . outta trouble."

"And when I say, 'Jump'?"

"I ask, 'How high?' " I reply without thought.

"Not bad. Not bad at all!" Mother leers. "But I do think It requires another lesson. Perhaps this will teach you . . . teach It. . . ."

I can hear a swishing sound. I brace my arms for the impact. My upper body is rock solid, but I have no way of telling which direction the sound is coming from. A jolting thud strikes the side of my neck. My knees buckle as I turn inside the doorway and lean against Mother's body. Without thinking I reach out to Mother. Her eyes shine with pleasure. She slaps my hands away. As my feet slip, my head jerks backward.

I can feel my throat collapse the same way it did when Mother had me swallow teaspoons full of ammonia. I fight to swallow a breath of air, but my brain is too slow to respond. My eyes lock on to Mother's. "So, do you still think you can fly?"

I glance down and see Mother's hand in motion. A moment later I can feel myself floating, my arms flung above my face. Suddenly, a rush of air fills my chest as the back of my head smashes against the staircase. I reach out, but I can't stop my body from bouncing backward down the stairs. At the bottom of the staircase, my chest heaves; I want to find a bucket and throw up. At the door above me, Mother bends over with laughter. "Look at you! You're a hoot!"

Her face becomes taut. In an ice-cold voice Mother says, "You're not even worth the effort." With a jerk of her hand she flings the broom at me, then slams the door shut. My only form of protection is to close my eyes. I don't even bother to turn away or cover my face. I can hear the broom topple down the stairs before missing me completely.

Alone in the garage I let go and cry like a baby. I don't care if Mother, or anyone else in the world, can hear me. I have no dignity, no self-worth. Rage slowly builds inside my soul. I clench my hands together and begin taking my frustration out on the floor. *Why, why, why? What in the hell did I ever do to you to make you hate me so much?*

With every blow I can feel my strength drain away. The whitish-yellow garage light begins to fade as I lose consciousness. Without thinking of Mother catching me, I lie on my side, pull my shirt over my face, bury my hands between my legs, and close my eyes. Before I pass out, I clasp my hands together and mutter, "Take me."

"Wake up! Wake up, I tell you!" My eyes flicker open. I'm trapped in a mental haze as I stand in front of Mother in the kitchen. I have no idea how I got here. And somehow I know it's almost time for me to run to school. My mind struggles to recall why I keep losing track of time.

"I said, wake up!" Mother barks. She leans over and slaps my face. I'm fascinated that I can no longer feel the pain. "What in the hell is wrong with you?" she asks with some concern.

Forgetting who I am, I rub my face and reply, "I dunno." Immediately I know I've just committed a double crime of *moving* and *speaking* without Mother's permission. Before I can stop myself, I commit *another* offense by looking right at her and shaking my head. "I don't understand . . . what's happening to me?"

"You're fine," Mother states. I lean forward to catch what she said. I'm not sure, but I think Mother just spoke to me in a soft tone. "Listen. Listen up. Tell 'em . . . uhm, tell them that you were . . ." I strain to pay attention to Mother's instructions, but her words seem mumbled and confusing. Mother snaps her fingers, indicating a breakthrough for her latest cover story. "If those nosy teachers ask, you tell them that you were wrestling and you got out of control . . . so your brothers had to put you in your place. Do you understand?"

I'm trying to digest Mother's new set of instructions.

"Do you understand?" Mother probes, fighting to keep her anger under control.

"Ah, yes," I chuckle. I cannot believe how easily Mother can come up with her off-the-wall lies every single day of school. I'm also amazed that I no longer care about masking my emotions in front of her. "Tell 'em I was wrong. I was bad."

"And . . . ?" Mother whines, trying to draw me out further.

"Tell them . . . I was . . . I was playing, I mean wrestling! I was wrestling and . . . I got out of control. Yes, I understand," I stammer.

Mother tilts her head to one side as she inspects her latest damage. She holds her gaze for a few moments before losing her balance, stumbling toward me. In a jerking motion I flinch backward. "Shh . . . no, it's okay. Relax," Mother calmly says with an outstretched hand as she keeps her distance, acting as if I were a stray dog. "No one's going to hurt you. Shh . . ." Mother circles around me before backing into her kitchen chair. Bending her head down, she stares into space.

My head begins to slump forward when Mother's hacking cough makes me snap upright. "It wasn't always like this, you know," she whimpers in a scratchy voice. "If you knew . . . if you only understood. I wish I could somehow make you, make *them* understand. . . ." Mother stops in mid-sentence to collect herself. I can feel her eyes scan my body. "Things just got outta control, that's all. I never meant to . . . to live like this. No one does. I tried, God knows I did—to be the good wife, the perfect mother. I did everything: den mother this, PTA that, hosting the perfect parties. I really did try.

"You, you're the only one who knows, who really knows. You're the only one I can really talk to," Mother whispers. "I can't trust *them*. But you, you're the perfect outlet, the perfect audience, anytime it damn well pleases *me*. You don't talk, so no one will hear your pain. You don't have any friends, and you never go outside, so you know what it's like to be all alone inside. Hell, besides school, no one knows you. It's as if you were never . . .

"No. You'll never tell anyone . . . never!" Mother brags as she nods her head up and down to reinforce her warning.

Without stealing a glance, I can hear Mother sniffle as she struggles not to let down her guard. I realize she's only using me to talk to herself. She always has. When I was younger, Mother would drag me out of bed in the middle of the night, have me stand in front of her as she poured herself glass after glass and raved on for hours. But now as I stand in front of her, I'm too numb to understand her ramblings. *What in the hell does she want?* Can she be totally smashed so early in the morning, or is she still under the effects from last night's stupor? Maybe she's testing my reaction? I hate not knowing what Mother expects of me.

"You," she continues, "oh, you were so cute! At parties everyone loved *you!* Everyone wanted to take you home. Always polite, always with manners. Wouldn't speak unless spoken to. Oh, I remember whenever you couldn't sleep, you'd crawl up into my lap and sing me Christmas songs, even in the middle of July. Whenever I felt bad I could always count on you to 'croon a tune.' " Mother smiles as she remembers the past. She can no longer control the tears that stream down her cheeks. I've never seen her like this before. "You had the sweetest voice, David. Why is it you don't sing for me anymore? How come?" Mother stares at me as if I were a ghost.

"I don't . . . I dunno." My grogginess vanishes. I realize this is not one of Mother's sinister Games. I know, deep inside Mother, that something is different. She's reaching out. Mother's never been this emotional about her past. I wish I had a clear head to analyze what she's trying to tell me. I know it's not the booze talking, but my real mother, the one who's been trapped inside herself for so many years. "Mommy?"

Mother's head jerks up as she covers her mouth. *"Mommy?* Oh Lord, David, do you know how long it's been since I've been someone's *Mommy?* My God!" She closes her eyes to hide her pain. "You were so fragile, so timid. You don't remember, but you were always the slow one. It took you forever to tie your shoes. I thought I'd go crazy trying to teach you that damn square knot for your Cub Scouts badge. But you never gave up. I'd find you in a corner of the room trying to tie knots. No, that's one thing about you, you never gave up. Hey," Mother asks with a wide smile, "do you remember that summer when you were seven or eight years old, and you and I spent forever trying to catch that fish at Memorial Park?"

With perfect clarity I recall how Mommy and I sat at the far edge of a giant fallen log that hung over a small stream. I couldn't believe she had chosen me—over my younger brother Stan, who constantly fought for Mother's attention. As Stan threw a temper tantrum on the beach below us, I thought Mother would realize her mistake. But Mommy had paid no attention to Stan's commotion; she simply tightened her grip on my belt, in case I slipped, and whispered encouragement into my ear. After a few minutes of fishing, I deliberately kept the pink salmon egg bait just above the water. I never wanted my adventure with my mommy to end. Now, as I shake my head clear of the memory, my voice becomes choked up. "I, ah, I prayed we'd never catch that fish," I confessed to her.

"Why's that?"

"So . . . we could spend more time together . . . as mother and son."

"Oh, your brother Stan was red with jealousy, stomping up and down beside the creek, throwing rocks into the water, trying to scare off that fish of yours. My God." Mother tosses her hair back, revealing a rare smile.

I'm not sure if she failed to hear or understand the true meaning of what I said.

"David?" Mother pleads. "You do remember, don't you?"

"Yes," I cry, shaking my head, "I do. I remember everything. Like the first day of school when the teacher had us color a picture of what we did that summer. I drew you and me sitting on that old tree with a happy-face sun shining above us. Remember, I gave it to you that day after school?"

Mother turns away from me. She clutches her coffee mug, then puts a finger to her lips. The excitement from her face drains away. "No!" Mother states in a strict tone, as if our fishing adventure were a hoax.

"Oh, sure you do—"

"I said no, goddammit!" Mother interrupts. She clamps her eyes shut and covers her ears. "No, no, no! I don't remember. You can't make me! No one can force me to remember the past if I don't want to. Not you or anybody else. No one tells *me* what to do! You got that, mister?"

"Yes, ma'am," I automatically respond.

Mother's face turns beet red as the muscles in her neck tighten. Her upper body begins to shake. I'm not sure, but I think Mother is having a violent seizure. I want to yell out, but I'm too scared. I stand in front of Mother like a helpless fool. I don't know what to do.

After a few seconds the redness from her face disappears. She lets out a deep sigh. "I just don't know anymore . . . if I'm coming or going. I don't know . . . I didn't mean for things to happen this way; no one did. You can't blame me, I did my best . . ."

The sweetness in her voice fades. I want so badly to run and hug *Mommy* before she completely slips away, but, like always, I know in a few hours *Mother* won't remember a single word of our conversation. I back away from the kitchen table and resume the position of address.

"Oh, Jesus!" Mother snaps. "Now look what you've done! I've got to drive my boys to school! Forget the dishes; you can finish them after school. And listen up: I don't want to hear a peep from any of those nosy teachers today, so you keep that carcass of yours the hell out of trouble! You got me, mister?" Mother raises her voice to her usual evil tone.

"Yes, ma'am," I mutter.

"Then get the hell out of my house! Run!" Mother bellows.

"What about lunch . . . ?" I ask.

"Too bad. You took my time, then I take your lousy sandwich. You'll just have to go diggin' for food today. Now get the hell out of here! Don't make me get the broom! Now run!"

In a flash I race through Mother's house. I can hear her evil laugh as I slam the front door shut before sprinting off to school.

Minutes later, after running to school at top speed, I stagger into the nurse's office with my hands slapping on my knees. With every breath I take in, the muscles around my throat tighten. An enormous pressure from behind my eyes begins to build. I slap my knees as if that will somehow make air rush into my lungs. The school nurse spins around from behind her desk. My mind fumbles to yell, but I cannot form the words. But I try again. *"C-a-n-'t b-r-e-a-t-h-e!"* I finally sputter, pointing at my neck.

The nurse leaps up with lightning speed, grabs a brown bag, turns it upside down spilling its contents onto the floor, and kneels down in front of me. Through my tears I can see the terror in her eyes. I want to cry out, but I'm too scared. The nurse pulls on my hand, but I slap her away as I continue to pound my knees. The more I try to draw air into my lungs, the more the invisible bands tighten around my chest. "No!" the nurse shouts. "David, stop it! Don't fight it! You're hyper-ventilating!"

"Hipper ventle . . . ?" I gasp.

"Slow down. You're going to be fine. I'm just going to put this bag over your—"

"Nooo! I can't . . . won't be able . . . to see. I . . . have to see!"

"Shh, I'm right here. Close your eyes and concentrate on the sound of my voice. Good. Now slow down. Take tiny puffs of air. Breathe through your nose. That's it," the nurse whis-pers in a soothing voice. With her I feel safe. "That's much better; tiny breaths. Reach out, take my hand. I'm right here. I'm not going to leave you. You're going to be fine."

I obey the nurse and shut my eyes. As the nurse places the bag over my face, I can instantly feel warm air circulate. It feels good, but after a few breaths my exhaled air becomes too hot. My legs begin to lock up. By accident I jerk the nurse's hand.

"Shh. David, trust me, you're fine. You're doing better. Much better. That's it, slow down. See? Now, lean your head back and relax."

As I tilt my head backward, a rush of air escapes from my mouth. The pressure is so intense that I fight to keep myself from throwing up. I rip the bag from my face before my legs buckle, and I fall to the floor gasping for more air. Within seconds the bands around my chest begin to ease.

After a few minutes, the fire from inside my neck begins to

cool. "Here," the nurse says, holding a glass of ice cubes in front of me, "take one of these to suck on."

I try to pick up a piece of ice, but my trembling fingers cannot grasp the cube. Without a second thought the nurse reaches into the glass and picks one out. "Open up."

I lower my head, trying to hide. The moment I do, the searing pain returns. "David, what's wrong? Come on now, open up," she instructs in a more commanding tone. I close my eyes. I know what's coming next: questions. *I'd give anything to avoid another round of questions.* All they do is make everyone at school upset and somehow Mother always finds out. Whenever the principal has called Mother, the staff at school would see the results the next day. As I continue to avoid the nurse's eyes, I fantasize about crawling into a corner so I can disappear.

I slowly open my eyes when I feel the nurse lift my head with her fingers. Her face turns chalky white.

"Oh . . . my . . . Lord! What in heaven's name happened to your neck?" the nurse exclaims as she peers from side to side.

I wring my hands, hoping she'll drop the subject. *"Please!"* I wheeze. *"Let it go."*

"The side of your Adam's apple is so swollen!" The nurse flies away to snatch a tongue depressor from one of her glass jars. "Let's have a look. Open up." I let out a raspy sigh before obeying. "I need you to open just a little bit wider. Can you do that for me?" she asks gently.

"Can't," I whimper. "Hurts too much."

At last the nurse allows me to close my mouth. Again, I try to avoid her stare. I bury my trembling fingers in my lap. She shakes her head before standing up and grabbing her clipboard. Every school day, for over a year, the nurse has inspected my body from head to toe before documenting her examinations. Now she mutters to herself as she scribbles her latest findings. Kneeling back down, she delicately massages the palms of my hands. I bite my lip in anticipation. The nurse stares into my eyes as if not knowing what to say.

Now I'm really scared.

"I'm sorry, David," she says as tears seep from behind her glasses. "I was wrong. You weren't hyperventilating. Your, ah, your larynx . . . your epiglottis is swollen and your trachea is inflamed. What I'm saying is: this is why you are having trouble breathing. The opening to your throat was cutting off your flow of oxygen. Do you understand?"

I take a moment to visualize in my mind the nurse's meaning. I don't want her to think I'm stupid.

"When did this happen?" she asks.

I look away from the nurse's gaze and stare at my shoes. "I was, uhm . . ." I fumble for the exact wording to Mother's cover story, but my brain still feels trapped in a fog bank. "I was . . . I fell . . . I fell down the stairs."

"David?" she replies, raising her eyebrows.

"It's my fault!" I snap back. "I was wrestling and I got out of control and my brothers—"

"Poppycock!" the nurse interrupts. "You mean your mother knew of your condition . . . and she still made you run to school? Do you realize what might have happened to you? For goodness sakes, you could have . . ."

"Uhm, no, ma'am. Please, I'm better now. Really, I'm fine," I say as softly and as quickly as I can, before the burning sensation returns. "Please! It's not her fault! Let it go!"

The nurse lifts her glasses to wipe away her tears. "No! Not this time! I won't let it go. I've had enough. This is the last straw. This has to be reported to the principal. Something has got to be done." She stands up and slaps her clipboard against her leg as she marches for the door.

"No! Pleeze!" I beg. "You don't understand! If you tell, she'll—"

"She'll what?" The nurse spins around. "Tell me, David, tell me so I have something, anything, to go on! I know it's her—we know it's her—but you've got to help us, to help you," she pleads.

In an effort to relieve the pain I stare up at the ceiling. I wring my hands and concentrate on inhaling tiny puffs of air through my nose. From the corner of my eye I can see the nurse still standing by the door. I slowly turn my head toward her. Tears run down my cheeks. "I, ah . . . I can't."

"Why? In heaven's name, why do you protect her? What are you waiting for?" she barks in a rattling voice. "Something has to be done!"

The nurse's words pound through my skull. I bite down on my lip until it bleeds. My arms begin to shake. "Dammit!" I blurt out in a squeaky voice. *"Don't you understand?* There's nothing, *nothing,* that anyone can do! It's my fault! *It's always my fault.* 'Boy' this, 'It' that, blah, blah, blah. Every day is a repeat of the day before. Even you," I state with my finger thrust at the nurse, "every day I come in, take off my clothes, you look me over, you ask me about this, about that . . . for what? Nothing changes, and nothing ever will!" The band around my throat begins to tighten, but I don't care. I can no longer control my flood of emotions. "Miss Moss tried—"

"Miss Moss?" the nurse asks.

"My, ah, my second-grade teacher. She tried . . . she tried to help and she's gone. . . ."

"David?" the nurse says in a disbelieving tone.

I bury my face in my hands. "Father tried . . . and he's gone, too. You have to understand: everything I am, everything I do, is bad. Everything's wrong. If you get too close, she'll . . . she'll deal with you, too! No one wins!" I cry. "No one wins against The Mother!" I bend over in a coughing fit. Whatever energy I had drains away. I lean against the nurse's examination bed. I fight to slow down my breathing. "I, ah . . . when I sat at the bottom of the garage stairs and they'd watch TV or eat dinner, I tried to figure things out, to understand why." I shake my head clear of the countless hours spent in the garage. "You know the one thing I wanted the most?"

Her mouth hangs open. She's never seen me like this before. "No," she answers.

"I just wanted to be *real.* To be a real kid—with clothes and stuff. I don't mean just toys, but to be outside. I always wanted to play on the jungle gym after school. I'd really like to do that." For a moment I smile at my fantasy. "But I know I won't, be able to. *Never.* I have to run to The House fast or I get into trouble. Sometimes, on really sunny days, as I'm running from school, I cheat and stop to watch the kids play."

My vision becomes blurred as I rattle off my deepest secrets to the nurse. Because I am not allowed to speak at Mother's house and have no friends at school, I have no one to express my feelings to. "Other times in the garage, at night, when I lay on my cot, I'd think hard to figure out what I could do. I mean, to fix things between Mother and me, to make things better. I wanted to know why, how, things became so bad. I really thought if I tried hard enough—if I prayed with all my spirit—I'd find my answers. They never came.

"I . . . I, ah, tri—tried," I stutter. I'm holding back my tears. "I spent so much time . . . I, ah, I just . . . I just wanted to know why. That's all. Why me, why us? I just wanted to know. Why?" I stare into the nurse's eyes. "I don't care anymore! I just want to go to sleep! I'm tired of everything! The games, the secrets, the lies, hoping one day Mother will wake up and everything will be better again! I can't take it anymore!

"If you could just let me sleep, for just a while, please?" I beg.

She shakes her head. "This has to end, David. Look at you. You're—"

"It's okay," I interrupt in a calm voice. "I'm not . . . when I'm at school, I'm not afraid. Just promise me you won't tell. *Not today, please?*"

"David, you know I can't do that," the nurse replies in a flat tone.

"If you . . . if you tell," I pant, "then you know what will happen. Please, let it go!"

She nods her head in agreement. "Just for today."

"Promise?"

"Promise." She takes my hand and leads me to the small bed in the corner of the room.

"Cross your heart and hope to die?" I ask, making an X mark on my chest with my finger.

"Cross my heart," she repeats in a choked-up voice. She covers me with a thick wool blanket.

". . . And hope to die?" I repeat. The nurse's lips part with a smile as she gently strokes my matted hair. I take her hands and cup them around mine. ". . . And hope to die?"

The nurse gives my hands a gentle squeeze. "And hope to die."

In the deepest part of my soul, I feel at peace. I am no longer afraid. *I am ready to die.*

CHAPTER 2

FLY AWAY

AUGUST 24, 1979

Thick, sticky sweat coated every pore of my skin. My stomach seized with fear. My fingers seemed fused together as they clawed the armrest. I wanted to shut my eyes, but the combination of exhilaration, fascination, and terror inside me kept them glued to the small Plexiglas window. I studied every feature of the Bay Area—my home for the last eighteen years.

"I'm flying?" I asked, to my own amazement.

My body slid from my seat, and I thought for sure I'd fall out of the plane as the Boeing 727 made a sudden sharp roll to the right. To help contain my fear, I forced my eyes shut. *I'm okay. I'm all right. I'm fine. My God, I can't believe it! I'm flying! I'm actually flying!* I could feel myself drifting off. Because of the excitement of finally enlisting in the U.S. Air Force, saying good-bye to my foster parents, and struggling with my past, I had not slept in days. As the roar of the jet's engines began to fade, I started to unwind. The more my tension disappeared, the more I began to think of how far I had come.

As a child surviving in the garage of Mother's house, I had never dreamed of making it out alive. Somehow, I had known Mother was close to killing me, and yet I did not care. I had given up all hope. Yet on March 5, 1973, the day after Mother had thrown me down the garage stairs, my teachers called the police, who immediately placed me into protective custody. I was free. As elated as I was, I sensed that my freedom was a hollow victory. At the county's court proceedings, I felt that Mother had given me away. I felt as if *I* was not good enough for *her*. When my angel of mercy—my social worker, Ms. Gold—informed me that I was never to have any contact with Mother or her children ever again, I was crushed.

It was then that I became obsessed with finding answers to my past. Even though I was still terrified of Mother, who wanted nothing to do with me, I still struggled to prove that I was worthy of her love and worthy enough to be a member of her family.

As a foster child, I soon learned that I knew absolutely nothing about *living in the real world.* My former life as Mother's prisoner had been dominated by elemental needs of survival. But after my rescue I felt like a toddler—learning and growing by leaps and bounds. The simplest things taught to preschool children became major obstacles for me. Because I had spent years in the garage with my head bent backward in a POW position, I developed very bad posture. As a foster child, I had to learn to focus and walk upright. Whenever I became nervous, I stuttered or slurred every word. It would take me forever to complete one simple sentence. My foster mother, Mrs. Turnbough, spent hours with me every day after school, teaching me phonics and helping me to imagine my words flowing from my mouth, like water cascading over a fall. Mrs. Turnbough's valiant efforts were perhaps her undoing. Within a few months, I was driving my foster parents up the wall with all I had to say. They had all they could do to shut me up. I wanted to show off my new form of communication to everyone, every minute. But my mouth soon became my Achilles' heel. Because I was so skinny and awkward, I became easy prey for others, and my only form of defense was my mouth. Whenever I felt backed in a corner, words of intense anger and hatred seemed to erupt before I could analyze what I was saying or why.

The only way I felt I could make friends was stealing for acceptance or doing whatever else I could to gain recognition. I knew that what I was doing was completely wrong, but after years of being an outcast and totally isolated, the need to fit in was too powerful to resist. My foster parents struggled to keep me on the straight and narrow, and teach me the seriousness of my decisions.

On the lighter side, they were dismayed at my naivete and ignorance. The first few times I took a bath, I filled the tub to the rim *before* stepping into it, causing water to spill over the sides. I would then squeeze every drop I could from what I thought was "fancy-smelling bubble bath" into the tub, then stir the water like a whirlpool trying to form as much lather as possible. As much as my foster parents laughed at my water frolics, my foster sisters were not amused and hid their bottles of Vidal Sassoon in their bedrooms. Up until then I had never heard of the word shampoo.

I thought that in order to survive, I had to work. Early on as a foster child, it was drummed into me that foster kids—labeled as "F-kids"—never amounted to anything, never graduated high school, let alone go on to college. I also discovered that by the time I turned eighteen years old, I would no longer be a ward of the court—a minor that was provided for by the county—and since I didn't have parents to rely on, I would be all alone. The closer I came to reaching adulthood, the more I became terrified of being broke and homeless. Deep down I feared I would not be strong enough to make it on my own. As a frightened child living in my mother's garage, one of the promises I had made was that if I ever escaped, I would always have enough money to eat. So, as a young teenager, I abandoned my Lego and Erector sets and my Hot Wheels toy cars and focused on earning a living. By the age of fifteen I was shining shoes. I lied about my age to get work as a busboy. I did whatever I could to put in at least forty hours a week. As a freshman in high school, I slaved six days a week to put in over sixty hours. I did anything I could to squeeze in an extra hour a week to earn an additional $2.65. Only after I'd show up to school and collapse on top of my desk and get sick from total exhaustion did I begin to slack off. On one level, thinking that I was ahead of the game, I was proud, almost to the point of being cocky. But on the inside I felt hollow and lonely. As other boys my age were dating beautiful girls with short dresses and fancy makeup, driving their parents' cars and whining about their ten-hour work weeks, I became increasingly jealous of their good fortune.

Whenever I felt a little depressed, I would bury myself even more in my work. The harder I applied myself, the more the cravings of wanting to be a normal teenager disappeared. And more important, the inner voice bubbling inside me, fighting for the answers to my past, remained quiet.

For me, work meant peace.

In the summer of 1978, at age eighteen, in order to further my career as top-rated car salesman, I decided to drop out of high school. But months later, after a statewide recession, I found myself as a legal adult, with no diploma, no job, and my life savings quickly draining away. My worst nightmare had come true. All of my well-thought-out plans of getting ahead and sacrificing while others played vanished into thin air. Because of my lack of education, the only jobs available were at fast-food restaurants. I knew I could not make it by working those jobs for the rest of my life.

Ever since I had been Mother's prisoner, I had dreamed of making something of myself. The more she would scream, curse at me, and leave me sprawled out on the floor in my own blood, the more I would fight back and smile inside, telling myself over and over again, *One day, you'll see. One of these days I'll make you proud.* But Mother's prediction was right: I had failed. And for that I hated myself to the core. My idle time awakened my inner voice. I began to think that maybe Mother had been right all along. Maybe I was a loser, and I had been treated as such because I deserved it. I became so paranoid about my future that I could no longer sleep. I spent my free evenings trying to form any strategy I could to survive. It was during one of those endless nights that I remembered the only piece of advice my father ever gave me.

In six years as a foster child, I had seen my father less than a dozen times. At the end of my last visit, he proudly showed me one of the only possessions he had left: his badge, representing his retirement from the San Francisco Fire Department. Before loading me onto a Greyhound bus, Father mumbled in a dejected voice, "Get out of here, David. Get as far away from here as you can. You're almost at that age. Get out." As he looked at me with darkened circles under his eyes, Father's final words were: "Do what you have to. Don't end up . . . don't end up like me."

In my heart I sensed that Father was a homeless alcoholic. After spending a lifetime saving others from burning buildings, Father had been helpless to save himself. That day as the bus pulled away, I cried from the depths of my soul. Every time the bus passed someone sleeping beside a building, I'd imagine Father shivering in the night. As much as I felt sorry for him, though, I knew I did not want to—I could not—end up like him. I felt selfish thinking of myself rather than my stricken father, but his advice, *Don't end up like me,* became my personal commandment.

I decided that joining the service was my only chance. I even fantasized about serving in the air force as a fireman, then one day returning to the Bay Area and showing Father my badge. Trying to enlist proved to be an ordeal. After struggling to obtain my GED, I had to fill out mounds of paperwork for every time I had been bounced from one foster home to another, then explain on separate forms why I was placed in another home. Whenever the air force recruiter pressed me about my past, I became so terrified that I stuttered like an idiot. After weeks of evading these questions, I caved in and gave the sergeant a brief explanation about why Mother and I did not get along. I waited for his reaction. I held my breath knowing that if the recruiter thought I was a troublemaker, he could refuse my application.

Every morning, for weeks, I stood outside the door, waiting for the office to open, before I hurried in to fill out more paperwork, and studied films and whatever booklets the recruiter had available. I became possessed to enlist. The air force was my ticket to a new life.

After the paperwork was filled out, double-checked, then reverified, I had to get a physical examination. During the battery of tests I was poked and prodded on every inch of my rail-thin body. At the end, as I sat nearly naked, the doctor kept circling around me as he questioned the ancient bumps on my scalp, the scars on my body, the marks on my right arm where Mother had burned me on the gas stove. I simply shrugged off the doctor's questions, telling him I had been a clumsy kid. The doctor let out a sigh and raised his eyebrows. Immediately my heart seized. I just knew I had said the wrong thing. Fearing my statement would disqualify me, I quickly added that it was a stage I had gone through when I was a kid. "A kid?" the doctor asked, as if he were not buying my story.

"Yeah, you know, when I was six, seven years old. But"—I raised a finger to stress the importance of this point—"I'm not clumsy now! Nope, not anymore. Not me. No sireee . . ." The doctor waved me off and told me to get dressed. I felt a surge of relief as I saw him mark the block that claimed I was medically qualified to enlist. I was on top of the world, right up until the moment I leaned too far and crashed against the table. Folders containing other recruits' paperwork exploded in every direction, and, still struggling to pull on my pants, I tried to grab the papers, only scattering them more. The doctor ordered me to stop trying to help and get out of his office as fast as humanly possible. As I hurried out the door, the doctor flashed a smile. "Over that clumsy period, eh?"

Hours later that same day, I sat frozen in front of a computer next to an air force sergeant who typed in an endless stream of information. Finally, the sergeant paused, turned toward me, and nonchalantly asked, "So, what day do you want to enlist?"

I shook my head, not sure I had heard what the sergeant just asked. I leaned forward and whispered, "You mean, I'm in? I can join? You're actually asking me if I want to join?"

"Don't make a federal case out of it. Yeah, you're in—that is, unless the FBI tells us you're a criminal," the sergeant teased.

My mind immediately flashed back to all the close calls I had had with the police for speeding tickets when I was a teenager. My heart skipped a beat. I knew that if the air force found out about my past, I was a goner. The sergeant startled me when he tapped on my shoulder. "Hey, Pelz-ter, relax. So . . . when do you want to enlist?"

I was lost in a daze. *Now you have the chance to make something of yourself. Now is your time to build a life.* I simply could not believe that after struggling over six months, I had actually made it.

I allowed myself the reward of smiling. "When's the soonest I can join?"

He snapped back, "Girlfriend problems, eh?" Before I had a chance to respond, the man bowed his head and feverishly pounded on the computer keyboard. "Well," he began, "if you really feel the need for speed, I can have you on a plane and in basic training by . . . tonight. Or, if that doesn't suit you, you can enlist next week. So, what will it be?"

I immediately knew what I had to do, but a wave of shame washed over me. For months I had lied to my foster parents, telling them that I was taking specialized tests and interviewing for a job, which in a way I felt I was. The Turnboughs had no idea what I was really up to. I felt a sudden urge to run off and enlist and then simply phone them from boot camp. Besides my foster parents and a handful of close friends, I had no one in my life. No girlfriends, no work buddies, no friends who picked me up to go cruising or see movies, no relatives to speak of—no one. I felt that if I fell off the face of the earth, less than half a dozen people would even notice. But deep in my heart I knew that I owed my *real* family—my foster parents and whatever friends I had—more than a long-distance phone call. Above all, it was a matter of honor. I let out a deep sigh before answering the sergeant. "Next week."

"All right, next week. You sure about this?" he politely asked.

Without blinking an eye, I nodded my head. "Yes, sir!"

The sergeant pressed a button, and the computer began printing a stream of papers. "Sign here, here, here, here and . . . here," he informed me without a trace of emotion. I stared at the blocks with the bright red Xs. *This is it!* I told myself. I snatched the government pen and scribbled my name so hard that I nearly tore through the sheets of papers. As the sergeant took the paperwork and typed in more commands to his computer, I killed time by looking at the framed glossy photographs of the high-tech air force fighter jets. My mouth began to water at the sleek, crisp lines of the airplanes against the endless blue sky.

"Sir, is that the F-15 jet fighter?" I asked, pointing at a photograph above his desk.

Without looking up from the computer, the sergeant replied, "Nope . . . F-16."

I nodded my head to the sergeant's answer, then stated before thinking, "Excuse me, sir, but if I'm not mistaken, that's the McDonnell Douglas F-15 Eagle: first strike, air superior fighter, capable of speeds in excess of Mach 2.5, produced by a pair of G.E. F-100 after-burning engines. . . ."

The sergeant turned toward me with his mouth hung open.

"Did I say something wrong, sir?" I thought for a moment of what I had just said, and even I was surprised how easy the basic technical aspects of the airplane came from my mouth. All these facts I had learned from the recruitment brochures and stream of books I had digested over the last few months.

He simply nodded for me to continue.

Immediately I thought this was part of some strange test. I closed my eyes to recall as much as I could. "Uhm, I know it has a comple . . . dent—I mean, complement of AIM-7 Sparrow and AIM-9 Sidewinder missiles. And . . . I think . . . it was two, maybe three years ago that a modified F-15 Streak Eagle beat the time-to-climb altitude record held by a Russian MeG." I paused to catch my breath and waited for his reaction. Craving acceptance, I didn't want the sergeant to think I was trying to show off. By the smile in his eyes I realized he was not only impressed, but interested in planes as well.

"That's 'MiG' Pelz-ter, not 'MeG,' " he countered. "Okay, smart guy: What base did they launch the Streak Eagle from?"

"Grand Forks, North Dakota!" I stated with confidence.

"All right, not bad. Now," he said, "the big one: Why Grand Forks?"

I smiled back, enjoying the game. "Molecule compression. The colder air allows the plane to reach speeds and altitudes quicker while at the same time consuming less fuel. I mean . . . I think that's the idea."

The sergeant responded with a wide grin and slapped me on the shoulder. "Where in the hell did you . . . ?"

By instinct, I hesitated. For a second I thought I had just revealed military secrets. "I read, sir."

"You read?"

"Ah . . . yes, sir. I read a lot. I've always wanted to . . . I mean, Sergeant?" I asked in a low voice. "You think they'd ever let me fly?"

"My Lord!" He coughed. "You're a piece of work, aren't you?

"Hey, Max," he bellowed to the next cubicle. "I got the next Chuck Yeager over here! Wants to know if he can fly!" As a small roar of laughter erupted, I closed my eyes. I always seemed to say the wrong thing at the wrong time and make a jerk out of myself.

After I let out a deep breath, the sergeant caught my eye. I stated in a firm tone, "Chuck Yeager was *enlisted* before he flew."

The sergeant thumbed through my paperwork. "Listen, Pelz, you barely made it in. You're a high school dropout, your aptitude scores are *way* below average, and you have the body of a skinny rat with the eyesight of Stevie Wonder. A fly boy? Thought you wanted to be a fireman. Listen," he said, "here's what you do: Learn your trade as a fireman and get some college classes under your belt. Heck, the air force will pay for your tuition. And then after a few years if you want to reenlist, you can apply for a slot. That's a major goal, but if you're serious, we'll meet you halfway. Okay?"

I swallowed hard, realizing how lucky I was to even enlist. "Yes, sir. I understand. Thanks for the advice."

"Hey, that's what I'm here for." He stood up, indicating he was through with me. "Not to worry, Pelz. You keep studying and they'll have you piloting the SR-71." He then raised his eyebrows. "I assume with your plethora of aeronautical knowledge, you do know about the Blackbird, *don't you?*"

My eyes lit up at the mention of my favorite plane. "Yes, sir!" I exclaimed. "I know about the Blackbird, like nobody's business!"

"Well then, we'll see you next week." He extended his hand.

"Thank you, sir," I said as I shook it. "I'll make you proud. You'll see."

The sergeant let out a chuckle, released my hand, then snapped to attention and gave me a crisp salute. "See ya, *Airman Pelz-a-Yeager!*"

Later that afternoon, before I chickened out and changed my mind, I informed my foster parents, "I enlisted in the air force! I leave next week!"

"Oh, really?" my foster father, Harold Turnbough, casually replied.

I searched their eyes for any kind of reaction to my explosive news. After what seemed like an eternity of silence, I broke the ice. "I'm going nowhere. I've been working myself stupid. I thought I could find the answers—to my past, to Mother—trying to numb myself about my dad. And now, now it's my time. My time to make something of myself. I've already missed so much, but if I stay focused and work hard, maybe someday I can turn this around." I stopped to gauge their response. My foster parents continued to just sit there. "Isn't that what you've tried to teach me; I mean, to become self-reliant? Well . . . ?" I asked, frustrated.

Alice and Harold, who years ago had adopted me into their hearts, began to nod their heads before exploding with laughter. I shook my head in disgust. Because of the day's mounting tensions—the test and examinations, my fear of not being good enough to enlist, my lack of sleep, and hiding my secret for so long—I felt sick to my stomach. "Stop it!" I shouted. "What's so funny? This is serious! I mean it! I already signed the paperwork."

Alice leaned over to embrace me. "We've known for a while, David."

Harold said with a crooked smile, "With all those brochures layin' around and your babblin' 'bout airplanes this, airplanes that, what else would you be up to?"

"So, you're not mad? I mean . . . ?"

"Of course not, David. But answer this: Why the service? Three years is a long time," said Alice.

"Four years; I'll be in for four," I corrected her. "I'm just fed up. I'm tired of living hand to mouth. Working my butt off, for what? For nothing! I've been scrimping and slaving away, and I have nothing to show for it. Check it out: In four years I can grow and learn, I can explore and see things beyond any picture of any magazine." I stopped and lowered my head. "Maybe getting away will help me . . . help me find my answers. . . ."

Mrs. Turnbough reached over to cup my hand. "David, you

may never know. Sometimes, bad things happen. For some things there are no absolutes."

"No," I interrupted, "it's wrong. I have to know. I have to find out. If I don't deal with this, all I'm doing is hiding 'the secret' like everyone else, and if I do that, then what's to say I don't become like her or like my dad? Something made them the way they are. Things do happen for a reason. I want to understand; I want to know. And if I don't find out and do something, who will? How many kids have you taken in who came from the same kind of homes as me? The problem's not going to go away by turning our backs or sweeping it underneath the carpet anymore. Every day *things* happen, and everyone acts as if nothing's wrong. No one wants to talk about *things,* let alone deal with the consequences afterward. It's wrong, and it's about time to take a stand. Isn't that what you and everyone else has pounded into my head since I was rescued? Be good, be honest and fair, find something I believe in, work hard and keep the faith no matter how long it takes? Well . . . ?"

My foster parents sat in front of me totally mesmerized. In all the years I had known them, they had never seen me so intense, so articulate about my past. I continued in a softer tone. "Listen, it's going to be okay, I can handle it. I'll be fine, but please understand, I don't want to turn out like them. This is something *I've* got to do."

I took a moment to compose my thoughts. I did not want to screw up and tell them in the wrong way what I felt in my heart. "You know I love you both very much. You've treated me as if I were a *real* person. But while I'm in the air force, I'm gonna save every dollar I can. I want a home . . . *my home.* I want to buy a home in Guerneville, on the Russian River. Ever since kindergarten, I knew that's what I wanted. That's my lifelong dream. When I lived in Mother's house, when things were really bad, I'd go inside and dream of a log home by the river with a warm fireplace and the smell of redwood trees. It made me feel safe. Of all the things she did to me, Mother could never get me when I thought about the river. As a kid, that dream gave me something to live for. I want *my* home." I hesitated as my throat tightened. Tears began to trickle down the sides of my face. I tried to hold back my emotions, but the years of extreme pressure were just too much.

"David, what is it? What's wrong?" Mrs. Turnbough whispered.

I closed my eyes before bursting with a flood of tears. "All his life, all he wanted was to have something. . . . And now he's alone, living on the streets, and has nothing. It's not right."

"Who's alone? Who are you talking about?" Alice probed.

"My father!" I cried. "I'm gonna buy a house and have Dad live with me. It's the right thing to do. And," I said, renewing my vow, "I'm going to find my answers, and when I'm ready, I'm going to do what I can to make a difference." I wiped my tears away, feeling foolish.

"So, you're joining the air force?" Harold asked with a hint of humor. "Do you think you can manage to stay out of *the brig*?"

My smile matched Harold's. "Yes, sir!" I said. "I'll make you proud, you watch. One day, you'll see. I'll make you proud!"

"Well," Alice broke in, "now that you've made your decision, when are you going to tell your parents?"

I took a long, deep breath. As I inhaled, I felt clean. I could feel my entire body relax. I suddenly felt as if I could curl up in a big, soft bed and sleep forever. For the first time in nearly half a year I found myself at peace. In front of me the Turnboughs sat hand in hand. I gently placed my hands around theirs. "As far as I'm concerned, *Mom*," I said as I gazed into Alice's eyes, *"and Dad,"* I said, looking at Harold, "I've enlisted in the United States Air Force. I leave next week. Any questions?"

* * *

The Boeing 727's sudden downward lurch shook me from my trance. I blinked, struggling to focus on the San Antonio skyline outside the airplane window. The more I stared through the Plexiglas, the more the faces and serenity of my parents faded away. I was on the threshold of my new life. I took a deep breath, then smiled. *And so it begins!*

CHAPTER 3

LETTER FROM HOME

Air force basic training was no cakewalk, but after stumbling through the first two weeks, I began to get into the groove and felt comfortable with the expectations of my drill sergeants, which in an odd sense reminded me of living with Mother. I had sense enough to keep a low profile and never make eye contact with the instructors whenever they lashed out at my squadron. I performed my duties as quickly and precisely as possible, and, most important, I made certain to keep my stuttering mouth clamped shut. Whenever I had a free moment, I'd crank out epic letters of my *mis*adventures to my foster parents, my "aviation mentor" Michael Marsh from my days in foster care, and my father. Every day in the late afternoon our squadron received mail call, and every day my heart pounded with excitement. But the only letters I received regularly were crumpled ones addressed to my father with RETURN TO SENDER stamped on the envelope. After a few weeks I gave up trying to reach Father through the mail, so I tried to keep close to him through my prayers.

After saying my evening prayers I would roll over, feeling relieved that I had truly escaped Mother's tangled web of hate and deceit. I knew she could no longer manipulate or harm me in any way. For the first time in my life, I was my own person. I had finally locked Mother away in the deep recesses of my mind. I felt so elated, my lifelong quest no longer seemed that important. I was free.

At night, though, I discovered, as I had in foster care, that The Mother still lived in my dreams. As always, she would stand before me like a marble statue at the end of a long hallway. I stood in front of her—in full view and helpless—but somehow thinking her sculpture could do me no harm. And then her eyes blink open. She smiles before gazing down at her bony hand and pulling out a gleaming silver carving knife. I know I should do something, anything, but my fear paralyzes any defenses. In slow motion The Mother steps toward me. Her glazed eyes pierce my soul. A split second before her foot touches the floor, I turn and flee down the hallway at full speed. As my heart races, I know I am miles ahead of The Mother, but I can somehow feel her presence inches behind me. I run forever, but there is no escape. I frantically hunt for a way out of the maze-like corridors, but I stumble and fall into a void. Above me The Mother stands poised, revealing her yellow teeth and putrid, steamy breath. As I look into her eyes for mercy, her expression seems to laugh before she raises her arm and lunges at me. I close my eyes as the shiny-silvered knife flings from The Mother's hand and flies through the air. I empty my lungs, screeching, *"Why . . . ?"*

"Hey, Pelz, wake up, man!" my air force "bunk buddy," Randy, whispered low enough so no one else could hear. "You havin' one of those dreams again."

I wiped the sticky sweat from my forehead as I scanned the outline of the sleeping bay of my fellow airmen. I thanked God that I didn't wake up my squad, let alone the entire training base. I checked my chest, making certain that The Mother had not crossed over and stabbed me. I thanked Randy for his concern, then spent the remainder of the night sitting on the edge of my cot.

The next morning after inspection, my drill instructor summoned me into his office. As I stood at attention in front of his desk, I became so terrified that my body began to weave. I kept my eyes glued straight ahead and held my breath, praying the instructor had no idea of my latest anxiety attack. "At ease, airman," the master sergeant commanded. "Says here," he stated as he casually read, "in last night's report . . . you had one of your episodes . . . again. Third time this week. *What's your problem?* You homesick for Momma?"

As my mind raced for an answer, I somehow had enough sense to evade the truth. Instead I bellowed, "Negative, sir! I'm not homesick, not for a moment, sir!" I glanced down at the sergeant, who wasn't fazed by my off-the-cuff response. My lips trembled as I tried to make up for lost ground. "Won't happen again, sir! Ever!" I promised in a quavering voice.

"Make certain it doesn't, *airman.* Damn sure! Understand this," the master sergeant said as he shot up from his chair and stood inches in front of my nose, "the United States Air Force has no room *whatsoever* for whiny little momma's boys. Our sole objective, our sole purpose, is to protect the freedom of this nation's democracy. *Is that clear?* If you can't handle the magnitude of that responsibility, then get out! If you continue on your present course, I will have no alternative but to have you undergo psychiatric evaluation for possible medical discharge. *Do I make myself clear . . .* Airman *Pelzer?*"

I swallowed hard. "Crystal clear, sir!" But even as the words came out of my mouth, I could feel my "master plan" evaporating. In my mind, I could see my dream—my log cabin, with Father and me sitting on the porch or fishing together on the Russian River—fading away. After being dismissed by my drill instructor, I gave a crisp salute and marched out of his office. Immediately I fled to the latrine and threw up. On my hands and knees I cursed myself for allowing Mother to continue controlling me. I became filled with shame.

After wiping away the vomit, I became furious—not at Mother but with myself. Everything I had accomplished— from studying books on big adventure in the darkness of Mother's garage to working endless hours as a teenager at fast-

food restaurants—was to somehow better myself and to prepare myself to live a better life, a *real life.* If I was kicked out of
the air force, it was *my* fault, not anyone else's. Therefore, as
the sergeant had stressed in his underlying message: *I had to
do something to change my present course.*

That morning I schemed to come up with a way to somehow save me from another *episode* and a possible lifetime of
disgrace. To be booted out of the armed forces for having im-
mature, childish dreams was not an option. Since I'd been
having the nightmares in the early hours of the morning and
my bunk buddy, Randy, was a slight sleeper, I bribed him to
wake me at the first sign of trouble. But after a couple of
nights, I felt I was stretching Randy's Southern generosity to
its limit. So I decided to volunteer for the guard-duty shift that
began at two a.m. until reveille at six a.m. My idea was an
immediate success, but days later my lack of sleep made it
impossible for me to concentrate on my academics. Whenever
I'd study my manuals in class, the words became blurred and
ran together. I'd slump forward at my desk only to be awakened by a furious drill sergeant. During parade practice I'd
misstep nearly every move and was soon abandoned to practice precision movements alone in the blistering Texas sun, so
not to further embarrass my squadron. I was ridiculed by my
air force instructors for my lack of concentration and never
ending clumsiness.

But I refused to cave in. I didn't mind being condemned; if
anything, my weakness in certain areas kept my mind off my
inner struggles. As long as I kept myself out of the shrink's
office, I would have gladly practiced my marching routine
barefoot on the searing tarmac.

Because of my awkwardness and the spreading rumors of
my nightmares, I found myself isolated from my squadron,
which had begun to break into cliques. The only friends I had
were the ones assigned with me for latrine duty. During the
latter part of training, our class was awarded afternoon weekend passes. I refused mine and stayed behind to catch up on

my studies, practice my marching movements in the long, empty hallways, starch-iron my uniforms to a razor's edge, and polish my boots with a wet cotton ball until they had a mirror finish. Hours later, groups of my squadron returned, bragging about their adventure of sneaking beers and showing off their dress-blue uniforms to the local girls. I simply counted the days until I could begin my training as a fireman. More important I mentally counted the money I had saved by remaining at the barracks. The more dollars I began to hoard, the more my pride grew with the fact that I was finally getting a foothold on buying my home on the Russian River.

During the last week of basic training, as I reported to the career counselor's office for my fireman position, I knew by the distant look on the sergeant's face that my goal was not meant to be. Without looking at me, the counselor rummaged through a stack of forms and mumbled, "Airman . . . there was a slight holdup in your specialty request, and, well, by the time it was rectified, well . . . don't ask me why, but these things happen . . . so . . ." As the sergeant's words trailed off, I could feel a sense of doom hanging over me.

For a moment I thought my paperwork problems were due to my constant screw-ups and the ever-looming "psych eval." I shook my head clear, praying that the sergeant was somehow toying with me and that this was a trick the career counselors played on young, gullible airmen. "Sir, I don't understand. What is it you're saying, sir?"

The sergeant cleared his throat and stated that all firefighter positions had been filled.

"That's okay," I said. "I can wait."

"Negative!" the counselor shot back. "There are no available positions. *You,*" he said, jabbing a finger in front of my plastic black-rimmed glasses, *"are not,* I repeat, *are not,* going to be a fireman!"

Breaking all rules of protocol, I blurted, "But . . . that's what I signed up for. That's why I joined. I—"

"I am sorry," the sergeant broke in. "I truly am. But mission necessities come first—"

"But, sir!" I interrupted, "it took me forever to get in . . . to fill out all that paperwork, passing the interviews. . . . This can't happen. I mean, my whole life, all I wanted. . . . My father!" I shrieked. "He was a—"

"At ease! Stand down, airman," the sergeant snapped. "The air force could care less what *you* want! Listen," he spoke in a softer tone, "I realize your position. I've got half a dozen other troops outside this office with the same problem. You knew when you enlisted that mission necessity has priority. So, for now, the air force dictates that it needs 62210s."

"62210s?" I asked as I leaned closer to his desk.

The sergeant flipped through a manual, matching the coded numbers with the job description. I knew by his reaction that I was in for another shock. "Uh, food service specialist."

"Sir?" I asked, shaking my head.

"A cook, Airman Pelzer. You'd be a cook. Come on," the sergeant said in a cheerful voice, "it's a slack job. You go in for a few hours, then you go home—nine to five. Bankers' hours. It's a cakewalk. Hey, at most bases you're in charge of the civilians; they're the ones who cook, they do all the work. You'll just supervise!"

"So . . . in my off time I can go to college or get a part-time job?" I inquired. I had instantly accepted my fate and somehow was trying to formulate a plan to turn my negative setback into a positive outcome.

"Listen," the counselor said, "you'll have so much time on your hands, you'll be bored stiff—that is, unless you get assigned to a field unit. Then you'll work your tail off in some godforsaken boondocks. But hey, I've yet to see that happen. Don't sweat it. In three years, if you keep your nose clean, you can cross-train and then become a fireman."

"But if I stay in, I wanna fly. That's why I gotta go to college," I said.

"Yeah, sure, whatever. Not to worry. Just sign this paper that I briefed you in this little snafu. And don't worry, you keep pluggin' away. Things have a way of turning up. Aim high!"

Without hesitation I snatched a pen and scribbled my name, rank, and date. I found it strange that after my months of intense longing, my life's course was again heading in a direction in which I had no control. I felt completely helpless. My childhood ambitions were instantly erased with a stroke of a pen. Afterward, I stared at the cheap, black ballpoint that had U.S. GOVERNMENT stamped on it and flung it on top of a stack of papers. I was so numb that I strolled out of the office without being dismissed, let alone saluting my superior.

Weeks after graduating basic training and being transferred to my specialty training base, the shock of serving in the air force as a mere cook began to fade away. I was so ashamed that I didn't tell my foster parents. I wrestled with the fact that I had, in a sense, failed my father. I knew being a fire-fighter meant the world to him, and he had seemed so proud when I phoned him days before I enlisted. I had wanted so badly to impress him, to surprise him that David Pelzer—the unwanted one, the child called "It"—would someday be en-trusted with saving the lives of others, like my once-upon-a-time hero . . . my dad.

The more I had boasted to Father on the phone that day about my worldly plans of obtaining a degree in fire science after my initial qualification training, the more happy he seemed. His violent coughing attacks, caused by a lifetime of smoking, eased for a few moments, and his voice seemed less tense and more warm. I nearly broke down and cried after he let out a strained laugh, saying how proud he was of me. "You're going to make good, Tiger. You'll be fine." I clutched the phone with both hands and pressed it against my ear at the mention of the word "Tiger." As a young boy, before my world had turned black, the highest compliment Father could pay his adoring children was the word Tiger. After I hung up the phone, I stood mesmerized. After all these years Father had still remembered a single precious word. I felt from the bottom of my soul how desperately I craved to someday make both Mother and Father proud. But more so, I had hoped that by becoming a fireman, I would somehow ease the loneliness and pain I felt that Father had lived with every day—because of a son, a wife, and a family *he could not, would not save.*

I swallowed my dreams and my dignity and focused on applying myself as best as I could. Because of my years of working in various fast-food chains, I found the training classes boring. I blazed through the study materials while maintaining a near perfect score, and my hands-on skills surpassed the entire class. Whereas some of my peers would haphazardly throw their meals together, I would analyze every measurement, every ingredient, then time each move of whatever I was assigned to prepare for that particular shift. No matter what I cooked—a fluffy omelet with cheese oozing from both ends, perfectly crisp vegetables, or BBQ ribs that melted in one's mouth—I felt I had somehow prepared the perfect entree, and I surged with pride whenever my instructor, or anyone who came through the food line, especially an air crew member, threw me a compliment for my efforts.

During my off-duty hours, while most of my classmates partied at the Airman's Club, I maintained my vow of pinching pennies and stayed in the barracks. I buried myself in books about the history of the air force or adventures of combat flying. I soon became addicted and began to build my own aeronautical library, one book at a time. Every payday I would retrieve my crumpled shopping list of specific planes that, to me, had changed the course of history. I soon became a walking encyclopedia, and I wished that someday I, too, could make a difference in my new world of flight.

No matter what time of day or night, whenever I thought my mind would explode from the constant studying, I'd take long walks around the base. I would go to my postal box with my eyes widened. I would utter a quick prayer before speed-dialing the combination. At times I would become so frantic that I would spin past my number, and have to clasp the fingers of my right hand together to keep them from shaking. But even before I flipped open the box, I knew the outcome. It got to the point that I'd shrug my shoulders as if I didn't care. Just as I had years ago in Mother's house, in order to protect myself I'd turn off my emotions and remain tough inside. So I'd simply take a few laps around the air base and return three or four more times, hoping that someone from the post office had made a mistake, found my misplaced letter on the floor, and stuffed it in that precious box. For the most part I'd become numb, for I'd know that tomorrow was another day.

One day during my lunch break, I decided not to check my box. I dared myself to stroll past without giving it a thought. The disappointment had become too much. I got only as far as five feet before I spun around and hurried back. Seconds later my fingers trembled as I pulled out a crumpled, soiled letter. With my mouth gaping open, I focused on the childish scribbling. My heart raced as I tore open the envelope. I impatiently scanned the length of the paper but lost my grip, then stood paralyzed as I watched it flutter to the floor. The distinctive penmanship belonged to Father.

From behind, a friend woke me from my trance when he bent down and picked up my letter. "What's wrong?"

I took forever to form the words. "My . . . ah, my dad . . . he's not doing too well."

My friend shook his head. "Hey, man, don't sweat it. Parents they get old, but hey, his old lady can take care of him. Come on . . . shit happens."

No! I wanted to scream. *You don't understand* . . . But before I could justify my fears, my friend became lost in the crowd of other airmen retrieving their mail and letting out whoops of joy as they clutched their prizes over their heads. I lowered my head and disappeared in the opposite direction. I wished I had never received that letter.

I wandered outside, found a bench, and sat down. It took me more than half a dozen tries to comprehend the contents of the letter. The more I digested, the more my heart sank. Father had written that times were very tough for him. He could no longer find part-time work either washing dishes or filling in as a short-order cook. Feeling ashamed, Father gave up on asking friends to stay at their home for a few nights at a time. With no one to turn to and no money, society's old hero was now alone with no place to live. I wanted to mail Father some money to ease some of his pain.

Rereading both the envelope and the letter, I frantically hunted for the return address, but there was none. Father's handwriting had always been barely legible, but this letter was almost impossible to read. Nearly every sentence was incomplete or rambled on without any conclusion. Words were either misspelled, jumbled, or ran off the page altogether. I concentrated so hard on Father's writing that my head began to throb with pain. Suddenly it struck me: he probably had been drunk when he scrawled out the letter. That had to be the only conclusion. That would explain the condition of the soiled envelope, his penmanship, and, more important, the reason he forgot a return address.

In the blink of an eye I became furious. I was so ashamed of the life Father was living. *How,* I wondered, *could he be so foolish to keep drinking?* He had to realize his binges—his entire lifestyle—would be the death of him. *Why?* I yelled at myself. *Why couldn't Father just quit once and for all?* He had been so courageous as a fireman; why couldn't he muster the willpower to deal with something so relatively simple? *How hard was it to throw away the bottle?*

I closed my eyes, replaying the countless times Father had nearly passed out, literally on top of me, with his eyes bloodshot and his clothes reeking from days-old perspiration and spilled drinks. Dad had always promised that he would someday, somehow, take me away from Mother's evil clutches. But even back then I realized it was the booze talking. As brave as

Father had been on the job, he had no intention of crossing Mother. Sitting outside the air force barracks, I felt utterly helpless. To me, Father wasn't a bad man. *Maybe,* I justified, *Mother's fury forced him to drink.* Maybe . . . his drinking was his only outlet to deal with . . . ? "Oh, my God!" I cried out. What if Father's boozing began as his way to escape all the hell between Mother and me? What if I was the reason for Father's drinking problem?

My body shuddered from humiliation. My thoughts swayed between the intense guilt of Father's plight and wanting him to find the determination to help himself. I thought if I was the reason for Father's alcoholic condition . . . then I was responsible for the family's devastation, my parents' separation, and for Father's downfall at the fire station; *I was the reason for his current condition.* The sudden wave of shame was so overwhelming that I began to weep. In some sense, in the back of my mind I had always known this. As a child, I knew I was the bad seed. Somehow I had made everyone I had come into contact with miserable. As an adult, I had to make things right—buying a home for Father and me was not enough. Who knew what condition Father would be in by the time my enlistment was complete? I was the only one who could ease his pain, and I had to do it now.

I decided to wire Father some money. Even if he used the funds to buy booze, I didn't care. *Who was I,* my conscience argued, *to judge a grown man when in so many ways I was still a pitiful child?* After all the hell I had put Father through, this was the least I could do for him. If the money helped to numb his loneliness and despair for a few hours, then so be it.

After I reached a definite decision, my fingers quit shaking. I wiped my tears away and stared at the crumpled envelope. Seconds later I shook my head in disgust after remembering that Father left no return address. "Goddammit!" I exploded. "Why?" I cried as I clutched the letter. "Why is my life constantly plagued with so much bullshit!" When my own mother tried, for twelve years, to kill me, I never fought back.

I never ran away. I had just taken the abuse by adapting every moment of every single day to surviving. And foster care was no breeze, but I made the best of it. As a teenager I'd worked my tail off while normal kids were having the time of their lives. While scores of others waltzed into the recruiter's office to enlist, it took me forever to join the air force. When my lifelong dream of becoming a fireman was shattered because of some foul-up in the paperwork, I bit my lip and pressed on. And now I couldn't even help my father because he had no address or no phone number for me to call. I couldn't even disturb Mother and beg her for information on Father because I have been excommunicated from *her precious family*—I was not worthy of the privilege of having her unlisted phone number. As I sat and stewed at my latest predicament, I so badly wanted to be anyone other than David James Pelzer. I covered my face with my hands as if to squeeze an answer from my brain.

The only alternative I could think of was if Father by some chance wrote me again. Maybe then he would scribble his address. Whenever I was faced with overwhelming, impossible odds, I always turned to God. As a child I always felt guilty, begging for His time to help me, but now I pleaded for God to keep my father safe and warm. Mostly I begged for God to somehow ease my father's pain. "Please," I whispered, "do what you can to protect my dad. And please, deliver him from all evil. Amen." After pleading with God I discovered that a film of snow covered my fatigues, the bench I was sitting on, and the entire air base. Even though the tips of my fingers had turned purple and my ear lobes raged with pain, I somehow felt warm inside. As I stood up and walked back toward the barracks, a howling wind blew in my face. I didn't blink an eye. "It's up to God," I said to myself. "Only He can save my father now."

Days turned into weeks, which turned into months. As much as I waited, as much as I prayed, I never heard from Father.

After graduating from specialty training, I was transferred to my permanent base in the Florida panhandle. Just as my counselor in basic training had boasted, I expected to serve in a typical setting while overseeing civilians who ran the kitchen. But it was not meant to be. I was stationed with a combat engineering group, which entailed spending most of my time laboring under the cover of a tent rather than simply monitoring others in an air-conditioned building. I dreaded rolling out of bed in the early morning, before driving over an hour, in the middle of nowhere, to the field site, and work straight through without a break, then finish the day at eight that evening, only to repeat the cycle the next day. I detested the job, and I felt as worthless and degraded as I had when I lived with Mother.

As always, I swallowed my pride and rose to the challenge. However, as much as I tried, it seemed that I could do nothing right for my two hard-nosed supervisors, who berated me every minute of the day. I refused to cave in. Because I had a hard time getting the field burner units, which cooked the meals, up and running in time, I had to begin my day at three a.m. rather than four-thirty. By the time others showed up to begin their shift, I had almost everything cooked and on the serving line and ready to be dished out. But that was not good enough for the sergeants. When I accomplished that feat, I only found myself being chewed out for something else. Every week, it seemed to me, the harder that I'd focus on my tasks, the more I'd screw up. I seemed to be in the middle of a never ending cycle. It never failed: I always had everything under control, right up until the moment the sergeants peeked in on my progress, only to find me fighting off my latest blunder. A short time later I discovered I was the only cook preparing all the meals, while the sergeants and other airmen seemed content to watch me sweat away.

Then one afternoon, out of the blue, my supervisor, Technical Sergeant Campbell, a towering black man who always bellowed at me while his gleaming white teeth maintained a vise lock on one of his huge cigars, called me for what I thought was another lecture on my shortcomings. "I tell you, Airman Pelt-der, you a working fool," he stated with a wide smile.

My eyes dodged down at my splattered boots. "I'm trying hard, Sergeant Campbell."

"You need to understand, squadron's job's to build bases from nothin' and fix runways in the event they've been damaged after an enemy attack. Runway's not fixed, planes don't take off. Mind can't be on business of buildin' and fixin' if everyone's hungry. It's that simple. You get what I'm sayin'?" I nodded my head. "I get you to work hard, to see if you quit. That's why I ride ya. Ride ya hard. Gets the job done, that's all that matters to me. We're in this together. You still needs to work on adjusting that attitude, though. Ain't no shame being a cook. I know you want something else; you can do whatever you like in the future. But for now you stay with us," Sergeant Campbell said. "You done good! No need to be ridin' on your behind no more," he stated with a grin as he slapped me on the back.

It was then that I understood why I had been constantly harassed and forced to carry the load more than others: I was being tested. I let out a sigh. *At least,* I told myself, *I tackled a job I detested and was willing to give it my best shot.* Above all, I knew that I would never give up and with my determination I would find honor.

A short time later I found myself on my first temporary duty assignment (TDY). Because of Sergeant Campbell's faith in me, two peers and I were the sole cooks to feed a small group of pilots and support staff in a remote location. The two senior airmen and I worked from dusk to dawn, and our efforts were rewarded with praise. During my stay I began to feel a certain pride that I, in some small way, had contributed to a team effort.

That evening, while the other cooks cruised to the local bars, I stayed behind and studied one of my books. Part of the reason was that I felt enormously intimidated in front of other people. While others would tell wild stories of where they grew up and adventures in school or dating, I would become afraid, lock up like a statue and stutter. I couldn't look at anyone in the face, let alone maintain eye contact long enough to tell a joke. So I had decided that I'd rather be alone than make myself out to be more of a fool than they already knew.

Hours later, after reading several chapters of my book, after filing away another written letter to Father that I would never mail, and after staring at the ceiling, I still could not fall asleep. For some reason something seemed to keep me from relaxing. I was wide awake even after my cohorts stumbled in and collapsed on their beds, As usual, whenever I'd become uptight about something, I'd doze off literally minutes before I had to begin another day.

The next day, after serving lunch, one of the cooks thrust a phone in my hand, refusing to look at me. Confused, I shook my head. My eyes darted between my friend standing a few feet away and the phone cradled in my fingers. For a moment I hesitated before pressing the receiver end against my ear. "Hello?" I uttered.

"David?" The voice seemed to crackle from a million miles away.

My heart skipped a beat. "Mom, is that you? What is it? What's wrong? How did you get this number? Why are you calling?" I asked my foster mother as fast as the words could spill from my mouth.

"My God!" Alice exclaimed. "David, I'm so sorry. I beg of you, please forgive me. It took days, and I mean *days*, to reach you. Your squadron . . . in Florida. . . . they weren't sure where you were. . . . I tried every number they gave me. Please know that I—"

"Wait! Slow down, I can barely hear you! The line . . . it's too much static. Just tell me, what is it? What's wrong?!"

"Harold's fine. I'm fine. . . . David, just believe me when I tell you how hard I tried. Honest to God, I tried. . . ."

My stomach began to clench. The more my mind ran

through every possible option, the more the answer became crystal clear. "Tell me," I said as I clamped my eyes shut and uttered a quick prayer, "just tell me. Tell me he's not . . ."

On the other end of the line I could hear Alice lose control. "Come home, David. Come home," she sobbed. "Your father's in the hospital. They say he's not going to . . . he only has a few days. . . . Come home, David. Just come home."

As the words sank in, the receiver dropped from my hand. I fell to my knees as a static shrill from the phone filled my head.

CHAPTER 4

WISHFUL THINKING

Nothing could have prepared me for seeing my father. I had zero tolerance for the assistant at the nurses' station at Kaiser Hospital, in the heart of San Francisco, who stood in front of Alice Turnbough and me as if we were invisible, while refusing to say if Stephen Pelzer was indeed on that particular floor, let alone admitted to the premises. Because of my insomnia, zigzagging across the country in the middle of the night, and the anxiety of seeing Father, I was ready to explode.

Whatever scenarios I had formulated during the flight over, dealing with the actual situation was far more stressful than I had planned. Aboard the plane, every option seemed cut and dried, but now, I strained just to lean my upper body against the counter to keep from collapsing. I could feel my resistance to stay razor sharp, to retain a crystal-clear focus, drain away. The sterile pine smell nearly caused my nose to bleed and triggered memories of being trapped in the bathroom with Mother's concoction of ammonia and Chlorox. The thought of not only coming face to face but actually dealing with Mother whenever she showed up would be hellish at best. My only wish was that somehow Mother would for once find it in her heart to bury her immense hatred and permit me a few moments alone with Father without unleashing her explosive fury.

But maybe, I imagined, I was the one going too far. It was

in fact Mother who had called Alice to tell her of Father's condition. Maybe, there was already a crack in Mother's defensive armor. When I had spoken to her before joining the air force, she had seemed overly pleasant, even proud of my efforts. For a fleeting moment her soothing tone reminded me of the mommy I had once adored. *What if,* I thought, *Dad's condition brought them back together?* As a small child, before events turned the family upside down, I knew my parents had been deeply in love with each other. I had always heard that a crisis could bring strained relationships back together. There had to be a reason why Mom and Dad never divorced after all those years of separation. So now there was hope. I knew it! The scare of Father being in the hospital could be the best thing to happen for the entire family.

The more I thought about this possible outcome, the more my anticipation of seeing Father grew. Like a lot of folks in similar situations, I, too, had initially overreacted. As my optimism grew, I pictured myself with Father, checking him out of the hospital in a few days, spending time with him one on one, then maybe . . . one day soon . . . I could return again on military leave, and all of us could sit down to a dinner. I told myself, feeling replenished with energy, that no matter what the consequences, nothing was going to be the same. The winds of change had begun to stir the moment Mother broke down and telephoned Mrs. Turnbough. The entire charade would be over. Nodding my head in agreement to myself, but nodding more to the deranged woman at the nurses' station, who continued to act as if she was engaged in more important matters, it no longer fazed me. I was in control of my emotions, and I knew that everything would work out for the better.

From out of nowhere, a male nurse wearing a name tag STEVE slid behind the station and took immediate control of the situation. Before I could badger him, Steve read my name, stitched on my green air force fatigues, and let out a heavy sigh.

"My father, Stephen Pelzer, he's here? I mean, he's okay and he's *in this hospital* on *this floor.* Right?" I blurted out. I stared down the arrogant woman, who turned away after tossing her hair in disgust.

Steve began to reply but raised a hand to his mouth as if to first collect his thoughts. "Man, we've been waiting on you. Yeah, kid, your father's here, and . . . yeah, he's on this floor. But chill for a sec. There's a few things you need to know."

I rolled my eyes as if to say, *Yeah, yeah, come on, out with it.* "So . . ." I nagged, "what's the deal? What happened? He fell down, broke an arm? What is it? When does he check out?"

As Steve rapped his fingers on the countertop, wondering how to deal with me, my ears picked up the faint sound of a hacking cough. Without thinking, I spun to the right and marched into the room next to the nurses' station. It took a few seconds for my eyes to adjust. Before me, shaking like a leaf in a flimsy hospital gown, was the skeleton-like figure of my father. His arms were twitching uncontrollably as he struggled to slide his bare feet in front of him. He seemed to be using whatever strength he could muster to make it to the bathroom. By the vacant look in his eyes I could tell he had no idea of who I was, or even that someone else was in the room with him. Coming around behind him, I slung his arm around my shoulder and helped him into the bathroom. His wafer-thin body trembled against mine as he fought to stand straight while relieving himself. My mind was spinning, and I kept questioning like an idiot, "Are you all right? Are you okay?" over and over again.

Only after helping Father to his bed did I realize how bad his appearance was. His eyes were blank. They rolled to whatever caught his attention for that split second before drifting off somewhere else. As he lay flat on his back, the only time his arms were still was when he would drag his bony hand over to the other and hold it. Looking into Father's face, I smiled, hoping to catch his darting eyes. The skin around his cheeks was crimson red and stretched thin. I noticed a large white patch taped to the right side of his neck and shoulder but paid no attention to it. Instead I reached out to cup Father's hands. "Dad," I gently whispered, "it's David."

No reaction.

"Dad," I said in a firmer tone, "can you hear me?"

Father's only response was a raspy exhale.

I could hear Alice sniffling from the entrance of the room. Out of frustration, I lay my body next to Father, while keeping my face just above his. "Dad? Hey, Dad! Can you . . . do you hear me? It's me, David. *Say something,* anything. Dad?"

Studying Father's eyes, I looked for the slightest response. I thought if he couldn't speak, at least he could communicate with his eyes. Minutes crawled by with no answer. I wanted to grab the sides of his face and squeeze out some type of reply that Father indeed knew I was with him.

From the right side of my shoulder I could feel a firm but gentle squeeze. I smiled, knowing Father had snapped out of his trance. "I'm here, Dad. I'm right here," I said with a wave of relief. Patting the hand, I nearly jumped off the bed when I discovered it belonged not to Father but to the nurse Steve.

"We need to talk," he said without the slightest trace of embarrassment.

"But my dad . . . ?" I asked, thinking I could not leave his side.

"I'll stay," Mrs. Turnbough said, as she now stood over my father.

When we were both outside of the room, Steve carefully closed the heavy oak door. "What's wrong with him?" I demanded. Feeling my anxiety take hold, I pressed for hard answers. "What type of medication do you have him on? How come he doesn't recognize me? Is it the drugs? How long will it be until he gets better and gains some weight? When do you expect him to be released?"

"Hey, man," Steve said, raising his hand, "give it a rest. Didn't your mother tell you . . . ? You don't know, do you?"

"Know what? If I knew, I wouldn't be bugging you!" I sarcastically shot back. "Just tell me, what in the heck is going on? Please!" I now begged, "I gotta know."

Leading me down the corridor, Steve searched for a more private setting. At the end of the hallway, he stopped to offer me a chair. I refused, feeling the need to stand. "It was about four months ago when your father was admitted—"

"Four months!" I yelled. "Admitted? Admitted for what? Why didn't anybody call me? Why now?"

"Please," he interjected, "give me a chance. Your father . . . he wanted to keep things discreet. A lot of patients are like that. Anyway, it was only after we ran all the tests that our diagnosis was confirmed. David, your father has cancer. I'm afraid it's terminal. He's in the advanced stages. I'm sorry." Steve reached out for my hands. "There is nothing we can do."

"Hang on!" I said, stepping away from his gesture. "What do you mean, *terminal*? I don't get it. . . ."

"David," Steve said in a deliberate, slow voice, gripping me by the shoulders, "your father . . . *he's not going to make it.*"

"You mean . . . you're saying he's going to die? *My dad* is going to die? No way!" I shook my head in complete denial. "Can't you give him a shot of something . . . or I thought there's some kind of chemo treatment. If it's money you need . . . just don't let him die. Not now. Please!" I begged, as if he alone decided the fate of my father.

"David, listen, chill for a sec. I don't know, *no one knows* exactly how long your father has, but," he emphasized in a strong tone, "the thing I do know for certain is this: *your father is not going to make it.* And there is nothing, *nothing*, that you, I, or anyone else can do about it. Come on, you're not a kid. You understand these things. It's a fact of life. Your father's lived a full life, and now it's his time." Steve paused to collect his thoughts. Looking at him, I realized the immense strain he was under and how hard he was trying to help me. For a brief moment I wondered how many times a week he spent with others like me. I felt foolish and ashamed. "David," he said, taking my hand, "I am sorry. I truly am."

My thoughts refused to come together. Whatever reserves of energy I had left suddenly disappeared. Finally, at the one time I needed to be in control, to be strong, I found myself completely, pitifully helpless. I had so many questions, but it took everything I had to form a single sentence. I simply stood in front of Steve like a zombie. I wanted to release everything and cry. A heartbeat later, I suppressed the urge. "Four months?" I asked incoherently. "You're telling me my dad's been here that long? How long has he been . . . like he is now? Why can't he talk? Is he doped up? I mean, he acts like he doesn't even recognize me. . . . I don't, I just don't understand," I stammered. "I just wanna know. That's all."

"Well," Steve began, sliding a chair for me next to his, "as I was saying, your father checked in a few months ago. Since then his condition has rapidly deteriorated. The growth was primarily centered on the side of his neck, but has since spread to his throat. He is on medication, and under the circumstances I'm sure you can understand why. That is the reason he lacks discernment. If we take him off the 'meds,' his understanding might improve, but the pain would be unbearable."

"So . . . he'll never be able to say anything again? Ever . . . ?" I asked as my voice trailed off.

"That is correct. Not any longer," Steve replied, nodding his head.

I sat on the edge of the wooden chair, rubbing my hands together, wondering what I could do to comfort Father. For once in my life, I was actually glad when I thought of Mother. With all her diabolical, scheming tactics, *she* would know how to deal with Father's situation.

Breaking the silence, Steve spoke up. "Ya know, when your dad first checked in, I don't think he fully understood the seriousness of his condition. A great deal of patients are like that. They won't allow themselves to be examined until it's almost always too late. Call it embarrassment, ignorance, ego, whatever. But please know that we did all that we could for your father. It's important for you to know that."

"Yeah, I understand. Thanks, but," I probed, "was he able to speak when he first came in?"

Steve barely nodded his head.

"So, why didn't he call anyone?" I inquired.

"He did." Steve frowned. "He must have, right after he was admitted, 'cause his other son, your brother Ronald, came over to visit. They spent a few days together. I guess he's in the military, too."

Ronald? I gasped. Ronald, the oldest of my four siblings, who I hadn't seen since my rescue in 1973, had finally escaped Mother's wrath a few years ago by joining the army as soon as he turned eighteen years old. I hadn't thought of Ron in years. "He was able to talk? I mean, talk to Ronald?"

"Well, as much as he could. Your father was in a great deal of pain. It was soon after your brother's visit that he lost his ability to speak," Steve gently explained.

"How long ago . . . I mean, when Ronald came to visit?"

"Uhm, I have to say about two, almost three months ago," Steve answered.

"What about the others? Mother and my brothers, Father's firemen buddies? Were they able to talk with him? I mean, my father was coherent? He knew who came to see him?"

"Hey, man," Steve interrupted, "what others? Ronald was the only one who came to see him. No one else saw your father."

"But Mother, she must have seen . . . ?"

"No one," Steve adamantly stated. "And I mean *no one*. We didn't even realize he was married until we rechecked his admission papers. I understand, after talking to your father, that they're not exactly in close contact. There is a chance, knowing how your father guarded his condition, that your mother doesn't even—"

"Oh, she knows," I objected as my entire body suddenly tensed.

"I'm sure if she—" Steve countered.

"No way," I said. "You don't know. You don't know her."

"And how do you know?" he asked.

"Come on, Steve, think about it. Who do you think called my brother Ron and Mrs. Turnbough?" I returned.

Steve paused, then switched the focus off of Mother's total lack of compassion. "Well, right now, since you're the only relative available, you need to be thinking about your father's arrangements."

I still refused to admit I could be losing Father. "So . . . what can I do?" I asked. I somehow wanted to uncover something, anything that the staff had forgotten or overlooked which might be a cure to Father's disease. Everything was hitting me at once. "So! Why doesn't he look at me? Does he know, I mean, is he capable of knowing I'm even here?"

Steve sighed as if growing tired of my endless stream of questions. "For the most part, it's fifty-fifty at best. He seems more coherent in the morning but, for the most part, no more than a few minutes at a time. He's at the stage when he drifts off quite a bit. Part of the reason is due to his meds. Again, this is all normal for his condition."

The more the nurse talked, the more I began to feel a crushing weight bearing down on my shoulders. My mouth hung open as I stared upward at Steve.

"I know it's a lot to deal with," he stated, shaking his head, "but first things first. Spend time with your father. That's priority one. I can walk you through the paperwork and all the other things you need to do when the time comes. For now, just spend time with your dad."

"But . . . I, ah, I don't know what to say," I replied. "I mean, he doesn't even know that I'm with him."

"Well, David, he's been in seclusion for nearly the entire time since he checked in. Your father doesn't show it, but he's scared. He knows he's not going to make it. Anything you can

do would mean the world to him. He's all alone in there."
Steve gently scolded, "You have to do this! Just . . . just remi-
nisce about all those good times you spent together. Keep him
'up.' He'll know."

Yeah, all those good times, I said mockingly to myself.

I thanked Steve for the umpteenth time, while he assured
me that he would stay in close contact. But even as I reluc-
tantly returned to Father's room, I somehow believed that my
dad would miraculously pull through.

As I cautiously reentered the Lysol-scented room, Mrs.
Turnbough turned and flashed me a bright smile. "Your father
and I are having a nice chat. I'm just telling him what a fine
young man you've become," she said as she patted Father's
hand.

"Oh, my God! He can talk?" I nearly screeched.

"Oh, you don't need to blabber away to hold a conversation, right, Mr. Pelzer?" Alice returned in a smooth tone, as
she continued to smile at Father. "I'm gonna leave you two
dashing gents alone for now." She laid down Father's hand
and eased out of the room.

Not knowing what to say or do, I felt paralyzed. For the first
time in nearly two years, I finally had the chance to be with
my father. As I stared at him, I suddenly realized I knew nothing about him. As long as I could remember, my visits with
Father had probably amounted to less than ten, maybe twenty
hours together, so now I wondered, had I been caught up over
the last few years craving to love Dad, hoping he *may* love me
in return? As a child, I so badly wanted to be with him, but
watching Father's body writhe as he struggled to breathe, I so
desperately wanted to flee. Without warning tears began to
swell in my eyes. "I, ah . . . I tried to write. I mean, I wrote . . .
but I wasn't sure of your address." I shook my head, knowing
I sounded like a complete idiot, but I stammered on. "I got
your letter when I was stationed at the base in Colorado. I
didn't—I mean, I couldn't find your address. I'm sorry. I truly

am. I didn't know. I would have come sooner. I just didn't know."

I turned away to compose myself. The last thing I wanted was to lose it in front of my father. My focus had to be his needs rather than my sorrow. After a few minutes of silence, I remembered Steve's advice about keeping Father uplifted. Out of nowhere, a memory of Father and me, when I was a preschooler, sprang from my mind. I sat on Father's bed while tucking the sheet under his frail back. "You may not remember," I began, "but when I was four, maybe five, all of us went to the Russian River. . . . Early one evening, after dinner, you stepped out for a walk, and I tagged along behind you. . . ." The more I spoke, the more that fragment of time crystallized. "I snuck out and walked behind you, tracing your steps. I had those little Forest Ranger boots, and I tried to keep up while being as quiet as I could. I think I made it five, maybe ten feet away from the cabin, when you heard me. You spun around so fast I thought you were going to bite my head off, but you—" I stopped for a second to smile at Father's face. "You simply extended your giant hand and scooped my fingers into yours. . . . Then, without a word, you let me walk with you.

"I have to say, as a kid that was pretty cool. At the time, between Ron, Stan, and me, to be able to hog a few minutes alone with you, well, back then that was all I talked about after our walk. It was that summer when I knew that's where I wanted to live. The trees, the river, the smell, those precious moments with you, that's when I knew. Back then, with you, I was safe. Back then you were my superhero; you were my Superman. I know it sounds kinda dumb," I scoffed, "but that was the only time you held my hand. When *you* wanted to be with *me*."

I stopped for a moment to close my eyes. As I did, my vision with Father faded away. I could feel my insides swell up. As a teenager in foster care, I couldn't wait to become an adult so Father and I could work through our past. I had somehow hoped it would bring us closer together. I had no intention of making him upset or trying to use what happened to pin the blame on anyone. I simply thought if I had the answers, I would free myself from being doomed to repeat the tragedy of mindless hate and violence. Looking down at Father, I felt that Mother had deliberately manipulated this situation, calling me only *after* Father was unable to utter a single syllable.

"When I was at The House, I remember all those times you'd come home from the fire station for just a few minutes to check in on me. Mother didn't know it, but I made sure I timed your arrival when I was washing the dishes so I could actually see you. Sometimes I got too far behind with my chores and . . . well, you know Mother . . . I paid the price when you were gone. I knew she'd never allow you to go down to the basement, so I'd wash the dishes over and over until I heard you open the front door." I paused to stare directly into Father's eyes. "You saved me. Even though it was only for a few seconds alone in the kitchen, it made all the difference. Sometimes if you brushed against me, I'd breathe in your Old Spice cologne. You were my invisible force field. I'm just sorry you, the boys—everyone—had to deal with so much crap. I somehow thought I'd be able to make it up to you—to everyone.

"You see, Dad, I knew. I always knew you came back to the house for me. And now, no matter what happens, I'm here for you. No matter what anybody says, I'll protect your honor."

From behind me I heard Alice close the door. Without breaking my train of thought, I nodded at Mrs. Turnbough and continued talking. For the first time in my life I was actually opening up to my father.

"As a kid, I was always proud of you being a fireman. I . . . I, ah, remember when Mom was a den mother for the Club Scouts and she drove the pack down to your fire station on Post Street. You looked so cool in your dark blue uniform, leaning against the polished fire truck. I think I was maybe in the first grade. It was then that I knew I wanted to be a fireman. That's why I joined the air force." I abruptly stopped. I didn't have the guts to tell him the truth: I was a pathetic "Food Service Specialist." Even if I lied, I knew Father would hear it in my voice. I so badly wanted him to be proud of me. I wanted to prove to him that I was not a loser, that I would not end up like . . . like . . .

A flash of embarrassment washed over me. The more I gazed at Father, the more I saw myself as a hopeless creature that, no matter how hard I tried, would not amount to anything.

As I cleared my head, my mind flashed to Father's fireman badge. "Dad," I asked, "Dad, do you . . . do . . . do you still have your badge? Your fireman's badge?"

I pictured the time he had blushed with pride as he displayed his silver badge, with his identification numbers stamped above the seal. "It's the only thing he has," I said to Alice in a soft voice, "that showed what he did. After everything, it's all he has. . . ."

"David!" Alice gently whispered. "Your father, look!"

My head snapped back toward Father. His head continued to twitch, but now more to the right, while his eyes strained as if telling me to look into . . . "The closet!" I exclaimed. "You want me to look in the closet?"

I searched Father's face for any type of reaction. It seemed as if he was committing whatever strength he had on leaning toward the closet. I jumped from the bed and flung open the door. Neatly hung were a pair of worn pants, a pressed shirt, and a heavy overcoat. My eyes darted to the bottom of the closet. I searched for Father's Pan Am travel bag he had used to pack his belongings when he worked at the fire station. All I could find was a pair of scuffed shoes, brushed off and placed neatly together. An odd sense of fear began to overtake me as I flung open the drawers, only to find a pair of white socks. No clothes, papers, wallet, and no fireman's badge. I turned to Father, shaking my head. In a moment of stillness, as he kept his eyes locked onto mine, I understood what he was trying to convey.

I gave Father a slight nod before my hands patted down his coat. Part of me felt jittery for invading, of all things, my father's privacy, while a deeper side couldn't wait to find his prize. I found a set of official-looking papers that I stuffed into my back pocket without thinking. I could read them later. The only thing that mattered was Father's badge. After two attempts, I slowed down my pace. I used the tips of my fingers to trace every outline, for any opening, while I studied Father's face. I felt a small bulge. Without looking I yanked out a small, black-leather casing.

"Is that your father's—?" Mrs. Turnbough began to ask.

"Yeah." I interrupted as I opened the small case, revealing the silver emblem inches in front of Father's twitching face.

Immediately his breathing eased. While holding his badge, I began to feel the magnitude of what it meant to him. The only thing that represented Father's adult life—besides his broken marriage—was what I now held in my hand. Father shut his eyes as if in concentration. I then noticed his lips quivering. I bent my head down, but much as I tried, I could not decipher any sounds escaping his mouth. When his eyes blinked open they again locked onto mine. Out of fright I shook my head. "I don't know!" I snapped. "I don't know what you're trying to . . ." Suddenly I felt the slightest sensation on my right hand. Glancing down, I saw Father's bony crimson fingers wrapped around my hand clutching his fireman's badge. As my hand began shaking from Father's trembling, he sealed my fingers around the black leather case. Searching his eyes, I understood. I whispered into his ear, praying he could hear me, "As God is my witness, I will protect and keep your badge. I will carry it as a sign of honor."

As Father's grip eased, I could tell he had fallen asleep. Before his fingers could slip away, I kissed his hand. Standing beside his bed, I gently laid Father's vibrating hand on his chest. Turning toward the door, I saw Steve standing beside Alice. "He'll be able to rest now. You've made him very happy. He told me months ago, when he checked in, that he wanted you to have it." We both looked down at my right hand, still clutching Father's badge. "It's the right thing to do," he said in a broken voice. "Today was a good day for your father. A very good day."

"How do you—I mean, I don't know if he can understand me. If he could just talk—"

"He is talking," Steve replied, "and you're learning to listen. It's hard, but as long as he knows you're there, beside him, that's all that matters."

"He's not . . . my dad's not going to . . . to make it?" I cried, choking on the words. Staring at Father, I felt as if a sledgehammer crushed my skull. "He's going to die," I whispered to Alice. Instantly, out of humiliation, I gasped, slapping my hand against my mouth. I couldn't believe I had uttered those words. Up until that exact moment I had still held out for some dramatic turn. In some odd sense, I felt that by saving Father from his life of despair, I would in effect save myself.

Returning to Steve, I stood half frozen. "So, how will I know . . . when it's time?"

"You still have some time. Someone is always watching over your father. We'll let you know if there're any changes." Steve had returned to his official nurse's tone. "It's going to be all right."

After assurances that Father would be resting for some time, I found myself driving Mr. Turnbough's whale-sized, oxidized blue Plymouth Fury. With Alice beside me, I slowly cruised through Golden Gate Park on John F. Kennedy Drive. At Rainbow Falls, I stopped "The Blue Humpback" and rolled down the window. I recalled the hundreds of times both Mother and Father had driven Ron, Stan, and me through the park. With our noses pressed against the glass of our beat-up station wagon, we'd stare at the endless rows of freshly planted flowers in brilliant colors. If one of us dared to crack open a window, I'd suck in the distinctive scent of the eucalyptus trees. And if Ron, Stan, and I were lucky, we were able to catch a glimpse of the red-ear turtles basking in the sun as the silver station wagon rolled by Lloyd's Lake. Back then, as a preschooler, even though I knew Mother and I had our secret, I felt safe when all of us were together as a family. Back then I had prayed that my life could someday be as serene and as beautiful as the park.

Snapping out of my trance, I realized what I had to do. "I have to see her," I stated without emotion.

"I know," Mrs. Turnbough answered, nodding her head in agreement.

I was surprised. I had expected her to challenge me. When Mother had called me hours before I joined the air force, it was Alice who had rightly stopped me from seeing her. Whenever I had a question regarding Mother, I had always run it by Mrs. Turnbough first. But now, I realized, Alice was giving me a wide berth, allowing me to make my own decisions.

After taking a final mental snapshot of the cascading water at Rainbow Falls, I shifted the car into drive, eased my foot off the brake, and coasted from Golden Gate Park . . . to Crestline Avenue in Daly City.

CHAPTER 5

SLIP AWAY

I walked hesitantly up the red steps that led to Mother's house, knowing there was no turning back. For the life of me, I didn't understand why I still felt drawn to her. By choice, I left Mrs. Turnbough in the Plymouth. Above all, I didn't want to drag her into my slimy world any more than I already had. At the top of the steps, before I could chicken out, I gave a strong rap on the front door. The moment I did, I saw there was no way for me to control my trembling hand. I hid it behind my back, taking up my military stance. I was thinking about straightening my hair or anything else that would make me more presentable when the front door opened.

A small boy's eyes ran up my air force fatigues. "Hey, are you a Pelzer, too?" The child turned his head and yelled, "Mom! There's a Pelzer here to see—"

"My God, Kevin?" The words flew out of my mouth. With perfect clarity I remembered one Saturday, years before, when Kevin was a baby crawling on the floors, dressed in his blue outfit. Back then his shrieks of joy had melted my ice-cold heart. Now, as I studied his features, I was certain Kevin had no idea who I was.

His eyes grew wide. Total shock was etched in his face. "Mom?"

From the back another figure emerged. A taller, freckle-faced teenager shoved Kevin aside, taking an offensive stance—as if to protect his home. He put on his best tough-guy act as he stared me down. As much as Russell tried not to show it, though, I could tell by his fidgety movements that he was nervous, too. "So . . . what do you want?"

In a deliberate tone I replied, "I need to see her. Please?" I added, attempting to defuse my younger brother's hostile attitude.

"Yeah, right," Russell nodded, as if I had an appointment.

Extending his arm toward the living room, Russell permitted me to enter but followed behind me like a prison guard escorting me to the warden. Part of me felt that Russell's disposition was due to Mother's years of psychotic brainwashing, or maybe jealousy that I had escaped her wrath while he and my other brothers remained behind. I also felt in some odd sense that Russell resented me, perhaps because he might have become my replacement.

With Kevin bouncing in front of me, I scanned the living room. In seven years nothing had changed. Every piece of furniture seemed as if it were glued to the same position, as it had for years even before I was rescued. The only thing that appeared different was how small and dark the room had become, due to the paper-thin, soiled drapes and nicotine-stained walls. An overpowering stench of urine, from what I assumed was Mother's small herd of dogs and cats over the years, nearly made my eyes water. I let out a cough and shook my head in disgust. This was a woman who when I was a tiny child had hosted elegant parties and prided herself on her home's grandeur.

Upon stepping into the kitchen and seeing Mother's silhouette, my entire body locked up—my hands fused to my sides, my chin fastened to my chest, and my eyes staring at the multicolored spots on the floor. A split second passed before I regained my senses. But it was too late. By the sickening sound of her chuckle, Mother had just witnessed my automatic response. Standing a safe distance away, putting my hands behind my back in the at-rest position, I leaned against the countertop to stabilize my dizziness.

Mother was emptying a brown paper bag full of groceries. As she grabbed a loaf of Wonder Bread, she flashed me one of her snake-like smiles, and asked, "So . . . I can assume you've at least seen him?"

"Yes, ma'am," I replied with no emotion.

"And how is *he*?" Mother sarcastically probed as she began folding her grocery bags for future use.

Calculating my every word, I asked, "You haven't seen Dad, have you?"

With the speed of lightning, Mother slapped her hands on her hips and took three steps toward me. Surprisingly, I didn't back away. I stood my ground. "That's none of your goddamn business!" she ranted. "Listen to me, you little shit! *I'm* the one who did *you* a favor! I didn't have to phone that—that *foster* person. I didn't have to do that, you know."

"Mrs. Turnbough," I calmly corrected her.

"Whoever." Mother returned to the kitchen table and started to cough, emptying her lungs. She acted as if she were under an overwhelming strain. Hearing her agony, Russell slid closer to Mother, as if she might collapse at any second. With a dramatic flair Mother threw up her hands, tilted her head back, and cried, "*I'm* fine. *I'm* all right." Only when Russell moved behind her again did Mother drop her hands. Then in a vindictive tone she hissed, "*You* of all people, you have no right. No right whatsoever to judge me." Her face went from bright red to ghost white. "No one knows," Mother sobbed, "no one knows how hard this is . . . *for me!*"

"Now look what you did!" Russell yelled.

For a moment I stood there confused. *Is my direct questioning truly setting her off,* I thought to myself, *or perhaps my presence is too much for her?* This could also be another dramatic performance of hers, trying to shift the focus of sympathy onto Mother and not to the situation at hand. With little to lose I dug further. "I just don't understand. How is it that Dad's been in the hospital all this time and you haven't seen him once?"

I hit pay dirt. "The pain would be too much for me to bear. Don't you understand? I've known him longer . . . than any-one. It's just, it's all just too much."

Outwardly I nodded at Mother, as if I agreed with her state-ment. But inside I was saying to myself, *And the Oscar for best performance—under fake duress—goes to . . . Catherine Roerva Pelzer!*

Interrupting my thought, Mother went on to claim, "You have no idea. He was never there for me or his children. If he wasn't at work, he was with his pals out drinking God knows where."

Again I nodded, knowing full well that Mother was throw-ing out whatever excuses she could to justify her lack of com-mon decency and compassion.

"Boys," Mother announced, "excuse us," she decreed, with a wave of her hands.

"But, Mom," Kevin said.

"I said, leave!" she screeched. "Before I really give you something to cry about!" Like magic, the boys scurried from the room.

As Mother rambled on about her anxiety, my head began to throb from the day's overload. I didn't know how much longer I could stay in this house. "So," I interrupted, "what about Father?"

"I told you!" Mother roared.

"No, ma'am," I said in a soothing tone. I met her gaze, and she knew I wasn't going to back down. "He's still your hus-band. He's all alone. He's not doing well—" I caught myself before I lost control. In front of Mother—*in her house*—I had to maintain total composure. "Dad's not going to . . . make it. There's not much time." I waited for Mother to respond, to wake up and throw on her jacket and race off to see Father. Knowing that I was passing the point of no return, I stepped toward Mother and said, for her ears only, "He's the father of your children. Don't end it like this. Please, I beg you. Do the right thing. See him."

By the strain on Mother's face, I knew I was getting to her. Ever so slightly she nodded her head in agreement. Behind her faded silver-framed glasses I could see her eyes begin to water. The last time Mother had lowered her guard like this was the day before I was rescued in March 1973, when we had both stood in the same room, while she broke down and began talking about her past. Standing in front of her now, I prayed I didn't lose her . . . again. My sole objective was for Mother to be with Father. *Maybe, somehow,* I thought, *a few minutes alone might wash away the years of animosity.* "Come on," I softly pleaded, "let's all go see Dad. Come on." I smiled as I extended my hand to hers.

"Oh, David," Mother cried as she stretched out her trembling arm. Without hesitation I took her hand. Mother let out a sigh as I cupped the palm of her hand. "It's going to be fine. It's going to be okay," I told her. Her body began to weave. Mother closed her eyes tightly, as if washing away all the pain she had kept locked in her heart. She let out another, deeper sigh, as if cleansing herself. As I looked at Mother's face, her color seemed to change. A reddened look began to take over. Before she opened her eyes, I knew what was coming. Suddenly her hand felt ice cold. "Don't go," I softly pleaded. "Please, don't go."

The same moment I released her hand, Mother jerked it away. Just as years before, I had enough sense to back away from her. By the evil smile I knew *The Mother* had returned with a vengeance. "Oh, what a manipulating little shit you are! How I bet those foster people of yours are ever so proud! And here you come traipsing into *my* house, telling *me* what to do. Who made you the Messiah?" Mother paused to reload, while she struggled to light a cigarette. It took several attempts for her—not only to light it but to take a drag—due to her violent shakes. "You"—she thrust a finger at my face while smoke poured from her mouth—"of all people, have no right.

You might be something to the *United States Air Force,* but you know . . ." Mother hesitated, as if to have me feel the full meaning of her words, ". . . you know what you are. Deep down, you're nothing. You don't even deserve to breathe the same air as me or my children. How could you march into my house, as if you owned the place, and tell me what I should or shouldn't do? How could you, after all I've done for you? What gives you the right to come back?"

I tried to maintain an unthreatening stance. As I had years before, I simply shut down and became a cyborg: part man, part machine. Yet her words "after all I've done for you" caught me by total surprise.

"Done for me?" I muttered.

"You still don't get it, do you?" she sneered after taking a long drag. "I didn't have to release you. No! *I let you go.* I was done with you. You gave me no pleasure, so you were disposed of." It took me a few seconds to comprehend what Mother was saying. "You were trash, and like trash I simply tossed you away." Mother struck the pose of a refined aristocrat and said in a sarcastic voice, "Oh, dear me, how rude. Am I bursting your bubble? And all this time I bet you thought your blessed little saviors at your school were the ones responsible for your dramatic deliverance." Then in a tone barely audible, Mother whispered, "You don't know how fortunate you were. I could have ended it all. Just . . . like . . . that," Mother emphasized with the snap of her fingers. "You know what you are, so if I were you, I'd keep that little trap of yours shut. Don't push it. You were lucky once, so don't think I haven't done anything for you."

Behind her, Kevin popped his head in from the dining room. Seeing him, Mother assumed the role of the grieving wife. With a fresh stream of tears rolling down her face, Mother tilted her head back as if to ease the intensity of her pain. As if the effort of standing was too much for her, Mother struggled to sit down. In all, I thought it was a fair performance. I also was certain that Ron, Stan, Russell, and Kevin had seen her charades many times before.

"Care?" Mother reached out to Kevin with an exaggerated trembling hand. "Oh, I care about your fath—about *him,*" Mother corrected herself. "I care. That's the problem, I care too much." Mother finished by wiping away her tears.

I deliberately remained stoic. I had already pushed her too far, so I did not want to say anything that might reignite the situation. Still, I had surprised myself by not caving in. I couldn't believe I had actually penetrated her defenses, let alone stood up and questioned her status as a wife. Either I was exceptionally lucky or Mother was losing her grasp.

Kevin broke the tension. "So, you used to live here?"

Surely, I assumed, Mother must have told him something about me and why I no longer lived with them. She had to justify my going away. As much as she reigned over everything, snippets of the truth must have seeped out. I flashed Kevin a smile, who smiled back. "Yes," I stated with confidence, "I lived here, but that was a long time ago—"

"Oh no, he didn't!" Mother retaliated. "Don't listen to him! He's . . . he's a liar. He's not one of us." To emphasize her point, Mother raised a finger. "Remember what I told you? About . . . about bad people?"

I locked into Mother's eyes, thinking to myself, *You're right. You are absolutely right. I am not like you.*

Before Mother could continue, Kevin broke in, "So, you wanna see my house?"

An overwhelming sense of curiosity took hold as I passed Mother and followed Kevin into the dining room. I walked around the table before stopping to gaze at the red towers of the Golden Gate Bridge. Distant memories from childhood began to flood my mind. I looked down at the backyard, where I had spent countless hours sitting on my hands on top of a bed of rocks—as a form of twisted punishment for whatever crime I had committed. I remembered shivering in the chilling fog, scarcely dressed, but too terrified to remove my hands and rub them together for fear of being caught. Feeling myself weaken, I turned from the sight. I remembered the good times, when Ron, Stan, and I were preschoolers and played in the sandbox, and how one summer afternoon Mother had taught us all how to catch a lifeline—just in case, she said. Back then Mother seemed so devoted about every aspect of her children's well-being. I could still picture Mother, on her hands and knees, wearing her gardening gloves, weeding her flower beds that she had taken so much pride in, and how she used to fill the home with the orchids she had meticulously cared for. Even now I could still see the remnants of what had once been.

"That's the waterfall Stan built," Mother pointed out, breaking my trance. I was startled. I was so tired that I hadn't heard her approaching. "He's so good with his hands. He keeps everything up and running. He's such the handyman, you know. And with Ronald serving his country, I don't know what I'd do. Stan, he's the man of the house now," Mother boasted with pride. From behind I could hear Russell let out a sigh of frustration. By the look I stole at Russell, I knew there was a power struggle between him and Stan, who as a baby had suffered a massive fever and was never the same. In the early years Mother had always gone out of her way to shield Stan, by showering him with praise—telling him how brave, strong, and smart he was. But even as a child, Stan became jealous of Ronald, the firstborn, who had Father's confidence while Father was at work.

Continuing the tour, Kevin led me through the living room, then down the narrow hallway. As I walked down the passage, an odor from years ago filled my senses. I glanced down at the worn carpet and paused in front of the bathroom. Kevin stopped and gave me a puzzled look, asking, "Gotta go?" I stood transfixed at the tiny room, where I had almost died from being locked in the bathroom after Mother's lethal concoction of ammonia and Clorox. I stared at the far left side of the bathroom floor at the vent—where I had prayed that fresh air would come through before I gagged to death. Turning toward the mirror above the sink, I remembered looking at the fresh pink scars on my chin and my tongue that had skin peeled away from swallowing teaspoons of ammonia. As a child I'd usually steal time to look into the mirror and yell at myself for whatever I did wrong—that had made Mother despise me so much. I had hated everything about myself—how I looked, how I stuttered, everything. Back then I so desperately wanted to somehow transfer myself to the other side of the mirror. But as I grew and became aware of my situation as Mother's prisoner, I knew I could never rid myself of that person in the mirror. For that reason, I still refused to look at myself in a mirror.

"You gotta go to the bathroom?" Kevin again interjected.

"No, I'm fine," I said with a trembling voice.

From behind, I caught one of Mother's snide smiles. "Something amiss?" she said in a low tone.

Making our way forward, Kevin led me into the bedroom that I assumed he shared with Russell. The last time I had seen it was when Kevin was sleeping in his crib. Growing tired of the tour, I simply nodded and turned away. "And this," Kevin stated grandly, "is Mom's room." Still amazed at how small everything seemed, I stepped into Mother's sanctuary and gawked at her mirrored bureau, where her once cherished perfumes and figurines were coated with dust.

As I turned to leave Mother's bedroom, I noticed a set of photographs. The upper left picture was a color bust shot of Ronald in his army uniform. By the tone of his expression, Ron was his own man. He looked fantastic in uniform, and I was proud of him. He had escaped. My eyes then darted to the outdated school photos of Stan, Russell, and Kevin. In the middle of the surrounding pictures was a black-and-white portrait of Mother on her wedding day. Catherine Roerva Pelzer was absolutely stunning. Her eyes glowed with love. Her complexion was flawless. She seemed to radiate the model of a young bride who couldn't wait to live a lifetime filled with happiness. As I admired Mother's portrait, I suddenly realized that Father was nowhere in the set of pictures. Looking closer, I discovered that I, too, had been excluded. I now understood why Mother refused to have anything to do with Father. How could she help Father, if, in her mind, he had already died?

I turned around to search for Mother, but she had retreated to the safety of her kitchen. I could not understand how one person could hate so much. I could only imagine how she had validated her cover story to the boys. *How easily she could make anything that troubled her completely disappear.*

"So, what'd you think of my family?" Kevin chimed. Turning away from the set of pictures, I saw Russell's face, which revealed a crocodile smile acting as if everything was exactly as it should be. *So be it,* I thought to myself.

"Fine," I replied to Kevin with a grin before pushing myself past Russell.

At the end of the hallway Mother stood, puffing on a cigarette. "So, I can assume you found everything you came to see?" she said in a belittling tone. Facing her, I became too distraught to reply. I knew I should leave, that it was useless to try to convince Mother to see Dad. Sensing my weakness, Mother added, "Ronald's in the army, you know. *He's* doing quite well. He sends me all of his medals." Mother turned away, then produced a box of assorted medals. Dumbfounded, I could only look into the box as Mother bragged on, "This one's for sharpshooting . . . and this one's for basic training . . . ah, this . . . I'm not quite sure. There are so many of them, it's hard for me . . . anyway, he's stationed in Alaska. They don't just station *anybody* there. He won't say it, but I know better. He's one of the best military police they've ever had. I'm so proud that one of my boys is serving their country. You can't imagine how proud I am," Mother sighed, laying it on as thick as ever.

"I'm . . . in the air force."

Mother glanced up from her prized box in bewilderment, as if she had no idea, even though I was wearing my air force fatigues. "Ah, yes, well, isn't that nice. Army wouldn't take your kind, eh?" she said. "So, what is it you do to protect our country?"

I smiled triumphantly. "I'm a cook."

As soon as the words came out of my mouth, I felt like an idiot.

"*A cook?*" Russell broke out laughing.

"Didn't you enlist to become a firefighter?" Mother asked bitingly. "What happened, did they boot you out of that too? I thought the air force was about jets. No one's a cook."

The silence that followed extended into infinity. Without a word I nodded my head, as if to thank Mother for her time and for her hospitality, before seeing myself out. I could feel all eyes on my back as I closed the front door behind me, and only then did the living room erupt into a burst of laughter. Easing back into Mr. Turnbough's car, I let out a deep breath.

"Had to do it?" Mrs. Turnbough asked.

"Had to. She doesn't have, nor ever did have, any intention of helping Dad," I stated in a cold voice.

"My Lord," Alice replied, "how does a person like that—"

I interrupted Mrs. Turnbough by raising my hand. "I only hope she gets hers. It's just not fair." I struggled to control my breathing. I thought my head would explode from the surge of hatred I had for my mother. Sensing that *her boys* were spying on me through their bedroom windows, I regained my composure, started the car, and coasted away. I had somehow thought things would be different. But, like always, when dealing with Mother, I had been foolishly wrong.

The next morning, I returned to Father's room. With my head slumped, I bumped into a chaplain, who simply nodded at me without a word and patted my shoulder as if I were some stray dog.

I debated what to do next. I felt the urge to do something. I wanted to kidnap Dad and take him to a baseball game, take a walk through the park, even sit in the back of a dingy bar and simply shoot the bull, go anywhere as long as we were together. But there was no way I could do anything.

Excusing myself, I reached into the back of my flimsy wallet and pulled out a crumpled note before making a telephone call to Mother's mother, to tell her about my dad.

Seemingly within moments of replacing the phone in its cradle, Uncle Dan, Mother's brother, flew out from the elevator. After a crushing hug, he pulled up a chair next to Father's bed and whispered in his ear. I stood against the door beside Alice to give the two men their time together. I knew I did the right thing. As Uncle Dan held me, he fell over himself with apologies. "We didn't know about him. No one knew," Dan said.

Watching Uncle Dan and Father together, I sensed the closeness they once must have shared. "Hey, Steve," Dan grumbled, "come on, you gotta get dressed. I got a few good bottles and a couple of nice-looking dames in the car. Come on, we can't keep 'em waitin'." I nearly jumped out of my skin from the audacity of what Uncle Dan said. Of all the settings, it was the most tasteless thing I could possibly imagine. But by the response from Father's eyes, I realized the true meaning of Dan's statement. I selfishly felt as if I were babying Father, protecting him from anything I deemed might be harmful. Quietly, Alice and I slipped from the room, where I found a couch, closed my eyes, and pondered what to do.

Sometime later Uncle Dan woke me with a shake, pleading for me to go home with Alice. Peeking in on Father, I felt that my weak need for rest was somehow a betrayal to him. Emotions of guilt over Father, elation at seeing Uncle Dan, and the rage I still felt about Mother swirled inside my head all the way home until I lay down again, this time on Alice's couch.

Almost the moment I fell asleep, Mrs. Turnbough shook me awake. I bolted up, thinking the worst. But before I could race into the kitchen and seize the phone, Alice gently informed me it was not Kaiser Hospital but my grandmother. Dealing with Mother's mother had never been easy. As a child, Mother

and Grandmother always had an intense love-hate relationship, which my brothers and I had seen whenever one of the
women had a run-in with the other. Though we were by no
means close, I had always felt as a child that Grandmother
was a covert ally.

Wiping my eyes, I fought to regain my focus. Knowing that
Grandmother was getting older, I had made sure when I called
her hours ago that I deliberately downplayed the drama of
Father's condition. Because of Mother's complete lack of re-
gard for Father, I suddenly felt like an arbitrator. I was proud.
For the first time, I was truly helping "The Family." Reminding myself not to frighten her, I smiled and said in my most
cheerful voice, "Grandma! I'm so glad you called. Everything's fine. Father's sleeping and there's really been no
change since this after—"

"What in the goddamn hell is going on down there? What
in the hell are *you* doing?" Grandma blasted.

"What is it?" I said, stumbling. "What's wrong? Father's
okay. I—I just . . . left him." With Grandmother's silence on
the other end, I became seized with anxiety. "I just left over
an hour ago. I'm sorry; I only wanted to catch a quick nap. I
checked with the nurse. He said it was okay and that he'd call
if there was any change. I swear it. Since I've been back, I
haven't had an hour's sleep. I'm so sorry," I said as I felt a wall
of guilt crashing down on top of me. I knew I shouldn't have
left the hospital, so *I* could relax, while Father fought for every
breath just a few miles away.

Grandmother broke in, "What in hell's bells are you bab-
bling about? I don't give a damn about your father at the moment. Right now all I want is an explanation. *What did you
do?* How could you . . . at a time like this? Holy Mother of God
. . . you've got some explaining to do, young man!"

I was totally confused. "What?" I begged. "Grandma,
please, slow down. Did what? What are you—?"

"Don't you interrupt me. Don't get too big for your brit-
ches. I'm sick and tired of you, of everyone talking over me.

I'll be goddamned if I have to sit here, sit here all alone and put up with . . . with this!" I couldn't believe my ears. I slapped my hand against my forehead for the crime of committing yet another atrocity. Biting my tongue, I readied myself for the next volley.

"You know damn well what you did—storming into your mother's house this afternoon . . . ranting and raving like a mad man . . . terrorizing her and tearing up everything in sight . . . throwing things . . . demanding this and that . . . inspecting every room as if you were goddamn General Patton! You're lucky she didn't call the police. Just who in the hell do you think you are? How in the world could you act like that at a time like this? Does anybody care to think about . . . to think how I feel?" Grandmother paused to cry into the phone. "I'm all alone here. I'm not getting any younger. If I live to be a hundred . . . I am very, very ashamed of you, David James Pelzer!"

All I could do was shake my head as Grandmother continued to berate me. I knew it was pointless to inform her that I, in fact, had not threatened Mother nor had I destroyed her house. Even the timing was off by a day. But much like Mother, no one could tell Grandmother anything. All I could do was reply with an occasional "Yes, ma'am" or "No, ma'am" whenever I felt a response was needed. An hour later, and after repeating herself for the umpteenth time, I broke in. "Grandma, I saw her *yesterday,* not today. And when you talked to Mother, just before you called me, was she . . . was she drunk?"

Hundreds of miles away, I could hear Grandmother suck in a deep breath. Intentionally, I had pushed her buttons. I was in no way trying to be disrespectful, but rather calming Grandmother down before she drove herself to a frenzy. Sensing she was close to a meltdown, I thought it best to bring her back to reality with a question so startling she had to see the situation for what it was: one of Mother's futile ravings. "Well," she insisted, "you know damn well she was! Drunk?

She's always drunk. I'm just sick and tired of her calling me. I mind my own business, you know. I don't bother a soul, and every day it's always something about *her* that *I* have to deal with. I've told everyone and now I'm telling you: I'm not getting any younger out here. It's not easy . . . but does anyone care to think about how I feel? Do they? Well . . . ?"

Grandmother's self-pity sounded word for word like Mother's self-centered speech just one day ago. "Grandma?" I lightly interjected. "If Mom's drunk when she calls you, maybe you should, you know . . . not take what she says to heart." Grandmother was by no means feebleminded; on the contrary, she was an intelligent, overbearing individual, who seemed at times to relish demeaning her daughter. As I carefully tiptoed past Grandmother, I suddenly realized the problem: her attention was never on the crisis at hand, but rather on *her* and how *she felt* at the time of the problem.

Feeling drained, and before Grandmother could fire off another round, I said, "Listen, I know it's late back there, so I'll call you later. Sorry to have disturbed you. I gotta go. I'll give Father your best. Bye."

As I gently lowered the telephone, I could hear Grandmother erupt like a volcano. "David James Pelzer! Don't you even think about hanging up on me! I'm sick and tired of everyone walking all over me, like some doormat. You'd think as much as I've done, that someone would be kind enough to think about my feelings. . . ."

As I dragged myself back to the living room couch, Alice exclaimed, "My Lord, you look a mess!" Since I avoided mirrors as much as possible, I could only imagine my appearance. "You haven't slept in Lord knows how long, and you eat like a bird. And now your face and neck are beet red . . ." Mrs. Turnbough placed her hand on my forehead. She shook her head in dismay. ". . . and now you're burning up."

As Alice disappeared into the bathroom, I exploded, "Man, *what is their problem?*" Returning a moment later, she presented me with some aspirin and a glass of water. With one swoop I tossed the aspirin into my mouth and gulped down the water. "I don't get it," I said to her. "They don't care. Not one of them. Mother nor Grandmother even asked about Father. And now," I shouted as my frustration spilled over, "it's like Father doesn't exist. It's too much for them. Or he's not important enough? I don't know. They didn't ask about him—how he's doing, what's going on, nothing. They didn't offer to lift a finger. Everything, all the time, is always *them*. How they feel their pain. Poor pitiful them. Dammit!" I swore, hitting my knee.

I quickly caught myself. "I'm sorry." I didn't want Alice to think I was upset at her. Feeling myself run out of steam, I added, "I don't know what I'm doing . . . I mean, about Father. I just wish I had a real family who loved each other or for once could bury their hate and do what's right. That's all I wanna do."

"David!" Alice cried. "Wake up, we're late. It's after nine. We've overslept." Before she could finish, I shot up from the couch, brushed my crumpled fatigues, which I had worn for the last four days, and bolted to the front door. In record time Alice and I arrived at the hospital.

Sprinting down the hallway, I met Steve at the entrance to Father's room. Extending his arm, Steve blocked me from entering. "We need to talk," he stated. Peeking in on Father, I noticed that except for his intensified breathing he seemed the same. But I knew by Steve's forced smile all I needed to know. "David, you need to understand . . . sometimes they can't . . . they won't go . . . until they know the ones they love will be fine. You . . . ah, get what I'm saying, David?"

I fully understood, but the moment was too much for me. "Hey, David," he went on, "your dad, he's in pain. You have to tell him you'll be fine. You have to let him go. You understand, right, David? He won't pass until you do this. Ease his suffering. It's the right thing for him. It's the proper thing to do. He won't pass until . . ."

I turned to Alice. "Could you go in and talk to him, please?" I begged, before fleeing to the far end of the hall, where I found a wooden bench. With a million thoughts running through my mind, I became fixated with my cheap Timex watch. It showed a few minutes to ten. Clasping my hands together, I prayed. "I've never really asked you for much. And you know what I've been through. I guess I thought I could save him. . . . So, if you could grant me this . . . if there's no way that he can get better . . . then take him. Ease his pain and take my dad. Amen."

Not knowing what to do next, I wiped away my tears, cleared my mind, and made my way to Father's room. A small legion of nurses and specialists, who had probably been Father's only contact with the outside world for the past few months, cleared a pathway as I stepped into his room. Alice turned toward me after patting Father's arm. "You're a good man, Mr. Pelzer. God be with you," Alice said with tears swelling in her eyes, then left the room. From behind me Steve whispered, "Let him go." Everyone else filed out after him.

Alone now, I noticed how huge the room seemed. The drapes were wide open, and the sun poured through the windows. Besides the bed, all the other furniture and medical equipment had been removed. The sheet to Father's bed was crisp, and his gown seemed new. The only sound to be heard was Father's raspy breathing. Taking a long, hard look, I saw for the first time, below the left side of his neck, that Father's bandage had been removed. It exposed the blackened area where the cancer had literally eaten his skin. Even then, as much as I wanted to ease his pain, I could not say good-bye.

Standing by his bed, I took Father's trembling hand. From behind my eyes I could feel the pressure build, and fought to bury the pain.

"I, ah, got . . . some great news," I lied. "The doctor says everything's gonna be fine . . . and that . . . they can have you up and outta here real soon." Part of me felt like a heel, and yet the more I talked, the more my fantasy seemed to take hold. Peering into Father's face, I stated with confidence, "I didn't tell you this before, but I got a home on the Russian River." I paused, beaming at Father, who seemed to understand. "It's got knotty pine walls and ceilings. A stone fireplace, your own room. It's always warm and sunny. It's really nice. It's got everything. It's on the river, and when the sun goes down, the water's as smooth as glass. At night you can smell the redwood trees . . . it's a piece of heaven, Dad. Heaven.

"Remember that time when I was a kid and you let me walk with you that summer at the river . . . you said it was like heaven. You and I can live there . . . and go fishing, sit at Johnson's Beach, or do anything we want. And in the summer . . . we can go to San Fran and catch a game at Candlestick— just like you always said we'd do. We can be like a real father and son. Just the two of us.

"We made it, Dad! We really made it! Everything's gonna be fine. We can be together . . . and live at peace. We got a home, a real home. No more fighting, no more troubles, no one's gonna kick us out. We got it made! It's gonna be fine. You just relax and . . . I'll take care of you . . . I'll take care of everything. . . ."

I broke off when I felt Father's trembling fingers clutch my hand. Never before in my entire life had both of us looked deep into each other. His dark eyes were perfectly clear as they bore into mine. I could somehow feel the immense shame, loneliness, sorrow, and pain in Father's gaze. "I've always been proud of you. You've always been my hero. And as your son, I swear to God, one day I will, *I will* make you proud. I always have and always will love you, Father. Now you relax . . . and I'll meet you at the river."

With whatever strength Father had, he strained to lift his head to mine to kiss me on the mouth. With my free hand I held him from behind his neck as delicately as possible. The two of us had finally joined as father and son. I returned the gesture by smiling at him and kissing him on the forehead. Then, like so many years ago, as he had that summer when we strolled together at the Russian River, my father winked at me before he slipped away.

I held Father's body as long as possible before I eased his head back onto the white pillow. Looking at Father's face, I felt so utterly stupid for thinking that I could have somehow saved him. Time seemed to come to a halt as I gazed at the man I had so long wanted to be with. After closing Father's eyes, I thanked God for allowing me to be with him during his last moments. With the tips of my fingers I rubbed my lips, thinking how Father had never kissed me before. No matter what void had existed between Father and me in the past, I now had the memory of being with him when it counted most. It was something I would forever cherish.

Stepping outside the room, I saw that Steve understood. With a piece of paper in his hand, he dialed the phone and gave it to me. "What?" I asked in a daze.

Not looking at me directly, Steve muttered, "Your mother . . . she wanted to know as soon as it happened . . . the moment he passed away."

Closing my eyes, I could feel myself drift. At the lowest point of my life, Mother, in all her grandeur, had maintained control of the situation. As always, I wasn't even worthy of the privilege of her majesty's unlisted line, but was somehow good enough to do her dirty work. At the other end of the phone line, I could hear Mother's heaving voice. I swallowed hard and performed my function. "This phone call is to inform you that your husband, Stephen Joseph Pelzer, has just passed away."

I stopped for a second, surprised by my deadpan tone and lack of compassion. As much as I prided myself on manners, at that moment I didn't give a damn about Mother or her dramatic, self-centered exploits. Mother didn't even flinch.

"Well . . . yes. It's really better that way, isn't it? Uhm . . ." A moment later the line went dead.

I stared at the phone, which seemed welded to my hand. From behind the nurses' station, Steve pried the phone from my fingers. "We need to talk," he said with a bright smile. "Remember, when I told you that he wouldn't go until he was ready?"

With tears now freely running down my face, it was all I could do to nod my head yes.

"Your father wasn't ready. He held on . . . he waited . . . he waited for you."

"For me?" I repeated.

"Yes!" Steve said with conviction. "Out of all the people he's met during his life, your father hung on so he could say good-bye to you."

"But," I babbled, "he, ah . . . he couldn't even speak, not even with his eyes. He couldn't—"

"Doesn't matter," Steve replied as he came from behind the counter. "He knew what he was doing. David, listen carefully, your father fought as long and as hard as anyone I've ever known under those conditions. He could have given up a long time ago. He knew the outcome; he knew he wasn't going to walk out of here. He waited. He waited for *you!*

"You get what I'm saying?" Steve asked as he held my shoulders.

"Yeah," I said, "I understand now. I really do." Wiping away my tears, I said, "I appreciate everything you and everyone else did for him. At least"—I stopped to look at the small group of staff—"at least he wasn't alone. For that I'm grateful. I truly am. Thank you. Thank you all."

Shaking everyone's hand, I saved my appreciation for Steve last. All I could do was nod my head, up and down. "It's all right, man, I understand," he said before embracing me. Reaching behind to my back pocket, I pulled out a faded piece of black leather. "It's my father's badge," I announced triumphantly.

"He wanted you to have it. He told me so," Steve said, taking my hand.

"It's the only thing he had that was his . . . that no one could take away." I paused to collect myself. Without warning I felt an overwhelming urge to crawl into bed, hide from everything and everyone, and sleep forever. "One day I'm gonna make my dad proud," I adamantly stated. "I will!"

"David," Steve said, shaking his head, "not to worry. You already have. He told me himself. He's proud of you. He told me you made it . . . that you made it *out* of whatever situation you were in.

"Your father's 'up there' right now. He can see you." Steve stopped for a moment of introspection. "Maybe he was never physically with you. But up there, he'll be with you . . . always."

Four days later, on a foggy Monday morning, I parked Mr. Turnbough's car in front of the same Catholic church Ron, Stan, and I had briefly attended with our aunt years ago as preschoolers. Upon entering, I thought I was late—the services were apparently under way. Trying to be as inconspicuous as possible, in my olive green air force fatigues, I stepped with Alice lightly yet quickly down the left side of the aisle before sliding into one of the front pews.

While praying on my knees, I couldn't believe that I had dishonored my father by being late for his service. After thanking God for relieving Father's pain, I concentrated on the service. In an odd sense, I was excited to hear the good things others would say about Father. Maybe, I thought, I could learn something about him. I had always wondered about my parents' pasts, their ideas, their outlooks for the future, how they met, fell in love, why things turned sour, how as a couple they seemed to have it all but lost everything. I especially wondered about the love that I felt they had at one time for each other. But instead the priest began to hastily run down a list of announcements. "This Wednesday evening's sermon will be canceled. But the potluck dinner will still be served at the regular time. . . ." I turned to Alice in disgust.

It was then that I noticed behind the pulpit there were no bouquets, wreaths, or even a casket for Father. "Look." I elbowed Alice.

Mrs. Turnbough leaned over and whispered, "Your mother said your father's wishes were to be cremated."

"No way!" I erupted. "He was a fireman! Get it, *a firefighter!* They're paranoid of getting burned. . . . No!" I said, trying to restrain my fury, "This is wrong. Totally wrong. Dad wouldn't want this!"

"I know," Alice gently replied, "but it's too late. She already . . ."

Not wanting to hear my father's fate, I turned away and caught a hateful glance from Mother, who sat directly across the aisle from Alice and me. By her look she seemed outraged that I was in the same building with her and her precious children, who for the most part appeared to be bored at the whole affair. My concentration returned to the priest, who cleared his throat before chanting his final blessing, ". . . of the Father, the Son, and the Holy Spirit. May the Lord be with you."

"And also with you," the congregation answered.

"Go in peace," the priest concluded.

A surge of anger took over me. *How could I have screwed up and missed Father's service?* On my knees I cursed myself for somehow misunderstanding the time of the funeral. Alice leaned over, saying, "I could swear that your mother said nine o'clock." I nodded, checking my watch, which read a few minutes after the hour.

Turning from the crowd, the priest bowed before stepping away from the podium. But by the sudden change in his face, the priest must have looked at Mother. Without breaking stride, he returned to his pulpit and unfolded a paper. "Pardon me," he said, "the church wishes to recognize the passing of Stephen Pelzer, who now rests in the hands of our Heavenly

Father. A retired fireman of San Francisco, Stephen is survived by . . ." the priest paused to read his notes. ". . . Stephen is survived by his beloved wife, Catherine, and his four children: Ronald, Stan, Russell, and Kevin. Let us pray."

As I bowed my head, I realized: *That was my father's entire eulogy.* Ten, twenty words. A lifespan said in a single breath. My father wasn't even worth a single flower, a prayer offering, anything. *How empty,* I thought, *his entire life spoken within a blink of an eye.* Then I recalled the words: *his four children.* "Oh, my God!" I swore to myself. "She did it again!"

I fired a glance at Mother, who wiped her swollen red eyes with a clean white handkerchief. As always, she didn't miss the opportunity to make herself the center of attention. Surrounded by *her children* for others to behold, the beloved Mrs. Pelzer played the role of the grieving widow to the hilt.

The priest broke my trance. "Peace be with you."

"And also with you," the congregation again answered.

"This mass is ended. Go in peace."

While standing, I maintained my hard stare at Mother, who lost her footing as she struggled to get up. I could hear a series of muffled gasps from the crowd. Per her dramatic display, all eyes turned to Mother. From behind me, I could hear people rushing toward the widow. I shook my head in disgust.

"Dah-veed?" someone called. "Dah-veed, do you remember? You remember us?"

I turned toward an elderly couple standing before me. It took me a moment to realize that they were my old next-door neighbors, Tony and Alice. "You remember us, yah?" Tony asked in broken English. I could remember him smoking his pipe while he pushed his wooden lawn mower across the grass when I was a preschooler. But when I was older, I also recalled that winter when Mother's game was having me skate up and down the block, nonstop in near-freezing weather, wearing only a worn-out T-shirt and a pair of shorts. Once Tony stepped outside, bundled in a thick jacket, to pick up his evening paper. All we could do was nod at each other. Somehow we both understood. The last time I had seen him was days before I was rescued. Because of the closeness of the houses, you could walk up the stairs that led to the front door and easily see into the small kitchen window of the neighbor's house, which was just a few feet away. Late in the afternoon, Mother drove her foot into my face as I laid sprawled on the kitchen floor. For a second Tony's eyes had met mine. Blood was pouring from my mouth and nose. As always, he understood, but was unable to do anything. Times were different back then.

"You be okay now. I see you in the army air corps. You be fine," Tony said with pride as he held my shoulders. With his wife, Alice, standing beside him, he stated, "We proud of you. Everyone knows. You a goot boy. We all, de whole neighborhood, know about you and Ronald, joining the service. You goot boys. Always goot boys."

Out of embarrassment, all I could do was nod. "You come to see Tony and Alice when army gives you time to come home."

Before I could reply, a band of men in dark blue uniforms stepped forward. I swallowed in awe as the group of firemen from Father's station stopped in front of me. For a moment I thought they had mistaken me for a member of Mother's party. A man, who I assumed by his commanding presence was the captain of the station, took my hand and whispered into my ear, "Your father was a good man and one hell of a firefighter. Don't you ever forget that, son."

"Yes, sir, I'll remember, Captain," I promised.

"And do you remember your favorite uncle?" a voice from the past asked.

Among the group Uncle Lee, my father's longtime partner, emerged, giving me a hug. One by one the men from the station paid their respects, in the process seeming to form a protective shield from Mother.

"Thanks, Lee," I blurted.

"For what?"

"You know . . . for *acknowledging* me. I was there when . . . he passed away. But you guys shouldn't be with me. I don't want to do anything that may set her off," I said, glancing over at Mother.

" 'Acknowledge,' my ass. Ain't nothin' can pry us away. He loved you boys. You, David, need to know that. Maybe he didn't say it, and maybe he wasn't there for ya, but he always thought about you kids. Things just . . . well, they didn't work out. And if Ronald was here, I'd tell him the same thing. You boys need to know. No one's perfect. Your father did things I didn't approve of, but," Uncle Lee adamantly asserted, "your father wasn't evil. Whatever his shortcomings, it was never intentional. Get my meaning?"

I nodded my head. "I understand. Thanks, Lee."

"Listen," Lee knelt down, "your father gave his helmet to Ron. Do you have his badge?"

Checking behind me to ensure I was safe from prying eyes, I confided, "Yeah, but I'm not so sure I'm supposed to have it. Am I supposed to give it to you guys? What do I do?" I swallowed hard. "Give it to her?"

"Not on your life!" Uncle Lee cried. "Listen up. It's your father's way of saying how much you meant to him. He wanted so much to give you kids something, instead of all the hell you boys were put through. David, you got shortchanged quite a bit and"—Lee paused to look in the direction of the pulpit—"and I expect you're going to get the shaft before this matter is through. You keep it. To your father . . . well, that badge represents the kind of man he longed to be—on and off the job. To him it's worth more than any amount of money. Do we have an understanding? What your mother doesn't know won't hurt her. So, keep your mouth shut and keep that badge. Do your namesake proud."

I felt as if I were ten feet tall. For a shining moment, I was a real person.

Outside the church, I shivered from the morning chill. A thick gray blanket of fog swirled above. *"Excuse me!"* Mother interrupted in her best sarcastic, pompous tone, *"Mrs. Trewn-bow,* I require a moment alone to speak with *The Boy."*

Alice—who had suffered years of Mother's psychotic "disciplinary instructions" on what a burden I was to society in general during late-night drunken ramblings—had had her fill of Mother. Before Mrs. Turnbough could give Mother a piece of her mind, I intervened and led Mother to the side of the church. Alone in the empty parking lot, Mother grabbed my shoulder and spun me around. "Just who in the hell do you think you are? What gives you the right to show up at a function like this?"

With my resistance completely drained, I returned to my former position of address—with my head down and my arms locked to my sides. "You called," I interjected.

"I don't ever remember placing a call to you. . . . I can't keep track of everything . . . and don't . . . don't *you* of all people contradict me . . . not today . . . you little shit! I'm not saying I called or didn't call, and if I did, I did so out of *courtesy.* You should've had enough sense to understand that you weren't welcome. But you were never that bright, were you?

"And what in hell's bells do you mean by having all those men fondle you as if you were something special?" Stealing a glance at her, I could tell that Mother was truly upset.

"You listen up! I only brought you out here, from your measly air force base, out of the kindness of my heart. I didn't have to do that, you know. So you stay the hell away from me and my boys! You know *who you are* and *what you are.* You don't belong. Don't you ever, ever, step foot in my house again!" Mother hissed. This time she didn't use her finger to lift my chin, as she had when I was her prisoner. I looked up on my own and into Mother's firey-red eyes. Not backing down, Mother leaned closer to me. "Don't you have something for me? Didn't *he* give you anything before he passed away?"

Ever so slightly, I uncoiled my fingers on my right hand and ran them across my back pocket. I became less tense when I felt the outline of Father's prized badge. Without batting an eye, I returned Mother's cold stare. "No," I said. "Father did not give me a thing."

"You're lying!" Mother shrieked. In the same instant I felt the sting of her hand slapping my face. Maintaining my stance, I let the blood from my bitten lip trickle to the pavement. Her physical assaults no longer hurt me. Mother's act of aggression was the final nail to her coffin—she had absolutely no control over me, and the only way to dominate me was to beat me. It never really worked when I was a child, and it certainly wouldn't work now. It also meant that Mother must be desperate to resort to this form of treatment, especially in public.

"I called the hospital . . . and they checked his belongings. They said he had the papers when he checked in, so don't stand here and tell me those papers just up and disappeared! And what in the hell gives you the right to dispose of his clothes at his motel? I called and they said you had come by and simply gave them away. So, tell me, tell me just who in the hell gave you the right to march in and—"

"You did!" I interrupted. "When you didn't visit him. When you deliberately went out of your way not to lift a finger. When you let the father of your children, your husband, someone you've known for years, rot away in a deathbed for months. You did *nothing* to help, but everything you could do to make him feel unworthy and isolated," I fired back, venting my anguish over Father's treatment. "Whatever I did, I did my best. At least *I* would have had the decency to give Father a proper burial service. I don't know why you . . . you hate everybody and everything so much!

"You think you're the only one who's been through hell? You're the source. You made everyone's, every single person's life a *living nightmare,* and you thoroughly enjoyed it. You relished it. You had everything. You blew it. Not me, not Father, Grandma, the teachers, the neighbors, your friends, Uncle Dan, Ron, Stan, Russell, or Kevin. It's not my fault, not then as a kid, and not now! Father deserved better. No matter all the fights, his fault or yours, he deserved better!"

"Why, you pompous, filthy piece of . . ." Mother muttered under her breath. Again she raised a hand to strike me down.

"Don't you even think about it!" I shot back. "Know this," I stated in a low, clear voice, "everything you've done to me, to Father, to everyone, will come back to you. The pain, the suffering, the hell . . . everything!"

"Don't you—you . . . try and change the subject," Mother fumbled. "One of the nurses . . . told me . . . he said he saw you . . . go through his jacket pockets stealing the papers."

Papers? I truly had no idea what Mother had been ranting about. *Unless she was referring to when I was first searching for his badge in the hospital . . . and found a set of documents and stuffed them into my back pocket near my wallet.* My only concern had been for Father's badge. In all the chaos of dealing with Mother, Grandmother, and the lack of sleep, let alone Father's needs, I had stupidly forgotten to look over the papers. For all I knew . . .

My facial expression must have given me away. "Yeah," I hesitated, "I have 'em. I didn't mean to . . . I mean, I meant to give them—"

"Shut up and give me the fuckin' papers!" Mother ordered.

I could only guess that the papers were some gigantic insurance policy that Father had taken out years ago. Part of me wanted to whip out the papers and watch Mother grovel on her hands and knees as I ripped them to shreds. After years of enduring Mother's misery, head games, and torture, I now had control over something she desperately craved. *I now called the shots.* But as I stood in front of this pitiful wreck, I realized that my passing fantasy was not the outcome Father would have intended. In all, I still had the prize of prizes. But by withholding the documents, I thought I would somehow discredit whatever dignity Father had. *No matter how many times Mother had plotted to kill me, stooping to her level was something I could not do.*

"Here," I said as I unfolded and presented her the papers. "It was a mistake. I forgot I had them. Really, I did. I never meant to keep anything from you. I would have given them to—"

In a flash Mother snatched the papers. The only time she ever moved with such speed was years ago when she used to beat me. Her eyes sparkled and she sighed with relief. "And now, young man, I indeed have everything I will ever need."

"You lose," I smiled.

"What?" Mother asked as she leafed through the papers.

"All those years you tried your best to break me, *and I'm still here*. Father's finally free, Ron's in the service, and soon the boys will move out on their own. I'm a good person. I try my best in everything I set out to do. I make mistakes, I screw up, but I learn. I don't blame others for my problems. I stand on my own. And one day you'll see, I'm going to make something out of myself. Whether I dig ditches or flip burgers for the air force, I'll be the best, and somehow, some way, I won't waste my life away. If you taught me anything, you taught me that." Turning, I saw Mother's boys milling around at a safe distance with a small group of adults. I took a half step forward and pointed a finger in Mother's reddened face. *"Stay away from me.* Everything you've done to others . . ." I stopped as my voice quavered. I could feel whatever energy I had fade away. The last seven days had taken their toll on me. Taking a deep breath, I lowered my finger and backed away. "I pray for you every night, I swear to God, I really do. You may have your papers, your money, whatever. You can hate everybody and everything on this planet, but *you* lose!"

Mother stood with her mouth gaping. Before I left her, I clasped my hands together, then made the sign of the cross and leaned toward her ear, whispering, *"May God be with you, Mrs. Pelzer, for no one else will be."*

* * *

Ten hours and three thousand miles later, I returned to Hurl-burt Field, in Florida, only to discover my somber mood was no match for that of the base. After a small fleet of specially outfitted C-130 cargo aircraft landed, I learned that the air unit had been directly involved in the ill-fated rescue attempt of the American hostages held in Iran. Five of the eight men who gave their lives when a helicopter accidentally sliced into the C-130 had been assigned to Hurlburt Field. To make matters worse, I learned that the men had died the same day Father did.

I woke up in the early morning hours the next day to find I could barely breathe—the sides of my throat had swelled to the size of oranges. After a quick examination at the base's clinic, I was rushed to the hospital and admitted for severe mononucleosis. Since it was the first time I had ever been admitted as a hospital patient, and coupled with the strain of just losing my father, I was terrified. Because of my condition, I was heavily sedated. As the medicine took effect, I was finally able to lose myself and whatever problems I had through sleep.

During the night, I dreamed I was lying next to Father. I tried to stretch my arm toward him and hold his hand, but I could not budge. I fought to scream out to Father, to say something, anything. But, just like Father, I could not utter a single word.

CHAPTER 6

REGROUP

Because of severe mononucleosis, I was heavily sedated in a hospital bed for over a week. Even after being released, I found myself without a clear-cut purpose for the first time in my life. I was devastated that I had lost my father. My sole objective for the past few years had been to push myself beyond any normal limits in order to save every penny, which would enable me to buy my home, then scour San Francisco until I found Dad. Without him, though, sharing the cabin in the serenity of the redwood trees, fishing at the river, talking over a crackling fire, or anything that might resemble an ordinary family life was a complete delusion.

As a shivering child in the garage, I had always dealt with my challenges by pushing down my feelings, thinking of what I could learn from the situation, and do whatever it took to somehow make things better. I had always formulated the ultimate plans and broken them down to the tiniest detail. This strategy helped me prevail over Mother, served as my protective shield while I was in foster care, and propelled me into the air force. As long as I had a chance—a glimmer of hope in a tunnel of darkness—all I had to do was clear my head, rid myself of any self-pity, and forge ahead.

And yet another part of me felt that my best-laid plans of becoming a knight in shining armor to my father were nothing but an idiotic pipe dream. Since Father and I spent so little time together during his lifetime, we were obviously not that close. But I had always believed that if I could put all the large-scale pieces in place, I could smooth out the minor details of a relationship later. This delicate process had become a guilt-filled obsession. How dare I go to the beach with my air force friends, buy records or even clothes while Father was out in the cold somewhere. It had gotten to the point that I never did anything beyond waking up, working my tail off, returning to the barracks to catch a bit of sleep, then repeating the cycle the next day. Whenever I had a day off, I'd simply sleep in, watch television, or read. To do anything more meant taking money away from my goals. Yet, I had to admit to myself, it was also because of my lack of social skills, taking a chance at making a jerk of myself in front of people. Even as a young man in my early twenties, I'd continue to say the wrong things at the wrong time, and whenever I became nervous, I dug a deeper hole by stuttering uncontrollably.

By focusing on my future, I was able to reject the present.

Months dragged on, and I came to realize that I had used Father as an escape from dealing with my new life as a young adult. Now with Father's death, I had to learn to deal with myself.

I coped with Father's death the only way I knew how: working. I would get off work and rush to the barracks to change clothes before putting in a full shift as a short-order cook at the local Denny's restaurant. After an eight-hour shift I would get off from Denny's with just enough time to change back into my rumpled air force fatigues and head out to the field for a day's work. At times I went without sleep for several days. I really didn't care. I hated my jobs. I hated my life. After a while, when I'd sleep, I often had intense nightmares of being late for either my air force or restaurant job.

At least now when I slept, I no longer had nightmares of Mother trying to kill me. She used to always appear in my dreams standing at the end of a hallway surrounded by a gray mist. But now as Mother moved forward to attack me, instead of fleeing, I'd march toward her, step for step. When Mother would raise the knife above her head, I would rip open my shirt and hiss, "Do it . . . ! C'mon, do it!" The gleaming knife would remain frozen beside Mother's red face. Stepping within inches of her, I'd whisper, "Kill me now or let me be!" Even though I was still intimidated by Mother in real life, she no longer had control of my dreams. I had been terrified for so long, yet with Father's passing, day by day I believed I was finally releasing myself from her grasp.

Soon I found out my squadron had been chosen to fly to Egypt and build a temporary air base. Nearly all of the four hundred men assigned to the unit were tasked for the mission. I found myself desperately wanting to be a part of the extraordinary adventure. As a low-ranking airman who had been in the squadron for less than a year I was not considered, but a major officer in charge of logistics spoke with my hardhearted supervisors to give me a chance. And they did. When I was finally selected, I was so elated that I waltzed into Denny's, quit my job, and packed my duffel bag.

The exercise, dubbed "Proud Phantom," gave me a different perspective on being part of a team. As a cook in the middle of the desert, just outside Cairo, I'd work ten to twelve hours in furnace-like heat during the day, then in bone-chilling temperatures at night, without any breaks. I was proud to sweat side by side with others who also pushed themselves beyond the norm in our combined effort to achieve a military mission. Whenever I'd steal a few moments for myself, I would step outside the sweltering dark green tent and scan the skies for the vintage American F-4 Phantom fighter jets as they raced overhead, showing off to the Egyptian pilots by either making diving passes or pushing their planes through Mach 1, shaking the ground like a volcanic eruption. The shock wave would practically demolish our cooking tent, scattering pots, pans, and every other piece of equipment in every direction. During more serene times, I'd stand outside mesmerized by the streaks of powder blue and bright orange skies before the sun set beyond the brown-speckled dunes. At other times, just before dawn, when an eerie quietness filled the base camp, I'd gaze at the thin layer of fog, minutes before the rising sun, and watch as a blanket of purple evaporated the mist. Halfway across the world, it was a relief not to worry about my future or be locked away in my past. I had finally found some peace.

Immediately upon returning from Egypt, I called Alice. Barely giving her a chance to talk, I began recalling my adventures of putting in grueling hours at the base camp, my visit to the pyramids and the sphinx, and the loads of postcards I had mailed her and Harold. Finally she broke in, telling me that my uncle Dan had passed away. Cutting the conversation short, I phoned Grandmother so I could get the telephone number of Uncle Dan's wife, Jane. As always, I didn't know what to expect, so I took a deep breath, waiting to see what mood she was in. I was not prepared for the frail tone of Grandmother's voice. In all my years of knowing her, even as a child in Mother's house, I had never heard her so vulnerable. "I am truly sorry to hear about Uncle Dan," I gently said.

Thousands of miles away, outside the limits of Salt Lake City, I could hear Grandmother whimper. After crying for a few minutes, her entire manner began to change. As much as I wanted to "be there" for Grandmother on the phone, I knew I was just her captive audience. "No one knows what it's like," she began, "to lose your children, to be all alone. No one knows."

"What?" I exclaimed. "Did you say she's dead? Mom's dead?"

"Well," Grandmother sniffled, "she sure as hell might as well be. You'd think the least she could do is visit her own mother."

"So she's alive? I'm sorry, I misunderstood, I thought you just said . . ." My words trailed off.

"You know damn well, young man, that when your mother sold the house to some foreigner—and let me tell you, I heard she got a pretty penny for it, too. That house sold so fast it would have made your head spin. And does she offer me anything? Hell no! Not one red cent, let alone grant a kind word to her own mother. . . ."

I steadied myself, trying to clear my head. I had no idea Mother had moved. And I truly did not care. All I could think about was my brothers—if they were still with her, if they were safe. Maybe they even had a new chance of happiness. Slowly I came out of my trance, wondering how the conversation had turned. I knew the unspoken rules of speaking with Grandmother: Let her rant as long as she wanted, never question her opinion, never interrupt, and, above all, never ask a question. Any questions could mean dire consequences. "Grandma, I am sorry, but . . . could I please have the number to Aunt Jane's? I just would like to pay my respects. I've been away for a while, and I don't want her to think . . ."

"Well," Grandmother said, "I just don't know if I can find it. I just don't know *what* I'm going to do." After a lengthy pause, she let out a labored sigh. "And if that weren't enough, can you believe she settled here?" I could hear Grandmother stab her finger into the phone. "Here of all places? She doesn't even have the decency to come see me. Not once. Well, if she's waiting for me to traipse over to her place and bow down before her holiness, well, she can wait till hell freezes over! I don't need this, you know."

Standing in the cramped phone booth, I automatically nodded in agreement. "Yes, Grandma," I replied, "I understand." Yet, as I thought about it, Mother moving near Salt Lake City made absolutely no sense. I recalled as a small child that Mother had told stories to Ron, Stan, and me about how she despised Utah, the extreme winters, and what she dubbed, "the inner society of 'The Church.'" I would have never guessed that Mother would, of all places, move near her own mother—a person that she treated with absolute malice.

Clutching the telephone, I recalled Mother's instantaneous change of attitude whenever Grandmother dropped by. Even when I had sat at the bottom of the stairs in the basement, I could distinctively hear Mother's unique way of being both slightly submissive and coldly dispassionate. Mother seemed to attempt to appease Grandmother but only to a limit. The more Grandmother tried to reach out, the more Mother refused Grandmother and whatever offers she made. Whenever Grandmother left Mother's home, there was always hell to pay, and I was usually Mother's outlet. Now, leaning against the metal ledge of the phone booth, I could not remember a single gesture of love or compassion between the two women. Straining to pick up what Grandmother was saying, I could not help but make the connection between mother and daughter—both consumed by their mutual hatred and yet they were a mirror image of each other.

From the books I was studying on psychology and human development, I could only assume that Mother's drinking, vindictive behavior, and her treatment of me were somehow linked to her past.

Grandmother's labored breathing caught my attention. "And . . ." she huffed, "I just don't know what to do about Stan. I give him odd jobs and I pay him, of course, but I'm not going to be around forever, you know. I've told him time and time again, he needs to finish school and get a high school diploma. I've told him over and over that I'd pay for a tutor. You'd think he'd listen to me. You'll see, when he's on his own without a pot to piss in, he'll come running to me. You'd think with all I've done . . ."

I had to jump in to keep her from belittling my younger brother, Stan, who had been mildly retarded since suffering a severe fever as a small child. "Grandma," I interjected, "I'm sorry about Stan, but could I please, *please* get the phone number for Aunt Jane?" By the extended pause on her end, I knew I had pushed too hard, but I also knew that the simplest request was always met with a wall of resistance. After several more gentle nudges, Grandmother finally relented. I hung up the phone feeling completely drained. Part of me felt I should mail Grandmother a card, send her some flowers, or maybe take some military leave to visit her. I had been outside the family fold for so long that I wasn't sure what to do or how my intentions would be received. For years I had wanted to do the right thing and make up for years of loss. As always, a blanket of guilt covered me and I wasn't sure how to proceed. Stepping outside the booth, I took in a few deep breaths to clear my head. Yes, I told myself, Grandmother was obviously having a hard time, but I had gotten so wrapped up in her grief that I almost forgot about my uncle Dan.

Thinking of our conversation, I realized Grandmother had said little of Aunt Jane and how her children were coping. When I had asked about my brothers, the question was brushed aside. Like Mother, the center of attention had shifted to Grandmother and *her* anguish.

Speaking with Aunt Jane was completely different than with Grandmother just minutes before. She was more concerned about my feelings than her loss. Trying to take Aunt Jane's mind off Uncle Dan, I told her of my trip to Egypt and my hopes of going to college to make something of myself. "You already have, David. Dan was proud of you, and all of us here are, too. Don't push too hard and just live life. Take time and enjoy a little." As we spoke back and forth, I remembered Uncle Dan as a hard-nosed man who had lived as the ultimate outdoor sportsman, and who also drank as much as Mother and Father. I remembered as a child looking deep into his eyes, and sensing that Dan was like Mother—a person with a volatile temper that could erupt at any moment. As Aunt Jane opened up to me a little more on the phone, I felt that her marriage to Dan and the lifestyle that went with it was not a smooth one. "It wasn't easy for anyone back then, David. Back then things were different . . . the drinking, everything. It was considered the norm back then; 'The days of wine and roses.' "

"I'm not trying to pry," I asserted, "I just want to know so . . . so I don't do the same as . . ."

I could almost see Aunt Jane nodding in approval. "I understand. Don't be too judgmental. Like I said, it was a different era back then; for your parents, and their parents before them. Whatever problems we had were swept under the rug. Family skeletons were kept locked in the closet. A lot of us had high hopes that situations we dealt with or how we were raised wouldn't be passed on to our children. It was hard on all of us. If you children can break the cycle, that's all any of us as adults can ever wish for. There are no guarantees in life, so learn from others' mistakes. Enjoy what you can, while you can. Don't let it consume you like . . . well, just let go and let life happen."

For me, Aunt Jane said it all in a nutshell. Afterward, I replayed every word in my mind, even months after we spoke. Aunt Jane did not know, but her words "Don't let it consume you" were the last words Father had said to me before I enlisted in the air force: "Do what you have to. Don't end up like me." My aunt helped me to realize that whatever had happened between Mother and me had deeper causes than her drinking and abuse. I could only guess whatever anxiety Mother or even Grandmother carried within their heart of hearts. I was in no way looking to place blame on either of them; if anything, I felt a certain sadness for what it must have been like for both of them during their childhoods.

I vividly recalled as a preschooler how, when I called her Mommy, she showered Ron, Stan, and me with endless love, attention, and anything we could wish for. At times, whenever Grandmother left from one of her visits, the four of us would celebrate. It was as if Grandmother was still a parental figure in Mommy's house, and once she departed, Mom was able to do as she pleased. One time, when Grandmother was adamant about Mommy not allowing my brothers and me to play the game Twister for fear of us contorting ourselves into bone-snapping positions, Mom rolled out the plastic sheet and played with us the moment the front door closed. "Oh, don't mind her," Mommy cooed. "She doesn't know how to play. Let's have some fun!" Looking back, I thought perhaps some black hole from Mommy's past had caught hold and sucked in all the goodness and any chance for her to relive her childhood. As a boy sleeping on an army cot, I had always prayed for "Mommy" to come back and rescue me from "The Mother." I truly believed that "Mommy" would someday wake up, and once she did, all of us would forever live our lives as one perfect, happy family.

In some peculiar sense, I began to feel a certain pity for Mother. Did she, I wonder, have a happy childhood? Was Mother resentful toward Grandmother because of the way she was raised? If so, perhaps Mother became a hateful person because she had not dealt with her unresolved issues? Maybe Mother turned her back on her past, while hoping for the best in her future. Barely in my twenties, I already knew that unless a drastic change is made, the way a person is raised will most likely be the way that person will raise their children. For me it was not a matter of placing blame on Mother, or pointing the finger at my grandparents, but to ensure my freedom to live a life free of misery and despair. And I had to make certain whatever pushed Mommy into the abyss would not suck me in, too. I was still confused and, strangely enough, I still craved Mother's acceptance. For now, all I could do was take Aunt Jane's advice and get on with my life.

After more than two years of being a field cook, I was reassigned to the training section of the squadron, enabling me to work a basic eight-to-five schedule. No longer having to get up at three a.m. to put in ten to fourteen hours a day, let alone the hour drive to the work site each way, I welcomed the opportunity. The timing of my assignment was perfect. Since I desperately wanted to become an air crew member, I needed to take college classes. As a field cook, there was no way I could take time off even to register. But now I had all the time I needed.

Attempting to better myself through college courses after normal duty hours was frustrating. I had never taken anything beyond basic math while in high school before I dropped out, so fundamental algebra was way beyond my comprehension. Even one of the simplest rules—negative plus a negative equals a positive—was too hard for me to grasp; I could not understand the logic. Even after the instructor explained, "It just is," like a broken record, the equation still did not add up for me. Because I could not apply the most basic of rules, I would spend hours trying to solve a single problem until I would literally bang my head against the desk.

Because I'd still mispronounce words at times and stutter when I became nervous, I'd spend hours in front of the mirror, studying the way I formed my lips as the sound came out. Due to my low self-esteem, I was terrified of girls, and had a complete lack of any social finesse, so I hardly ever went out with friends. I had always known the kind of person I was and where I fit in. It was as it had always been for me: break down the situation, analyze the different scenarios, make a decision about the problem at hand, and cut my losses the moment the issue looked hopeless. My life was black and white.

I got so far behind in class that the only thing I learned was how to curse myself for my stupidity. Part of me felt as if I were trying to become someone that I knew in my heart I wasn't. I thought college classes were the big leagues. While everyone else seemed to pick up on the material, I became completely lost. I had always prided myself on knowing my limitations, and now I was in way over my head. Late one evening I asked myself out loud, "Who am I kidding?" I threw the math book against the wall and quit the class.

Initially, I was relieved. I was free of the mind-numbing pressures from the class. I spent my free evenings consuming books like *Operation Overflight,* written by the U-2 pilot Gary Powers, who was shot down over Russia. The U-2 was the product of the same engineer who designed the SR-71, Kelly Johnson. As I studied other books that pertained to unique jets constructed by this famed aeronautical wizard—Johnson formed his own division dubbed *Skunk Works*—I realized that in order to have even a remote chance of becoming an air crew member, I needed to return to college. To reaffirm this, I phoned an air crew boom operator who in midair refueled the SR-71 Blackbird, Sergeant D. K. Smith, who told me straight out that not only did the air force require advance courses in math, but the slots to become a boom operator were few and those who applied for the position fought for them with a ferocious intensity. The issue had come down to a simple matter of how badly did I want it, and was I willing to stick it out in order to achieve my dream.

It took two more attempts, and an instructor with the patience of a saint, for me to muddle through the material, until one day something clicked and I understood the hows and whys of algebra—everything suddenly made complete sense. I actually enjoyed solving equations. I regarded math as absolute—no maybes, no ifs, no letting things be and seeing if it works out somewhere down the road. X always equaled something. In math, and as I had always lived my life, there were no gray areas.

With the first hurdle behind me, I applied my efforts to advanced algebra, then tackled trigonometry. My instructors were outstanding. I began to build upon a good foundation, helping me grasp complicated equations with relative ease. My esteem began to take root. I lived in the breathtaking state of Florida, I spoiled myself by purchasing a monstrous motorcycle I owned free and clear, went through intensive prequalifications, and officially applied for a slot as an elite air crew member. I had a fantastic job and even completed rigorous training as a paratrooper. Ever so slowly, I was doing what I could to better myself. For once my efforts were beginning to pay off. Life was great. I felt as I had when I first entered foster care—every day was a precious gift.

One day, out of the blue, in the last few days of May 1983, I received a letter from my brother Russell. Since I had not been in direct contact with Grandmother for nearly three years, I wondered how Russell knew where to write me. As I sped through the letter, I had to force myself to slow down, so I could digest each word. I was thrilled to hear from one of my brothers, to hear from an actual family member. But as the contents of the letter began to sink in, I could feel my stomach turn. Russell's letter confirmed what Grandmother had told me years ago, that after Father had passed away, Mother had moved and now lived just outside Salt Lake City. Russell also stated that before he died, Mother's primary focus of malice was mainly directed at Father. As evil as Mother had been when I lived in her house, she seemed to have reached new levels of hatred. With Father gone and me removed, it appeared as if Russell had become the target of Mother's rage.

I remembered one time when I was a foster child, I ran into Russell at a nearby school. By the haunted look on his face, I knew. While I was safely tucked away in the county's protective arms, Mother must have been putting my brothers through hell. As a child, I lived with Mother for only twelve years, while my brothers had to endure her vindictiveness until they were at least eighteen.

My thoughts turned to Stan. In the letter, Russell wrote that he was worried about Stan, who had become financially dependent on Mother and was now resenting his situation. He was proud and wanted to be his own person. What, I wondered, if anything happened to Mother or Grandmother? What would become of Stan? What could I do?

Even my older brother, Ron, who had recently married, was not beyond Mother's reach. The letter stated that although Ron and his wife, Linda, lived in Colorado, for Mother's benefit they were only a phone call away. It was not hard to imagine Mother in the middle of one of her drunken binges, telephoning late in the evening and ranting for hours. Knowing Ron was still a military police officer in the army, I could envision him getting only a few hours of sleep before he had to go to work. This poor man, I thought, was bombarded from both sides. When did *he* ever get a moment of peace? How in the world was Ron able to tell Linda about Mother and the

history of the family? If Mother kept to her pattern, she probably cleaned herself up for Linda, playing the role of the loving,
overly gracious parental figure who lived the picture-perfect
life. While Mother's act may have worked for her years ago, it
hardly seemed she could carry on with the charade any
longer.

Thinking ahead, I promised myself that if I ever became
involved with someone, I would have to protect her from the
sickening relationship between Mother and me. Even if it
meant going against everything I stood for, I would have to
lie. In order to have a chance of a future with anyone special,
I would have to bury my past.

At least Russell's letter stated that Kevin, my youngest
brother, had little idea of what had happened or what was
going on around him now. For Kevin, Mother's way of life and
the hell that went with it were perfectly normal. In an odd
sense I felt that Ron, Russell, and even Stan did what they
could to shield their younger brother. If anything happened
to Kevin, perhaps Grandmother could offer him safe refuge.
As I reread the letter, I began to feel a deep remorse. All in all,
without a doubt, *I was the lucky one.*

The letter ended with a positive statement. Russell would
soon be enlisting in the Marine Corps. He seemed proud to
join the elite force, and I felt that its camaraderie and values
of duty and honor would serve Russell well. At the very least,
getting as far away from Mother as possible would do Russell
good. I smiled at the thought. Three down, two to go.

As the weeks passed, though, the letter from Russell gnawed
at me. Every night as I unfolded the papers that I kept in my
Bible, I'd reread the letter. Why, after so many years, had Russell written to me? What did he really want? What, if anything, could I do? After years of working myself stupid on my
hopeless quest, I was just now getting a foothold on my life.
As much as I still craved answers to my past, part of me did

not give a damn. After years of feeling totally worthless, I was now the guy with the fancy motorcycle, with the chance of making something of myself by becoming an air crew member. Overall, I thought I was a good person: I worked hard, was self-reliant, kept to myself, stayed out of trouble, and did whatever I could to better myself. I had all anyone could ask for. As time passed, my childhood was increasingly becoming an illusion.

During one of these evening readings of Russell's letter, I came to a realization. Though I knew my brothers were still exposed to Mother's lifestyle, I, like my father at the time, remained passive to the situation. I never wrote anyone, called, or even mailed a simple Christmas card. After years of trying to fit in, it was I who had become reclusive. I had conveniently become nonexistent. Part of me wanted to tear up the letter in the same way I almost ripped up Father's insurance papers. If I did, I would no longer have Russell's letter tugging on my conscience. I would be saving myself by not being sucked in by my past. Closing my eyes, I clutched the letter. I took a deep breath, envisioning myself shredding it into tiny pieces. Suddenly my hands began to tremble. A wave of shame crashed over me. Opening my eyes, I broke down and cried. I ran the tips of my fingers down the length of the papers. After over ten years of exile, Russell's letter was the only form of contact I had with my family. Maybe the letter was a subliminal open line to my brothers. The least I could do was keep it. For now all I could do was replace my brother's letter in my Bible, and pray for the best.

Three months later, I took military leave for the first time in years, and after a short visit to the Turnboughs, I rode my motorcycle from the Bay Area nonstop to Salt Lake City. Although I would be staying with Grandmother, my intention was to spend as much time as possible with my brothers, and if all went as planned, I would finally come face to face with Mother. Over the last few months since Russell's letter, Grandmother and I had established a fragile truce. Even though at times I was still her sounding board, Grandmother now treated me like an adult capable of making my own decisions. But before my journey, when I had told Grandmother of my intentions, I knew by her sarcastic reply that I had hit a raw nerve. I did not understand what I had said that set her off. As I drew nearer to Utah, I only hoped that Grandmother would not interfere for once. Perhaps spending time with her would not only help us grow closer, but maybe, just maybe, would shed some light on how Mother came to be the way she was. The answers were within my grasp. The only thing that was certain, as I raced my super bike toward the sun, was that I was heading into the heart of my childhood, and my life would be forever changed.

CHAPTER 7

FOOLISH CRUSADE

By the time I found Grandmother's home in the midst of the trailer park, it was well past midnight. I repeatedly knocked on the door, but because of the late hour she had gone to bed. Being exhausted from the nonstop ride from California and frustrated from the built-up anticipation, all I could do was roll out my sleeping bag, which was strapped on the motorcycle, and sleep on one of the patio chairs on the deck.

The next morning I awoke to the sound of the sliding door opening. For years I had fantasized of greeting Grandmother with a warm embrace, as I had seen in so many movies, but before I could unzip my sleeping bag Grandmother was standing over me with her hands on her hips. "So, I see you made it," she stated more than asked. "Sorry," I yawned, rubbing my eyes, "it was a long drive." I smiled as I stood close to Grandmother, then awkwardly leaned forward to hug her. For a second I thought she flinched. I gently held her, wrapping my long arms around her back. Although she returned the gesture, the hug seemed mechanical to me—it had no emotional significance. As Grandmother pulled back, I let go and followed her into her mobile home. An overwhelming scent brought back to me the days when Mother would bring Ron, Stan, and me over to Grandmother's apartment in San Francisco, where we would spend the entire day decorating her artificial Christmas tree. My God, I thought. I must have been five, maybe six years old. After all those years Grandmother seemed to have the same pieces of furniture in the same perfect condition. I stood with my mouth open as my fingers ran over her piano. Grandmother's house was like stepping into a time warp.

Still a whirlwind of energy in her seventies, Grandmother took me on a trip to the local bakery to purchase a few loaves of day-old bread, then a brief but spastic tour of the city in which her stop-and-start driving left me nauseous—pointing in one direction, while flooring the accelerator and wheeling the car in a completely different direction. Afterward we both settled outside on her patio for lunch.

For whatever reason, I could not get myself to relax. All I could think about was not saying or doing anything that might make Grandmother upset. So far my visit was nothing like I had hoped for. I couldn't even look at Grandmother's face for more than a few seconds. I found myself turning away whenever I spoke. As I picked at my food, I realized that I was intimidated. Being with Grandmother in person was completely different than our relationship on the phone. In front of her, I was a pathetic child.

The situation became unbearable. Clearing my throat, I broke the ice by asking, "Are you still getting some good golf time in?"

By the flash in Grandmother's eyes, I knew I opened with the right question. "Just last week I played a round with a general from Hill Air Force Base. He's a general officer, you know. I asked if he knew you and, well, I guess there are so many of you soldiers—"

"Airmen," I corrected.

With a sandwich in her hand, Grandmother stopped cold, staring me square in the eye. After a long silence I apologized. "Well, anyway, you should take time and visit the Air Force Academy in Colorado Springs. Yes," Grandmother stated, "you must go and see the chapel. I have a map here somewhere. Now, where did I leave that map?" As she stood up to leave, I accidentally brushed against her arm. "It's okay," I said, "we'll find it later." In a flash Grandmother pulled away and stomped into the house. From outside I could hear her going through various drawers, searching for the elusive map. Minutes later, Grandmother returned to the patio looking defeated. "We'll just have to go to AAA. I go there all the time. The girls there are so nice."

The thought of another drive with Grandmother made my stomach flip. "Grandma, I'm sorry. I didn't mean to have you go through all that trouble, but I'm not going anywhere near the academy. My leave is up in a few days. I'll have just enough time to make it back to the base."

"Then you just make time, young man," Grandmother snapped.

I nearly dropped my sandwich. Looking into her eyes, I was met with another cold, hard stare. It took me an instant to realize my error. I was in no way trying to be impolite or disrespectful. I was only trying to make a point that to me seemed perfectly clear. Traveling over twelve hours a day on a motorcycle on the interstate for three days meant I truly did not have time for any side trips.

Trying to redeem myself, I changed the subject. "Anyway, about two months ago I got a letter from Russell. I hear he's going to join the marines. You must be so proud—the three of your grand kids in different branches of the service."

"Russell?" Grandmother exclaimed. "Let me tell you something about Russell! He borrowed my metal chest. I loaned it to him . . . going off with some church group to Hawaii, picking pineapples for the harvest . . . or whatever they do over there. I don't understand why their people don't do their own work. If you ask me, it's nothing but a vacation. Back in my day, when you worked, it certainly wasn't over there among the palm trees, that I can tell you. It was hard work, all day every day.

"Anyway, ever since he came back—high and mighty, I might add—he comes over telling me that I'll get my chest next time; he forgot it or he's too busy. By the time I got the damn thing, it was in terrible condition. That's *not* the way I had loaned it to him, I can tell you that!"

I sat with every muscle in my face frozen. I could not believe the floodgates I had opened. Grandmother was on one of her spiteful rolls. With my back against the chair, I asked myself if there was any subject, any person, safe to talk about. She went on. "The chest is useless to me now. You'd think as much as I do, it wouldn't be too much to ask to have my chest returned in the condition I loaned it to him!"

"Grandma!" I halfheartedly interjected, "you've traveled a lot. You know how it is. Things get banged up. You probably had that chest for what, years? I'm sure Russell didn't know how much it meant to you. Besides"—I shrugged my shoulders—"he can't help what happens when it's loaded from plane to plane all over Hawaii."

"Doesn't matter!" she huffed. "I paid a great deal for that chest. He should have apologized. I may have accepted that rather than his—his treachery. I can't and won't tolerate a liar!"

I wanted to reach over and hug Grandmother's frustration away. I couldn't believe that she had become so worked up over something so petty. "Maybe," I said, "Russell was embarrassed. Maybe he was afraid to bring the chest back to you after he returned from Hawaii. Do you think that might be the reason he might have avoided you?" I delicately asked, trying once again to defuse the situation.

"Doesn't matter. If you can't keep your word, then keep your mouth shut!" Grandmother replied, as if telling me a coded message.

I took the hint and sighed, trying to clear my head. "Well," I smiled, changing the subject, "the place looks great. Did you say Stan keeps it up for you? He does a great—"

"Stan? Let me tell you something about Stan!" Before I could blink, Grandmother launched into another tirade. "I've told him to finish school so he can make something of himself. I told him what he needs to do. I've offered to help with his reading. If he doesn't get some schooling, well," she huffed, "I don't know what will become of him. You can only be a pizza delivery boy for so long. He needs to go to school and learn a trade. I can tell you what I'm not going to do: I'm not going to be the one responsible for him."

I had had enough. Without her knowing, I clenched my fist under the table. "Grandma," I coldly stated, *"Stan is mentally retarded. It's not his fault."*

"I'm well aware of that. Doesn't mean Stan can go around life looking for a handout," she retorted. At least she now addressed Stan as a person.

"There's a limit to his understanding, his comprehension. Can you imagine what it's like to read something and not only not understand it, but forget whatever you've read? Believe me, I know. Some of that stuff can be pretty intimidating. And quite frankly, well, I really think he's embarrassed. I think he knows he'll have to break his back and work hard for the rest of his life. I—I . . ." I stammered, "I don't know him very well, but . . . Stan's . . . well, he's too proud to admit it."

Grandmother's eyes flashed. "You don't know a thing about him—or anyone else, for that matter! Like I said, if you don't know what you're talking about, then you should keep your trap shut." She paused for a moment as if for effect. "Besides, he needs to be humbled a peg or two."

My emotions began to swallow me up. Even though the person in front of me was my relative, an elder whom I respected, I truly detested her vindictiveness. Before I said anything, though, I excused myself to the bathroom, where I splashed cool water on my face. Taking a rare look at myself in the mirror, I saw my eyes were still red from the spine-numbing ride of traveling six hundred miles on a motorcycle with no protection against the wind and rain. As I rubbed the back of my neck with a face cloth, my thoughts returned to Grandmother. I could not understand why nearly everything that spewed from her mouth was filled with malice. The manner in which Grandmother spoke, the tone of her words, was nearly a carbon copy of Mother's.

A heartbeat later, I made the connection. *"Oh, my God!"*

Outside the bathroom, I scanned Grandmother's living room. As meticulous as it was—every item, no matter how small or how many, was placed in such a deliberate fashion—I could not find a single picture of Mother. Besides a few scattered photos of her grandchildren, there were none of Grandmother's husband, who, I was told when I was a child, had passed away when I was a baby, or any other adult relative. I could not help but think the lack of portraits was just like Mother's bedroom when I had visited before Father died.

Grandmother startled me as she came through the sliding door. Her look said she did not approve of my snooping. As she sat in a chair, I could tell by her posture she was upset with me. My fingers grazed a photo of Ronald in his uniform—the same picture I had seen at Mother's years ago. "Tell me about Mom. I mean, as a kid, when she was young. Was she ever happy?"

Grandmother's head shot up. She sputtered for a second before placing a hand under her chin. "Happy? Well, uhm . . ." Her voice cracked as she struggled to regain control. She cleared her throat. "No one was happy back then," she said as if I should have known all along. "Things were tough all over. I remember, when I was a young girl . . ."

As she went on, I patiently waited for her to finish. After her ancient clock struck twice, I broke in, "Yes, but, what about Mom? Do you realize I know absolutely nothing about my own mother?"

"Hard to please. Never appreciative. You'd think for once she'd show an act of kindness." Grandmother paused as she looked upward. "I told her she'd *never* finish nursing school," she said in her "I told you so" attitude.

"Never finished? But I thought that's how she met Dad. I mean, as a nurse."

"Hell's bells! She worked at the pharmacy across the street

from the fire station. Always been that way, out to impress. Always showing off. Never accepted who she really was. Never sees things as they are," Grandmother grumbled.

I was completely surprised. It had been ingrained in my memory that "Mommy's" lifetime dream was becoming a nurse so she could help others in need. As a child, I recalled, whenever a kid scraped their knee or bumped an elbow, Mommy, the neighborhood nurse, was always there. My mind began to reel. *Is anything in my life real? Must everything be secrets within secrets? Why are there so many lies?*

Grandmother never broke her stride. "I told her—over and over and over again—she would never make it as a nurse. She never listened. *Never has, never will.* Never appreciated one damn thing I did for her. Even now, all she does is call me, I don't know how many times a day, drunk as a skunk. Sometimes I just put the phone down and walk off."

"But why do you think?" I gently probed. "What made Mom become the way she is? Come on, Grandma, something in her past had to—"

"Don't you even . . . !" Grandmother commanded, shaking a finger at me as she leaned forward. "I never, *never* abused her! I might have given Roerva a good swat on the behind; she might have gone without a few meals when she didn't appreciate it, but I never, never abused her!" Grandmother slapped the back of one hand against the palm of the other with such force that I thought her hand would break. "If you ask me, she had it too easy.

"What you people today call abuse . . . times were different back then. Anyway . . ." She began to calm down. She repositioned herself into the rear of the chair. "I have no idea what happened back then. That's not my affair. What happens in someone's house stays in their house. It's no one else's business. I see no need to open up Pandora's box. It can't do anybody any good." Grandmother regarded me as if I were supposed to obediently agree.

All I could do was nod my head in agreement. I heard. And more important, I *understood* Grandmother's message.

After a lapse of silence, she announced to me, "I was the one who called the county's social services before you were removed."

I sat dazed by the sudden change of subject. "I don't understand. I—"

"Don't act so naive. The woman who visited the house, when your mother dressed you up and paraded you around, I know all about it. And who do you think purchased that bike of yours that last Christmas before you were taken away? Your mother sure as hell didn't do it, I can tell you that! She had new bicycles for all the boys, except Kevin; he was too young. Your mother said she simply forgot to get one for you, and by the time she remembered, well, she was over budget. Or so she said. I didn't have to get you one, you know. I paid for it in more ways than you could know."

I was overcome with shock. Of all people, my grandmother, who had just adamantly stated, "What happens in someone's house should stay in their house," was the one who initially called the authorities. As I sat in front of her, I could not believe my ears.

I remembered that bike, too. As a child in Mother's house, my only possessions were the ragged clothes that I had washed by hand in the basement sink. Even though I was allowed to ride the candy apple red Murray bicycle only a couple of times that winter, the thrill of freedom was still phenomenal. I had no idea; I had always thought, that Christmas of 1972, Mother, out of kindness, had broken down and purchased the bicycle.

I smiled and thanked Grandmother for calling social services. But then Grandmother, like everyone else, had always known how I was treated. On one visit Grandmother found me standing in front of the bedroom mirror yelling at myself, "I'm a bad boy! I'm a bad boy!" over and over again. With tears streaming down my cheeks, I had confessed how sorry I was for making Mommy upset. Another time Grandmother, the overly stern disciplinarian, had cupped my face with both her hands, saying, "You're the sorriest child I ever met! Quit feeling so sorry for yourself and do something about it!" At the time I didn't know that what was happening to me was wrong—I simply thought I was a bad boy.

Although I had an impulse to reach out and hug Grandmother for all the times she had silently helped me, I held back. Still not one word of compassion or sorrow had escaped Grandmother's lips about the past. She never showed or expressed to me any remorse about Father's death, what my brothers had been put through, or whatever I had suffered by the hands of her own daughter. Maybe, I thought, from Grandmother's point of view, life was full of suffering. You couldn't engage in self-pity, but rather had to do whatever you could to get out of bad circumstances, no matter how young. And, I guessed, you became hardened from the process.

What had made Grandmother the way she was? What was it that had hardened her heart? In her day, I assumed, she had to be rigid just to survive the times. However spiteful she may be, at least she was a self-reliant adult.

Maybe after dedicating a majority of her adult life fighting just to survive as a widow, while raising two children, she was worn down and fed up with how hard life could be. Perhaps that was one of the reasons Father advised me, before I enlisted in the air force, when I had brought up my childhood: "You'd be better off forgetting about it. The whole thing. It never happened." At that time I thought Father was ordering me to sweep the family secret under the rug. But maybe he was protecting me from taking on a lost cause. Maybe that's why Father had become a broken man. As much as he might have tried, his efforts were futile. That might be the reason, I assumed, why Grandmother always referred to the past as Pandora's box—once opened, uncontrollable agony of human suffering would follow. And in the end nothing would change. The back of my head began to throb from the over-load. *Maybe,* I told myself, *I just think too much.*

"Well," I announced as I stood up, stretching my legs, "I'm off to see Russell. I should only be gone a couple of hours."

"Oh no, you're not!" Grandmother said. "You're not to go there. I don't want you seeing her."

"It's okay, Grandma," I calmly corrected, thinking she had misunderstood. "I'm not going to see Mother. I'm only going to see Russell. It's all worked out; Mother won't know. It's okay, honest," I reassured her.

"You're not to see her. I forbid it!" Grandmother choked up. "You're not here. Ron's away. Nobody knows; I'm all alone. All she does is call—all the time, night and day. I'm surprised she hasn't phoned today. I don't initiate anything. She's the one who gets drunk and goes on and on and on. The hell she puts her own mother through. If she catches a whiff of you being here, there'll be hell to pay, and I'm the one who'll have to pay the price!"

All I could do was shake my head. I didn't mean to hurt anyone, but in my short visit here, every move, every inten-tion, was being questioned and scrutinized. Once again, I was caught between pleasing Grandmother or visiting my own brother, whom I had not spoken to in ten years. A familiar wave of guilt came over me.

"Grandma," I consoled, "don't put yourself through it. If Mother calls and goes off like she does, hang up. It's that sim-ple. Don't let her get your goat. Just hang up the phone and walk away. I don't mean to be disrespectful, but let Mother stay in her own little world. Go out and play golf. You'll be fine. It's only a game to Mother, if you play along."

"You don't know, *no one knows,* the hell she puts her own mother through. . . ."

It was then that I felt as if I was being manipulated. As a grown, independent adult, I was growing tired of walking on eggs with every subject that was brought up, constantly smoothing the waves while practically begging for permission to do something any normal person could do freely. "I gave Russell my word," I said. "I have to see him."

In a heartbeat Grandmother's tone changed from utter despair to cold vindictiveness. "Russell, Russell, Russell! He's not worth the time of day. I don't see any good in it. There's no need to run off all over the place just to see him. Nothing good can become of it. If you ask me, he's not worth rubbing two pennies together. That's what I think. I'm not telling you what to do, but if you want my two cents worth . . ."

I stood in front of Grandmother, waiting for her to order me to stay. And I would have. Without hesitation—just as I always had when faced with a confrontation that dealt with others' feelings—I appeased her by shutting up, swallowing my pride, and forgetting about it. After a lapse of silence, I grabbed my motorcycle helmet, saying, "It's gonna be all right, Grandma. It's not the end of the world. It's only a visit with my brother."

Minutes later I was guiding my motorcycle through a maze of road construction, freeing my mind of deserting Grandmother. I parked the Honda CBX on Mulberry Way, where, because of Mother, Russell had been recently taken in by friends from his church. I walked up the pathway not knowing what to expect. My heart raced with apprehension until a tall young man with freckles flung open the door and greeted me with a quick hug. After a fast round of introductions, Russell hopped on the back of the motorcycle, and we sped off to find a place to get to know each other.

Less than a mile away I parked my Honda next to a pool hall. Stepping inside such a place with one of my brothers was a fantasy of mine—male bonding. I marched up to the long bar, looked the bartender in the eye, slapped the palm of my hand against the bar showing off a twenty, and bellowed, "A beer for my brother, future marine extraordinaire. In fact, a round's on me! Set us up!"

Dead silence filled the hall. Not accustomed to social drinking, I thought the response was normal, maybe even a sign of respect. I could feel Russell tugging on the sleeve of my shirt. "Hey, man, relax," I stated in my "I'm king of the world" attitude. "It's on me." In reality I was broke. But this was a once-in-a-lifetime opportunity. I smiled, patting Russell on the shoulder, thinking of him as another escapee from the asylum. A prisoner of war repatriated. A young man taking the plunge into adulthood. Yes, indeed, a proud moment.

"David?" my brother whispered, breaking my concentration.

"Hey, man." I cut him off. "Don't sweat it; you're eighteen, right? Don't worry, they'll serve ya. I know my way around these places. Tip 'em a fin and they'll keep 'em coming. Come on, man, relax, you only live twice," I advised, jabbing Russell's shoulder. For once in my life, I threw caution to the wind and lived for the moment. I was a regular guy with no problems, living outside my shell. "Come on, man, don't be a killjoy."

"David, listen to me," Russell barked, "they don't serve beer."

"Get the—" I responded.

"This is Salt Lake City, Utah, get it? No bars."

As my younger brother educated me on the local customs, the look from the bartender confirmed my blunder. By the man's intense red face, I knew I had, once again, stepped out of bounds. I muttered to the older man, "I'm sorry. I truly am. I in no way mean to be rude, sir." Whatever adrenaline I had had moments before ebbed away. I politely asked for two Cokes, left a massive tip, and took a table in the back beyond the hard gaze of the construction workers playing pool.

"As you can see, I'm still working on my social graces," I confessed.

"Don't get out much?" Russell chided.

"Bingo," I said after taking a swallow. It was time to move on to something else. "Man, I just can't get over it. You look great. So, how's things?"

"Better," Russell sighed, "now that I'm out of *that house*!" I instantly picked up on his meaning. "Man, you have no idea what she's like. I don't mean to say you had it easy, but believe me, you got off pretty good. It's become a lot worse." Russell was ready to pour out his soul. "I tell ya, sometimes she'd chase me around the house. I told her if she ever laid a hand on me . . . I just couldn't take it anymore," he said with a heavy sigh. "If she's not on some rampage, then she's constantly complaining about everyone, everything, every second of the day.

"When she's done with me as a sounding board, Mom makes the rounds to Grandma and even Ron and his wife, Linda. No one's safe. Ron doesn't even take her calls, but Mom just doesn't get it." Russell paused to collect his thoughts. "And Stan thinks he's a he-man. I mean, what's he gonna do? He's bummed; he knows he needs Mom for financial help, and he hates it. If something ever happened to her, he'd never make it. He really thinks he's Mr. Fix-it. Bob Villa Jr." Russell smiled.

"I understand," I replied, thinking of what Grandmother had told me.

"I'm not trying to down him, but some of his electrical wiring projects almost started a few fires in the lower part of the house. Mom, of course, used to think that Ron and I were picking on him, but Stan can't do half the things Mom thinks he can, and she's so drunk she can't tell the difference. Stan just doesn't understand. It ain't his fault, but Mom's smothered him so much."

"What about Kevin?" I asked.

"He drinks so much Coke all the time that he's practically lost all his teeth."

"What?" I asked. "No way!"

"You don't get it, man. The whole setup: it's all normal to him. Kevin's a kid, he's oblivious. He doesn't know anything else."

The more Russell described the situation, the more I realized how on the mark he was. *I was indeed the lucky one.* I had been Mother's outlet as a child, and once I was taken away, psychologically she became a wounded animal, attacking anyone who crossed her path. The main difference was that by then my brothers were older and knew better than to take Mother's physical abuse, but unfortunately they had to put up with her psychological torture and self-destructive life-style.

And yet it all seemed surreal to me, how Mother could turn her hatred against her other children. Part of me had always feared for them. As a young boy surviving in darkness, I had known what to expect from Mother, to the point that I could predict her moods. Thinking ahead, staying a step or two ahead of her, not only kept me alive and gave me a protective armor, but became a way of life for me. Before Kevin was born, I was never sure if Mother would suddenly strike out against Ron, Russell, or even Stan. Before I was taken away, as I sat on my hands in the basement, I would cringe whenever I heard my brothers come through the front door and walk into the house as if they were entering a minefield. With every step Mother could, without warning, detonate, spreading her shrapnel-like fury in every direction. Weeks prior to my rescue I became so cold inside, I was nearly obsessed with hatred toward Ron, Stan, and especially Russell—who used to be Mother's little brainwashed Nazi—but at the same time I'd still pray for their safety.

As I sat in front of Russell now, I could not imagine the hellish nightmare Mother had put my brothers through. All I could do now was pray that whatever they had experienced would somehow not carry over into their future. Like a broken record, all I could hear in my head was, "Three down, two to go." Every one of them had endured more from Mother than I ever possibly could. They were indeed the strong ones, while I was fortunate enough to be rescued.

"If this means anything," I choked up, "I'm sorry . . . about everything. That's no way to live. Maybe, maybe as a kid I drove her crazy. But," I added with remorse, "she wasn't always like this." I smiled at distant memories, before Russell was born. Mommy had been the adoring parent who cherished her children, taking them on springtime picnics in the park, week-long camping adventures under the stars, glorious trips to the Russian River. Mommy had embellished her home with lights, candles, and ornaments during the Christmas season. "There were good times," I confessed. "And for me, sometimes that's enough to pull me through."

"I could never understand what you could have done that was so bad," Russell said. "All I could remember, since I was a kid, was . . . you were always in trouble. As if that was why she had to beat you," Russell softly stated. "And that one summer . . . I remember when she . . . she threw the knife at you, right in front of me . . ."

I flashed back to a memory of Russell as a small child, clamped onto Mother's leg, gently rocking as she swayed drunkenly. Mother had snatched up a knife, screaming that she would kill me if I did not finish washing the dinner dishes within the specified time. At the time, I knew she didn't mean it. Afterward, as I regained consciousness in the bathroom, while blood poured from my chest, Mother announced to my dismay that she could never take me to hospital for fear of exposing the secret. Yet I knew what she meant. "It was an accident," I boomed, startling the group of men around the bar.

Russell shook his head. "No way. It didn't look like an accident to me."

How could I tell him that I truly believed Mother never intended to stab me? I assumed, from Mother's point of view, it was just another twisted game she had played to strengthen her position over me. Mother was a control freak who tried to dominate me through threatening and forbidding tactics. Mother would threaten me any way she could, but because of the bizarre nature of her ongoing progressive "games," she had to constantly up the ante, at times to the point that she drove me to the brink of death. I went from being no longer a member of "the family" to *The Boy* to a child called *It.* As an adult, I believed Mother used those labels not just to demean me, but to somehow justify her treatment, to protect her psyche from some type of traumatic meltdown, from the fact that she was a mother who was brutalizing her own son.

Russell nervously rubbed his hands. "I asked her," he said, "about when you were in her bedroom . . . she was beating you bad. I peeked through the door and . . . when she marched out, I remember her wiping her hands . . . like she just finished washing the dishes. I asked Mom why she beat you up, and without blinking she says, 'Mommy loves It and wants It to be good.' "

I nearly lost my breath as I visualized the scene.

"With Dad gone," Russell continued, "she's worse. If Mom's not on my case, then she's on the phone with Ron and Linda, or Grandma . . . it never stops."

Changing the subject, I interrupted. "Can you get word to Stan and tell him I said hello? As kids, before you were born, before things were bad, we used to be tight. Ron and Stan saved my butt a few times."

Russell merely nodded. "Okay, it's just . . . Stan thinks he knows it all and that he's the man of the house; you can't tell him anything."

"Well," I said, "tell him I said hi. And can you get word to Ron?"

Russell hesitated. "I can give you his number."

"I'd rather you give him a call first. I know it sounds stupid, but I'm kinda embarrassed. I don't know, I mean, I haven't seen or talked to him in years . . . with him being married and all . . . being he's in the army. I don't want to do anything that might mess with his head." My heavy breathing made me stop for a moment to collect myself. "Man, what a family. What a waste. At least *we* made it out alive."

"So," Russell said, smiling, "the big question: You gonna see Mom?"

Swallowing hard, I muttered, "I dunno. In some odd sense,

I want to. I know it sounds kinda weird, but . . . I dunno." I paused. "I can't explain it."

"Man," Russell howled, "you see Mom and Grandma's gonna have a cow!"

"Trust me," I laughed. "She's having a litter of kittens as we speak. Gram gave me so much static over seeing you. It's like . . . if something's not her idea, you shouldn't do it. I mean, I feel for Grandma and I know she did a lot for us when we were kids and all, but I just can't help but think that when it comes to dealing with Mom, she doesn't help the situation any."

"Man, you're not there to see it," Russell broke it. "I'm not pointing fingers, but it's like they feed off each other. The more miserable one can make the other, the happier they think their world will be."

Clutching my Coke, I nodded in agreement.

"So, you gonna see her?" Russell again asked.

Feeling gutless, I said, "It ain't worth it, maybe next time. . . ." My voice trailed off.

"Yeah," Russell replied, "I understand, maybe next time."

We drifted to other matters, until I dropped Russell off hours later. Back at Grandmother's, she gave me the cold shoulder. The next day I aggravated our situation further when I told Grandmother that I had invited Russell on the trip Grandmother and I had planned to the border of Idaho. Hours later, I again made her upset when I was shopping at a bookstore, buying a novel for Kevin. Grandmother became impatient, announcing she had had enough and stormed out of the mall. Part of me felt bad for her—she had driven Russell and me to Idaho and fed us a nice picnic lunch—but yet I felt I was somehow being manipulated again. No matter what anyone was doing, if Grandmother wanted to go, everyone had to leave at once.

All I could do was continue to wait in line, make my purchase, and sprint after her, for I felt she would leave without me. But in a small sense I was giving Grandmother a message:

I would respect her and be polite, but I was not a child whom she could snap her fingers at whenever it pleased her. As I entered Grandmother's two-door sedan—with the engine running and her clutching the steering wheel—I proudly held Kevin's book in my hand.

My last afternoon at Grandmother's, I phoned the air force office that was handling my cross training request of becoming an air crew member. As hectic as my military leave had been, at least I felt that I stood a good chance of fulfilling my lifelong dream. When the sergeant recognized my name, his tone seemed positive. "Ah, yes, Sergeant Pelzer. I saw your file. I got it right here somewhere, hang on. . . . Yep, ah, give me a second." I could feel my excitement grow. "You've been at my heels for a while now, haven't you? All righty now, here it is . . ." he triumphantly announced. "Everything seems to be in order . . . uh . . . um . . . hang on a second."

My heart sank. "I don't know how to say this," the sergeant's tone softened, "but it seems there's been a mistake. Somehow your paperwork went to ground refueling, not mid-air refueling. Not to worry, this happens all the time—"

"Excuse me, sir," I interrupted. "What does this mean? It's fixable, right? I mean, you can correct it, especially since it's not my fault?"

"I'm sorry," he answered. "I know how bad you wanted it, but by the time I received your paperwork, it was too late; the slots had been filled. You just missed the cutoff. Don't sweat it. If this is any consolation, I know in about eight, maybe nine months or so, we'll have another batch of slots to fill. I can't make any promises, but as much as you check in, I can advise you when to resubmit directly to my office. I have to be fair to everyone who applies, but I can guarantee you'll get a fair shot."

"But, Sergeant!" I pleaded, "I don't have eight months! My enlistment is up in six, seven weeks! I don't understand; I did everything. I took math, even trig. I studied planes inside and out. I've got good annual progress reports. I've got medals. I graduated jump school. I even got a letter from Kelly John-son." I was yammering like an idiot. "I've wanted this forever. What else can I do?"

"Your package is not being questioned. It's sound. If there was a slot open, I'd give it to you. But right now that's not the issue. I am sorry. I feel for you, but there is nothing, nothing I can do."

I stood in a frozen state, still clutching the phone. I had strongly believed I had a chance. I thought *this time* my hard work and determination would pay off. Ever since Father passed away, I had found something I could focus my efforts toward, a longtime dream that I could achieve for myself. For months, in the barracks on Friday and Saturday evenings, while the other guys would party outside on the building's ledge, I'd dangle my legs over the same ledge and absorb my latest mathematical equation. Around the squadron, I'd dis-covered that peers that I didn't really know were silently root-ing for me, a mere cook, to cross over and become an air crew member.

As Grandmother came toward me, I could see she was not happy. I remembered that she had lectured me to keep the phone call short. I had been speaking to the sergeant for at least ten minutes, which I assumed was nine minutes too long. Besides being overly polite and careful where to tread, I felt my visit with Grandmother was not the tender homecom-ing I had imagined. I genuinely did not know this relative, and she did not know me.

"The phone," she snipped.

I looked down at my hand grasping the phone. It felt ice cold. "Oh, yeah, sorry." My eyes darted toward the floor as I replaced the phone in its cradle. Grandmother remained by my side, as if waiting for a report.

"So?" she asked.

I shook my head like a scolded puppy. "Oh . . . sorry," I said. "It was nothing. Just air force stuff, no big deal. It's nothing, nothing at all." I wanted to tell her. To grab her frail body and open my heart to her. Not to necessarily moan about my latest futile crusade, but rather as a way to finally come to know Grandmother as a real person—her hopes, her dreams, her anxieties. To know of her life experiences as a child, as a woman, and a single parent who raised two children during hard times. There was much I admired about her. Grandmother was one of the original "pull yourself up by the bootstraps" people. In a way I still believed she and I were alike. The whole purpose of spending a few days with her was to get to know her better. All my life I had been led to believe that any sensitive matter was to be instantly buried. As an adult, I still knew nothing about my parents and how they came to be. Yet as I stood beside Grandmother, I knew that all we could manage was idle chitchat, at best, praying one of us didn't step into forbidden territory.

"Well, then," Grandmother heaved, breaking the tension, "did I tell you about the time I played golf with an officer from Hill Air Force Base? I think he's a general . . . anyway . . ." And so did Grandmother and I kill time on my last evening, until we finally went to bed.

Early the next morning, I strapped my oversized green sleeping bag, my military backpack, and, upon Grandmother's unwavering insistence, a coffee can containing her homemade snickerdoodle cookies onto my motorcycle. After an impassive departing embrace, I rode off. Hours later, in the blazing heat, as my body became numb and dehydrated from the miles of endless interstate, my sole thought was getting back to my Florida base, where I could begin my out-processing. I was quitting the air force.

Chapter 8

CHANGES

I barely made it back from Utah to Hurlburt Field in Florida. The chain from my motorcycle stretched so much from the cross-country trek, that nearly all the teeth from the rear sprocket sheared off, almost leaving me stranded in Texas at the height of a heat wave. By the time I limped through Mississippi, my rear tire became bald, and all I could do was disregard it. I had to spend the remainder of my funds filling up my gas tank, praying every mile I'd make it.

Hours after coasting into the base, I reported to the office that handled out-processing. As luck would have it, I no sooner came before a young airman—newly assigned, frantic, and confused—before he informed me to report to the section chief, pronto! *Great,* I thought, *now what?* I was exhausted, ready to give the next person I met a piece of my mind. As I stormed through the passageways, I felt betrayed. After four years, none of my efforts had paid off. Joining the air force to become a fireman was nothing more than a joke. I slaved away like I had years ago, but this time from the swamps of Florida to the Egyptian desert. And for what? I didn't mind paying my dues, but for once, just once, I wished I could get lucky.

The more I felt myself getting hot under the collar, the more I tried to brush aside my ego. Okay, I was a cook, but one with jump wings who had actually seen the great pyramids. I'd had a chance to be reassigned to work in an office where I was appreciated, enabling me, a high school dropout, to go to college. I had a couple of bucks socked away, and for four years the air force had given me a home. In all, what did I really have to complain about? So I didn't snatch the golden ring of becoming an air crew member; big deal. What truly mattered to me was that I had done my best. There was a sense of satisfaction knowing I hadn't faltered. I had taken a few hard knocks and I never quit. By the time the receptionist ushered me into a captain's office, I was back to my old self. Standing ramrod straight, I popped out a crisp salute. "Sergeant Pelzer reporting, sir!"

A towering black gentleman rose from behind his gray metal desk. He maintained a thin smile as his eyes ran up my pressed uniform. "Take a seat. So," the captain paused, "we have a situation?"

"Sir?"

"You still want to be a crew member?"

I wasn't sure what he was asking. "Well, I do . . . I mean, I did, but that's no longer—"

"The bottom line is," he interjected, "the way your submission was processed, the air force made a mistake. *I* have a problem with that," the captain stated with pride. "So, I have a proposition for you. The air force is willing to grant an extension on your enlistment. You can use it to resubmit your paperwork. If you get accepted as a crew member, you reenlist. If you don't, you can out-process, then get out. Understand, just by getting an extension in no way means getting a slot as a crew dawg. But," he said with a sly grin, "*you'll* be able to track your paperwork along the way. You'll be jumping through a lot of hoops, and in the end there are no guarantees, but this is a square offer."

I had just pulled an ace out of thin air. "I'll take the deal!"

Dashing to my supervisors, I informed them of my luck. Without hesitation, they varied my work schedule so I could indeed oversee the necessary paperwork, which had to start from scratch. The next several weeks flew by as I literally ran around the entire base collecting the right forms, dropping them off at the appropriate office or, if I was lucky, hovering over them as I collected either signatures, initials, or boxes properly checked off. Then I had to collect additional forms that required further verification, again in the proper sequence, until, finally, I returned to the captain's office with a perfectly completed package.

"Got a whiff from Sergeant Blue," the officer began, "the guy who handles your specialty request. Says he may have some slots open pretty soon." This time he broke into a wide smile. "I'll Q.C.—quality control—the paperwork, give it my blessing, and send it up the pike. You maintain tabs, and within a week you should be getting a call from Sergeant Blue."

"Thanks . . . Cap," I saluted.

He returned the gesture. "Like I said, air force made a mistake. *I* had a problem with that."

Weeks dragged by with no word. I desperately wanted to call the sergeant, but feared that pestering him would blow my opportunity. I kept myself busy any way I could, fighting to keep my mind off the package. After another week I caved in and phoned. "Been expecting your call," Sergeant Blue nonchalantly began. "We had a problem . . ." I exhaled, waiting for the sky to come crashing down. "You're not going to believe this, but it seems the paperwork ended up in the hands of ground refueling again." As he paused, I wondered, What did I have to do? After all I had been through, I was not going to roll over and quit. "Anyways, like I said, we *had* a problem," Sergeant Blue went on.

"Say again?" I asked, catching his emphasis on the word *had*.

"Let me just say this: they've been educated on the errors of their ways. I got the paperwork in time. Now," he added, "we have *another* problem." My stomach turned. Clearing his throat, Sergeant Blue stammered, "It—it seems I won't be able to grant you your base request."

I quickly saw my opening. "I'll take anything you have. Anything! Even Minot!" I thundered, knowing that Minot Air Force Base was located in the far region of North Dakota and was infamous for its extreme arctic-like winters.

"No can do," he informed me.

In my head I calculated. I would never have a chance of resubmitting another package. I had run out of time. There were no other options. Suddenly, I thought of a different tactic. "What do you have?"

"Well, the best I could do is . . ."—I could sense Sergeant Blue's restrained excitement, and the hairs on my arms began to rise—". . . this base out in California, west of the Sierra Nevadas."

"Beale!" I shouted.

"Home of the Sled. Congratulations. Once you've earned your crew wings, you'll be an in-flight boom operator for the SR-71—known to crew dawgs as the Sled. I was just waiting for your call."

In a swirl of emotions I profusely thanked Sergeant Blue. Hanging up the phone, I clasped my hands together. Calming down, I began praying, thanking God.

Ten months later, in the summer of 1984, an SR-71 Blackbird stabilized in a hovering state, flying ten feet below and forty feet behind a KC-135 Q model refueling tanker, waiting on me—a recently certified crew member—to fulfill my part of the mission. Staring out of the glass that not only protected me at an altitude of twenty-five thousand feet, but gave me an unlimited view of everything within hundreds of miles, I drew in a deep breath to collect myself. I felt the unique sensation of needing to merely reach out through the glass and touch the Blackbird, as both planes made their way south at speeds exceeding five hundred miles per hour on a specialized refueling track above Idaho's aqua blue Salmon River. It wasn't the heavenly scenery or being lucky enough to be a part of a distinctive air force program that was important to me, but that it was my first solo flight. I was fulfilling a childhood dream. I was no longer confined to a dark, torturous environment, hopelessly wishing I could "fly away" from danger. After years of sacrifice, my life had made a turn for the better. *For the first time in my life, I began to feel good about myself.* I always knew as a child, deep down inside, I could make it if I had the chance. And now my entire life was on track. I no longer wore a mantle of shame. I was becoming a real person. I could lower my guard, relax, and live life.

"Aspen 31, Bandit 27," I relayed to the waiting SR-71, using his identification call sign immediately followed by mine, "you are clear for contact!"

"Hey, boom!" the pilot in the flight deck echoed, "make Kelly Johnson proud!"

"Roger that!" I smiled. For me, it didn't get any better than this.

Now that I was an air crew member, every day was an adventure. Every time I zipped up my flight suit, I felt like my childhood hero, Superman, out to save the world from impending doom. My green Nomex uniform was my red cape, taking me to places I had dreamed about when I was a prisoner in Mother's war. I was appreciative that I was with a unique organization that carried a sense of honor and camaraderie. The more I became involved as a boom operator, the more I cherished my position, and a deep sense of pride was growing. I was part of a family.

My new career carried a new level of responsibility. Besides flying two, sometimes three times a week, at any hour of the day or night, my crew and I would have to spend the day before planning the most minute segments—from preflight-

ing the aircraft before takeoff to engine shutdown after landing. I quickly learned the seriousness of the job. If there was a
major political or military situation anywhere in the world,
the Blackbird would be deployed to collect real-time photographs of a hot spot that could be in the hands of the President, if needed, in a period of twenty-four hours. The Q model
KC-135 Stratotanker was the tanker that fed precious, one-of-
a-kind JP-7 fuel to the Blackbird, enabling the SR-71 to accomplish its mission. There was a sense of excitement knowing
that my bags were packed and that I could be called upon to
fly off into the sunset at a moment's notice.

Because I never slept the evening prior to a flight, there
were times after a late-night mission that I would be so exhausted, I'd collapse at the pool of my apartment complex.
Yet still I'd be smiling. I'd gaze up at the stars that hours ago
seemed close enough to cup in my hand.

I lived a grand life. I had my own apartment, *my home,*
where no one could kick me out or make me feel unwanted. I
could go to bed as early as I wanted without being disturbed,
as I had been when I was an airman living in a dormitory. I
kept my tiny one-bedroom home apartment sparkling clean.
Financially, I was barely getting by, but what I was losing in
salary was easily made up for in peace of mind. I was proud
that my first home was fully furnished and paid for from my
years of saving. My life also included two close friends that I
had met as a foster child, Dave Howard and J. D. Thom. They
still lived in the Bay Area, and I'd drive down to goof off with
them during the weekends whenever possible. I kept close
tabs with Alice and Harold as well by calling them several
times a week. I felt I had more than anyone could ask for.

Although I was feeling good about myself, something continued to gnaw at me. During my rare time off at the apartment complex, whenever I would go down to the pool, I
could not relax like my neighbors—working on a tan, drinking beer, swimming, or celebrating that they had survived another week of work. I was known only as "Fly Boy": a skinny,

pasty white geek in shorts and a tank top; a bookworm who absorbed mounds of technical flight manuals. Unlike the majority of those by the poolside, I was not smooth, cool, or a tough-guy with endless tattoos. I didn't drink until I passed out, smoke like a chimney, use drugs daily to escape my pain, or rant nonstop about how someone or something did me wrong. Nor was I on federal aid. Yet I didn't even feel good enough about myself to be among "them."

It was at the pool where I first met Patsy. Even though she hung out with a wild group of friends, she seemed different. She wasn't as rowdy or aimless as the others. I felt awkward, as I studied my work, whenever we'd make eye contact, but flattered that she would even look at me. Since I could never hold a gaze, I'd immediately snap my head back down to my papers. Within days we were greeting each other with a quick hello. One Friday afternoon, in passing, I told Patsy I was going to the Bay Area. Her eyes lit up. "San Francisco? Can I come?"

I hesitated. No woman had ever asked to be with me. "Well . . ." I stammered, "I'm not going to the city, but . . ."

"You'd be doing me a favor. These guys are driving me crazy." Patsy pointed at the small herd in the pool thrashing around, screeching at the top of their lungs. "I'm not like them. Really," she gently added.

"Okay," I finally answered, "let's go."

The next day Patsy joined me as I drove west to see the Turnboughs. I could not believe how easy it was to talk to her. Whatever apprehension I had evaporated within minutes. She even fed off my humor, laughing at whatever spilled from my mouth. In the midst of my chattering, I realized how lonely I had become. Beyond small talk, I could hardly get over how she appeared to be *interested in me*. "So," Patsy asked when my mouth was still for a brief moment, "what is it you do?"

"I'm a boomer," I automatically replied.

"A what?"

"Oh, excuse me," I said, translating, "sometimes I get

ahead of myself. I'm a boom operator. . . . I midair-refuel jets
for the air force."

"Oh, yeah, I get it." Patsy politely nodded, but by the look
on her face I knew she did not understand. "So what's with
that green overall thing I see you in?"

"It's a flight suit."

"Well . . . it's just," she said, "well, some of us were trying
to figure you out. You know, you don't go out. The word is
out: you don't *party*. I don't know anyone who reads or writes
that much." I began to imagine the word *dweeb* etched on my
forehead as Patsy continued. "You come and go at all hours.
You're always alone. The only time I've seen you with anyone
else is when you're with those other guys in those green over-
alls. It's just, well, some of us thought you were . . . you
know."

Not understanding, I shook my head. "What are you getting at?"

"Oh, shit!" Patsy covered her mouth. "I didn't mean to . . .
it's just, well, some of us, not me, have had a hard time figur-
ing you out."

I was stunned by the thought that if I didn't party, or if I
spent my time alone applying myself, that I was considered
so abnormal. "Those guys you see me with are some of the
men I fly with."

I could tell Patsy was embarrassed. She in no way meant to
hurt my feelings. I could only assume that in her world I was
quite the outsider, and for years, strangely enough, I had been
curious to discover what it would be like to fit in.

Several quiet miles passed between us until I relieved the
tension by trying to make small talk again. Even after I apologized for putting her in an odd position, I felt Patsy thought
badly of me. Even as we regained momentum in our conversation, I discovered that Patsy, as kind as she was to me, gave no
thought to the happenings of the world, politics, her local
surroundings, or anything beyond the latest Indiana Jones
film or the pop group Duran Duran's newest album.

A couple of hours later, when Alice saw me with Patsy, her eyes lit up. As she hugged me, Alice whispered, "Thank God you're finally dating. I was getting worried about you." Still holding my hand, she spun around toward Patsy. "So, how long have you two been going together?"

Patsy stepped back. "Oh, we just met."

I suddenly felt like a complete idiot, bringing a woman I barely knew over to my parents' place and it wasn't even a date. Alice, who continued to radiate happiness, plopped down between Patsy and me, snapping her head left and right to keep the conversation going. Every time she turned toward me, she would smirk and raise her eyebrows. I felt like an awkward teenager, trying to be kind to my mother while protecting Patsy from total boredom. I could only pray Alice didn't slip up and tell Patsy something from my past. After some small talk I excused myself to spend time with Harold. Though I had seen him a few months ago, Harold suddenly looked years older. He appeared so frail, and he struggled to make simple conversation. His eyes were distant, while he did his best to hide his trembling hands. After a few minutes, I gave up and cupped his hands in mine. We spent the remainder of our time in silence. In the back of my mind, the memory of my biological father suffering came back in full force.

When Patsy and I were leaving, I whispered to Alice as I hugged her good-bye, "What's with Pop?"

Her eyes darted toward the floor. "Oh, it's nothing. Harold's just got a touch of the flu. He's been working too hard lately. He's got an appointment to see the doctor next week. Listen," she said, "don't you fret, you two have fun. And I tell you something else." Alice looked at both Patsy and me. "You two look good together."

"It's not what you think," I again whispered. "We just met a few days ago, okay?"

"Well," Mom said, "if you ask me, I've got a good feeling about you two."

"You'll have to forgive my mom," I said to Patsy as we

pulled away, "I think she's playing matchmaker." I did not want Patsy to get the wrong impression. "Besides," I added in a Yiddish voice, "I think she's seen *Fiddler on the Roof* too many times." I was making a reference to the movie's persistent matchmaker, but I could see Patsy did not get the joke.

"So," Patsy asked, "are they your real parents?"

"Well, yeah," I immediately responded. But after a few moments of silence, I exhaled, saying, "They are to me. They're my foster parents. My mother, my real mom, well, she had a drinking problem and sometimes used to, you know, go off on me. Sometimes . . ." I trailed off, hoping not to scare Patsy off. I had no intention of telling her about my former life. I clutched the steering wheel, afraid Patsy would suddenly fling open the car door and bail out. I had never exposed my childhood to anyone like this before, let alone the magnitude of my mother's twisted sickness.

For some time now I had been resigned to the fact that my past would probably keep me from being with someone. Even at age twenty-three, with all I had been fortunate enough to accomplish on my own, against the odds, I had the self-esteem of an ant. I was deathly afraid of women. I felt unworthy even of looking at them for more than a few quick seconds, let alone talking with one. That's why I was so overwhelmed, confused, and yet enchanted by Patsy's interest in me.

I found myself rambling about how I came into foster care. At least I had sense enough to graze the surface. Since my past was so mired in lies and deceit, I valued honesty above everything else. I believed that if I was to have a relationship with anyone, it was important to me to be truthful as possible, yet at the same time maintain a veil to protect that person from whatever pain or embarrassment that came from being with me. I knew I was walking a fine line and in doing so was now living a true lie. I had been doing so for some time in the air force, especially during the extensive psychological evaluations that I had to undertake to become an air crew member. I had simply deflected what I felt necessary in order to protect my security clearance. I could only pray someday it didn't backfire on me or on anyone else. The last thing I wanted was to cause anyone any pain whatsoever.

"I know what it's like . . . I was the black sheep of my family," Patsy confessed.

She went on to explain that she was picked on as a child, felt out of place among her siblings, had trouble getting along with her overbearing mother, and as a teenager felt the only way to escape was to run away. "I hooked up with some guy. We both worked to get by, partied a lot, ya know." As Patsy opened up, not only could I relate to her feelings of being alienated, but to me everything seemed to fall into place on how she carried herself and why she hung out with that rambunctious crowd. I felt that Patsy, too, was looking for acceptance. "But," she sighed, "when my father passed away, Mom had to sell the house and move into an apartment. I moved back in to help out; no one else will lift a finger. Hell, I'm sleeping on the couch. As much as she drives me crazy, I'm the only one who will take care of her."

Even though I picked up on her slight resentment, I knew Patsy was grazing the surface, too. "I am sorry," I said. "I truly am. No one deserves to be treated bad." I stopped for a moment. "My real father passed away, too—"

Patsy jumped in before I could complete my thought. "What the hell. Shit happens! That's my motto."

Without thinking I let out a laugh. I had never heard that expression before. And I picked up on Patsy's subliminal message of brushing off whatever problems came her way.

During the drive back home, both Patsy and I gabbed nonstop. I had never been with a woman for such an extended time in my life. I didn't want our time together to end. Late into the evening, at my apartment, I proudly showed off my new home. Patsy was the first person to step into my world. We sat down on the couch, sipping wine while listening to acoustical jazz. My mind swam between saying good night and wanting to talk longer. Without warning, Patsy leaned forward. I flinched as she wrapped her arms around my neck before kissing me. Neither of us had any premonitions. We both seemed surprised that we had fallen for each other.

The next few weeks became a whirlwind. Of all people, I had a girlfriend. I had everything going for me. I was enthralled with my job, and for the first time I had someone who wanted to be with me, someone who cared about me. The sensation of coming home after an exhausting flight to spend time with Patsy was beyond elation. Patsy blew me away when she would cook dinner or leave me notes inside my lunch bag that I'd discover when I'd fly. I adored the attention. I felt complete.

When I had to fly overseas for weeks at a time, Patsy volunteered to watch my place, watering my plants and feeding Chuck, my box turtle. I was slightly apprehensive because I was overly cautious and felt things were happening way too fast. I knew I was caught up with her, and yet I could hardly control myself. I had always been alone. No one had ever wanted me, let alone found me attractive enough to give me the time of day. I gave Patsy an extra key, on the condition that she simply watch over my apartment.

Weeks later when I returned home, Patsy met me at the door. As I unpacked, I noticed my closet space had been taken over by her clothes and the bathroom countertop was filled with her makeup items. As I stood at the entrance to the bedroom, Patsy rushed over, hugging me and crying, "It's not what you think! I didn't plan to, but my mom's driving me crazy! We got into a huge argument. I'm tired of being under her thumb. You know what it's like. Besides, I'm here almost all the time anyway. I missed you so much. You're not like the others. What are we waiting for? You know how I feel about you. Please?" she sobbed.

Patsy had never been so emotional before. I wanted to sit her down and calmly, logically explain that we were now considering moving in together. This was no longer a date to the movies, a romantic dinner, or a passionate affair. While overseas, I had told myself to let things cool off between Patsy and me. But as I held her, I was tired of overanalyzing every detail in my life. Looking into her tear-stained eyes, I realized how much I missed her. As her whimpering eased, Patsy kissed me on the neck and face and said, "Sometimes it's so hard. I'm tired of being put down, always being told what to do. And no matter what I do, it's never good enough."

It had always troubled me how Patsy was treated at times. Her mother, Dottie Mae, had seemed overly nice when I first met her, but I could sense how closely she watched Patsy's every move or corrected her on the slightest thing. When I asked Patsy why her mother acted that way, she waved a hand at me. "It's her way of watching over me. She's afraid I'll blow it and get into trouble again. When I was younger I was pretty wild."

One time, before I had to fly overseas, Patsy rushed into my apartment, telling me how her mother and siblings were again berating her. Before I could console her, one by one her family barged in, without knocking, screaming at the top of their lungs at Patsy before turning on each other. I even found one person gorging on anything he could from my refrigerator and someone else rummaging through my bureau drawers in my bedroom. Only after I had kicked everyone but Patsy out did I learn how common this sort of outburst was for her family.

I knew how hard Patsy had it in her mother's cramped two-bedroom apartment. Because Patsy's mother occupied one bedroom and Patsy's brother and his girlfriend the other, Patsy slept on the living room couch. Her brother, though, spent his time waterskiing, cruising around in his prized truck he had purchased after winning a legal dispute, or partying. Due to Dottie Mae's bad hips, Patsy felt she was the only one who had to take care of cleaning the apartment, do all the cooking, and run a multitude of daily errands for her mother. "Now you know why I go out and party," Patsy once explained to me.

"But why don't you get a job, save some money, and move out?" I had replied.

"Job? What jobs? I tried a couple of times, and why bother? The best I could do would be a waitress. Who wants to do that? Besides . . . I have a bad back. My mom gives me money when I need it." Patsy shrugged, as if it was no big deal.

At the time I couldn't believe my ears. All my life I had never thought about *not* working to provide for myself. I had a hard time accepting Patsy's family dynamics and how they treated her, but, thinking about my own family, who in the hell was I to judge? At least I knew, as Patsy once pointed out to me, "I know at times we're at each other's throats, but if someone else messes with either one of us, I tell you what: we'll kick that person's ass. Now, that's how much we love each other." I thought at the time that maybe Patsy's family wasn't so abnormal and that, once again, my standards were too high.

As I held Patsy's quivering body, she whispered, "If you let me move in, my mom will leave me alone; she'll have to. And then I can be happy. You'll see. We'll be so happy." My heart ached for Patsy. I knew she deserved better. Maybe, I thought, because of our pasts we had a good chance of making a good couple. We'd be strong enough to weather any storm. Besides, I told myself, no one could ever treat me as well as Patsy.

"Okay," I said, my voice cracking, "let's do it. Let's move in together."

In her excitement, Patsy nearly crushed my ribs. "Thank you, thank you, thank you! Finally, now *I* have a home!" Her eyes again swelled with tears. Patsy swallowed hard before bursting, "I love you, David. I have for the longest time. I really love you. You're the one, the only one for me."

I was paralyzed. I couldn't look at her. All I could do was continue to hold her. Time sped by and I still could not open my mouth. Here was a woman in my arms, now a major part of my life, who had just opened her soul to me and I . . .

I could not say the words. And for that I despised myself.

How could I allow someone into my home and not in my heart? I thought after everything Patsy had done for me and all she had been through, she deserved better. "It's okay," Patsy sniffed as she wiped away her tears, "I understand, I know, I do. But one day you will, I know it. One day you'll love me."

Later, in the early morning hours, I lay wide awake with Patsy snoring beside me. Part of the reason I could not sleep was due to the time-zone changes of flying back from England. But I knew the true reason for my lack of sleep: my guilty conscience eating at me. I was now living with someone, and as I searched my heart, I didn't know if I could ever have the same strong feelings for Patsy that she seemed to have for me. How could I be so cold when Patsy was filled with joy? Was it because after years of toughening myself to survive, I couldn't break the pattern? Or was it because I didn't want to? As much as I struggled, I could not find an answer. I only knew that I was getting myself deeper into something I did not fully understand. All I could do now was follow through with my commitment.

The next afternoon I phoned Alice. After I told her of my overseas trip, the anxiety grew too much for me. "Mom," I stammered, "Patsy and I, well . . . we decided, we're living together now. If that's all right?"

I could hear Mom take a deep breath. "Well, I guess you've both given this some serious thought."

"Oh, yeah," I broke in, "we ah, we've talked a lot."

"And she has the same feelings for you as you do for her?"

I felt crushed. "Yeah," I swallowed. "Patsy, she—she treats me great . . . and she's had some hard times, too." I caught myself. I was saying anything I could think of that would make this easier. "I'm sorry, Mom, I know you don't agree. I just, I just respect you and Pop too much. I didn't want to live a lie." I paused, waiting for Alice to lay into me. I didn't even hear her breathe. "Mom, Mom, are you there?"

"Yes, I'm here. It's just . . ." She stopped, and as she did, I hated myself. All I could do was wait for the bomb to drop. "It's just, well . . . I took Harold to the doctor . . ."

I felt a surge of relief that the subject had shifted away from Patsy and me. "So," I put in, "it's the flu, right? And all Pop has to do is stay home and rest for a while?"

"David," Alice said, "Harold has cancer. He's scheduled for therapy, but . . . the doctor thinks it's too advanced. He's gonna fight it, so for right now all we can do is pray. I'm happy for the two of you, but for now let's keep this between us."

Hanging up the phone, I turned to Patsy and told her the news. What I did not tell her was how ashamed I felt. That evening I thought of how selfish I had become. My flying, my globe-trotting adventures, my apartment, my live-in girl-friend—me, me, me. The next morning after returning from work, I sat down with Patsy. "I've given this some thought, and I think on the weekends I should go down and spend time with my parents."

"I understand. Remember, I just lost my dad, too," Patsy responded. I nodded in agreement. "Listen, I've got a great idea, I can go with you! I can help out Alice, and this way we can spend time together."

My answer was not what Patsy had hoped for. "But I barely get to see you now, what about us?" she cried.

"When I lost my dad, he couldn't even say good-bye. No one was there for him." I stopped, imagining my father alone in the room, covered in white hospital sheets. "When I first came to the Turnboughs as a foster kid, no one, and I mean no one, would take me in. We'll have time together, but for now this is something I have to . . . it's the right thing to do."

Patsy nodded. "I understand." She reached out to hug me, but by the time I saw it I had already stood up and walked away.

When I wasn't overseas flying, I spent nearly every free weekend I could with the Turnboughs, sometimes even show-ing up after a Friday afternoon mission wearing my sweaty flight suit. Whenever Harold was not taking one of his lengthy naps, we'd sit outside in the closed-in screen porch he had constructed a few months before. For a person who had never spoken to me that much as a teenager, Harold now told me stories of when he served during World War II as a driver for the officers, and upon his return home from Europe how he and other veterans cried when they saw the Statue of Liberty. While some of his army buddies stayed in New York to celebrate, Harold caught the first train back to Missouri so he could get up early at home, grab his box of carpentry tools, and go from door to door to find work. For me it didn't matter what he said, just as long as we spent time together. It was during those times, while a cool breeze blew in through the screen porch, that Harold and I accomplished something my biological father and I had never done: bond as father and son.

As the months went by, I saw Harold slowly deteriorate. Those times Patsy joined me, she had to hold back her shock at Harold's appearance. Leaving her with Alice, I'd sit with Harold as he drifted in and out of sleep. We all knew the cancer had spread too far and the chemotherapy wasn't helping. Harold somehow held on, but his strength, coordination, and eyes were failing him to the point he could no longer drive his truck or do his woodworking. That's when he knew the end was near.

"I was gonna build that home for Alice, you know, in Nevada," Harold said during one of my Saturday visits. "Had to wait to retire."

I nodded my head in agreement. "Yes."

"No time now." He paused, rubbing his callused hands. "So . . . what is it you want?"

"Excuse me?" I blurted from embarrassment. In all the years I had known him, Harold had never asked such a probing question. "Well . . ." I stuttered; "I—I like flying. I've al-

ways wanted a home at the river. Ever since my father passed
away, I was kinda hoping you and I could maybe build it together."

"No!" His voice cracked as he clasped my hands with his.
"What is it you really want?"

Our eyes locked, just as my father's and mine had before he
passed away. I bent closer to his ear. "No matter where I'm at,
or what I have, or what I'm doing, I just want to be happy."

"Yes," Harold said. His grip intensified. "You've found it.
You make a difference. Do good, do your best, and do it now."

Suddenly his grip loosened. His head rolled back. For a
fleeting moment I panicked. By the time Alice and Patsy raced
onto the porch, Harold had regained consciousness, snapped
his neck back up, and smiled before drifting off to sleep. I was
never able to speak to him again.

Days later, Alice called on the verge of tears to say Harold
was near death. Patsy and I jumped into my tiny Toyota Cel-
ica, weaving through the Bay Area rush-hour traffic until I
came to a screeching halt in front of my old home. As I
stepped through the front door, I knew I was too late by the
look that was etched on everyone's face. Alice came over and
simply said, "David, I'm sorry . . . he just passed away."

At the funeral, I received the American flag, then walked
over to present it to Alice. Standing above her, I stated, "Of all
the men I have known, Harold's had the most profound effect
on me." During the eulogy I tried to remain strong, but completely lost control after Harold's light oak casket was lowered.
As scores of people shuffled back to their cars, I found myself
standing alone filled with rage. My body shuddered as I
looked up at the deep blue sky. All I could think of was: *why?
Why Harold?* He was a man who had spent a lifetime living
the theme of a "good day's work for a good day's pay," was so
close to retiring, to just lose it all? While someone like my
mother, a cold, vindictive person who hated everyone and
everything, whose passion seemed to be destroying anything
close to her as if it were some kind of sport, lived on while

never having to lift a finger. This was beyond any form of reasoning for me. Harold didn't drink, he wasn't abusive, he never even raised his voice. He led a clean life; he took in kids that other families turned away. Why? As I felt myself slump to my knees, Alice's son-in-law, Del, a man I highly respected, embraced me until my anger dissipated.

Weeks after Harold's passing, I still made a point of calling Alice several times a week. Whenever possible during the weekends, I'd make the trip down to see her. I felt drawn to Alice and wanted to be there for her. We spent time strolling through malls, or when I took her to dinner I'd make her laugh by confessing some of my wild stories she had never known while I was a teenager under her care. My motives weren't entirely altruistic, though. Being there for Alice was a way for me to hide from some of my own problems.

"You look tired," Alice said, rubbing my head during one visit. "Are you losing weight?"

"It's the flying. It's dehydration," I lied. "Sometimes it's just hard for me to get some rest before a flight, that's all."

"And how are things with you and Patsy?" Alice pressed.

"Fine," I nodded, "just fine."

"You've been with someone for . . . not even a year and things are just fine? I'm not so sure of that," she replied.

While she was still mourning the loss of her husband, there was no way I could tell her that during that time I had discovered how vastly different Patsy and I were. Even after eleven months together, I didn't feel for her what she did me. For the life of me, I could not understand why I felt closed in. Part of me didn't trust her as much as I thought I should. I found myself becoming irritated over the smallest things. Yet when I was overseas for weeks at a time, I longed for Patsy. The question was, did I miss her for the right reasons?

Whenever I came home from my extended assignments, the first couple of days were great. We'd go out to dinner, have a few beers at her favorite bar, or see the latest movie. But within a week the elation wore off and frustrations grew.

While I was away, Patsy always claimed to have just gotten a job. Yet upon my return Patsy not only "suddenly lost her job" for no apparent reason, but was never paid. I was never able to find out what was happening with her jobs. Several times when I offered to assist Patsy by approaching her employers about the money owed to her, she somehow forgot who her employers were, or if she did remember, they had somehow fled the area. Once, when I persisted in trying to find where she had worked, Patsy broke down in tears and we had an argument.

The pattern always seemed to repeat itself. Patsy seemed surprised that I recalled her continual crises that she had forgotten over the short period of time. It seemed like an obvious lie, but I could not understand why she would concoct such elaborate stories. And I couldn't get myself to confront Patsy. Part of the reason was I so desperately wanted to believe her. I knew deep inside Patsy was a terrific person. But every time I tried to trust her, some bizarre situation would come between us.

Sometimes we'd clash because I didn't go out enough. I understood that Patsy liked to go out and party, but, as I tried to explain to her, the night life just wasn't for me. At times the disagreements ended with Patsy storming from the apartment, only to return drunk hours later. She'd stumble into the bathroom to throw up. As I tried to get her to lie down in bed, Patsy would wail that no one loved her, or that everyone was trying to take advantage of her. Several times before she passed out from the booze and exhaustion, she clutched my hand, sobbing, "Don't leave me, please. Everybody else does . . . don't you leave me, too."

Because I was worried, I always stood over Patsy until I was sure she was asleep. At times, because of the hour, I wouldn't get any sleep. All I could do was take a shower, zip on my flight suit, and drive off to report for a flight, praying I didn't lose my focus and make a critical mistake during a mission.

Sometimes upon returning home, either late in the afternoon or early evening, I'd find Patsy, seemingly embarrassed, looking as if she had just rolled out of bed. What was it that made her drink to the point of losing control? Something had to be eating at her. I knew part of it was me. As the pattern progressed, I sometimes became so frustrated when Patsy, in all sincerity, tried to make up. I'd retreat inside myself, ignoring her for days at a time. As much as I wanted to believe the line "It won't happen again," the act was wearing pretty thin.

Probing only made matters worse. My only concern was to stop the cycle, as I desperately wanted to ease her pain. Having seen my parents deteriorate in front of my eyes, I couldn't allow it to happen to someone else. No matter what had upset Patsy in the first place, though, her responses were always evasive. "Oh, it was nothing," "I got into an argument with my mom," "I met an old friend," or "Someone just pissed me off. It's no big deal, it's all right."

After months with no change, one evening I lit into Patsy. "Enough! It's not all right! We live together . . . and when you come home like that and I have to take care of you, it *is* my business. I feel like, at times, you expect it of me. Okay, I realize I have a few beers, but I know my limit, I don't lose control. Do you have any idea how many times I've broken crew rest before a flight just to take care of you? Do you realize if the air force found out I've lost sleep prior to a flight, they could pull my wings? I could be grounded!"

Patsy broke in with a vindictive tone, "Oh, Mr. Perfect, Mr. Control, Mr. Self-righteous—"

"No!" I cut Patsy off, fighting to explain. I was not trying to be overbearing, but after months of closing my eyes to the situation, I had to get my feelings off my chest. "Where do you get that? I am in no way perfect. You know I'm not like that. I just don't live like this. This whole thing is a problem for me and . . . if that makes me self-righteous . . . well, so be it. I thought you knew: my parents' drinking destroyed my family." I was breathing hard as I raised my finger. "I cannot and will not live through that again. For some folks, like your friends, I know it's okay and a part of their everyday lives. I don't care. I'm not better than anybody else. It's simply not for me." I began to cool down. "That's not my way of life. You've got to get this under control. Please?" I pleaded.

"You're not my father!" Patsy fired back. "No one, no one tells me what to do! Not you, my mother, my family, no one! All my life everyone's been bossing me around. You have no idea the shit I've been put through! I'll do what I want, when I want. Why do you care what happens to me? You can't even say the words. I know you don't love me."

I surprised myself by responding, "How can I love you when we live like this? I want to get close to you, but how can I if you don't tell me what's eating at you?"

My only hope was if I dug deep enough, or approached the subject in a different way, Patsy and I could find the answers to our problems. I became driven to make things right. Unfortunately, our arguments usually ended with her fleeing from the apartment. At times, late at night, I would still be wide awake when Patsy came in. She would slip into bed beside me and wrap her arms around my chest. Acting as if I were asleep, I'd shrug Patsy off, then roll over to the far side of the bed in the fetal position. I didn't know why, but whenever she'd reach out to defuse the situation, I always seemed to push her away.

From the bits and pieces Patsy revealed to me, I could relate to her difficult childhood. I truly believed our unfortunate experiences would make us closer; our past would make us appreciate our future. I knew Patsy was in pain, and as much as I was affected, I knew she was battling herself.

For the most part it was Patsy who tried to make amends. At times when flying at twenty-nine thousand feet, I'd open my lunch to find a note she had taken hours to say on paper what she could not tell me in person. Or I'd come home to find the apartment immaculate and an elaborate dinner waiting for me. When things were smooth between us, no one was kinder or sweeter than Patsy. I doubted if she even realized her own potential. Just as Patsy was there for me, during the rough times with Harold, I owed it to her to stick it out. I believed working through the little bumps on the road was exactly what a relationship was all about. I had thought for many years of being alone that I was not good enough to be with anyone, and now I had a chance. If these were the dues I had to pay, then so be it.

When I next saw Alice, I kept replaying everything Patsy and I had been through in my head. Since I had become an air crew member, I had lost my focus. I began to live a little too much. I went out to bars, and I spent, for the first time in my life, rather than saved for my future. I began to throw away years of self-discipline. But I thought that whatever my problems, I should have known better; I had brought them upon myself.

Sadly enough, I also knew I could not leave Patsy.

"Things are fine with you and Patsy?" Alice probed.

Turning away to avoid looking at my foster mother, I paused before nodding yes. "Mind if I spend the night?" I yawned. "It's a long drive and . . . I just wanted to spend some time together."

Alice nodded. By the look in her eyes, I sensed she understood.

A weekend with my foster mother gave me a chance to catch up on some badly needed sleep and time to clear my head. But within days of returning home, another problem between Patsy and me surfaced. After living together for nearly a year, the money that had taken me years to save was nearly depleted. Ever since Patsy had moved in, I was spending more than the air force paid me, and I had to draw from my savings to get by. Patsy always claimed she'd help out. I knew she meant it at the time, but the funds never materialized. After wrestling in my mind whether to bring up the subject or not, finally I did, and hell followed. I was not trying to seem like a miser, for I wanted to make Patsy happy, and would have gladly given her anything I could, but even with only rent, groceries, the very basics of utilities, and a car payment, I couldn't hold out much longer. Once we even squabbled because I could not afford to buy Patsy a television set, let alone cable to keep her company while I was either flying for the day or out of the country for weeks at a time.

By the end of the summer of 1985, when I finally sat her down to thoroughly explain my situation, Patsy became upset. "What's the deal?" she fumed. "I know you fly boys make a ton of dough."

"Say again?" I couldn't believe my ears. Was Patsy totally clueless about how hard it was for me to bring up the subject, let alone, support her for as long as I had? "What are you talking about?" I shook my head. "A ton of money? I'm enlisted! I make seventy-five, maybe one hundred bucks extra a month!"

Confused, Patsy shook her head. *"Enlisted,* what's that?"

It was then that I understood the misconception. Patsy must have assumed because I flew for the air force, I was an officer who was paid three to four times more than enlisted personnel, as they rightly deserved for the fact that officers graduated college and had more extensive technical training. But how, I wondered, could she be so naive about such a simple issue, especially since she lived near the air base all her life? How could she not know?

As I began to think this through, I questioned myself. Was I being taken advantage of? Nearly two years ago, when I had first in-processed into the air base, one of the lectures I'd attended warned about the possibility of women in the local community latching on to air force personnel, particularly air crew members. I had actually laughed out loud in total disbelief. But now, as I gazed at Patsy's hardened stance . . .

I knew she was not that kind of person. She was simply upset because she must have thought I had unlimited funds. Besides, Patsy had mentioned to me before how bad off she and her family had been ever since her father's death. From our time together, I understood Patsy was an emotional person and had a hard edge whenever she felt backed into a corner. I also knew Patsy was a wonderful woman, and I was grateful for all her kindness she'd shown me, especially during Harold's illness. So, I surmised, if I could relieve whatever strain that had surfaced, we would be that much better off. I wanted, as Patsy did, to work things out. At times I knew it was I, not Patsy, who could be overly petty. I breathed with relief when Patsy assured me she would indeed pitch in. Without hesitation, I accepted her word.

Because we lived in a cramped apartment, with her mother so close by driving Patsy crazy, we decided to move a few miles to a nicer, roomier house. I felt like a heel, but I had to have Patsy's absolute assurance that she would indeed help with the rent and utilities, since I was now financially way over my head. For a couple of months everything seemed fine. When I was not flying in Asia or Europe, Patsy's stress evaporated, her drinking stopped, and our arguments were a thing of the past. She landed a job as a waitress, making her feel needed and appreciated, which in turn made her esteem flourish. To top everything, Patsy loved being out from under her mother's thumb.

But upon returning home from another overseas assignment, I discovered, after nearly interrogating Patsy to get some answer, not one but several bills now months overdue. "What happened to the money?"

"Well . . ." Patsy hesitated. "I spent some of it."

"Some of it? That money was specifically for—"

Patsy deflected, "Take a chill pill, I'll pay you back. What's the deal? Everyone gets a few months behind."

"No," I exploded, "not me, not now, not ever! I gave my word!"

"Words . . . ? You can't even say it!" Patsy huffed while raising her eyebrows as if giving me a message.

What? I said to myself. My feelings toward her had nothing to do with our latest crisis.

"I really don't see why you're having such a shit fit. What's the big deal, just take care of it. You always do. I know you've got the money, just make a withdrawal. I bet lots of your air force buddies get behind. Get over it, it's a fact of life."

"It's called financial obligations. 'They' can get drummed out of the service, and if I don't meet my obligations, I can lose my clearance. Without my clearance, I can't fly, which means I can be kicked out. I don't care what happens to they, them, or anybody else. Don't you get it? *I* meet *my* commitments. Always have, always will."

"Really? We'll just see about that."

I felt I was being led down another twisted path rather than dealing with the root of the problem . . . again. My brain was spinning with emotions. I had to constantly pry everything from Patsy, figure out what had happened to our funds. I felt manipulated, as if my trust was a welcome mat she could stomp on whenever she felt the need.

Patsy continued to stand with her hands on her hips. "You're too hard. You think you're so perfect. You're . . . you're not my father!"

I knew that last statement was coming. Whenever she became irate, she always seemed to bring up her father. I tried to calm myself and her down. "Listen, please, I'm not trying to be your father. I'm not trying to boss you around or control you. If I have, I'm wrong. I'm sorry. I truly am. All I'm trying to do is—"

"You act as if I'm some, some leech. . . . I give, too! I'm here for you. I take care of your things, feed your stupid little turtle. I cook for you, pack your lunch, write you letters. I love you. And you . . . Mr. Perfect, Mr. 'what happened to my money' . . . you can't even say the words. Just three fuckin' words!" Patsy stepped forward, waving three fingers in my face.

"It's not like you have women beating down your door. When I met you, you were just a skinny bookworm geek, reading at the pool." Patsy stopped for a moment. "I'm with a geek. Me, with a geek," she announced, as if she had discovered a revelation. "*I* can be with anyone, you know. I was with someone before you, and I can be with someone else in a heartbeat! I see your fly boy buddies lookin' at me, I know what they want. You take good care of me, but why can't you say the words?"

"Why can't you be responsible?" I fired back. To me, everything was either right or wrong. To me life was not that complicated. If I saw a problem, rather than brush it aside, hoping it would simply disappear, I addressed the situation head-on. At the same time I'd make sure I did all that I could to prevent the problem from occurring again. To me, those who kept sweeping their problems under the rug were fooling themselves. A serious, unsolved issue would *sooner or later* suck a person into a black hole. That was one of the many lessons I had learned from living with Mother.

Battling Patsy whenever I was home, I came to believe that she thought it was all simply about money and all I had to do was "take care of it." But our core problem was that I didn't trust her as much as I wanted. At times, in the middle of a heated argument, I wanted nothing to do with her. But while alone overseas, I'd miss Patsy dearly and felt I was being too hard on her. I knew I drove her crazy with my idiosyncrasies. Maybe, I thought when I played back the arguments in my head, my standards were too high. After all I had been through, Patsy was the only person who had ever shown me any affection. Deep inside, I knew I didn't deserve any better.

But as much as I wanted to, as deceptions and confrontations continued to mount up, I could never trust the one person I wanted to love.

Because Patsy and I were so far behind in our rent, I moved from the condominium and into a smaller apartment that was closer to the base. I tried to break up with Patsy, but I couldn't bring myself to do it. Whenever I came close to explaining that we were just two different people, Patsy and I would both cry and make up, promising each other we would indeed, this time, work things out.

By Christmas of 1985, as I drove Patsy to the house of Alice's daughter's, the feeling from the year before had completely evaporated. On the way to the Bay Area, I yelled at her until she cried all over her new dress just moments before I pulled up to Mary's home. Recently I had found myself becoming petty, cold, and resentful. My feelings came from how I felt about myself, but I had begun to take them out on Patsy. Even after I erupted on her, blaming her for all my problems, she didn't say a word. After I parked the car, she took my hand, saying I worried too much and assuring me everything would work out. Of all the things I disliked about Patsy, at times she carried me when I fought myself.

Hours later, as I hugged Alice good-bye, Patsy leaned close, whispering, "Oh I forgot to tell you, Alice is coming with us. She's gonna spend a few days with my mom. Alice has been looking forward to this for a while now."

By the look on Alice's face, I knew it was another lie. For some reason I could not understand, I felt Patsy was beginning to manipulate, of all people, my foster mother. But after blowing up at Patsy just hours ago, I thought maybe once again I was being overly paranoid. After all, Alice and Patsy's mother Dottie Mae had been friends for some time, taking trips to Reno, and Alice had stayed at Dottie Mae's apartment for weeks at a time. My only fear was having Alice sucked into Patsy's and my bizarre world.

"My mom doesn't even have an overnight bag," I quietly stated to Patsy while trying to read her true intentions.

"Loosen up, you worry too much. If you must know," Patsy said, smiling, "I've been planning a surprise birthday party for you, and, well, Alice wanted to come." I felt like a complete idiot. Suddenly everything made sense. The last couple of weeks I had known Patsy was up to something, to the point that some of my friends at the squadron were acting strange. Now more than ever, I knew I needed to let down my guard.

"I'm gonna gain your trust," Patsy said as she kissed me. "You'll see."

Two mornings later I awoke to a ringing phone. I shot up, thinking it was an emergency squadron recall. That meant I had to report to the base as soon as possible. I was relieved to discover Patsy's chipper voice on the other line. "David," she shouted, "I'm at the hospital!"

"Oh, my God!" I said. "Are you okay?" Not fully awake yet, I wasn't even aware that Patsy had left that early in the morning.

"Chill out, I'm fine. Listen," she said with glee, "my mom and Alice are with me. . . . I've got great news. . . ." In the background I could hear Alice and Dottie Mae trying to speak over Patsy. "They're so happy to be grandparents!"

"What?" I cried, trying to shake my head clear, "Say again!"

"David," Patsy announced, "I'm going to have your baby!"

CHAPTER 9

HEAVEN SENT

There was no romantic proposal. Patsy and I became "engaged" at a local Mexican restaurant. While there, because I felt overwhelmed with shame about the pregnancy, I spilled over with apologizes to Alice at one table while Patsy chatted away with her mother, Dottie Mae, at another. After an hour of sulking in front of my foster mother, the four of us ate dinner, followed by Dottie Mae and Alice springing up and announcing our imminent marriage to strangers enjoying their dinners, who clapped feverishly while I squirmed in my seat. Since I soon was leaving to fly overseas for over a month, Patsy and I set the date for the second week in February.

Days later, on New Year's Eve, I was still consumed with a combination of guilt and rage—not against Patsy but myself. After years of self-discipline and going to great lengths to build a good life, I had thrown caution to the wind. I never had the guts to confront Patsy and sever our ties once and for all. And yet part of me began to feel maybe I had led her on. As unnerving and irresponsible as Patsy was, it was I who had held on.

It didn't really matter what I thought, how I felt, or how I analyzed the situation. The bottom line was Patsy and I—who had similar childhoods but at the same time as adults saw the world in different ways—were to become parents.

Ever since Patsy had phoned me days ago from the hospital,

I had been seized with fear. It wasn't an issue of escaping parenthood; it was a matter of responsibility. For most of my life I had felt rejected and inferior, so now as an adult, how could I abandon my own child? More than that, knowing full well that children who were severely abused stood a strong chance of becoming abusers themselves made me all the more terrified. As much as I had told Patsy about my childhood, she only knew the tip of the iceberg. As I promised myself years ago, in order to protect the person I was with, I had for the most part maintained my vow of burying the past. To compound the situation, since living with Patsy, I had come to realize how petty and argumentative I could be. If that wasn't enough, air crew members in general had an extremely high divorce rate. As these thoughts clashed in my mind, I became consumed with the single thought of doing what was right for my baby.

Here I was lying in bed, next to my future wife, a person I would spend the rest of my life with, hours before the fresh start to a new year, and yet I did not trust her, let alone have the love for Patsy that she claimed to have for me. I truly didn't mean to, but at times I displayed the affection of a statue. To the outside world, I had a great career, but on the inside, after years of pushing down my emotions in order to survive, I had become robotic. How in the world, I asked myself, could I raise my baby with love and encouragement when I barely had feelings for my fiancée and far less for myself?

Patsy was far more optimistic. "I've always wanted to have a baby," she cried. "My mom's got all boys for grand kids, and maybe, maybe we'll have a girl. This is going to be so great. I can dress and bathe the baby; I'll never be alone. This baby will be the answer to my prayers. A baby will make my life whole. We are going to be so happy."

The more Patsy prattled on, the more I felt she lacked the seriousness and all that having a baby entailed. Only days ago, we had been arguing for the umpteenth time, and now because of her pregnancy, suddenly everything was going to be roses. I couldn't help but think: How could a person who constantly scraped by in everyday life manage a baby?

Clearing my head of Patsy, my thoughts turned to the one person I had to inform of my upcoming marriage. With the phone shaking in my hand, I punched the numbers to Mother's private line. Even though I had secretly had her telephone number for years, this was the first time, since Father's funeral, I had made contact with her. Holding my breath, I asked myself why I was doing this. Nothing was going to change. Mother still hated me and always would. But I still felt a bizarre need for her approval, and I thought maybe, because of the years gone by, the holiday season coming, and the good news of getting married just might soften her heart. I shook my head at the thought, but before I could hang up the phone, Mother's hacking voice came on. "Yes, hello?" Mother coughed.

I swallowed hard. "Mrs. Pelzer?"

At the other end I could hear her gagging reply. "Yes, and who is this?"

"Mrs. Pelzer, this is David"—for a split second I panicked before completing the sentence—"David Pelzer."

"And how did *you* get this number?" Mother bellowed.

As calmly as possible I stated, "I only called to wish you a Happy New Year, and . . . I, uh, wanted to tell you that, ah, I'm—I'm going to get . . . get married."

After a few seconds of dead silence Mother replied, "Well, yes, that's good of you."

I wasn't sure of Mother's meaning, or if she had really heard what I had just told her. "I said, I'm getting married . . . a little after New Year's."

"And the same to you," Mother chimed.

"Thank you . . . but I'm getting . . ." As I stumbled in my vain attempt to draw her out, the line clicked dead. All I could do was lean against the headboard while still clutching the phone. In the course of a few days, my life had spun out of control. With the phone still in my hand, I began to shake from anxiety. My thoughts continued to shoot off in a thousand different directions, until just a few minutes before midnight when I finally drifted off in an uneasy sleep. My last thought of 1985 was how unworthy I felt of becoming a father.

Patsy and I were married in mid-February, in a small church of the town where she had been raised. Not a single member of my squadron—my air force family—came to the wedding. After several of them had given me excuses before the ceremony, I learned through the grapevine that they did not support my decision. One of my female co-pilots was so upset that she pinned me against a wall days before the wedding. "This is the real deal, Pelz," the lieutenant stated. "I know why you're doing this. We all do. There's something you should know. . . . It's not easy for me to say, you're like a brother to me. . . . I'm not saying your fiancée's a derelict, but I've seen her kind before."

By then the frustration was too much for me. "Don't you think I know? I gotta do this . . . you don't know, I mean, it's my responsibility."

"You're wrapped pretty tight, Pelz-man. You don't have to get married. You can still be the father, see the kid and all that. You better think about that baby and what happens if things don't work out," she warned.

Agitated, I grabbed my fellow crew member—an air force officer—by the lapels and flung her against the wall. "Don't *you* get it? That's all I do is think about the baby? What do you and the others want me to do? I see you, all of you, looking at me, talking about me behind my back, saying what an idiot I am for doing this. You think it's like I'm trapped into this. You're wrong, you're all wrong! You don't know, you really don't. You think I can just pack my bags, hit the bricks, and flee? Ride off into the sunset or fly off into the wild blue yonder? Well, I can't do that!

"I know the odds are against me. But you don't know me. I've beaten the odds before. I'll make it work, you'll see. Besides," I smiled, "Patsy loves me, she does. She really does."

My co-pilot leaned over to hug me. "Now, who's the one you're trying to convince? You don't have to do this. You say the word, and . . . I could round up the rest of the crew and we'll kidnap you and take you to Reno. We'll make it a no-notice deployment. I've got it all planned. You think about it. We're all just a phone call away."

"Thanks, Lisa." I swallowed. "That's about the kindest thing anybody ever said to me."

I had received the same response from David Howard, my childhood friend from foster care, who was so against the marriage that he refused to attend, even after I begged him to be my best man. Out of frustration, I blurted into the phone, "For God's sake, I'm begging you, stand with me. Please?" I groveled.

David and I had known each other for over ten years, and he was one of the first friends I ever had. He gave a deep sigh. "I know a lot's happening really fast, but I saw this coming. Did you know that Patsy practically bragged to my girlfriend that she'd do anything she could to marry you?"

I brushed David off. "Come on, man, you took it the wrong way. She meant it . . . in, ah, a romantic way."

David replied, "Get with it, man. I'm not downing Pats, but it's not like you've been 'out there' when it comes to dating. I know and respect what you're trying to do with your life, but man, what's it gonna be like for the kid with the two of you going at it all the time? You know what it's like. My old man was the same way. What then?" After a few seconds of silence he went on, "I'm sorry, man, I can't back your play on this. I love you bro, but—"

"Hey man," I jumped in, "I, ah, I understand." Thinking quickly, I tried one last time. "I know you two don't get along that well, but Patsy's really a great lady, a class act—"

"Yo, man, hold up. Don't even go there with that one!"

David interrupted. "Are you even listening to yourself? You two are as different as oil and water. Again, I'm not downing Patsy, but I know how this whole thing's gonna end."

Patsy, who I discovered had been straining to listen in, snatched the phone from my hand. "*We* don't need you or want you at *our* wedding. So . . . fuck off!"

David's and Lisa's warnings still rang in my ears as Patsy strolled down the aisle at the wedding. I gazed left, at the groom's side of the church. Besides Alice's daughter, Mary, and son-in-law, Del, and a handful of others, my side was virtually empty. Patsy's side spilled over with friends, relatives, and nearly every member of the town, who beamed as Patsy made her way to the minister. At least one friend from my days in foster care, J. D. Thom, stood with me as my best man. I was so nervous during the exchange of the vows, I dropped Patsy's ring. Later at the reception, one of Patsy's brothers smiled widely as he slapped me on the back, announcing to the world, "You's family now!"

Within a short time Patsy and I were fortunate enough to move into military base housing. Before I set off for another extended overseas assignment, the two of us set our ground rules. She surprised me by adamantly stating she had given up smoking and drinking, and from that moment on, Patsy claimed, she'd do whatever she could to make things right for our baby. "I married you, David. I can imagine what you think of me, but I married you for life. I wanna do right for our baby. Both of us had sucky childhoods, so let's do right with our own. But know this, I do love you, David. It's not the baby. I knew from the moment I saw you that you were the one for me. No more fighting, partying, running around. It's over."

I was relieved that Patsy had become serious about being a parent. At times when things were good between us I knew she loved me, but now as her husband, my sole concern was to ensure that I did anything I could for our child. "I wanna make sure our baby isn't treated like we were. I just want to do what's right."

Hugging me, she cried, "I love you, David."

I took a deep breath and closed my eyes before replying for the first time, "I . . . I love you, too."

"Thank you, David, thank you," Patsy whispered. "You'll see, the baby's gonna make everything different. Everything's gonna be fine, you'll see."

When not flying overseas, I dedicated every moment to redoing our house. I spent hours rearranging furniture, placing trinkets just the right way to capture as much light as possible. I wanted our home to be open and warm. I felt proud when I purchased a lawnmower and other garden tools. I'd wake up just after sunrise on Saturday mornings to spend the better part of the day mowing, raking, trimming, and watering or planting flowers to beautify our yard. I thought of myself as a husband providing for his family. I did my best to think ahead, trying to take care of every need to alleviate any friction between Patsy and me. Once all the bills were taken care of, I made certain Patsy received the bulk of our remaining funds. With each passing day my initial fears began to fade.

On payday I'd rush to the on-base department store and scour every aisle that had anything to do with babies. As the months progressed, I picked out toys, stuffed animals, or anything I knew the baby would enjoy. When I ran out of playthings to buy, I spent time in search of the perfect stroller, carrying basket, or clothes, even though I knew the baby wouldn't be able to wear some of the shorts and tank tops for years. I couldn't control my excitement. When overseas, because money was so tight, I skipped a few meals in order to buy the baby a cute stuffed yellow alligator, which I named

Wally. The more I did for my baby, the more my heart warmed.

When a member of my squadron asked if I wanted a boy or a girl, my instantaneous response was "A healthy child with ten fingers and ten toes." In the early spring, the air force doctors assured me that the fetus was perfectly healthy and was a boy. I was overjoyed with the news, but with my luck I had to think we weren't out of the woods yet. Not until I held my baby in my arms would I be convinced that everything was fine.

Since Patsy and I had set our rules, we got along better. Now whenever we had a disagreement, rather than argue I'd escape outside to putter in the yard until we both calmed down. I knew I had caused the disputes more than half the time, and it was Patsy who would make amends. Even though I still did not trust her as I felt I should, Patsy and I were now living together as husband and wife. All we could do was wait for our baby boy.

In June of 1986 I had to attend a six-week flight instructor school course. Patsy was due in late July, so on every flight I'd drop by the administration office to give them the plane's identifying call sign and frequency in case there was any news. On Fridays, after a lengthy day, I'd make the three-hour drive at warp speed, praying Patsy wasn't in labor yet. The weeks crawled by and still no baby. Even after flight school, when the doctor assured Patsy and me everything was normal, I worried that something was wrong. Finally, in mid-August, Patsy went into labor. For months we had known our baby was a boy, but we could not decide on a name. As Patsy was wheeled into the delivery room, I held her hand and bent down to whisper if we could name our child Stephen Joseph. "Why?" she groggily asked. "Isn't that your father's name?"

"Yeah, but it's another chance, *my* chance to set things right. Please?" I begged. "It will make things clean for me." Patsy smiled as she squeezed my hand. A short time later, I was the first person besides the doctor to hold my son, Stephen Joseph Pelzer.

Stephen was so tiny and delicate I thought for sure he'd break if I moved the wrong way. I could have held him forever, but the small group of nurses insisted I relinquish my son to their care. Hours later, in the middle of the night, I lay on my bed thankful that Stephen was indeed completely healthy. Before falling off to sleep, I began to feel an invisible weight bear down on me, for now I was a father.

Just over a week later, on a beautiful Saturday, Patsy and I made our first family trip. Before noon, with sunlight beaming through the towering redwood trees, I pulled up next to the same house where my father had taken his family on summer vacations seemingly a lifetime ago at 17426 Riverside Drive. Patsy and I had made countless trips to the Russian River, sometimes staying for only a few hours or even minutes at a time, and I had bored her to tears, constantly harping about one day living in Guerneville. And yet I could not explain to Patsy why I was so drawn to the area. With Stephen cradled in my arms, I sat on the old, decayed tree stump where my brothers and I had once played. As Stephen slept soundly, I shielded his sensitive eyes and whispered, "One day we'll live here. We'll live here at the river." Rocking Stephen, I couldn't help but think of my foolish pie-in-the-sky fantasy of my father and me having a relationship at the same spot my son and I now shared. "I'm gonna make things right," I promised Stephen, "What I do, I do for you. As God is my witness, I'll make things right *for you*."

That afternoon at the river was more than a family outing. Since that day my anxiety began to ease. Since Stephen was born, I had become paranoid, not only as a parent sustaining him, but other fears like illnesses, late-night fevers, and getting him all the appropriate shots at the right time. Back in our home at Beale Air Force Base, I discovered a million different ways my son could accidentally hurt himself—jamming his fingers into light sockets, crashing down the stairs, or even suffocating from his baby blanket. *"How,"* I asked myself, *"can. I protect him from all of this, all the time?"* It was at the river when Stephen unknowingly taught me my first lesson: Do everything I possibly could as situations arose, but ease up a little and let go. I realized I could not shield, fix, or control every aspect of my son's future, let alone my own.

From that point on, not a single day passed that I was not utterly amazed at Stephen. How he curled up and slept in my lap, the softness of his skin, or the gentle sounds that escaped his tiny mouth. When I returned home from a late-night flight, I would always tiptoe into his room and become lost in time as I stood over his crib to watch him sleep. Almost every time I did, after a few minutes of no movement from him, I would think Stephen was dead! My heart would seize as I reached down into the crib and snatched him up. I was always rewarded a split second later as Stephen's screeching cry became music to my ears. I would then take him into my bedroom, where I would lay him on my chest.

In the mornings while Patsy still slept, I always made sure I woke up early to spend time with Stephen, listening to him coo, watching him suck on his fingers or crawl through the sheets all over the bed. I was captivated by his constant smile and how every little thing made him laugh. At times I played with him so much that I was late for mission planning at work. At the squadron I'd show off stacks of Polaroid photos before sticking them in my in-flight checklist, so no matter where I flew I always had Stephen with me. After work I would race home, breezing by Patsy with a quick hello before playing with Stephen. By the time he was in his walker, I would chase him throughout the house as he sped away, giggling at the top of his lungs. I laughed as he learned to build up speed by pumping his tiny legs, then lean his walker before taking a sharp turn. More than once I kept my eyes on him instead of the wall that I smashed into at the end of the hallway. At the end of an exhausting day, I'd slowly read Dr. Seuss books to Stephen while he jabbed his finger at the pictures. Even though he was too young to understand, I wasn't concerned, just as long as we were together.

Before his first birthday, Stephen's room, which at one time had been vacant, had become a virtual Toys R Us warehouse. He had so many stuffed animals at one point that I would fill his entire crib to the brim and gently toss him in. He would disappear, only to resurface a few moments later, giggling for me to toss him again. To me, nothing was too much if it made Stephen happy.

With Stephen, Patsy gave her all. She always made sure he was bathed and covered with baby lotion. When she fed him she seemed happy and beamed whenever he did the smallest thing. As a couple, if we had a flare-up, all we had to do was gaze at Stephen and our anxiety disappeared. At times she'd joke that I spent more time with Stephen than I did her. I took the hint. I just didn't have the heart to confess that for the first time in my life I was filled with an emotion that I never felt before. Without a shred of hesitation, my son, Stephen, was the first and only person I adored—that I absolutely loved with all of my heart and soul.

CHAPTER 10

THE SOURCE

By the summer of 1987, just weeks prior to Stephen's first birthday, I took time off from the service and made our family's first long-range trip. Our destination: Salt Lake City, Utah. Since Patsy was complaining of being cooped up in the house, and, surprisingly to me, got along well with Grandmother, we decided to take the journey. I carefully explained to Patsy that Grandmother could be pleasant on the phone and yet once in person could be controlling and spiteful, but Patsy didn't care. She thought I was being paranoid. Once there, I knew Grandmother would drive Patsy and me crazy, but since becoming married and having Stephen, Grandmother had treated me like never before. On the phone she savored all updates of Stephen. In the back of my mind, though, I was extremely leery because of my last visit with her.

Secretly, I had another reason for traveling to Salt Lake City. For years I had had so many questions, and now I felt I was ready. With each day as Stephen grew before my eyes, I could not imagine how a person, let alone a mother, could concoct ways to dehumanize and torture their own child. As much as I craved closure to my past for myself, now as a father I felt I owed it to Stephen.

With Patsy and Stephen at Grandmother's house on a warm late morning, I drove the Toyota to Mother's and stopped a few houses away. Before getting out of the car, I stopped to collect myself. I checked my watch to make sure I wasn't late. I ensured every hair on my head was in place so to make a good impression. For the hundredth time that morning, I asked myself if I really wanted to go through with this. Part of me felt it was a hopeless quest. I knew Mother would never come out and tell me why she did all she did to me. After the countless ways Mother had made me suffer and the river of booze she had consumed over the years, she probably had no memory of it all. But, I thought, if I could walk out of there with even some information, maybe that would be enough to make me feel cleansed. As a matter of closure, if I could enter Mother's house without cowering down to her and display myself as the fair-minded, independent, responsible person that I strive to be, then by the time I left, I'd know in my heart I was no longer looked upon as a child called "It." After the years of self-doubt, I was beginning to feel I didn't need to prove myself to Mother anymore. Of all my tests, perhaps seeing Mother was the ultimate one for me.

Walking up to the house, I noticed how worn and lifeless the grass had become and how overgrown and unkempt the bushes were. Among the well-groomed houses on the street, Mother's gloomy, rundown home stood out. *"And years ago,"* I said to myself, *"her home was the Camelot of the block."* After knocking on the door, I caught a whiff of a rancid odor. When the door opened, I almost fell over from the smell. Before I could turn my head away, Mother flashed a smile. "Yes . . . well, right on time. Come in." Confused, I thought Mother was acting as if my seeing her was an everyday occurrence. Before I could offer a greeting, Mother spun around and made her way up a small flight of stairs. As I followed a few steps behind, a overwhelming stench began to flood my senses. Covering my mouth, I guessed that part of the smell came from the stairs, which were worn to the point there was nothing left but the bare wood. Whatever covering that remained was on the edges, but was layered in what I assumed was cat and dog hairs. The walls gave off an eerie glow from the dark yellow-brown stain from, it seemed, Mother's constant smoking.

After my youngest brother, Kevin, who by now I guessed to be sixteen, proudly showed off his bedroom, I returned to the living room to sit next to Mother. Kevin seemed to hover nervously as Mother and I strained to make small talk. After a few attempts, my mouth became dry. All I could do was nod my head as Mother made an occasional remark. An icy tension began to fill the room. For some odd reason, I was not afraid or even slightly intimidated by her. If anything, I could not help but stare at her. Since Father's funeral seven years ago, Mother had not only gained a great deal of weight, but her face now seemed pudgy and leathery. Her crimson features reminded me of Father's when I had found him at a bar across the street from the bus station in San Francisco during a visit before I joined the air force. Mother's fingers were swollen and twitched every few seconds. I fidgeted in my chair while trying to think of something to say. But Mother's appearance said it all. Her years of vindictiveness had left her a broken and lonely person. Whatever domination Mother once waved over others like a sword, allowing her to hurt anyone whenever she pleased, had now vanished.

Growing bored, Kevin barged out of the room, down the stairs, and from the house. Before the front door closed, Mother's head snapped upright. As if making sure the coast was clear, she murmured, "I want you to know, it was an *accident.*"

Realizing I was alone with Mother for the first time since that day in March before I was rescued—over fourteen years ago—made me feel weak. I couldn't believe I was actually sitting four feet away from someone who had tried to kill me. Mother's statement flew over my head. "I'm sorry," I apologized, "accident?"

Mother heaved as if she were already impatient with me. Raising her voice, she stated, "I want you to know *it* was an accident!" She nodded as if I should understand her coded message. All I could do was nod back. An eerie silence followed. Raising my eyebrows, I tried to get Mother to explain, but she simply grinned. Suddenly it hit me. Years ago, one summer when I was a child, during one of Mother's rages, she had snatched a knife and threatened to kill me. Back then I had known by her drunken condition and her flailing arms that Mother's threat was beyond the norm. Sitting in front of Mother now, I could visualize the terror in her eyes as the knife slipped from her grasp before stabbing me. I knew somehow, even back then, Mother had never meant to kill me. I had always felt it was one of her "games" that went too far.

Collecting myself, I leaned over in the chair. "Yes," I exclaimed, "an accident! I knew, I always knew you didn't mean . . . to kill me." As the words sputtered from my mouth, I could visualize the figure of a small child unconscious on the spotted kitchen floor, with blood oozing from his chest, while Mother stood above him, wiping her hands as if nothing had happened. Back then I had believed the stabbing would jolt Mother out of her vindictive madness and make her see how insane she had become. My injury would transform the evil Mother into the beautiful, loving Mommy I had prayed for. Only then could "the family" somehow reunite, like a fairy-tale ending.

Now, sitting with Mother in her dingy living room, I wondered why I was still drawn to her. Whenever I thought of Mother, I found myself constantly trying to prove that I was not the disobedient *monster child* that deserved to be *disciplined,* as Mother had drilled into my head for so many years, but that I was a human being of some self-worth. Because of my lack of self-esteem, even in foster care, I had always tried to uncover what I could do to prove myself to Mother, trying to accomplish something so phenomenal that the slate from my childhood would be wiped clean. As an adult I fully realized I was a fairly competent, independent person. I had not only gone from an almost animalistic child to a functional, married adult, an elite air crew member with the air force, but I was also the father to an incredible boy whom without a passing thought I showered with true love. I knew I had a long way to go, certainly when it came to issues of trust. The shame from my past still made me question myself. Especially in front of Mother, part of me felt that I had been the source of wrongdoing, that I was a failure. Only a wave of Mother's magical wand of acceptance would make my self-worth flourish.

Easing back into the chair, though, I realized I was not wrong. *I had not made Mother do those things to me.* I hadn't forced, let alone provoked her to stab me. And now, after sixteen years since the accident, Mother still could not bring herself to apologize for nearly killing me then, or for any other abuse she had inflicted on me during all those years. Mother's statement made her look as if *she* were the victim of the situation.

The booze had not erased Mother's memory—she knew exactly what she had done. She did not display any remorse, unless Mother's bringing it up was her feeble way of seeking forgiveness. If that was the case, did Mother actually bear some form of guilt? Was her statement revealing a shred of affection? Did she care? If I could just strip through the layers of vengeance . . .

With true sincerity, I gently probed, "What happened?" But before Mother could respond, I found myself spilling over with a list of questions. "Why me? I mean, what was it that I did to make you hate me?"

"Well . . ." Mother cleared her throat as she raised her head. "You have to understand, 'It' was bad, David." Mother's impassive explanation hung in the air. Shaking my head, I acted as if I had not heard her. I deliberately wanted Mother to repeat herself so she knew exactly what she had just stated. With a strained exhalation, Mother restated her justification, placing a further emphasis on "It" and "David," as if they were two separate entities. Still I was too dazed to respond. Mother's further elaboration only confused me more. "David, 'It' was always trying to steal food. 'It' deserved to be punished. The other boys had their share of chores, too, and I would have fed 'It' once 'It' was done with the chores . . . but . . . 'It' was always stealing food." Mother again gestured with a nod of her head, as if I should agree with her. "When you think about it, it's really not that difficult to understand, David."

For years I had believed if I ever confronted Mother as an adult, she would finally have to grasp the magnitude of the problem. I never meant to be vengeful. Part of me became concerned that the moment Mother realized the depth of her actions, she'd have a heart attack. But now Mother was carefully rationalizing her actions, guarding every word, making her treatment of "It" seem like nothing more than a parent disciplining a disobedient child; brutalizing "It" had not only been justified, but necessary.

"But why me? Was I really that bad? What did I do that was so wrong?"

"Oh, please," Mother said. "You may not remember, but you were always getting into everything. You could never keep that yap of yours shut. From one end of the house to the other I could always hear you wailing, more than Ron and Stan. You may not remember, but you were a handful."

Mother's testimony made me recall when I was four and how scared I was to speak. When my two brothers and I played in our bedroom, if I became too excited, Ron would cover my mouth so my voice didn't carry. Later on I was controlled to the point that I had to stand in front of Mother, with my chin resting on my chest, waiting for her to give me permission to speak so I could then ask her if I could go to the bathroom. More than once, with Mother towering over me, she'd contemplate aloud, "Well, I don't know what you want from me." Even then I felt trapped. Before I could ask her for approval, she would snap her fingers as a warning, as if I were a pet that required to be broken in. With my knees locked and my body weaving, sometimes I'd urinate on myself, which only sent Mother into a further rage.

Had that been Mother's way of disciplining me initially? Maybe I was too much for her to handle. Mother could have as easily picked on either Ron or Stan; it didn't really matter. Maybe Mother singled me out for something as simple as the irritating sound of my voice.

All I could do was think of Stephen. As I did, the outline of a child sprawled out on Mother's kitchen floor in a pool of blood suddenly became my son. Seeing my reaction, Mother's eyes flashed with pleasure. Once again I allowed her to feed off my emotions.

With my hands slid under my legs, I wanted to jump up and scream into Mother's repulsive face, *"You twisted, sick bitch! I was a toy for you to play with! A slave at your command! You humiliated me, took away my name, and tortured me to the brink of death, because . . . because my voice was too loud?"*

Breathing heavily, I continued to rage to myself, *Do you realize what I can do to you now, at this very moment? I could wrap my hands around that swollen neck of yours and squeeze the life out of you. Or make you suffer slowly, ever so slowly. I wouldn't kill you right away, but I'd strip away the very essence of your being. I could do it. I actually could."* I'd kidnap Mother, take her to some dingy hotel, lock her in a room, and deprive her of all the things that sustained normal life—food, water, light, heat, sleep, contact with others; I'd make her life hell. Afterward, I could tell the police that . . . I just flipped out . . . from some sort of post-traumatic stress from my treatment as a child. For once I could throw everything away and . . . become like her.

A freezing sensation crept up my spine. *Oh, my God! I* warned myself. With my wrist beginning to tremble, I wondered, Am I insane? Or were my thoughts normal considering what I'd been put through? Suddenly the light dawned on me: it was the chain, the chain linking me to my mother—a person who for whatever reason had become possessed with so much rage that over time the emotion grew into a cancer, passing itself on from one generation to the next . . . leading to my son in a single beat of my heart; I could become the person I despised the most.

Closing my eyes, I erased the thought of revenge and flushed away any feelings of hatred that I held against Mother. I could not believe the intensity of my rage. Taking a slow, deep breath, I cleared my head before raising my face and staring into Mother's eyes. For my own peace of mind I told myself, *"I'm never gonna be like you!"*

How different Mother looked to me now. To me as a child, in some ways Mommy was a princess, reminding me of Snow White. Her bright smile, her kind voice, and the way Mommy's hair smelled when she had wrapped me in her arms when I was a preschooler. I had watched Mommy glow as she laughed, as Ron, Stan, and I vied for her attention. And now, with Mother hunched over and her hips molded to her chair, her past had caught up with her, like Father's had years ago. Her life these days consisted of what she viewed from a television set. Her form of control was now a piece of plastic used to change channels to her world. Whatever light had kept her soul lit had been extinguished. *Mother had become her own prisoner.* Whatever harm I had just wished upon her moments ago could not compare to her self-created prison.

Mother's change of tone brought me out of my trance. "You may not think it by looking at me, but you and I are very much from the same piece of cloth."

I shook my head. "Excuse me?"

Mother seemed to make an effort to control her sniffling. "You think life is so easy, well . . ." she huffed, "before I was pregnant with Ron . . . I had a miscarriage." She stopped abruptly, as if for effect. Not knowing if she was sincere or again trying to feed off a tragedy, I wasn't sure how to react. Suddenly her face turned dark red. "You think this entire planet revolves around you! David, David, David! That's all I've heard about for years was David this, David that, 'feed the boy,' 'don't punish the boy,' every day since the day you were born!" Building up steam, Mother pointed a finger at me.

"And let me tell you something else: it was those teachers, those teachers at school, butting into my affairs! It's no one else's damn business! What happens in someone's house should stay in that person's house! But I tell you what: I taught that—that hippie teacher of yours, Ms. Moss, a thing or two when I had her little behind removed from the school. She was out of there so fast, you'd thought it made your head spin.

"You don't remember," Mother went on, "but when you were six, maybe seven, you were playing with matches one day and . . . you burned your arm. If I told you once," she said, "I told you a thousand times. Anyway, one day you showed up with a few marks on your arm. And that Moss teacher of yours had the audacity to accuse me of . . . well, we both know what happened, don't we?"

"Quite well," I said to myself. Mother's recollection was off by two years. I was eight when Mother held my arm over the kitchen stove. When she sent me off to school the next day, she claimed "the boy" had played with a match. Even back then, early on, everyone knew the reality of my situation. Somehow Mother must have believed she could not only hide the secret, but dispose of anyone who challenged her authority.

"And that principal of yours, Pete Hanson, calling me *every single day*! It got to the point every time the phone rang, well, I just knew who it was. I dreaded picking it up. If it wasn't one thing it was another, saying that boy of yours did this or that. How the boy got into a fight, pulled somebody's hair, stole food, clothes, or whatever it could get its hands on. *Every day.* Well, it just got to the point that it drives a person to drink. It wasn't me that was after you, it was those damn teachers! Always digging, always putting their noses in other people's business. It was them!" Mother stated as if her life depended upon it.

"You think you're the only one with troubles!" Mother continued. "You have no idea what it's like. It's not easy raising four boys all alone, barely scraping by, having a husband just pick up and walk out on you. Believe me, I could tell you things about your father!"

"Don't!" I coldly interjected. Lowering my voice, I said, "He was your husband, and you couldn't even step into the hospital once, just once, or have the decency to mail him a card. Of all the things—"

"Well!" Mother said. "I'm not all *that* cold-hearted. He wanted me to . . . to take him back before he even checked into Kaiser Hospital. We even had lunch. He practically begged me."

"You love it, don't you?" I blurted before thinking. I was so close to the edge, just a single breath away from opening up and *really* telling Mother off, but I kept myself in check. The last thing I wanted was to get sucked into one of Mother's games. "His name was *Stephen!*" I shook my head. "You must have known he was reaching out to you. You knew he was sick and you made him beg?"

"Oh, please! Enough with the dramatics. I told your father, and now I'm telling you: I wouldn't have taken him back for all the tea in China. You have no idea . . ." Mother wandered on.

Little did Mother know, weeks before enlisting in the air force, the day I had my records sealed, my juvenile officer, Gordon Hutchenson, allowed me a few hours to read through my files, which were in two separate folders and over ten inches thick. I spent the entire day reviewing reams of county paperwork, various forms, and even scribbled legal sheets. One report claimed that after I was removed, a social worker had made several attempts to visit Mother, to the point of pleading just to have Mother open the door. All efforts by the county were met with Mother's numerous excuses until she escalated to threats. Once, she slammed the door in the face of a social worker before laughing from the other side. Back then, as a teenager with the report in my hand, I could not believe her gall, how she seemingly got away with everything.

I turned to Mr. Hutchenson, asking how Mother could get off scot-free when the county should step in, rescue my brothers, and either have Mother arrested or be given some sort of psychiatric help. I wasn't out for blood, but I felt that if everyone within social services had told me how outrageous my situation was before I was placed into foster care, my brothers wouldn't have to live through the same hell.

Gordon had told me, "I agree with you, David, but back then in 1973 things were very different; your mother was never brought up on a single charge. We couldn't get her on assault, willful harm against a minor, failure to provide, or, in my estimation, attempted murder. Understand, there weren't a great deal of PCs to protect kids back then in '73. Even now, as we enter the 1980s, there are a majority of folks who are in total denial or believe parents are doing nothing more than 'disciplining' their children. Believe me, this whole thing's gonna blow up in our faces—these kids are gonna grow up, go on a rampage, wreak havoc on everything and everyone, contaminate themselves with every substance known to man, whack their kids as they were; then at the end of the day, when they face the judge, these people will either blame their deeds on society or plead that they were abused as kids, which of course made them the way they were. That's when there'll be an outcry from society to change the laws to protect children like you. Mark my words, it's gonna happen. We've come a long way, but we still have a ways to go."

"What are PCs?" I inquired.

"Penal codes. That's why we couldn't remove your brothers or even slap your mother on the wrist with a warning. So in essence, as you say, she got off scot-free. On the flip side, because of cases like yours, there are now laws on reporting abuse, intervention, the works. A lot has happened in the last six years since you've been 'placed.' Nowadays your mother would be hooked, booked, cuffed, and stuffed, if you get my meaning," Gordon had stressed.

Digging further through the file, reading a rare interview

Mother had given before my court hearing, I came across an official form stating one of the reasons she "may have" been distraught was she suspected her husband was having an affair with a woman whom was one of Mother's closest friends. Her defense also included how difficult it was for her to keep up with the housework while being left alone to raise *four* boys—the report corrected that it was *five*—while she worried sick when her husband was either at work or "God knows where," whenever Father disappeared for days at a time drinking with buddies from work. Being alone with no one to console her might have, Mother claimed in the report, made her tip the bottle and fly off the handle a little more than she normally would.

As I rubbed the dried sweat from my forehead, I still could not fathom even now as an adult, after eight years after reading the documents, that my father had had an affair. As a mature person, I fully understood that anyone was capable of anything. So, as Mother continued to play the role as the helpless victim in her never ending life tragedy, I felt the affair accusation was another sinister excuse she had strung out for so many years.

"You still have no idea of what I've been put through," Mother repeated, but this time with reddened eyes. "You think you had it bad? Well," she huffed, "back in my day, my mother, that person you're staying with, well . . . when I was a girl, she'd . . . she'd lock me in a closet for hours at a time. She did! She most certainly did!" Mother announced with a burst of tears. "And sometimes she wouldn't feed me . . . for days. Back then it wasn't like today, when children at school have a lunch program. And if that weren't enough, not one day, a single solitary day, passed that my mother didn't berate me, boss me around, telling me what to do and when to do it; what friends I could and couldn't have over for visits. My mother!" she bellowed. "My own mother! Can you imagine!"

With my chin resting on my hand, I nodded my head. I could in fact understand. As Mother cried, she appeared lost

in time, reliving her mistreatment at the hands of my grandmother. I could not help but think *if* what Mother said was
true, she had in turn done the exact same things to me, but for
far longer durations and in such obsessive, vindictive ways.

As much as I wanted to believe Mother's sobbing was partly
show, in an odd way her confession did make perfect sense.
From what I had learned, people like Mother abused their
children in the same manner they were abused; thus becoming a product of their environment.

But only a few years ago, during the summer of 1983, when
I had visited Grandmother, she steadfastly maintained that
she had *not* mistreated Mother in any way as a child. *Could it
be,* I thought, *by Grandmother's or even society's standard during
her time, it was not abuse but no more than stern discipline?*

Unless, I wondered, Mother was devious enough to concoct
a story about her childhood in order to take the blame off her,
transfer it to her mother, somehow freeing Mother from any
accountability?

"You know," I gently inserted, "I spoke to Grandma and . . .
well, I'm not pointing fingers . . . but she was adamant that
she never, under any circumstances, abused you."

"Well," Mother coughed as she rolled her eyes, "look at the
source. You know how she is. Who are you going to believe?"

The source, I repeated to myself. Look at the source. At that
moment in time I wasn't sure who did what to whom and
what for. Okay, I thought, maybe Grandmother was overbearing. When her husband passed away, leaving her to raise two
children in the middle of a depression, Grandmother had to
be stern. As a young woman, Mother might have craved her
independence, tried to get out from under Grandmother's rul-
ing thumb, then somewhere down the road became addicted
to booze, got married, had kids, while still carrying some resentment . . . that ate at the core of her soul. With my fingers
rubbing my temples, I was totally confused. But, I reflected, in
the final analysis did it truly matter? My only concerns were
that I make every day count, while trying to be the best person

I could possibly be, and to make certain that my son would never be exposed to anything but a safe and loving setting. Period.

Imagining my son, Stephen, with his bright blond hair and giggling smile, made me want to recapture the essence of "Mommy" I had always longed for. I wanted to fall on my knees, wrap my arms around Mother's waist, as if she still held a lifeline to my soul. And by my openly granting her amnesty, it would free me from being tied to my past and allow me to close that part of my life once and for all.

I stopped myself before I gave in to my foolish emotions that I always seemed to wear on my sleeves. For years I had felt I was either overly proving myself or giving myself away in the vain hope that someone would like me. As if the acceptance of other people were going to make all the difference.

Although I harbored no hate or ill feelings against Mother, breathing in the fumes from her lair, while surrounded by objects from our mutual past, made me feel nothing but pity for the person who was once my mommy.

Abruptly I stood up. "Thank you for allowing me to visit . . . Mrs. Pelzer."

Mother's facial expression changed, as if she were deeply saddened. "Come on now," she said, smiling, "for old times' sake, call me . . . call me Mom," she nearly pleaded.

I meant no disrespect, but I had to give myself some shield of protection. All I could do was extend my hand repeating, "Thank you, thank you for your time."

"Please?" Mother begged while she took my hand, but this time with a hint of *Mommy's* voice from years ago. I held my breath. I could feel the fingers from my left hand shake as I started to become light-headed. Part of me so desperately wanted to collapse in her arms, peer into her eyes, and hug her as if our lives depended on it. A moment later, although there was only an arm's length between us, I knew Mother and I were worlds apart.

With a slight nod of her head, she let go of my hand.

Mother understood. And yet I couldn't move. "If this means anything, the one thing I can give you is this: You," I said, pointing, with tears seeping from my eyes, "you made me strong. Because of . . . you made me want it more."

Mother cocked her head to the side. By her expression, I knew I had hit a raw nerve. Mother sucked in a deep breath, and I could feel the pressure build inside me. But a second later she let it pass. With the slightest nod, she understood my compliment.

As I walked down the stairs leading to the door, Mother burst out, "David!" With my hand on the doorknob I spun around. "Yes?"

"Do you love your son?" she asked.

Feeling choked up while a dam of pressure built up from behind my eyes, I stated, "Yes! With every fiber of my being!"

"Just remember," Mother cried, "at one time I did . . . I loved mine, too."

In the car I couldn't stop myself from shaking. A bone-chilling sensation crept up my spine. Once away from Mother's house, I pulled the car to the curb, opened the door, and threw up.

CHAPTER 11

A PERSONAL MATTER

Not a single day passed since my visit with Mother that I did not think about her. Whenever I found myself alone, my thoughts always turned to her. Usually I ended up wondering that if someone had stepped in early enough to actually dig at the root of the problem, then maybe things wouldn't have ended as they did. As Stephen grew from a toddler to a young boy before my eyes, I became haunted by Mother's condition. Part of me felt torn between the life I had with my son and the darkness of Mother's jail, as if someday, without warning, I could join her world. As if no matter what I did, no matter how hard I tried, I was destined to become like her. I felt in order to protect Stephen, I had to be a better person. I had to do more.

In a sense, Stephen was slowly becoming not only my outlet but my savior. When not at work, I'd squeeze in every minute I could to be with my son. Rushing home after a flight, I'd strip off my sticky flight suit, shower, then race outside to watch Stephen splash in his tiny play pool. When he wasn't playing in the water, he'd play baseball. Dressed in his brightly colored shorts, tank top, and no shoes, Stephen would clutch his oversized plastic red Bam Bam bat and cry out that it was time for "brasebrall." Since I had never played ball or any other games with my father, I was in complete awe of the smallest thing Stephen and I did together. Once, as the sun was setting, with Patsy across the street gabbing with her friends, I pitched a slow underhand ball to Stephen. He whacked the ball from the middle of our yard and across the street, zooming over Patsy's head and landing a few feet behind her. As Stephen ran in quasi circles, with his hand smacking the tree, the bumper of our car, or anything that he believed resembled a base, I hollered to tell Patsy of Stephen's accomplishment.

Since Patsy had seemingly missed Stephen's monster hit, I sprinted across the street to tell her and to pick up the ball. As I reached the sidewalk where Patsy stood, one of her friends, Debbie, grabbed her own toddler by the arm and yanked the girl toward her. "Put the ball down, it's not yours! You stupid little shit! You'd better listen up or I'll whack ya till ya do!"

Bending down, I thanked the little girl, Katie, as she dropped the ball into my hand. I could see her holding back tears. I stroked her head, turned up to Debbie, and said, "Katie's a real cutie!" Debbie gave me a hostile look before huffing at me, then at Patsy. Maintaining my stance, without pushing too far, all I could do was smile at Katie, stroll back to Stephen, and take him inside.

Later that night in bed, the incident with Katie continued to gnaw at me. For months I had heard Debbie lash out at Katie and then the sound of Katie's crying. At times when I played outside with Stephen, I'd catch glimpses of Debbie, between her chain-smoking puffs, screeching obscenities at Katie while the girl played. Reminding me of myself as a child, Katie always responded by slumping her shoulders. But whenever Stephen played with Katie, Debbie seemed overly kind. When I brought up the subject to Patsy, she agreed about Debbie's behavior, but brushed it off by saying, "Debbie's just a loud person." Since my upcoming deployment to Japan was only days away, I pleaded with Patsy to keep an eye out for Katie.

As much as my heart went out to little Katie, my mind was on my lengthy trip. As always, the evening prior to leaving, after packing, I sat down with Patsy to ensure all the bills were taken care of and she had enough money left over for anything extra. Saving the best for last, moments before heading out the door, I'd cradle Stephen in my arms while rocking him to sleep from the music of my stereo.

I didn't give Katie any thought until over six weeks later, when I flew back home from Japan. While scanning a newspaper I came across an article about a stepfather who had "accidentally" murdered a boy, then buried the body. Years later when the family moved, both the stepfather and his wife dug up the remains before placing the child in the trunk of the car. In court the man's defense was not only did he have a problem with drugs and his temper, but *he* was a victim of abuse at the hands of his father. I muttered out loud, "Can you believe this? This guy's getting ten years for offing his kid, which means he'll be out in . . . five, maybe six years for good behavior . . . 'cause he was abused? Man!"

Standing beside me, a senior officer from my squadron overheard my outburst. After striking up a conversation about the article, Major Wilson slid closer, telling me his wife volunteered with kids who had been abused and were now in foster care. "These kids come from scummy backgrounds. You wouldn't believe the stories my wife tells me. I gotta tell ya, it's heartbreaking. It's obvious you don't hail from that arena, but if you ever get a chance, maybe you could do something— talk to the kids, make 'em laugh, whatever. The smallest thing would mean the world to them." Patting my shoulder, Major Wilson added, "These kids, they have nothing. You, David, could make a difference."

Before Major Wilson had even finished, I had already made up my mind. In the last several months it seemed that every day I either read, watched on television, or saw firsthand from my neighbor something that related to child abuse, as if there were a sudden outbreak of children being brutalized. Since Stephen's birth I had become more sensitive and aware, but as Major Wilson spoke I realized the subject matter had always swirled around me, but I had conveniently shut my eyes. "Yeah, Major, I could do something," I said, committing myself. "I can imagine what it's like . . . for them." Besides, I said to myself, "it's time. It's about time."

Within a period of a few months, before Stephen's third birthday, I found myself volunteering for practically anything throughout the state of California that had to do with kids who came from troubled backgrounds. I began by speaking to older teenagers in foster care about not becoming swallowed up by their negative past, while praising them for overcoming their situations by their own determination. "And if you can do that as a kid, without any help, without a college degree, without any training, coaching, or guidance," I'd ask them, "what on earth could you now, as a *young adult,* not possibly achieve?" A few times a tough-acting teen would interrupt, asking, "Hey, man, what do you know? You ain't one of us. Man, you's a fly boy, what do you know?" I stopped for a moment to formulate my reply. "All right, I have no right to tell you what to do. I may not know exactly what every one of you has gone through, but I do know what's it's like to walk a few miles in your shoes." So in order to qualify my message, I felt I had to reveal parts of my childhood. I felt I owed them that much. And whenever I gave an illustration, I always told the audience what I had learned from the situation that somehow made me a stronger, better person. I had no need for bells and whistles or any other hype. I always spoke from my heart, treating every group like young adults instead of children. I always gave them total respect while challenging them to better themselves. My premise was never one of being a victim or exposing a dark secret for sympathy, but one of resilience.

Drawing further from my past, as I began working with adults who specialized with youth at risk, I offered reasons why some children who come from dysfunctional backgrounds react as they do and possible ideas to turn troubled kids around. To my horror, I discovered workers in these organizations rarely received any commendation, so as a matter of honor and respect, I would praise the individuals who struggled to make a difference with children.

Before I could give the matter much thought, I was overcoming one of my greatest anxieties. I was learning to talk to anyone, at any time, at any level. I became so consumed with my efforts that I conquered an enormous burden that had plagued me since I was a preschooler. But it didn't happen overnight. Before a presentation, alone in the car, I'd talk out loud, at various levels, paces, and tones to the point at times my voice almost gave out. At home, after tucking Stephen into bed, I'd sneak into the bathroom, close the door so not to disturb Patsy's sleep, and stand in front of the mirror for hours at a time, watching how my lips parted when I'd try to pronounce certain words. At work, I'd crack open my flight manual to learn long-syllable words; I also developed a technique to instantly replace a word if I became nervous and could not pronounce it correctly. Sometimes moments before a program, I'd become extremely nervous to the point of excusing myself and rushing to the bathroom to throw up. I quickly learned not to eat anything prior to speaking. Between my flight schedule and my present quest, I'd sometimes go without food for days. At times I'd still stutter, but somehow I'd find a calmness, tap into the audience, and let things happen. When the subject matter became too serious, I'd fire off comical impersonations, one after another, while maintaining my focus of driving my message home.

The more these individuals thanked me for my efforts, the more I'd open up and reach out with everything I had. I began to see my place in the world and the difference I could make to ease a bit of suffering, rather than turning my back as I had with little Katie. For years, in the back of my mind, I had always hoped something or someone else would fix the problem of not only children being brutalized, but the scores of individuals who blamed their current predicament on their past. As my father had years ago, I, too, had fantasized that if I swept the situation under the rug it would magically disappear. Now, as a parent, my conscience could no longer let me turn away.

My travels escalated to the point where after a night flight, I'd hop in my car at one in the morning, drive six hours without a break, to arrive just in time to spend the day at a teen conference. Other times I'd take leave to journey to the southern part of the state to speak to college students studying the psychological effects of abuse. I always relied on my own means. Whenever I was offered money for lodging or even gas, I'd refuse, asking instead that the sums be funneled back into the organization. As much as I felt the pinch, I believed it was wrong to accept payment. For me, changing a person's attitude for the better was payment enough.

As my activities increased, the problems of my childhood being exposed to the air force was becoming a reality. If discovered, I felt, I would lose my clearance. Whenever the squadron received a letter from one of the agencies I'd worked for, I'd casually reply that I was simply helping out. Even when I received an award from the governor's wife, Patsy accepted on my behalf and I never told my squadron. The extensive traveling and flurry of kudos from across the state were beginning to take their toll. I felt caught between two worlds. If I was to continue, I had to come up with a different tactic that would keep me local as well as provide a lower profile.

After assisting as a volunteer youth service worker, I was hired part-time in juvenile hall. I jumped at the opportunity to work directly with teens, who, like me at their age, were skating past the edge. Patsy liked my job because it kept me from constantly going all over the state, and working at juvenile hall added to our income. Patsy had been cross when I recently donated my award money to a local organization. "Do you know how much money that is?" she asked.

"It doesn't matter," I had pleaded at the time. "It's the right thing to do. Besides, we're doing fine."

"Oh, really? You may live in a high-horse morality world, but I live in a real one!" Patsy vented. As taken aback as I was,

Patsy was right. Even though I had checked with her every step of the way, I had in fact spent family funds for my cause. Over the course of a year, besides all the traveling expenses, I had sponsored a child abuse–awareness contest, providing scores of prizes and certificates for all the kids who entered. During Christmas I ran around town, collecting mounds of candy, hundreds of comics, and even a big Christmas tree for the kids at juvenile hall. Since I knew what it was like for some of them, I wanted to brighten their world if only for a day.

As upset as Patsy was, I knew she had a soft heart. When I ran out of Christmas stockings for the kids in juvenile hall, Patsy not only sewed makeshift stockings out of cloth by hand, but spent an entire day making cookies for the kids and staff. I was fully aware of other influences on her. She hung out with other wives from the block who seemed to complain about everything in their lives and how the air force somehow owed them for all their sacrifices. Caught up in the tide, more than once Patsy had brought up the subject when she was upset. Part of me understood her frustration of being alone while I was away, but she, unlike some of her friends, had family only minutes away, as well as everything she could desire. Once, when I thought she went too far, I adamantly stated, "Okay, it's not a mansion, but we live in a beautiful home, rent free. The only bills we have are car, gas, insurance, and food. Period. You don't work; you have a beautiful baby. So tell me; how bad can it be?"

"You don't know what it's like. Sometimes I just go crazy," Patsy fired back. "You're . . . you're always out there flying or doing God knows what. I support you in your little promotional things . . . helping the kids, making them laugh, or whatever . . . but I thought it would be different. I just . . . I just want something more, that's all."

At the time I simply thought Patsy was bored. Her moods seemed to change on a daily basis, and I didn't consider she was giving me a vital message. Wanting to get away, Patsy joined me during one of my long drives to the southern part of the state for another series of volunteer presentations to college students. In my heart I believed our time together—without interruptions from the air force, juvenile hall, the scores of agencies I worked for, or from Patsy's family tearing at her—would give us time to sort through some issues that were simmering below the surface. A part of me also wanted to peel away some of the layers of my past so I could finally be honest and open to Patsy. Maybe, I thought, hiding my past was interfering with my being able to trust Patsy. Due to our leaving at three in the morning, Patsy slept until we arrived at our destination. Moments before I left the motel to go to the campus, Patsy suddenly became ill and remained behind. But by the time I returned that night, Patsy had recovered and was now ready to paint the town. Because of the lengthy drive, the exhausting day, and the prospect of a long drive back home in order to mission-plan a flight with the air force, I was a walking zombie. As much as I wanted some time off to be with Patsy, once again I knew I had disappointed her by declining a night out. Bit by bit, without meaning to, I was adding to our strained marriage.

Still fuming on the drive back to Beale Air Force Base, Patsy said, "I don't get it! Why do you do this? This running around with the kids at 'the hall,' the colleges, collecting toys.... Half the time I don't know where you are or what you're doing. I just don't understand. It's not like it's gonna change anything."

I sighed as I rubbed my eyes. I knew as exhausted as I was, I would most likely make the situation worse. "Have you ever seen something that was wrong and . . . wanted to . . . to do something, anything? You know, just lend a hand and help out? I mean, I'm not trying to save the world, but if I can just—"

"Just what?" Patsy interrupted. "Hello? Earth to David? It's not our deal. Besides, don't you know that you're being laughed at? Come on, all anybody has to do is pick up the phone and tell you some sob story and boom: you're off saving the world. The least you can do is get something out of it. I know for a fact you've been offered some money."

My hands tightened on the steering wheel. "Really?" I asked. "Who's laughing?"

"Well," Patsy said, "my mom, for one thing—"

"Your mom," I retorted, as if she were a factor.

Losing steam, Patsy muttered, "And there's more . . . uhm, everyone on the block thinks you're stupid. Come on, who else would be stupid enough to drive off in the middle of the night and lose sleep just to talk to some college dweebs, knowing full well whatever you say to them, they can get from a book, huh? They're laughing, David. They're all laughing at you."

With sarcasm I said, "Is that so? Did *they* laugh when you met the governor's wife for the ceremony?"

She shot back, "Well, if you must know, it wasn't all that. In fact, at lunch the chicken was cold. All your work for what—a cold piece of chicken and some idiotic award? Like I said, someone gives you a call and you come runnin'. You may say it, but you don't owe anybody a damn thing. And if you do, it's me! You keep this up, and the day will come that you'll have to decide between what you're doing and me. The air force stuff I can take, but this 'we are the children' 'save the planet' thing is getting a bit too much."

"But," I defended myself, "what if I'm on to something? I don't know what it is, but I truly believe in what I'm doing. Maybe these late-night drives don't add up to a hill of beans, but in my heart if I can go to bed knowing I took a chance and gave it my best, that's good enough for me. That's why I push myself. When I commit, I give it my all. I can't explain it right now, but I feel I have this gift. I feel I'm making a difference. You gotta trust me on this, Patsy, for our sake, for the sake of Stephen. If we don't do something, who will? And if we don't step in now, then when? I'm just trying to make it a better place. You know what it's like. I'm just trying to make it better for you and for Stephen. I can't turn away. Please," I added, "you just gotta trust me."

"Making a difference? I don't see it," Patsy said with a snap of her fingers. "Besides, it's not like buying a kid a pair of shoes, giving them a video or a stupid Slurpie is gonna change anything," she finished with a roll of her eyes before nodding back off to sleep.

Patsy's reference to a Slurpie struck a chord in me. When I was a foster child, people like my social worker Ms. Gold had not only given me hope that I could make something of myself, but little things, like surprising me with an occasional Slurpie or Orange Julius. The sincerity of their gestures was something that I would never forget. And now seventeen years after others had made such an impact on my life, I reached out to lend a hand.

Yet with every program I did, every contest I promoted, donation I made or mile I logged in the wee hours of the night, I simply did what I believed was true and just. In the midst of my crusade I was becoming enveloped in a certain peace. Besides dedicating myself to being the best father I could, I had made a pact that I would do what I had to in order to ensure that no one became anything like my mother.

CHAPTER 12

THE LONG FAREWELL

In the summer of 1990, subtle changes began to take a toll on our marriage. As an air crew member it began in January with the retirement of the SR-71. After years of rumors of base closings and cutbacks in personnel, the Blackbird was deemed too expensive. The retirement festivities held an emotional significance for me. After years of studying and being part of the unique program, I had the chance to actually see my favorite plane up close. Dressed in my flight suit, with Stephen cradled in my arms, together for the first and only time we ran our hands lightly across the titanium skin of the spy plane.

Before the aircraft's last flight, as some personnel from the base worried about a new mission to fill the void left by the SR-71 Blackbird, a few members of my squadron, including myself, were tasked to mid-air refuel a new aircraft that was coming out from the highly shrouded world of "black operations"—the F-117 Stealth Fighter.

Working with the F-117 meant no more lengthy overseas deployments. After we had spent months apart for the last five years, my being home more seemed to amplify stresses between Patsy and me. Without meaning to, I drove her crazy. Patsy had always had the run of the house, and now I got in her way. Even after a few weeks of coming home from work every day, I still felt more like a guest. When I began to become frustrated over petty little things, Patsy bore it with the patience of a saint, but I could sense that the number of these situations, however insignificant, was forming a wedge between us.

But I knew my apprehension was due to matters of trust. After being together for nearly six years, I had grown to know by Patsy's sudden eruptions that something was brewing below the surface. During July 1990, two situations brought matters to a head. I discovered Patsy had a credit card under my name. After Patsy swore up and down that she had received the card out of the blue one day in the mail, she gave me the phone number to the company. As I dialed the number, Patsy snatched the receiver and slammed it back down. "I already called and talked to them . . . and they said it was okay if we're a little late."

I knew the only way to resolve this was to play out her game. When I probed for the person's name, Patsy could only come up with "Richard." She refused to give me a last name, position, or extension number. It seemed to be another obvious lie, but Patsy was steadfast to the point that even when I called in front of her, she acted as if everything was as she claimed. After explaining my situation to several people, finally I was able to speak to an account supervisor. He confirmed a signature on the card, and said no payments had been made since the card was activated months ago. Apologizing like a child, I informed the supervisor of what had actually happened and promised to make amends. I also begged him not to expose the issue to anyone outside his organization.

"Why?" I fumed as I hung up the phone. "You . . . you could have told me the truth. . . . You could have gotten a card under your own name. Why do you have to always drag me into your—?"

Patsy jumped in. "Duh! I can't get a card! You know that. I had credit problems."

I could not believe Patsy's gall. "That's not the point. The card, the spending, calling some guy from the card company whose name you can't remember, telling you it's okay for you to be late with a payment! With you it never ends. It's always something. I'm tired of being lied to. The games, the constant deceptions. You think, you really believe I'm that stupid? Feeding me a line that if you call some guy, from some company, it's gonna wave some magic wand over what you did and make things better? It's a matter of responsibility, and I'm tired of cleaning everything up!" I turned to leave the room, wondering if I was right to be accusing her. Had Patsy really deceived me or had I signed for a credit card long ago that I had forgotten about? Things were moving too fast for me to ever get to the bottom of it. I stopped as I approached the door. I spun back toward Patsy. "Do you know or even care that I have another security review coming up? If the air force finds out about this, they can pull me from—"

"From what?" Patsy lashed out. "I'm tired of air force this, air force that. You're so full of it! You ain't doin' nothin' and you know it. You never did. You ain't shit; you're enlisted. You just tried to make out that you're a part of something just to keep me in line, but I'm telling you this: I can do what I want when I want, and no one is going to tell me what to do!

"You wanna be truthful? You wanna talk about honesty? Come on, let's be honest! Tell me about you! Come on, I'm waiting, tell me!"

For almost a year as the SR-71 was being phased out, I had signed paperwork swearing to absolute secrecy about my involvement with the Stealth program, even though the aircraft had already been revealed to the public. Even after our squadron's involvement with the F-117 during its debut in Panama, as part of Operation Just Cause, we had been warned again of repercussions if anyone said anything, including being threatened with imprisonment.

To compound matters, I hadn't told Patsy about some of the organizations I was working for outside the air force. When I had tried to before, she was either too bored or simply wasn't interested. In my heart I had hoped Patsy would discover for herself the feeling of assisting others in need, and then, maybe, we could work as a couple, through issues that still seemed to tug at us both. But even after accepting the award from the state's first lady, Patsy still had not made the connection.

So, standing by the door with Patsy's face turning red, I knew if there was a hypocrite in the house it was me. Taking a deep breath, I meekly asked, "Talk to me, what's going on? Do you think we are having problems with money?"

"That's your problem," she said. "That's all you care about is money, money, money!"

"If there's anything you want, if it really means that much to you, I'll get it for you. You know that. It may take some time, but if there's something out there that would make you happy . . ." As I searched for the elusive answer, the more guilty I began to feel. Was I saying Patsy had to spend money in order to find happiness? If Patsy had everything she desired, that would somehow fill the void of whatever troubled her? I wondered if maybe Patsy spent so much in part because I did not provide for her emotional needs.

Suddenly, I felt I was being snowed. "Hold on! Wait up!" I said. "No, it's not about money—"

"Bullshit!" Patsy yelled. "Even your grandmother says so. Everybody knows that's all you care about. Money, money, money. That's all you're worried about. You need to chill out."

"You don't get it. It's like you don't want to understand. We have a son, we need to save for Stephen's college. We owe him that, and a home, a real home, that's ours. We're not going to be in the air force forever. You may not see it, but there's a lot of changes coming down the pike, and we're spending everything we have."

"Don't give me that 'poor house' attitude," Patsy said, shaking her head. "I know you always have some kind of secret stash. We'll be fine. You act as if the sky is always falling."

"Patsy," I said, "it's not about the money, it's about us! It's at the point you don't even care. I know you do, a lot, and I appreciate everything but . . . at times I feel like all I do is clean up after you. It's like you don't even think about the consequences of what you do. Do you really think I like battling you just to drag out a shred of information, just so I can fix something you did?

"Yeah," I went on, " I want a home! I want to save for our son's future! Does that really make me a bad guy? I've been working my tail off for what, since I was thirteen, and even before that as my mom's slave? A slave! And I'm tired of it. So, if having only one credit card and saving a few bucks makes me the bad guy . . . then I'm guilty. The bottom line is: I still have to fix your mess."

"Damn straight you will!" Patsy blared as she brushed past me. "Just fix it. Besides, what am I supposed to do? When you're home, you spend more time with Stephen than me."

"Hang on for a moment." I tried to stop her by grabbing her arm. But by the flash in her eyes, I knew I had pushed too far.

"Get your hand off of me, Mister Child Abuse Prevention Advocate." Dazed by her statement, I dropped my hand. "Got your attention, didn't I?" Patsy said. "Just fix it and get over it."

After Patsy stormed out of the house, I removed a piece of paper that I kept behind my checkbook. I scribbled the new bill next to the other bills that had mounted over the past several years. At least, I sighed to myself, I had my job at juvenile hall. It had started as a way to earn extra money, but had become necessary for survival. With my forehead resting on my hands, I began to shudder. All I could do was pray there weren't any more of my credit cards floating around.

It took me nearly a month to get over our latest crisis. As much as Patsy continued to say she was sorry, I brushed her off. After years of hearing the same thing over and over again, I had grown numb to anything that she did that was unrelated to Stephen. All I could do was pray every time I opened a piece of mail or answered the phone that I did not discover another catastrophe. My concern became more intense as rumors began to circulate that the air force might initiate cutbacks in my field. Fearful of the outside world and limited prospects, I worried about not being able to take care of my family.

Finally I got over my resentment. After dropping off Stephen at Dottie Mae's house for the weekend, I took Patsy out on a rare dinner date. As we ate, I held Patsy's hand and apologized for acting like a child. "I know it's not easy, and I don't wanna come off like some hard ass . . . but I just get scared. I know what it's like to go hungry, to be without, and I can't"—I stopped, shaking my head—"I won't allow that to happen to you and Stephen. I know you used some of that money to buy me some pants."

"You never do anything for yourself. I was gonna surprise you," Patsy said.

"Well," I laughed, "I was surprised. I also know by the credit card statement that you didn't buy a lot for yourself. I'm sorry. I feel like an ass that I can't do more for you. That's the reason why I work so hard. Someday, if we're lucky, we'll be able to do things. It's just, as of now, there's a lot of changes, and I don't know how it's gonna affect us. So, we gotta use our heads, watch our spending, and at the same time save for our future, our son's future. That's all."

"You just take everything so seriously," Patsy whispered with affection. "You worry too much. You need to pull back . . . just a bit."

"Yeah, I know. You're right," I confessed. "But let me say this: since the credit card thing, you've eased up. It's like you're a different person—the Patsy I knew when I first met you. That's why it tears me up. When you hang around those half-wit neighbors who bitch and moan, all they do is bring you down. You're better than that. Look at you: you don't need them messing with your head. You live a good life, and you're one hell of a mother." I paused, aching to say the one thing that would make Patsy believe in herself once and for all. "I just want you to be happy. With me, without me, it doesn't matter. You don't need Stephen, your family, those 'friends'—anybody to make you happy. All you need is this!" I said, pointing at Patsy's heart. "I know what a great person you are; all you have to do is make it happen."

With tears trickling down her cheeks, she nodded. "Thanks, David, for believing in me. Trust me, I won't let you down. Trust me."

The next evening after returning home, minutes before midnight due to working the swing shift at juvenile hall, I found the house completely dark and Patsy missing. After searching every room, I began to fear the worst. I phoned one of her friends, who answered with music exploding in the background. After I asked for Patsy more than a dozen times, an inebriated voice screamed back that she wasn't there, before dropping the phone. Covering all bases, I was about to telephone Dottie Mae when I heard Patsy fumbling at the back door. Rushing to meet her, I was knocked into the wall when she fell on top of me. " 'Unny, I'm 'ome," she slurred. "Like you said, gotta be me. But don't worry, *I'm happy.* This is me, and jou,"—Patsy jabbed her finger at my chest—"jou gotta love me for who I am. . . ." Suddenly her head rolled back. She opened her eyes wide a split second before she threw up on me.

Hours later, after stripping off Patsy's soiled and booze-soaked clothes, and assuring her she had nothing left in her to vomit, she allowed me to put her to bed. With Patsy taken care of, I cleaned the bathroom, threw our clothes in the washer, and showered off and got dressed to work the morning shift at juvenile hall.

As I drove from the air force base to the city of Marysville, I chuckled to myself. I knew Patsy had dropped by her friend's place and obviously had one too many. It wasn't her fault. She didn't mean to. Yet as the sun began to appear in my rearview mirror, a wave of rage engulfed me. The only reason I was killing myself was to pay her bills, and, to top it off, here I was trying to earn the trust and respect of these teenagers at "the hall" who had been through hell, so they could get on with their lives and be responsible rather than live their lives as helpless victims. All the while Patsy would spend the day in bed sleeping off another stupor. "Godammit!" I screamed, pounding the steering wheel. "How could I be so stupid?" Every single time I swallowed my pride, thinking I was too hard on her, and reached out with all my heart, something always happened. "Stupid, stupid, stupid! You're never gonna learn, Pelzer. She's never, ever going to fuckin' change, and you're an idiot for taking her shit!"

I fought to clear my head as I parked the Toyota at the juvenile hall parking lot. I didn't have time to think about Patsy, or analyze the situation I would face when I returned home, or even how exhausted I had now become. As I went up the walkway, all I knew was that it was the beginning of the end. Patsy would never again have my trust.

In August 1990, Saddam Hussein's invasion of Kuwait shifted my priorities. Whatever marital problems I was facing paled beside the prospect of fighting an actual war. For over a week every air crew at the base loaded jets with every conceivable piece of support equipment. We received countless briefings, varying from chemical warfare defense to our task of refueling the Stealth fighters. Knowing full well that the KC-135 aircraft had no defensive capabilities and since the Boeing jet was a "force multiplier"—meaning the various fighter aircraft could not fly to their targets without our plane's fuel—the Boeing tanker had the makings of a prime target. And because it was a flying gas station in the sky, if we took a single hit from enemy aircraft, my crew and I would be vaporized from the explosion. As the days passed, and as the base waited for our orders to deploy, worrying about Patsy, the checkbook, or whatever credit cards she might have acquired was the last thing on my mind. I had to set aside my mixed emotions about my marriage and focus on doing my part and coming home alive.

After endless delays and a series of last-minute standdowns, I received official notification that our squadron would deploy the next morning at three o'clock. I spent the night before with Patsy ensuring that she had everything she might possibly desire while I was away and knew what to do "just in case." I knew Patsy would be fine.

But my heart went out for Stephen. As I lay beside him on his bed, he clutched his red Sony Jr. Walkman I had just given him that day. Before drifting off to sleep, he whispered, "Daddy, where you gotta go?"

"I just have to fly off for a while," I softly said into his ear.

"You gonna bring me back something?"

"Yeah, but only if you take care of your mom." I then caught myself repeating what my father had said to Ron, my oldest brother, years ago before he left for work. "You be the man of the house for me. Can you do that?"

Stephen rolled over and fell asleep on my chest. As I stroked his spiky blond hair and kissed his forehead, I declared to myself that everything was going to be fine. *They won't shoot us down, Stephen. If they do, we won't blow up. I'll use my parachute. Once on the ground, I'll evade. They'll never take me prisoner. If they do, I'll escape. If I can't escape, I'll be fine. I'll come back. No matter what happens, I'll come back. I'll come back for you!*

In the midst of all the apprehension and wild sense of adventure, I felt an overwhelming calmness as I held my son. In an odd sense, it was the same feeling I had experienced as a child when I was ordered to sit on top of my hands in Mother's basement. Summoning all my willpower, I would tell myself that no matter what happened between Mother and me, I would survive. She could beat me, or do as she pleased, but God willing, I would somehow prevail. Now as the night slowly passed, I readied myself for another test. Hours later, I deployed for Operation Desert Shield on Stephen's fourth birthday.

* * *

The first few weeks in Saudi Arabia were like constantly walking on eggs. We weren't sure what to expect and when or if we were going to do anything. Whenever I spoke to Patsy on the phone, she seemed distraught, as if I somehow knew when I would be coming home.

By mid-January 1991, as the air force generals briefed us on the probable losses during the initial phase of the air campaign, the possibility of losing every third person opened my eyes. This was no longer a test of adulthood. My main concern was not to screw up on my part of the mission. As it turned out, though, after the first couple of weeks, the coalition maintained air superiority over Iraq, and the missions became routine.

Because we reported for a night flight in the afternoon and returned in the early morning hours, I found it nearly impossible to get any sleep. As I lay on my army cot, my thoughts always turned to Stephen. I became paranoid over things beyond my control. *What if he choked on food when Patsy wasn't looking? Or if he didn't look both ways before crossing the street and got hit by a car? What would I do?* At times I was so consumed by nightmares, I'd awake with my body soaked with sweat. Finally one evening after another anxiety attack, I strolled outside to marvel at the stars. In the stillness of the night, in the middle of the war, as a cool breeze blew from the desert, I somehow found serenity. What I still needed to understand was that there were so many things beyond my control. I needed to let go. After that morning, and on others to follow, I never slept as soundly as I did when I served in the gulf war.

I returned from Saudi Arabia in March 1991. I stepped off the plane, Patsy ran up to meet me. In the middle of a swirling rain shower, I held her like never before. "It's okay," I said. Patsy gave me a puzzled look. "Everything's gonna be fine. I am so sorry; I truly am, for everything. All the petty bullshit

I've put you through. Worrying about things that don't mean a hill of beans. No matter what happens, I know we're gonna be all right." I then sprinted and scooped up Stephen, who was wearing his little brown flight jacket. I crushed him to me until he cried out that he couldn't breathe. As my family and I walked through the sea of people waving flags and cheering, a surge of pride swelled within me. Not only had everyone from the base returned alive, without a scratch, I had everything anyone could ask for. I promised myself that I would do whatever it took to make things right between Patsy and me. After enduring all we had, I knew nothing could tear us apart.

After I came home, things that had seemed so critical months before were now insignificant. I continued to sleep soundly, and I no longer continually pushed myself to the limit as I had in the past. For a few weeks I felt like I was walking on a cloud. Patsy and I were closer than ever. And, for the first time, I could see changes in her attitude. She was upbeat and self-reliant; she faced her situations by herself, head on, without interference from her mother. One day while driving to nearby Sacramento, I reached over to take her hand. "I'm so proud of you, Patsy. I know it's not easy being married to me, putting up with all that you do, but you have really come a long way. You should be proud of yourself. You've made it, you truly have. No one can boss you around anymore, turn their nose down at you, 'cause you're better than that; you always have been. Maybe the war in the gulf was the best thing . . . for the both of us."

The euphoric honeymoon ended when I officially received transfer orders to Offutt Air Force Base in Nebraska. On a late evening in May, I was overwhelmed with sadness as I drove off from Beale Air Force Base—my home and surrogate family for over eight years. There were no good-bye parties or squadron ceremonies, since others, too, were quietly scattered to other bases. In the process of base closings and personal cutbacks, I was among the lucky ones. At least for now, I had a job.

A day later, while resting at Grandmother's home in Utah, I received a frantic call from Mother. Taking the phone, I wondered how she knew I was in the area, since I had no intention of visiting her. But as I listened to the sound of Mother's pleading voice, something in her tone compelled me to go see her. The next morning, after I became reaccustomed to the odor of her house, Mother and I initially chatted as we had before. Mother complained about her ailments, and this time I knew it was no longer a performance. I could not help but notice how her hands constantly shook. Even when she placed one hand on top of the other, she could not hide her tremors. Only after taking a gulp of what I guessed was vodka did Mother's shuddering ease. She went on to complain about how hard it was for her to walk and how at times she thought her feet would tear apart from the searing pain. After listening for more than an hour, I realized, even with Kevin still living with her, how desperately lonely Mother had become.

After a few moments of silence, I took a tremendous risk. "You know," I lightly said, "I'm involved . . . with helping kids and others who've . . . had problems."

"Yes," Mother replied with a nod. "Well . . . your grandmother . . . she ought to get a kick out of that."

We both suddenly broke out in a burst of laughter.

For a fleeting second the sound of Mother being happy brought me back in time. By her brightened eyes, she seemed to feel it as well. But I knew it was nothing more than a passing moment. I would never receive an acknowledgment of what had happened between us, let alone a sincere apology. And, after all I had been through, I felt I did need it. Yet the child within me felt a tremendous urge to wrap my mother in my arms and absorb every ounce of her anguish. In that moment I would have given my right arm to hear the sound of "Mommy's" laugh.

In my trance, my fingers grazed the edge of Mother's once

prized oak hutch. I caught my breath as my gaze became fix-ated on her assortment of towering red Christmas candles. I snapped my head around toward Mother. Then, looking back at the candles, I wiped off the accumulated dust from their bases. As long as I could remember, the one thing Mother had been adamant about was her treasured Christmas decorations. She always put up the decorations the day after Thanksgiving and put her ornaments away immediately after New Year's. *Why,* I asked myself—as I now discovered the sprayed-on snowflakes still in that window in the middle of May—*would Mother not tidy up the one element of her life that had meant so much to her?*

This went far beyond being lazy, I thought. If Mother hadn't taken care of Christmas decorations with summer ap-proaching, when would she? Unless . . . *Oh, my God!* I said to myself. *Mother knew . . . she somehow knew her time was limited.*

Her hands were again shaking, and by habit Mother cov-ered one with the other. But as her hands twitched with more intensity, she struggled to take another drink. Peering deep into her eyes, I stated, "Don't quit. Don't try to stop drinking."

Mother's face lit up. "You . . . *you understand?*"

I nodded. As I stood in front of Mother, my eyes scanned her every feature, in the vain hope of finding the person I had worshiped as a tiny child—the person I had so longed to love me. Yet, as I closed my eyes, I could not give Mother the hu-manity I gave to total strangers. With all the compassion I could muster, I swallowed hard before saying, "Go in peace."

As if she did not hear me, she lifted her head.

Feeling weak, I swallowed before repeating myself in a qua-vering tone. "I wish you no pain . . . Only for you to go—to go in peace."

"Yes, well, that's nice . . ." Mother said in her old conde-scending tone.

"No!" I lashed out, pointing my finger in her face. Raising my voice, I could feel my legs shudder. "Don't you even . . .

don't you spoil it. Not after all you've done. This is not one of
your little games that you can manipulate. You have . . . no
one, nothing left. Just stop it! For once put away your bullshit
and do what's right, for God's sake!" I pleaded, on the verge
of tears. "I swear to you, with all of my honor, I wish you no
pain, no suffering, I only wish you peace." I paused as my
chest seemed to heave. Calming myself, I said in a controlled
voice. "That's all I can . . . that's the best I can do."

Mother's eyes tried to bore right through me. After a few
moments, her intensity softened. I slowly shook my head
back and forth. Without saying the words, I mouthed, "I
can't. I can't do that."

With a nod Mother showed that she understood. Perhaps
she had thought that by calling me during her emotional
state, I would rush over and anoint her with forgiveness. To
my own dismay, and after a lifetime of constantly proving my
worthiness to others, I did not—I could not—forgive Mother.

As I walked down the stairs to the door Mother shouted
from her chair. "David?"

"Yes, Ma'am?"

"I want you to know . . ." She stopped as if to collect herself.
"I, uh, I'm proud of you. You turned out fine. I am proud of
you, David Pelzer."

I turned, looked up the staircase, and uttered a quick prayer
before closing the door behind me.

Mother died of a heart attack in her sleep in January 1992.

Twenty-four hours later, on Mulberry Street just outside Salt
Lake City, all five Pelzer brothers joined together. Initially it
was awkward for all of us, until Ron came up and hugged me.
There was so much to say, but we didn't seem to know how
to begin. Over a matter of days, as the five of us talked to each
other, I felt overtaken both by shame for what all of us had
experienced and pity for the life Mother had lived. We spent
nearly every waking moment covered with stench and grime

while we gutted out Mother's dilapidated house. Just before Mother's funeral, as we cleaned out her bedroom, one of us came across Mother's wedding portrait. I had seen the photo countless times, but for the first time I realized how stunning she was. Mother's face seemed silky smooth and her hair glistened, but what took me aback was her eyes. They seemed to radiate with pure joy. Mother's expression gave me the feeling that she was about to embark on an incredible life filled with happiness. With the frame shaking in my hand, I emptied my chest. I forgave her. I forgave "The Mother." Over the past several years, after I had visited Mother the summer of 1987, I had wavered on how I felt about her. When I had sat in front of mother just a few weeks before she died, I came within a heartbeat of stating my forgiveness. But because of giving myself away so many times, for so many years, only to appease others, in hope of their acceptance, I hesitated. Then, because of Stephen, part of me detested her. But, as I became involved with others who struggled, in part due to their past, I felt I had to rid myself of any feelings of resentment.

On a wintry, overcast day, only a handful of people came to Mother's funeral to pay their respects. A gentleman whom I later learned had met Mother a few times and worked part-time as a golf pro, gave Mother's eulogy. At Mother's gravesite, with scattered clumps of snow surrounding me, I knelt down and prayed. With my hands clasped, shivering from the chilling breeze, I prayed out loud for God to grant my mother peace. "May your soul finally be given eternal peace. And, may almighty God protect you and deliver you from evil . . . Amen."

As I finished, I could feel a gigantic weight lift from my soul.

Before I caught my departing flight, all five of us promised to stay in touch, but that was the last time the five Pelzer brothers would come together.

CHAPTER 13

THE LAST DANCE

I was not looking forward to returning to Nebraska. Once again, I discovered Patsy had borrowed money. This time she had begged Grandmother nearly a year ago, while I was flying in Saudi Arabia. I would have never known had I not asked Grandmother for a loan so I could use the money to give to my youngest brother, Kevin, who in his early twenties needed the money to find his own place to live. At first Grandmother was insistent that I had borrowed the money from her. When I assured her I knew nothing about the loan, she then became more livid because I *should* have known.

All the while Patsy fidgeted in her seat, claiming her innocence until she broke down in tears, saying she had forgotten to tell me and she was now too embarrassed to say anything in front of Grandmother. As I tried to stick up for my wife, Grandmother simply raised her head in a "I told you so" attitude, as if she enjoyed fueling the fire between Patsy and me. At the time I felt like a heel that my other brothers and I could do little to help Kevin, who eventually was able to provide for himself.

At my new air force base, even though I had been stationed there for over eight months, I was still adjusting. My job was completely different and absurd compared to Beale. I was now part of the EC-135 Looking Glass, whose mission had been to serve as an alternative airborne communication command post in the event of a nuclear war. But even though there was a refueling boom attached to the aircraft, the EC-135 rarely midair-refueled other planes. To confuse matters more, the Looking Glass was retired but continued to fly "unofficially."

During my in-processing I learned my biggest task as a boom operator was not learning to midair-refuel a different aircraft, but to ensure that the twenty plus members of the crew received their lunches.

On my first qualification flight, I found out how *serious* my job was when a low-ranking radio operator actually berated me in front of the entire crew because his lunch did not receive a mustard package. Upon landing I was immediately reprimanded by my superior, who rolled his eyes in mock dismay. Within days, because of my blunder, all boom operators were mandated to check every item on every meal prior to taking off.

At home, after settling into a nice condominium we could not afford, Patsy soon became bored. Because we lived off base, she felt even more isolated. When I first found out about my reassignment, I had prayed the move would somehow force us to rely on ourselves, as a couple, without "family" interference once and for all. During our drive to Nebraska. Patsy had even chatted about getting her GED and then taking courses in college. She had seemed so optimistic. But within weeks Patsy complained of missing her family in California.

I had assumed with the reduced flight times, due to budget cuts, I would be able to spend more time with my family, finish my college degree, and volunteer once in a while. But because of the ever changing flight schedule, I could not attend college or volunteer as I had in California, and I rarely saw Patsy or Stephen. To make matters worse, when I received my promotion to technical sergeant, I was assigned as the wing's senior in-flight evaluator, forcing me to work longer hours. At times I'd come home only long enough to throw a ball a few times with Stephen and give him a bath before reading to him in bed. At times I was so tired, I'd fall asleep with Stephen on his bed. As the months passed, I felt my job was completely worthless, and I began to detest myself as a father and a husband.

In the spring of 1992, rumors began to float of severe personnel cutbacks. I saw the writing on the wall. Since the Looking Glass was no longer an operational aircraft and boom operators were not allowed to perform their tasks, I believed I would be among the first to be relieved from active duty. I had always envisioned myself serving twenty years until I could retire, but now that was no longer an option. The air force was also offering early retirement bonuses but for a limited time, and after a certain cutoff, the air force claimed, they could legally dismiss anyone as they deemed necessary. Because of my years in service and my pay grade, I knew I was a prime candidate.

After months of speculating, I had a heart-to-heart with Patsy. So not to upset her, I had deliberately tried to keep her in the dark. "We've got to make a decision," I began. "Uhm, the air force, is going to announce—"

"Get out!" Patsy broke in. "Your job sucks, you're not happy. I'm miserable. I hate this place, there's nothing to do. Stephen needs . . . to be with his family. Let's take the money, bonus, separation thing, and go home before the air force gives you the boot and you have nothing to show for it."

"Okay." Patsy's outburst had stunned me. "How long . . . I mean, when did you know?"

Patsy raised her eyebrows. "I know a lot more than you think."

"Well, hang on, there's more. *If* we do this, you need to know, I mean fully understand what this means. It's a one-time payment; we won't have medical coverage—"

"How much?" Patsy quizzed.

"Well, if we don't have any unexpected bills," I said, "we should be able to put some money away for Stephen's college and, well, the rest we'll use to save up for a down payment on a home. But," I warned, "with me being the only one working—"

"I told you, I got a bad back," Patsy said defensively.

I waved her off. "I'm not saying that. But listen, I'll need to get at least a full-time job with lots of overtime, if not two jobs."

"So, they're not going to give you a lot of money?" Patsy asked, as if offended.

"The way I see it, the air force doesn't have to give me a thing."

"What will you do?"

"I've thought about this a great deal. I can't work full-time at juvenile hall; I need a degree, and aeronautics is not what they're looking for. If I'm lucky, I could work there part-time. Jobs right now are scarce with the recession and all, but . . . there is an option. . . ."

I spent the remainder of the time telling Patsy about a local speaker organization. "They've seen me speak a couple of times, and, well, Rich and Carl, the owners, think I have what it takes to become a speaker. It's not a bureau," I warned. "It's like having my own business. The firm, they provide the support staff. I can work out of California, and you know me, I'll work my tail off. In a couple of years, if we get lucky, maybe we can get a house and live on the river. Think of it, Patsy." I reached over to clasp her hand. "It's the best of both worlds. If I do this, I'll never be laid off. I can help kids, the people who work with kids, corporations, the works. I know I'll never be one of those motivational speakers you see on TV, and I don't want to be. I can't explain it, but I believe with all my heart I have a message that could really help a lot of people. We may not get rich, but who cares? Think about the impact we can make! And," I smiled, "they said they'll publish the book."

"*That* thing? You've been working on it for how long? Why is that so important to you?"

"*That book* is definitely going to change people's lives," I stated. *Besides,* I told myself, *it's a promise I made a long time ago.*

"Listen," I continued, "I know I'm hitting you with a lot. We still have some time. I don't want to jump into anything without both of our heads on straight. This is only the first of many steps we have to address. Either way, it's not gonna be overnight. I love the air force, it's been like a family for me . . . but I think my time has come.

"I'll promise you this. If I have to work a dozen jobs to pay the rent and put food on the table, I'll do it. I'll never put you or Stephen at risk. I promise."

Taking it all in, Patsy asked. "How much? With you speaking, how much can we make?"

"Well," I said, stumbling, "it's like being on commission. The more programs I do, the more I can make. But there are expenses; I'll be on the road a lot, and I'm going to have to fill the pipeline giving free programs. But, like I said, after a couple of years we should be able to make a living. I just wanna do a good job, that's all."

"One thing," Patsy asked, "what's the name of the book?"

"*A Child Called 'It.'* "

"*That's* a depressing title. It's about you, isn't it?"

Still trying to shield her, I shrugged my shoulders. "Let's just say it's a story about a kid who never quit." Looking at Patsy, I could tell I had lost her. I paused slightly before restating. "We don't need to decide now, but I just want to let you know—"

"Go for it!" Patsy grinned. "I say fuck 'em! Take the money and don't look back. We'll be fine. I know you'll take care of us. Let's do it! Get out!"

I received an honorable discharge from the air force that August. As much as I craved to live on the Russian River, we returned to the area where I had first met Patsy, outside

Marysville, so she could be close to her family. We enrolled
Stephen in a fantastic school and started anew.

In the fall of 1992, while doing a series of fact checks for *A
Child Called "It,"* I contacted my elementary school to discover that one of the teachers who had notified the authorities, Mr. Ziegler, was still teaching. He asked me to visit the
school. There was an odd note in my teacher's voice, as if
there was something he wanted to tell me.

One of the hardest things for me to confront, far more than
stepping into Mother's lair, was returning to my former
school. In the middle of October, on a beautiful, crisp morning, I stepped onto the school yard as if revisiting hallowed
ground. The first thing I recognized was the scent of food from
the cafeteria, where years ago I used to sneak in, run off with
a handful of hotdogs, only to gobble them down behind the
dumpster.

I met Mr. Ziegler as he accompanied his class into the library, where I gave my various presentations. Because we both
felt a little awkward, we gave each other a half-felt handshake
and a quick hello. As I spoke to his class, whenever I glanced
at Mr. Ziegler he seemed to avoid me by looking down and
away.

At the end of the day, as hundreds of kids scurried from the
school to play or run home, a young boy dressed in a worn-
out, oversized down jacket politely asked if he could talk to
me. In the heat of the afternoon sun, I noticed that the child
was nervously tugging on the ends of his jacket sleeves. After
calming the young boy down and assuring him everything
would be fine, I knelt down and held his hand. The boy suddenly exploded in a burst of tears, telling me how his uncle
would beat him and burn his arms with lit cigarettes. As his
little chest heaved, he sniffled. "I'm sorry, Mr. Pelzer, I don't
mean to take your time. I don't want to get anyone in trouble.
Please," he begged, "you can't tell. Please?"

I felt as if I had stepped into a time warp. I had met the
child I once was. "Listen," I said, still holding the boy's hand,

"you remember what I said about what happened to me when I was a kid?" The child nodded as he wiped away his tears. "Here's the deal. We need to get you some help. We're not here to get anyone in trouble, but that's no way to live. Am I right?" The boy again nodded. Thinking of my social worker Ms. Gold and what she had said to me when I had opened up to her about my secret, I relayed, "Listen, you're going to be fine. It takes a brave young man to tell a secret like you did, and it's the first step in making things better. You gotta be strong, but you gotta trust me." I stopped to look him in the eye. "You're going to be fine. I promise you"—with my finger I made an X sign on my chest—"cross my heart and hope to die, you have my word. You don't deserve to live like that, and we're going to turn things around."

I escorted the boy to the same room where I had waited before I was rescued nearly twenty years ago. After speaking to the school principal, Mr. Rizzo, I said good-bye to the young man, again assuring him that he was doing the right thing. I then stumbled toward the parking lot in a daze. As I watched a group of children in the playground, screeching with laughter—the same place I had once so desperately longed to be—I started hyperventilating. I couldn't stop myself. At last, with my hands on my knees, I recovered just before a group of children strolled past. I took a moment to pray for the young boy. I then thanked God for the strange twist of fate of having the privilege of returning to the school that meant so much to me, and how I had played a small part in helping a child in need.

Behind me the voice of my fifth-grade teacher startled me. "Just heard what you did. The kid's gonna be fine. You certainly have a way with them—the kids, I mean." Mr. Ziegler held out a hand. "Listen, I know you have a long drive ahead of you, but if you can spare the time . . . ?" A lump began to creep up my throat. All I could do was nod yes.

That evening, during supper in a local restaurant, both of us stumbled to keep the conversation going. I noticed that we made little to no eye contact. I was simply too ashamed. From across the table Mr. Ziegler turned away when I looked up from my food and spoke. Clearing his throat as he finished dinner, Mr. Ziegler said, "It's really good to see you. . . . It's been on my mind for a while, and I need to get this off my chest. I'm not sure if you even know, but . . . that day, when you came to my class, that day in March when you were taken away . . ."

I suddenly became paralyzed with fear. I had never known why my teachers finally intervened and called the police. I became so anxious that I thought my eyes would pop out of my head. With my left hand under the table, I squeezed my thigh. I almost raised my hand to stop Mr. Ziegler. I got as far as running my fingers through my hair.

"You . . . came to school that day . . . you were so small. But, uh—I just got to get this out—you came to school that day in March, with, uh . . . with no skin on your arms," Mr. Ziegler finished, then took a gulp of wine.

I dropped the fork that I was using. I sucked in a deep breath, staring at my right arm. "I, uh, I remember. I remember . . ." I felt almost in a trance-like state. "Yes, I remember, grayish flakes, dark grayish flakes, like patches, on my arms and . . . and my fingers. . . . Right?"

Looking as if he had seen a ghost himself, Mr. Ziegler stated, "Yes."

"I forgot—I mean, I never knew why. It's stupid, but I never thought it was anything she did different. . . . I mean, at times she, Mother, she was so careful . . ." I was sputtering as I struggled to find that one thing Mother had done to me that . . . "Holy shit! Excuse me." I shook my head. "That's it. The day—the morning you, all of you, called the police, I remember!" My eyes welled up. "I remember," I repeated, "my fingers and arms . . . they itched. I couldn't stop scratching . . . and uh, I didn't finish my chores on time. That Friday morning when you called the police . . . Mother had to drop me off at school that day. She never did before, but . . . I was so late,

late with my chores. Without skin . . . I couldn't grip anything
. . . I couldn't get them done on time. . . ."

I emptied my lungs in one deep breath. I could feel the tips
of my fingers beginning to twitch. "But . . . it was the afternoon, before Friday, she made me stick my arms in a bucket
that had . . . the mixture . . . ammonia and Chlorox. That's it.
That's what did it." I closed my eyes and shuddered from the
cold that crept up my spine. When I opened my eyes, I could
feel a small tear running down my cheek. "I'm sorry," I apologized to my teacher. "I, uh, always had to think ahead, I mean
to survive, to outsmart her, and I remember Mother tried, I
think, to force my head into the bucket, so, stupid me, all I
could do was . . . to think of . . . getting any air I could in case
. . . in case she put my head into the bucket." I stopped for a
moment. "I just forgot, the whole thing. My God. I remember
everything she did, every word she said, but, I just, I dunno.
For the life of me, I never knew what made all of you call the
police that morning. So much happened to me on a given
day . . ." I looked down at my hands, which were now shaking. "I know it sounds lame, but you . . . all of you . . . saved
my life."

"All we did was . . ." Mr. Ziegler said, downplaying the situation. "Anyway, anybody could see what she was doing. Back
then there was nothing we could have done, or were allowed
to do. Back then it was considered discipline, parental rights,
but we had to do something. Any one of us could see what
was going on. It's something you don't forget. Ever."

Afterward, in the parking lot we hugged each other good-
bye. "Thanks, Mr. Z."

"Call me Steven." He smiled.

"Thanks, but I can't," I said. "You mean that much to me.
You're my teacher."

Months later, the week of the twentieth anniversary of my
rescue, I returned to present Mr. Ziegler with the first signed

copy of *A Child Called "It."* The second signed copy I kept for my son, and the others were given to Mrs. Konstan, my fourth-grade teacher who still taught at the school, and Mrs. Woodworth, my English teacher who, because I had stuttered in class so badly, had encouraged me to communicate through writing. By dedicating and presenting the book to my saviors, I felt I was able to fulfill my vow of honoring them that I had made the day I was rescued.

Weeks following, I received a framed picture of my teachers taken the day of my visit. Engraved on the frame was WITH LOVE AND PRIDE. Like a child with a prized toy, I rushed to show Patsy, but she didn't seem too interested. For some time her patience with my new profession had been wearing thin. I tried to tell her, but I could not get her to understand how hard it was to start anew, especially since for years I had given programs for gratis, for organizations that had little to no funds. Somehow, it made it that much more difficult to make a living. To calm Patsy, I told her that because I had not received many bookings, the firm was kind enough to loan me advances. But in order to pay the rent and other bills, when not on the road I worked part-time at juvenile hall and took another job sanding kitchen door cabinets. It seemed no matter how hard I fought to convince Patsy, for some reason she thought I was going to be an overnight success.

I knew there was something wrong back in the Lincoln office. By now I should have received more bookings. But I felt too intimidated to say anything to the owners, Carl and Rich, especially since they were helping to feed my family. I hated myself for the position I was in. For the first time I was receiving money without earning it beforehand. Since my time in foster care, I always had pulled my own weight. For the most part I kept my apprehension to myself. A part of me felt I was being overly paranoid. I believed if I worked hard enough, somehow, someday, with a little luck, I would succeed.

My only concern was for Stephen. At times I would rush home after either flying, driving throughout the night, working at juvenile hall, or from putting in a full shift at the cabinet shop, to greet Patsy, jump in the shower, then race off to take Stephen to the latest Disney movie or spend the afternoon at the park playing baseball. Whenever Stephen came home from school, I always put aside my work so I could be with him; then later, after tucking him into bed, I'd return to complete my tasks. As much as I struggled to take care of my family, I didn't want to lose my son in the process.

For Patsy, the final straw came in July 1994. After waiting for me to break through, she had had enough. "It's been nearly two years," she said. "It shouldn't take this long. And you're still not making any—"

"I told you, it takes time."

"Two years, you promised. You said two years and you ain't made it yet. What about me? I had to wait around while you flew for the air force, and now, after two years, what do I have to show for it? We can't even afford to heat the house." Before I could defend myself, she went off in a different direction. "You're such a wimp. I know you're getting screwed from those—those speakers in Nebraska. They have no idea what the hell they're doing. They can't pitch you. For God's sake, they plug you as the child-abuse guy, and who wants to hear about that? Whatever happened to you giving those motivational-responsibility programs you gave before?" I shook my head, indicating I didn't have an answer. "You're so smart on some things but completely stupid on others. I don't trust them. Think about it: If you're such a *great speaker* and if your book is *so good,* tell me, how come you can't get any paid bookings?"

"Well, we got more than last year . . ."

"Oh, no, don't you even go there with that. Even after your little outstanding-American-person thing, you got nothing."

"Ten Outstanding Young Americans award," I proudly corrected.

"Excuse me! Whatever!" Patsy rolled her eyes. "If your re-
vered little award was all that, why didn't you get anything
out of it? It's been, what, a year and a half since you got that
thing, and I don't see anybody beating down your door. Huh,
come on, tell me."

If I had a lifetime, I could never explain to Patsy the mix
of unworthiness and absolute honor I had felt receiving the
recognition on the eve of the twentieth anniversary of my
rescue. The Ten Outstanding Young Americans trophy was the
same award presented to my childhood idols Chuck Yeager,
Orson Welles, the actor who played my all-time hero, Superman: Christopher Reeve, along with a league of others.

"Hello?" Patsy snapped her fingers, bringing me back to the
present. "The point is, you still didn't make it. You may have
been hot then, but you're nothing now. Those buttheads in
Lincoln should have handled you better. We could have been
rich!" Patsy cried. "After all you've done, after all these years,
you don't get it. It ain't happening! You ain't got it. You can act
all high and mighty saying whatever it is you say, but it don't
pay the rent. And," Patsy amplified, "if you want to know
something, I think you're full of shit. I read your book, if you
can call it that. They made it look more like a pamphlet, and,
it still didn't happen. Ain't no way no one could live through
all that. I should know. Think about it; if you were *that*
abused, if you didn't die . . . you'd be psycho, messed up on
drugs, an alcoholic, or whatever. I've been living in Marysville
and Yuba City all my life, and if what you claim is true, I know
the air force sure as hell wouldn't let you enlist, let alone be
involved with those jet planes. *If* you didn't lie about that,
too. No way!" Patsy shook her head. "No way! You're too
clean, everything's too perfect. What'd you do, pay off those
teachers so they could say you were abused? Oh, yeah, you
tried to hide it, but I found out. The only reason why you
wanted to hide your past from me is because it ain't true.
That's why you can't get paid bookings. That's why that piece
of shit book of yours ain't in any, I repeat, *any* bookstores. So

why you doing this? You wanna talk about trust? Come on, come clean, tell me, tell me the truth! After all the shit you put me through, I deserve to know!"

I had reached my boiling point. "You want to know what I do? Do you? Do you *really* want to know? I work with kids, begging them that no matter what happened to them, they can turn it around. At the 'hall' I restrain teenage girls who have so much meth in them, they want to kill themselves, 'cause they're tired of their fat, sick pimp stepdad hooking them out. Oh, it gets better! I have to stand in front of police officers and social workers, whose jobs are to find kids, babies, locked in cages, beaten to death, chained to toilets, and convince them to put on their jacket and tie, blouse and blazer, every single fuckin' day, and go out, eat shit, and see things that no one in our society wants to acknowledge. And these, these people are treated like the enemy!

"When I'm lucky enough to speak at the corporate gigs, I swear to you, I pray, I pray on my knees I don't speak too fast, come off the wall with my humor and give *them* something, just one thing they can use to better themselves. To tell them that if I can swallow ammonia and learn to speak after stuttering for years . . . if I could bandage myself up after being stabbed . . . if I didn't turn out, as you put it, *psycho* after all the shit I went through, what on God's green earth is stopping them? And you want to know the damned of it all? I pray to God that they—all those people—never see . . . how I feel on the inside. I can't even look into their eyes. Some of them think I'm all that, and I don't feel worthy enough to look them in the eye. Ever! I know I'm not smart. I know I ain't all that. I feel like such a fake. Even now, after all the awards, flying for the air force, getting a letter from the President, . . . I feel so guilty . . . and I rack my brain and I don't know why, after all of these years . . .

"I know I'll never be a motivational speaker—I'm not cool, smooth, I'm not polished—but I'm the real deal. I try. With every ounce, every breath, I try to give my best. That's why I land in Omaha, Nebraska, make the ten-hour drive to Bismarck, North Dakota, hit a deer that crashes through the windshield, so I can work all day and into the night, with a concussion, do a program for the kids in a youth jail, all the time hoping my insides don't bleed 'cause I swallowed shards of glass, just so I can save my client thirty-three dollars on the airfare! Why? 'Cause I feel guilty, that's why! You wanna know why I do this: reliving my past in front of my eyes *every single day?*" I fumed. "I work so you don't have to. I get up from fleabag motels with no hot water to shower with, praying my underwear I just washed in the sink three hours ago before I went to bed is dry, so I have a chance of giving my son a better life! I eat shit every single day, praying I can plant a seed—just one, that's all. I know I'm a joke, but I give it my all. I just want people to feel good about themselves. That's it. I know what it's like to be less than zero, and I want everyone I meet to feel they're the one. The one person who can go out there and make it better. And sometimes in the midst of all this crap, I can make 'em laugh. I have a gift, and if I can use it to better people's lives so they won't have to go through the hell my brothers and I went through, well . . . I'll do what I have to do," I concluded.

Not even a heartbeat later Patsy retorted, "It doesn't change the fact. You . . . you had your chance. You can pass off that Mister 'high and mighty, holier-than-thou, give my word' shit to others, but *you're a liar.* No matter how you slice it, you promised two years. I'm getting tired of waiting. What about me? I'm tired of waiting for something better to come along. Don't *you* get it? You're a loser! You ain't ever gonna make it. You're a loser with a big L," Patsy said, making an L sign with her hand. "That's it. I've waited and I've had enough. So here it is: Do you love me?"

Still angry, I hesitated to clear my head. After a few seconds I slowly nodded.

"No," Patsy insisted, "I want to hear it. After all the shit

you've put me through, I deserve to hear the words. Say it!"
she demanded.

Again, I exhaled before nodding. "I . . . I . . . love you."

Cocking her head to one side. Patsy sneered. "Well, then,
do you trust me?"

Without a moment's hesitation, I replied, "No!"

After years of hiding it, gently treading around the smallest
detail that might explode in my face at any second since I had
known her, I said it. I finally spoke the truth that had weighed
so heavily on my heart since I first knew Patsy. As much as I
was astounded by my revelation right in front of her, I felt
cleansed even more.

Patsy was paralyzed. As I waited for her to slap me across
the face, she continued to stare at me. "I'm sorry," I stuttered,
"I love you . . . and I always will . . . I'm sorry, but . . . I just
don't . . ."

"Well, if that don't . . . I can't believe it! After all I've put
up with. The sacrifices I've made. That's it! I've had enough. I
can't live with anyone who . . . You broke your word!" she
exclaimed. "Two years! You said two years. Trust? I don't trust
you. And I will not live with any man I can't trust. That's it!"
Patsy shrieked, "I want a divorce!"

CHAPTER 14

RESOLVE

After eight years of marriage, Patsy and I separated late July 1994. We sat down with Stephen to tell him the news. Even though he seemed to take it in stride, my heart went out to him. Above everything, I never wanted Stephen to experience the loss and suffering that I had felt when my parents split up. Since the day I was married, I had fought so hard to protect my son from every conceivable source of harm, and now I had failed at the most basic element of my role as a father—keeping my family together.

After several private conversations with Stephen, I realized he seemed more comfortable about the separation than I was. I promised him that no matter what happened between his mother and me, our devotion for him would never change.

It took a broken marriage and nearly thirty years for me to fulfill my childhood dream of living on the Russian River. Even though Patsy hinted that our current state of separation might be temporary, I couldn't bring myself to tell her that once I moved out, there was no turning back for me.

Because I was on the road, working when Patsy and I had decided our fate, she surprised me by taking the time to find me a one-bedroom summer home near the Russian River. The day I moved to Guerneville, Patsy graciously drove the U-Haul truck over one hundred eighty miles to my new home. Later that day, as we hugged good-bye and wiped away our tears, I thought we both felt the frustration and anxiety that had built up over the years begin to fade.

Due to the small size of the house and only a desk, bookshelf, and bureau for furniture, it took me less than two days to arrange my new home. Soon Stephen came to stay with me for two weeks. We were inseparable, spending our time stacking wood, fishing at the river, playing catch in the middle of the quiet street, or at nighttime, after we barbecued hot dogs, I'd hold him in my lap as we gazed up at the stars. When Patsy picked Stephen up, the magnitude of our separation exploded like a bomb in the pit of my stomach. As Patsy and Stephen drove off, part of me ached to race down the street, tear open the car door, clutch Stephen in my arms, and plead with Patsy that every problem we had could be worked out. But I could not, and would not, move a muscle to chase after them. All I did was try to capture the slightest trace of sound from Patsy's car, long after it disappeared from sight.

I stood in the middle of the street for what seemed like hours. After I began to tremble, I returned home, closed the door behind me, and cried for days. For nearly a week I shut myself completely off from the outside world. My days consisted of waking up at four or five in the morning, so I could scour every inch of every object within my surroundings. Every day, after more than nine hours of cleaning the house, I'd remove, wash, and restack the virtually empty refrigerator shelves; then on my hands and knees I'd scrub the baseboards until the paint nearly rubbed off. I thought if everything around me was perfectly immaculate, somehow my life, too, would be in order. I wouldn't stop until late into the evening and only after I'd scrub the telephone. With my body layered with sweat. I'd collapse in my chair with the sanitized telephone glued to my hand, as if I phoned Patsy she'd somehow take me back. Many times I dialed her number, but I always hung up before the number could ring through.

If I felt good about myself and felt I deserved it, late at night after a long shower I'd open the door to stand on the deck for

a few minutes and search for the group of stars Stephen and I
had found together. Sometimes as I listened as the tops of the
redwoods swayed, I'd catch a whiff of someone's fireplace or
the sweet scent from the trees before passing out on my leaky
air mattress. On a good day that was enough to get me
through.

After a week of solitude, I called the Lincoln office in the
vain hope that I had some upcoming work so I could somehow get away from my life. With each call my manager, Jerry,
assured me he was only days away from being flooded with
work. All I could do was thank him for believing in me and
pray for a breakthrough.

Then in the afternoon I'd sit and wait for Stephen to return
from school so I could call him and talk about his day. I
thanked God that with each conversation, he seemed upbeat
and happy. As Patsy had promised, she kept Stephen busy,
while letting me see or talk to him at any time.

Every time I hung up the phone with him, I could not help
but feel like a traitor—that somehow I had abandoned my
son. Even though my home was plastered with photos of Stephen and reams of his artwork from school covered the refrigerator and every inch of the kitchen cabinets, I still felt I had
deserted him. My guilt consumed me to the point that several
times when I dared myself to see a movie, I'd instead return
home, as if I could not allow myself to escape my reality for
just a few hours. Somehow I thought the pleasure of seeing a
movie took something away from Stephen.

My saving grace was the Rio Villa Resort in nearby Monte
Rio. For years after getting out of the service, Patsy, Stephen,
and I had been guests there, and I became close friends with
the owners, Ric and Don. Since my first visit, Ric and Don
knew of my passion of wanting to live on the Russian River.
And now, rather than keeping myself in a self-imposed exile,
they were kind enough to allow me to work on their grounds.
Whenever Stephen was not with me, I now felt some form of
purpose. After completing whatever assignment I had with

the speaking firm, I'd throw on a set of work clothes and race over to the Rio Villa, where I'd pull weeds, trim the rosebushes, or spend hours watering the grass in the late afternoon sun. Slowly, with the passing of summer, I began to feel a sense of worth and accomplishment.

But my shame never escaped me. Since my separation, whenever I spoke at a program and gave suggestions about facing issues and overcoming adversity, I felt like a hypocrite. The only time I felt halfway decent about myself was when I made the audience laugh. In humor I could forget about my pitiful life.

But when alone, even right after speaking, from deep within I felt as I had as a child—no matter how hard I worked, no matter how much effort I applied, I would never be good enough. I couldn't make my marriage work. I threw away a career with the air force so I could chase my tail trying to prove myself as a speaker, just to end up being labeled as a victim of abuse rather than a person with an inspirational message. And I had hurt the one true love of my life: Stephen. No matter what the future had in store for me, I could only pray my inadequacies would not come back to haunt my son.

As the days passed, some were better than others. On rare nights, I'd be able to sleep for more than three hours at a time. I'd ration myself with a yogurt in the morning and a Cup-O-Soup with a piece of French bread in the evening for dinner—so I could save money for whenever I was with Stephen—and for the most part I was beginning to keep my food down. Although I had lost a great deal of weight, I kept telling myself things were getting better. Besides being with my son, I was prepared to live my life alone. The last thing I wanted was to screw up another person's life, as I had with Patsy and Stephen.

During the late fall of that year, while on the road, I checked in with Jerry. He told me that the International Junior Chamber of Commerce had selected me as one of the Ten Outstanding Young Persons of the World. Before I could relish the moment, Jerry dropped his voice to a whisper and informed me the firm was in serious trouble. Immediately I thought about the advances the firm had initially provided me, that by now I should have paid back in full. But for some time now, whenever I had checked with Jerry on my accounting or other matters involving specifics, he would become frustrated and at times fiercely upset. Just being out of the military and because I was still adapting to dealing with the civilian world, and due to Jerry's position as the former vice president of the company, I always felt I was pushing too hard. All I could do was remain patient. But after months of promises, I still could not get answers to my questions, and whenever I'd probe, I felt belittled and I'd back down. As I had with Patsy before our separation, to spare myself any headaches I'd simply go along with things to avoid any confrontations. Before hanging up the phone, Jerry repeated his assurance for me not to worry and that he'd continue to stick his neck out for me.

Later that day, after I spoke to Stephen about his day, I told Patsy of the good news. Lately on the phone and whenever I had seen her in person, she seemed like a new woman. She was holding down a job she loved and raved about things she wanted to accomplish. Her attitude was one of confidence and independence. Even though I knew she was seeing someone else, I never let on. After the years of being with me, I simply desired that Patsy be happy. I felt I had dragged her down all those years. Before I flew to Japan to accept the TOYP award, Patsy was kind enough to write, thanking me for all that I had done for her and restating her newfound happiness. Patsy had moved on with her life.

I was on the road for over a week before arriving in Kobe, Japan, staying for just over twenty-four hours, then making several flights back and landing in Nebraska to drive several hours and speak at a school. Jerry had been insistent about my returning to Lincoln Saturday afternoon so that he could finally answer the concerns I had face to face. When I showed up at the high school, though, the principal was reluctant to have me speak to her students—I looked like I would faint from exhaustion. The principal also stated that she knew of my recent return from Japan, and she had told Jerry to have me come back to her school at another time. Jerry had joked with the principal, stating, "Don't worry about David; he won't mind." The stress, multiple time-zone changes, and lack of sleep had caught up with me. Assuring the principal that I wouldn't let her down, I stayed the entire day with the students and later made the four-hour drive back to Lincoln. After falling asleep behind the wheel and nearly crashing the car, I pulled over at a rest stop to catch a nap. Late that Friday evening I finally checked into a hotel, collapsing on top of the bed with my clothes still on. Before passing out, I felt a sense of pride—as tired as I was, I gave it my best and hopefully made an impact. Thinking about the day to come, I felt everything would fall into place.

Early the next morning, Carl, the senior partner of the firm, woke me with a phone call, asking me to come over to the office right away. I thought the reason was some surprise party for the award I had just received. The entire staff knew how hard I had worked to prove my worthiness, and since my separation they had gone out of their way to show me kindness.

With my award clutched in my hand, I nearly dropped it when I saw the look on everyone's face. I thought someone had died. Sitting down, I swallowed hard as I was told that Jerry had stolen funds from the organization. As I was presented with reams of paperwork and canceled checks made out to himself, everything suddenly made sense.

I didn't want anyone to think I had violated their trust, so I confessed to the group the advances that Jerry had instructed me to keep to myself, and that I felt Jerry was deliberately isolating me from the staff. When they looked at each other, then back at me, I thought I was doomed. The last thing I wanted was for anyone to think I, too, had cheated on them. With the award on the table in full view, I felt like a heel. I should have come forward months ago when I felt something was wrong. But when Rich, the co-founder, told me that the advances were not only legitimate but paid in full, only then did I feel a sense of relief. "Besides," Rich said to me later in private, "you're too Jimmy Olsen. Oh, yeah, by the way, congrats on the award."

I alone had to address Jerry. As much as I hated to, I phoned Jerry, and for the first time as a businessman, I showed a little backbone when he made excuses. Jerry tried to blame it on the firm, and told me to trust him, but I didn't want to get into finger pointing or blaming. Without disrespect or emotion, I simply stated, "I can never see you or talk to you again. Ever."

Days later, upon returning to Guerneville, I hated everything about myself. I felt like a joke. Because my place was a summer home, it had no insulation or heating unit except for an ancient wood stove, and the temperature inside the house was literally just above freezing. From the constant traveling and other roller-coaster–like events, I was emotionally drained. With a clean cloth I wiped off the statuette made of a pair of golden hands that held a silver globe, with my name engraved on the wooden base. In a flash of rage I almost threw the award—which I had received days ago in front of thousands of delegates throughout the world who showered me with praise I felt I did not deserve—into the fireplace. I shook my head with disgust. Here I was, an Outstanding Young Person of the World, separated from my wife and son because I had chased a dream, only to have my trust violated again, and if I didn't freeze to death due to my firewood being soaked from the rain, I could celebrate with a Cup-O-Soup for dinner. After pumping air back into my leaky air mattress, I covered myself with layers of worn-out sleeping bags. If I was lucky I'd fall asleep before hunger took over, so I could save my dinner for another time.

When I awoke the next day, I walked for miles in a cold drizzle. I reflected on the last few years and how within a short amount of time I had tossed away my air force career and my marriage. Patsy was right: she had given me two years and the results were I was now living like an Eskimo. By taking a chance and blindly charging ahead, I had put at risk all that I held sacred. As much as I thought my message was helping others, the personal results were obvious.

It was Patsy who had the guts to call it quits. I never had the nerve to walk away, and I felt she had worked on our relationship far more than I had. In the final analysis, we were simply two different people. Maybe in my desire to protect Patsy, I had unintentionally smothered her until my pettiness drove her away.

I didn't deserve to be with Patsy, or anyone else. But as much as I still cared for her, I could never trust her or, because of Jerry, anyone else. Maybe my ice-cold environment was the perfect penance for my stupidity. One thing I knew: I was meant to be alone. Because of the tangled feelings of unworthiness and self-preservation, I could never allow anyone, besides my son, into my hardened heart.

Within months, I rid myself of my self-pity, took stock in myself, and said good-bye to the Lincoln firm. I had heard Jerry and the firm had settled their issues, and I wished them the best of luck. I decided to run my own business. This way I could be independent and in control of my own destiny. If I was going to fall on my face, I wanted it to be from my doing. And for me, the bonus of being self-employed was seeing Stephen. Since he lived nearly two hundred miles away, I could take time off that I normally could not in a regular job. I could make the three-hour drive to watch him play a late-night game of baseball, spend long weekends with him, or schedule my work around his time off from school. With each day, as scared as I was, the long hours were good therapy. Because Jerry had rarely returned clients' calls who were interested in my programs, I now found myself with just enough work to survive. I knew things would work out, especially by the time I had saved enough money to purchase a cheap pedestal bed and a heating blanket. With each day I began to feel better about myself. But there was still one issue that needed closure.

One morning after returning home from church, I prayed for guidance before calling Patsy. We met hours later. After being separated for over a year, I owed it to her to get everything off my chest. Patsy arrived wearing a nice outfit and had obviously spent extra time making up her face and hair. Her appearance reminded me of the Patsy I had known when we had first met. I exhaled deeply as I began to speak, but when I opened my mouth nothing came out. After several attempts I finally blurted, "I want you to know . . . how sorry I am." Patsy's eyes lit up. "I was wrong . . . in so many ways, and I beg for your forgiveness."

Patsy reached out to seize my hand. "Does this mean you're ready to come back to . . . ?"

"No," I whispered. I turned my head down and away. "I'm sorry. I didn't mean to call you and give you the wrong impression." I shook my head. "I can't do that to you, to Stephen. I mean, we'd be okay for a while, but . . . I'd end up screwing everything up. . . ." Without warning, my chest started to shudder. I felt light-headed, and I could feel myself about to slide off the chair.

"David? David?" Patsy said. "Are you okay, what are . . . what are you saying?"

Again with my head hung low, I shook my head.

While Patsy and I sat in silence, around us people came in and out of the hotel lounge, ordering drinks, laughing, or watching the big-screen television.

After several minutes an overwhelming pressure built up behind my eyes. Patsy's expression told me not to say anything. "I owe you this much," I wept. "I could have . . . I *should* have treated you better. I—I was scared, all the time, of what might happen next. It wasn't your fault . . . I just couldn't let you in, and for that I am truly sorry. I swear to God, I know what an ass I was, and I beg for your forgiveness. I drove you crazy, and every time you reached out . . . I shut you out. How *could* I love you? I mean really love you, when I hated myself?" I said, pounding my hand. "There are so many things I did wrong, and for that I can never forgive myself. I should have stopped and listened to what you were really trying to say. As much as I provided for you, I was never there for you."

"Well," Patsy asked as she wiped her eyes, "I guess this means we're through?"

I bit my lip, and nodded.

"Just say it," Patsy pleaded. "Just tell me so I can go on. I can take it, be a man and tell me."

"Patsy," I swallowed as I gazed into her eyes, "I'm not good enough to be your husband and I think we should . . . should divorce."

Patsy closed her eyes before nodding that she agreed. After dabbing a tissue to her eyes and adjusting her blouse, she smiled. "Well, you can't blame a girl for trying."

"I'm flattered." I laughed. "Really I am."

We spent the remainder of the afternoon addressing every issue we could think of. "You realize Stephen will live with me. I'm a homebody and you're on the road too much. You can see or talk to him anytime you want. I'll never use him as a pawn. I think you and I both know what that's like. I won't do that to our son.

"The thing is," Patsy went on, "for both of us Stephen was the best thing in our lives. I just wanted something more, that's all."

"No matter what, I want to be friends," I said. Patsy immediately nodded. "I mean it. I don't have many friends, and I think we deserve to give each other that." I stopped to take in a deep breath. "One more thing . . ."

"Oh, my God!" Patsy gasped. "You're not going to tell me you're gay?"

I coughed before I could reply. "No! What made you think that?"

"Well," Patsy said, recovering, "I just thought, I mean, you live in Guerneville and all. You don't go out. What's a wife to think? You leave me to go live down there. . . ."

I brushed off the statement. "Listen, please. I just want you to know, you were right about the office in Lincoln. I found out a few months ago. I was mismanaged. That's why I couldn't get enough gigs. And the books, they were 'printed,' they were never published. They weren't even copyrighted! That's why they weren't in the stores."

"*The Lost Boy,* too?" Patsy inquired, my second book, which Jerry had about insisted that I write. I nodded. "Jesus," Patsy scolded, "how could you be that stupid and allow so many people to take advantage of you like that? As smart as you are, I'll never understand you."

I thought of myself from years ago. "I dunno," I replied. "Ever since I was a kid . . . I never had the guts to really speak up for myself. I was always too intimidated. Even now as an adult, whether it was Jerry at the Lincoln office, buying a car, sticking up for myself so no one could walk over me or, no offense, even with you, I couldn't do it. I . . . it was easy for me to do for others, but not for myself."

"David," Patsy sighed, "it's different with me . . . I'm your wife."

I nodded, but more to myself. "All that changes now."

"So, what are you going to do? Sue 'em?" Patsy had a gleam in her eye.

"No." I shook my head. "It's not the money, it never was. I don't want a dime of something I didn't earn first. It's a matter of honor. The worst thing I could do to them—to anyone that screws me—is have nothing to do with them."

"I think you're stupid. I'd stick it to them but good. So, what are you going to do to protect yourself?"

"Simple," I said, smiling, "trust no one."

"You do that, and you'll be a lonely old man, David Pelzer."

"I know," I sighed. "But I just can't allow myself to be hurt again."

"I don't know what you think of me; I know I've burned a lot of bridges with you, but I'd never screw you, David," she stated.

"I know. It's going to be okay. I swear, I just want you to be happy, that's all."

"Well," Patsy gushed. "I am. I mean—"

"I know," I interrupted. "I've known for a while. Are you happy? Is he good to you? To Stephen?"

"Yeah." Patsy beamed. "Guess you can say I finally got myself a real cowboy."

"And please," I begged, "be careful. We're adults, but I don't want Stephen to get hurt any more than he has."

"So, what are you gonna do?"

Without hesitation I said, "Be a good father and carry on. I'm not going to quit. I'm going to work hard and see it through."

"David," Patsy snapped, "I'm not talking about work, or Stephen. I know you'll be a good father for him. For once in your life, what about *you?* What are you going to do for you?"

For a moment I felt the magnitude of Patsy's question. I sat hunched over, stymied. "I don't . . . I don't know. Just live my life day by day. That's all I can do. I just don't want to repeat the same mistakes all over again."

Patsy shook her head in disbelief. "My God, after all these years . . . you're still carrying her shame."

I had no response. I truly felt like a leper when it came to being close to anyone besides my son.

As we got up to leave, Patsy and I embraced. "I'll always

hold a place in my heart for you, David Pelzer. You're a good man, and for God's sake go out there and live a little!"

"Thanks, Patsy, you have no idea what that means to me. I pray for you every day. Godspeed, Patsy," I stated.

"Good-bye, David."

"Good-bye, Patsy."

We soon filed for divorce. Less than thirty days after our divorce was finalized, Patsy remarried.

Between Stephen and my work, I deliberately stayed to myself. Overall I was content. On a good week, when I felt I earned it, I would venture "out there" and treat myself to a movie. Working for myself proved more difficult than I had expected, yet I loved every minute of it. After purchasing the rights to my books from the Lincoln firm, I quickly found two publishers who wanted to publish the books. Even though I knew I could receive a better deal with a New York publishing house, I signed with a smaller publisher in Florida, partly because for years I had admired the works of their authors John Bradshaw and Jack Canfield. I assumed a smaller publisher would be able to spend more time marketing and promoting my books.

Within a few weeks I received a call from an assistant editor who introduced herself as Marsha Donohoe. We spoke about the changes she wished to make and the schedule of publishing my first book. After hanging up the phone, I could not help but think what an incredible voice she had. Before my mind began to wander, I pushed Marsha out of my mind by burying myself in my work.

Months passed. The more Marsha and I discussed every page, every paragraph, analyzing every word of the book, the more I found myself becoming enthralled by her. Besides having the sweetest voice I ever heard, I respected the passion she had for her work. I understood that editors could not afford to spend much time on any particular project due to the overwhelming amount of deadlines within the publishing world, yet because Marsha and I cared so much about the story, we would spend more than an hour wrangling over a single sentence. "I don't want to get you in trouble," I told her one day. "I don't understand; I usually catch a lot of flak for trying to do my best. Why are *you* doing this?"

"I may be new here," Marsha confided, "but I've been involved with books all my life. And I gotta tell you, this book is one in a million. I swear to God, I couldn't put it down. Before I even called you, I believed in this book. With all my heart, I believe in what you are doing." Raising her voice with excitement, Marsha said, "Do you know how many lives you're going to change with this? I don't know you that well, Dave, but I think you're one incredible person."

I pressed the phone so hard against my ear that I thought it would bleed. Not being used to compliments, I immediately mocked her. "I bet you say that to all the authors!" A second later, I said, "You believe, I mean, you truly believe I'm doing the right thing?"

After our conversation I sat frozen in my chair. I couldn't believe my luck. After all these years and endless battles, I was working with someone who had the same values as I did. "She believes!" I said out loud. "Marsha actually believes in me!"

I never intended to cross the relationship between editor and author, but I lost myself as I savored every word of every minute Marsha and I spent on the phone. It was easy for me to become fascinated with her. At the end of editing each page, we would reward ourselves by telling stories and exchanging jokes. I soon became caught up not only in Marsha's sense of humor, but in her work ethic and her honor. Over time, as she began to tell me about her struggles and disappointments in life, I realized the incredible willpower she had. Marsha never quit. Whenever she applied herself, she gave it her all. We made a pact that we could talk to each other about anything at any time. Marsha became my one true friend.

* * *

Unexpectedly, weeks later after the end of one of our editing sessions, I leaned back in my chair, slowly exhaled as I closed my eyes, and imagined Marsha's smile and the way she might toss her hair when she laughed. Before I could allow myself any sense of pleasure, I buried my affections. I knew Marsha was way out of my league. She was by far the kindest, most sensitive person I knew, while I was a hyperkinetic geek boy with baggage, hiding my insecurities behind my work and manic sense of humor.

Marsha never gave up on me. Because of the graphic nature of some parts of the book, more than once she broke down and cried on the phone. One day, without thinking, I nearly swallowed the phone as if to get closer to her. "Mar, it's okay, honey, it's all right. That was a long time ago. It's over; it's over now." A second after the words slipped out, I backtracked, "Mar, listen, I'm sorry. I didn't mean to . . . I'm sorry, I didn't mean to seem forward . . . please forget what I just said. Please?"

"It's okay. Precious," Marsha sighed, "your book has become my baby. And when someone holds a place in my heart, I protect them. I just wish I could have been there for you. You're just so precious to me. Please don't apologize, we're friends. I've been waiting for you to say something to me."

"I, uh . . ." I paused, thinking of her. "I, uh, just don't want to hear you cry," I stammered, still holding back. "I just don't want you to be sad. Believe me, I'm fine. I don't want to hurt you, that's all."

"Dave, we've been working together for some time now. I know what you look like from the back cover of your book, but . . . can you see me?" Marsha whispered.

Hang up the phone! my brain screamed. *Before you screw up and say something, hang up!* As my grip tightened against the phone, a surge of energy seeped through my heart. "Yeah," I gasped into the phone—my only lifeline to Marsha. "Sometimes, at night, when everything is still, I'll walk outside and look up at the stars. . . . I'll close my eyes . . ." I stopped.

"Dave, please, go on. I know it's hard. I know you've been through a lot with your childhood, all you're trying to do, your divorce, your son . . . but just say something, say anything. I won't hurt you. I promise, it's okay."

Closing my eyes, I prayed for Marsha to keep talking. Letting out a deep sigh, I said, "Sometimes, at night, before I go to sleep . . . I can see your face. . . ."

We stayed on the phone from nine that evening until three in the morning. Afterward, I strolled out into a swirl of gray fog that had begun to settle in the trees. I knew everything about Marsha, down to the how she breathed. Looking up, I thanked God.

Maybe, I thought to myself, maybe.

Marsha and I began dating on the phone. Four months later, as our friendship and our personal feelings for each other grew stronger, we decided it was time to meet.

I was a nervous wreck the day Marsha was scheduled to fly in. I almost crashed my 4-Runner as I daydreamed about Marsha on the way. Hours later at the airport, I kept readjusting my clothes to look absolutely perfect for her. I felt like a schoolboy on a blind date, fearing she might think I was ugly, or laugh at me if I said the wrong thing. But by far my biggest anxiety was what if, after all our late-night conversations, romantic courtship, and reams of letters and cards we had exchanged, I froze up and never let her get close, just as I had with Patsy? What if I could not break through to how I wanted to feel? For me it was as it always had been: what if I could not open my heart and let Marsha in? I started to panic, and imagined myself fleeing before things became too deep. Part of me wanted to drop the yellow rose I was holding behind my back and run out of the airport terminal. "For God's sake," I said to myself, "who are you trying to kid?" With my head bent down, I found myself taking a step backward, then another step. I swallowed hard, thinking that in the end Marsha would understand—she was just too good for me.

As I turned away a sudden shimmer caught my eyes. As the passengers streamed from the terminal gate, one person stood out among the throng of people. Marsha's alluring eyes and shiny auburn hair almost made me faint. With my mind racing, I imagined myself strolling over to extend my hand to introduce myself properly. I didn't want to seem too desperate or too forward.

But I threw away my apprehension. To hell with that, I thought to myself.

We awkwardly ran into each other's open arms. Holding her tight, I could feel Marsha's heart race. "I can't believe it," she cried as tears fell down her face.

Lowering my defenses, I whispered, "Hello, princess." For a few moments the world stood still. When I finally took a long look at Marsha's face, rather than kissing her, I closed my eyes and ran my fingers along the side of her face to the base of her neck.

Leaning her face into my hand, she sighed, "Whatever you do, don't let go."

"Hardly a chance," I replied.

Wiping her tears away, Marsha shook her head. "Dave, I've dreamed about this day for a long time. Don't let me go."

The next several days Marsha and I were inseparable. We spent every waking moment together. While clutching our mugs of coffee, we'd chat outside for hours at a time. As I grew fascinated with her, Marsha seemed to absorb every detail of my life, to the point of insisting to see the summer cabin where I had stayed as a child. Trying to recapture the magic that had captivated me so many years ago as a child, we stood holding each other, watching the sun set beneath the redwood trees as the sky turned from blue to orange. With every passing hour, I found myself stripping away layers of armor that I had worn as my defense from years of internal battle. Marsha became the only person to whom I could bare my soul.

The days passed by too quickly. The day before Marsha had to return home, I began to pull back. For me, the cold reality was that Marsha lived thousands of miles away—with a job, a great family, and a real life. I didn't want her to become any more entangled in my warped world. As much as every fiber of my being craved to be with her, the only way keep her as a close friend, I thought, was to set her free.

After sitting outside, stirring our coffees that had grown cold in silence, Marsha tossed her hair and asked, "Dave, is it me? Did I get too close?"

With tears beginning to build, I shook my head. "No, it's not you. It's just, it's me," I stammered before swallowing hard. "I don't want to hurt you, that's all."

Reaching out to hold my hand, Marsha probed, "What is it, Dave? What are you so afraid of?"

I clamped my eyes shut. The pressure inside of me was too much for me to hold in any longer. "You!" I fired back. "I'm scared to death of you! I can't, I can't even look at you! I can't do it. I mean, you're too good, too good for me." Marsha sat back in her chair, dumbstruck. "For God's sake, look at you. You're perfect, a china doll. You're drop-dead gorgeous! You don't lie, cheat, or steal. You have no vices. You don't have a mean streak in your body. You believe in God and in doing your best. You're educated, you don't complain or blame others if things don't turn out. You have no baggage from your past, no skeletons in your closet. Come on. I'm waiting for you to peel off your mask. . . . You're just too perfect. I know who I am and where I belong. You're way too good for me. I'm sorry, but I don't . . . I don't deserve to be with you."

"Don't say that!" Marsha pleaded. "All your life you've carried this guilt. Don't you understand? It's not your fault! You're not to blame. I'm an adult. I can take it. I know everything, everything about you, and I'm still here."

Turning away, I raised my voice at Marsha for the first time. "Don't you get it? My grandmother hates me, my mother tried to kill me. I drove Patsy to the brink. . . . If you get too close . . . I'll somehow screw things up for you, too." With my chest beginning to heave, I murmured, "I'd rather stop before things get too serious and keep you as a friend. I'm just trying to save what we have. You mean that much to me. You're too important for me to lose. You deserve to be happy, and if you become involved with me—"

"It's too late. I'm already involved. I know what I'm getting into. I've been around the block; I've dated plenty of creeps. I've never met anyone out there like you. Don't you see how precious you are to me?"

I shook my head.

"And what about you. Dave? What do *you* deserve?" Marsha asked me. "My God, all your life you've worked your butt off, been taken advantage of; you've gotten truckloads of manure thrown at you and you get up, wipe yourself off, and carry on as if nothing happened. You never quit! What about you? You deserve to live a better life. I've never seen anybody work as hard as you. Look at how you sacrifice everything for your son. I've never seen any parent smother his child with as much love as you do. Okay, you had a bad marriage; but it takes two, *two* people to ruin something. You were not the only one responsible for the divorce. Maybe you couldn't love her because she broke your trust. I'm not even going to tell you what I think about her! You've been more honorable, forgiving, and self-blaming than you should have. You're the most broken person I know. What about Dave? When is Dave going to be happy? You deserve, Dave, *you* deserve to be happy. When is it going to be time for *Dave*?"

I continued to shake my head. "Some mistakes . . . can never be paid for."

"It's her, isn't it?" Marsha asked. "You can't stop thinking about her, can you?"

I nodded in agreement. "Every day," I began, "I try, I really do, but it's like something pulls me back and I can't break free—no matter what I do or how hard I try. Sometimes when I'm out there speaking, explaining what happened between Mother and me, it's like I'm searching, crawling for a fragment of something I could have done, anything to change all that . . . besides Stephen. It's like, it's one of the reasons why I'm out there. If I could just find—"

"No!" Marsha broke in. "You've got to let her go, it wasn't your fault that—"

"No. I could have—"

"My God!" Marsha now yelled. "Your mother was nuts! There's nothing you could have done to stop her!"

With my heart continuing to race, I frantically shook my head. "You're wrong. I could have . . ."

"Could have done what?" Marsha countered.

"Please," I begged, "don't push it. I really don't want to go there."

"No! We're going to confront it!" Marsha demanded. "All you do is give. You'd slit your wrists if you thought it would help someone. Just take a moment and help yourself. I'm here. I'm here for you, honey. There was nothing you could have done." Marsha leaned closer, to hold me, but before her fingers could touch my shoulders, I pulled away.

"You don't know, you weren't there. I could have done something! That's the worst part of it all. I never said no. I never stood up for myself. Don't you get it? I could have stopped it. I let it go too far. The day she—she stabbed me, I just stood there, like I was begging for it. My brothers would have never let anything like that happen to them, I could tell by the look in their eyes. But I did. I always did. I swallowed ammonia in front of my dad. When I cleaned the bathroom with that mixture of ammonia and Chlorox my throat was on fire, and all I had to do was dump that stuff down the toilet. I even ate the dog shit when she was in the other room. All I had to do was throw it down the disposal and she'd never know, but I did it, I did everything she wanted. I never stood up for myself. All I had to do was stop her, just one time. Maybe once and that could have changed everything." A stream of tears began to spatter the wooden deck. "I could have stopped her. I never . . . never said no."

Marsha began to cry as well. As I covered my face to hide my shame, a wave of anxiety made me slip from my chair and fall forward to the deck. I stayed on my knees as my body shook. "Everyone thinks I'm—I'm so damn courageous for telling my pathetic little tale. Part of me feels like a whore. The truth is, if I'm so brave, why didn't I have the guts to stop her? I could have left. I had hundreds of chances." In my mind I envisioned Mother parking her gray station wagon at the local Serramonte Mall. "Whenever she went shopping, when she kept me in the car, my hand would wrap around that door handle . . . sometimes my grip was so tight my entire arm would vibrate. All I had to do was turn the handle, open the door, and walk, just walk away. I could have ended it. It would have all been over. I could have stopped it." With my eyes clamped shut, I shook my head from side to side, so much so that I could feel myself beginning to pass out.

"Dave," Marsha cut in, "when you were with Patsy, did you work on your marriage?"

Stopping to look up at her, I shook my head. "Now that I've had time to think about it, it was Patsy who really put forth the effort—"

"No!" Marsha boomed, "it's not just your fault. So, I'm asking: when you were married, did you give it your best?"

"Yeah, I guess so." I stopped to collect myself. "Sure, I guess so."

"As a writer, how long did you say it takes you to construct a paragraph?"

"Anywhere from four to maybe six hours. Why?" I asked, feeling intimidated.

Marsha dug further. "Now, don't think, just answer: Why does it take you so long?"

"Because I can't type, I have no mechanics, because I'm stupid? What are you getting at?"

"No," Marsha calmly interjected. "Shh, slow down. Tell me, just open up and tell me. Dave. Why?"

I could feel myself about to erupt. "Because . . . I want to do my best, my best in everything I am and do! That's why!" I shouted.

"As a father, a husband when you were married . . . ?"

"I did my best!" I fired back.

"Flying for the air force, your volunteer work, the way you stack your firewood, fold your shirts, arrange your table when you barbecue dinner . . . ?"

"I try. I try and give everything my all. Stop it!" I begged. "Just let it go."

"Everything?" Marsha asked in a hushed tone. "You've always given everything your all?"

I nodded yes.

"As a son, did you give it your best?"

"Damn straight I did! I always did. The chores, trying to impress her with my work at school, praying every day that I wouldn't piss her off."

"And you didn't quit?" Marsha raised her eyebrows.

"No! I never quit!" I stated with conviction. "I never quit."

"You told me that when you were in foster care and the air force didn't want you that it took you years of proving to them that you wanted to fly for them. . . . When you were scammed by that man from Lincoln and left with nothing, you walked away. . . . After everything you've been through, why in heaven's name, why do you push yourself? As a child, Dave, you were a child; why did you . . . ?"

"Because that's all I had!" I cried. "I got nothing else! It's all I am! It's all I've ever known. If I quit back then, once, for just a second . . . it could have been all over. I got nothing else, all my life. . . ."

Falling to the deck, Marsha said, "I know, I know, baby, I know." Reaching over to cradle my head against her chest, she whispered, "You made that choice. Your mother made hers. It's not your fault. It wasn't your doing. She gave up on herself a long, long time ago. She quit—on her son, her family, everything she had, *she* quit. No one could have saved her, least of all her own baby that she treated like an animal. She was a broken woman long before you came into her life. You've got to give her up. It's not your doing. You deserve, Dave, you deserve to be free."

"I could have—" I protested.

"No!" Marsha shouted. "Tell me, tell yourself, what was the one thing you could have possibly done to prevent her self-destruction?"

"Been a better son? I dunno." I shook my head. "I just don't know."

"You're a good son now, and you always have been. No matter what happens to us, for your own peace of mind, after all your years of searching, you need to understand, it wasn't your doing."

Feeling the pressure beginning to ease, I stammered, "It's just, I feel my entire—and I mean my *entire* life, since I was a kid—it's like I saw everything swirling around me, and somehow I allowed things to take over, to take control of me because I never felt I deserved anything but that. My marriage, the firm in Lincoln, I deserve what I got. That's why I couldn't tell Patsy or anyone else. That's why I tried to bury the dirt; that's why I eat crap every day of my life. I don't deserve any better.

"I know there's nothing I could have done to stop her, but that doesn't help, doesn't stop it from gnawing at me every day. And because of that I feel so undeserving, especially when it comes to you. You're too pure."

I let out a deep breath. "I can't do it anymore. I'm just tired, tired of swimming against the tide, proving myself . . . I'm tired."

"After all you've been through, no matter what happens to us, Dave, you deserve everything life has to offer. I'm so proud of you, I could just bust. You're the most inspirational person I know. You're my Robin Williams and Jimmy Stewart rolled into one. And I'm not saying that because I've got some schoolgirl crush on you. No matter what, you're precious to me. No matter what, with all my heart, I believe. I believe in you, Dave Pelzer. You're my best friend. Okay," Marsha sighed, "I can see where you can drive people crazy, only because you want to do your best. But, Dave, you deserve, *we* deserve to give each other a chance. I'm not going to smother you or trick you into anything. With my hand on the Bible, if I live to be a hundred, if I know one thing: it's that we deserve—we deserve to be together."

Wiping away my tears, I locked onto Marsha's tear-filled eyes. "I'm your best friend?"

"Why do you think I came to see you?" she asked.

Closing my eyes, I shook off my fear of intimacy, and I stripped away my last protective layer. "When I'm with you, Marsha . . . I feel clean. You ease my shame."

"And you're my white knight. Together, back to back, we can do anything, Dave," Marsha cried. "Can't you see that all I want is to be with you?"

My insides became unglued. As much as I had tried to drive Marsha away, my heart ached for her to stay. With my anxiety spent and my heart bursting, I wrapped my arms around Marsha's waist with my head bent in her lap. "I'll never deserve you. You're my best friend. I love you. You're the one, Marsha. The only one . . . the only one I trust."

15

ALL GOOD THINGS

Now, this was completely different. Marsha stood with her back toward my chest, venting about the demands placed on her from the day, while I tried to calm her down by pleading for her not to take work so seriously. I had my reasons to get her mind off work, but whenever I tried to veer Marsha off the subject, it only seemed to intensify her passion.

But that was one of the many things I loved about Marsha: her steadfast commitment. Months after meeting in California, Marsha had given up her job as an editor and moved to Guerneville—not only to be close to me, but to take over and manage my business. Since Marsha knew me like no other, and because of the respect we had for each other, she was the perfect choice. While some scoffed at her decision, thinking that she would play the role of a mere secretary, answering phones and filing paperwork, Marsha faced many demands: arranging continuous media interviews, strategizing every aspect of the strenuous travel logistics, and keeping my calendar packed with engagements. At times when I was away, Marsha slaved twelve to sixteen hours, only to end her day by fighting to keep up with paperwork correspondence, which began as a trickle but soon flooded to the point she was answering thousands of pieces of mail a month from all over the world.

Since our lives were so crazy, we worked hard on our personal relationship. With Marsha I learned to listen and not father her, to offer advice when I thought it was needed. When we'd have a disagreement, we'd talk things through. When we'd have a heated discussion, we'd try our best to resolve the issue, learn from it, and move forward. Throughout every situation, every obstacle we faced together, Marsha remained sincere and dedicated and never broke my trust.

Allowing Marsha into the deepest recesses of my heart and, more important, introducing her to Stephen, was the highest compliment I could give to her. I was learning from my past mistakes and respecting her as a lady. Marsha resided in a cozy cottage near the Russian River across from me. After work we'd curl up on her futon to watch a movie or read well into the late evening, until I left after kissing her good night.

With Marsha I didn't have to spend my time worrying about when the sky would come crashing down. In business, she protected me in so many ways. She taught me the fine line between helping others and being taken advantage of. There were ways to help others, provide for my own son, and maintain my own self-worth—instead of constantly neglecting and sabotaging myself just to please others.

Marsha also helped me to grow as an individual, in ways I never thought possible. For years I had felt I was swimming against the tide, with lead weights cuffed to my ankles. But somehow Marsha seemed to part the waters, while coaching me along the way. She not only made me believe there was little I could not accomplish, but that I was indeed deserving and was destined to succeed. With Marsha I was invincible.

As a couple we went through a great many peaks and valleys. Marsha was in a completely different world. Since I was on the road so much, being pulled in every direction, combined with her getting to know Stephen, and a few difficult situations she encountered with Patsy, life for Marsha sometimes became too much. When times were tough and we could barely scrape together enough money to pay our bills, Marsha would huddle with me in my bone-chilling cabin and share a Cup-O-Soup and a loaf of day-old French bread. Yet somehow, together, we found a way to help others who we knew were worse off. For a while it seemed everything was against us. We'd question our business wisdom to the point that we'd break into tears. It seemed we were both working our tails off, but only keeping our heads above water. But together, we never lost faith, for Marsha and I knew tomorrow was indeed another day.

Over time, as we made solid progress, Marsha insisted that I move out of my moldy "icebox," into a warm, modern two-bedroom home among the redwood trees. It looked like a tree-house for grown-ups. After years of sacrificing and pinching every penny, Marsha basically kicked me in the behind, saying that I deserved to live like a normal human being. My proudest moment after moving into my new home was holding Stephen by the shoulders as I walked him into *his* bedroom—that was filled with brand-new furniture, toys, and video games that he had wanted. For years after the divorce, when Stephen would visit me at my old house, we'd shiver in bed—at first on my air mattress, then later on my cardboard-like pedestal bed. When I could not afford to make Stephen an elaborate meal, we simply heated up a frozen dinner. Because I did not have a dining room table then, Stephen would sit on a wobbly bar stool while I stood beside him. Stephen never complained. In an odd sense, maybe having him watch me struggle was good for his character. For only Marsha knew the extent of the sacrifices I placed upon myself, to provide for and protect my son.

As with everything in my life, ever so slowly things began to fall into place. When I was on the road, after going over an endless stream of business matters, Marsha and I would steal time to chat aimlessly. As before, when the phone had been our lifeline, I'd sit back and begin to ponder our future together.

Once back in town, as El Niño began to bear down on the Russian River, Marsha was standing in front of me, describing her day in every detail. Without her realizing, I had basically kidnapped her away from our office to the Rio Villa—to ask her the most important question of my life. For some time now I had planned to ask Marsha on Valentine's Day. I'd take her to her favorite city in the world—Carmel—and present her with a bouquet of yellow roses on the beach as the sun set. But that was over four weeks away. Like a child at Christmas. I could no longer hold back my excitement. When it came to Marsha, my willpower was as strong as jelly. I was a man possessed.

As Marsha chatted about her day, I kept trying to sidetrack her. But she was clueless as to my intentions. After a half hour of standing outside under the canopy, I nearly gave up all hope. My timing was completely off. I wanted everything to be perfectly magical for her. Yet deep inside I was terrified she would say no. I discovered, to my own horror, that I could not think of how to ask her. Here I was—a person who spoke for a living, and with a quick wit to take people's minds off their troubles—and I could not form the most important words of my life.

As Marsha slowly began to unwind, I stepped closer to her. I wrapped my arms around her waist. In a slow, deep voice I said. "Close your eyes. Take a deep breath." From the bottom of her chest I could feel Marsha's tension ease. With my mind spinning, I didn't know what to say next. Whispering into her ear, I asked, "What do you think of . . . of the Russian River?" Marsha's soothing response seemed to calm my shaking legs. "What do you think of . . . Stephen?" I continued, as my right hand cautiously retrieved the black velvet box from my pocket and stuck it between my thighs.

A swirl of mist coupled with the freezing rain made Marsha shiver. As she said how much she loved Stephen and how proud she was of him, I closed my eyes. Uttering a quick prayer, I reached for the box. As tears began to trickle from my eyes, I came around in front of Marsha and knelt down as I sprung open the box, asking, "What do you think of . . . spending the rest of your life with me?"

I thought by Marsha's scream that she was furious with me. She jumped up and down on the wooden deck for what seemed like an eternity. Only when she nearly snapped my neck off as she hugged me did I realize she was accepting my proposal.

A few hours later, in the middle of the worst series of storms to hit California, Marsha and I drove west toward the setting sun. We were putting away the world's problems for a day. Our only ambition was to spend the remainder of our lives together . . . happily ever after.

Another rare moment in time occurred during Stephen's summer vacation. In July 1998, after celebrating a beautiful day, topped off with a barbecue dinner, I went outside for my evening walk. As usual, Stephen joined me. For years, since he was able to walk, we had strolled together, and since moving to the Russian River, we had practically worn out pairs of shoes watching dusk turn into night as we held hands, taking in the majestic beauty around us. Now, as he approached adolescence, Stephen at times seemed apprehensive about his place in the world.

That evening the air held a certain crispness as the clouds above us seemed to melt away to streaks of orange as the sun vanished below the ridge. Taking a turn by a familiar road. Stephen looked up and asked, "Back then . . . was it hard?" Not understanding the question, I asked what he meant. Stephen ducked his head down. "You know, back then?"

"Oh," I lightly replied. As a parent, I always had felt my first obligation was to protect my son from the atrocities of the world, especially the horrors from my past. And yet in order to prepare him for adulthood, I felt I had to inform Stephen of the realities of life. As early as age six, he had begun inquiring about my past. Rather than break his trust by lying to him, I had skirted the issue by claiming "my mommy" was sick and sometimes said or did bad things. Back then a simple answer had seemed enough for Stephen's inquisitive mind. I never had any intention of revealing the magnitude of what had happened to me out of fear of scaring him. But now, after I had appeared on numerous television talk shows, with two books about my life on international best-seller lists, it was impossible to shield my past from him. "You know, Stephen, I never thought of it as being hard. It was just something I had to get through, that's all."

"But were you scared?" he probed.

Addressing the very topic I had fought so hard to protect him from, I said, "Sometimes, yeah. But . . . aren't you scared sometimes when you're in the batter's box . . . when you're facing a pitcher?"

His eyes lit up. "Oh yeah; I mean, sometimes."

"Well," I asked, "what do *you* do?"

"You know." Stephen shrugged.

"No, I don't," I claimed. "I never really played baseball. I never experienced what it's like to stare down a pitcher and have a ball coming at you in the blink of an eye. To tell you the truth, I don't see how you do it."

Shaking his head, Stephen said, "It ain't much. Just practice, that's all. I've been doing it all my life. You just do it; that's all there is to it."

"Even when you're behind on the count, with two strikes against you, and you can feel all the pressure, don't you ever thinking about quitting?" I inquired.

"No," Stephen stated, "I just do what I have to do."

"And that's all I did as a kid, Stephen. I dug in and made the best of things. Just like you and I did at the cabin when we didn't have enough wood to heat the house. You adjust, that's all."

"But your dad, didn't he know?"

"Yes and no. I think he didn't realize or want to understand what was going on, and by the time he did . . . it was too late. You see, my dad, like my mom, was an alcoholic. Back then things were very different. A lot of things happened, but they were kept in the closet. A secret, like cancer, AIDS, equal rights, and lots of other things were not supposed to be discussed, either out of embarrassment, shame, or whatever the reason. Hopefully, as a society, things are better now. We can openly talk about things that we would never speak of when I was your age. In fact, did you know," I asked, taking Stephen away from our subject matter, "the one thing you never said to a parent?"

His eyes grew wide. "What?"

"*No.* You never said the word no. As a kid, when a parent said, 'Jump,' you asked, 'How high?' "

"That's kinda stupid. I say no all the time. I wouldn't let anyone treat me like that."

"Yes." I raised my finger. "Because of the changes within society. Things . . . things were very different back then."

Stopping in front of me, Stephen asked, "Do you forgive her? I mean, your mom?"

Kneeling down, I held him by his shoulders. "Absolutely. Somehow, some way, something made my mom the way she was. Back then, when she was raised, she was not allowed to talk about things that might appear to be negative. I don't think she had anyone to turn to, to really help her deal with whatever it was that troubled her. From what I know, I don't believe anyone wakes up one day and wants to be bad, hurt others, or get high on drugs, but something leads them to that decision because of something they haven't dealt with. In a weird sense, as much as my mom did to me, I learned from her what *not* to do." Stephen nodded that he understood. "That's why I'm always on you for facing things as they come up. If you learn anything from my past, it's to hate no one. If you do, you'll become that person who did you wrong. As you grow older, you're going to face a lot of issues. If you have a problem, don't go to bed upset; talk to your mom, call me in the middle of the night, whatever. It's important because if you let things build up inside you, whatever the situation is, little by little it will eat away at you, like it did my mom. And that would be a waste, especially for all that you have going for yourself. Hate no one!"

"Did your dad and you ever spend time together?"

"Not a lot of time. But like I said, things were different back then. I'm sure part of him wanted to, but I don't know. . . ." My voice trailed off as I thought about Father and me.

"Did you two have a special time together?" Stephen asked, tilting his head.

Realizing where I was at that moment, I slowly turned Stephen to the right. "Well, as a matter of fact . . ." I choked for a split second, "I was maybe a little younger than you when one evening, on a night just like this, my dad was out for his evening smoke and I followed his footsteps to this exact spot, where my family and I would spend our summers together."

"Right here, at that cabin?" Stephen pointed as he asked in amazement.

"Yep, right here. We walked around the block, and that one time with Dad I felt like I was ten feet tall. I was a somebody. It's something I never forgot. Back then it meant the world to me. That's why I love walking with you; it's something I can pass on." I smiled.

Together in silence Stephen and I retraced a journey that had begun a lifetime ago. Only this time we held hands, and I kept my son close to my side. At the end of the block Stephen stopped to hug me around the waist. "Thanks, Dad."

"No." I again choked up. "Thank you, Stephen. You mean the world to me, and well, I know it hasn't been easy for you, but I try. I want you to know how much I love you. I truly do."

On the block near our house, Stephen shyly asked, "Dad . . . am I going to make it?"

I could only stroke his short blond hair in wonderment. That same question had plagued me for so many years.

"It's okay, Dad. I know it's a stupid question. I don't want to waste your time."

"Stephen, take all the time you want. Here, sit down," I instructed.

"Here, in the middle of the street?" he asked, looking around.

I sat down, folding my legs on the pavement. "Right here, right now, nothing else is more important. Relax, you're too young to be so serious. You're going to make it. Not a doubt in my mind. Absolutely!"

"How do you know? I mean . . ."

"I know." I nodded my head. "I know you. You're a terrific young man. You're kind, you're sensitive. You know right from wrong and, most important, you've got a good heart." Switching topics for a moment, I admitted, "I know our divorce wasn't easy, and I am sorry. I truly am. I know school isn't always easy, or dealing with other kids, or things you have to face on a daily basis. No offense, but that's life. Everybody has problems. Everyone.

"But you're different: you deal with things. It's not always easy, but that's the way it is. I'm not trying to be a tough guy about this, but no matter what happens to you, it doesn't give you an excuse to blame others or wallow in self-pity. Your mother, your teachers, others who love you, or even myself: we can only help you so far. It's going to be up to you to make it happen. No one's perfect. There are no sets of perfect parents; no one has a perfect life. Your mother and I tried to make it work out. But it didn't. And as you grow older, maybe you can learn something positive from our mistakes.

"You're going to be fine. You've got a strong heart. In life you're going to make mistakes, you're going to fall down, but it's getting up that counts. Just like in baseball: you'll get a few hits, but most likely, you'll strike out more than you'll get on base. But don't quit. Find your focus, relax, take a deep breath, and give it a good swing. I beg of you, Stephen, don't quit. There are so many people who cave in at the first sign of trouble. They quit school, they act like they know it all, and develop a habit of quitting on everything. You're better than that. If you quit, everything you fought for—your grades, baseball, your self-respect—would have been in vain. The thing is, at the end of the day you still have to face yourself. I know it's a lot to digest at your age, but I'm here to help you. Like I said, I can't do it all for you, but my job as a parent is to make you a responsible, functional, productive adult. I'm not here to raise a child, but a happy, caring, nurturing man. I see greatness within you. You have your whole life ahead of you. If I've learned anything from my past, the one thing I can teach you as a father is this: Stephen, there is nothing, and I mean nothing, *you* cannot accomplish if you want it bad enough. The choice is yours. Always has been, always will be. Stay on your course. Be true to yourself, and you'll be fine."

Smiling, Stephen asked, "You think so?"

Taking his hand, I stated, "I know so. You're going to be fine. I'm here for you. Even when I'm not physically with you, not a single day passes that I don't think about you and pray for you. Come on," I joked, "don't do what I did and be so serious all the time. Have fun! Relax, seize the day. Take a breath. 'In da nose . . . out da mouth,' I said in my Schwarzenegger voice. As we gazed up at the stars that filled the black sky, everything seemed within reach. Both Stephen and I filled our lungs. "Feel better?" I asked.

Wiping a tear from his eye, Stephen nodded. Leaning over, I brought him to my chest. "Love you, Dad."

"I love you, too, son, I truly do. Trust me, it's gonna be fine," I whispered.

"I'm sorry you had to go through that," Stephen said as he looked up at me.

"Well . . ." I deflected as another tear trickled down my cheek. "To, ah . . . to tell you the truth," I stumbled, "as I sit here with you, it's like it never happened. Just as long as I can look at you and know you're okay, for me that's all that matters. It's times like these . . . that's what I live for. I'll always remember this, our time right now, as one of my happy thoughts."

"Me, too." Stephen sprang up to walk over to the nearby fence. Taking a few seconds longer to work the cramp out from my leg, I followed him, wondering what he was up to. "Remember, Dad, how you always told me about you smelling the redwood trees, how it makes you feel good even when you're feeling down?" Still feeling emotional, all I could do was nod my head. "Well, this is going to be my smell. When I smell this, I'll think of us and our time together. It's going to be my happy thought."

"Good for you," I replied, walking over to pluck off a few strands of sweet jasmine from the vine. "So be it."

Later, after tucking Stephen in to bed and kissing him good night, with his beloved Wally, the stuffed alligator, cradled in his arm, I stood over him long after he drifted off to sleep. Before turning off the light, I closed my eyes and took in a deep breath from the jasmine, whose fragrance filled Stephen's room. "Happy thoughts," I prayed as I closed the door behind me.

Returning outside, I looked down at my watch. During our walk Stephen and I had become closer in four hours than I had with my parents in twelve years. Strolling in the early morning hours of the new day, beneath a canopy of towering redwoods, I felt more fortunate than ever before. After years of intense struggles and personal battles, everything seemed to be coming together. I was a father to a terrific young man who never had a childhood like I did, I had broken the shackles of my past and was fortunate enough to help others, and I finally had a lady in my life whom I loved and adored. I was happy, in every sense of the word. And fulfilling a lifetime fantasy, I was now living yards away from the cabin where my childhood desires first took root.

Before returning to my home, I stopped suddenly when I caught a scent of the redwoods' sweet aroma. Turning up to gaze at the silvery-white stars that twinkled far above the tops of the trees, I closed my eyes, thinking of the first time I breathed in that same smell that continued to possess me. As a five-year-old boy, as Ron, Stan, and I stood with Father by the Russian River, I had strained my neck to look up as the deep blue sky gave way to bright orange and purple streaks—as if someone had taken a paintbrush to heaven's canvas. I had shuddered when I felt someone brush up against me. I thought it was Father, but glanced up to see Mother's face beaming down at me as she wrapped me in her arms. "Take it in," she had said. "Take a deep breath, hold it, and never forget. Never forget this moment." And as I did, it was as if nature's aroma was Mother's perfume and the gentle rustling of the trees was Mother whispering to me. For an instant Mom, Dad, Ron, Stan, and I were the perfect family. I had never felt that safe or as loved by Mother as I did at that moment in time. Years later, at the depths of my despair, replaying the vision in my head over and over again had been enough to wash away my pain and loneliness.

Now, standing alone beneath God's creation, I closed my eyes, relaxed my body, and inhaled as much air as my lungs could hold. I could almost recapture the scent of Mother's perfume and Father's shiny jet black hair and beaming smile, as I recalled that evening so long ago. Opening my eyes, I found the north star and muttered, "Rest in peace. May God Almighty grant you both eternal peace. Amen."

EPILOGUE

Without a care in the world, I sip champagne as I gaze at the clear blue ocean. On the beach, dogs run back and forth into the water, chasing the ocean's foam or each other, or fetching sticks. A blanket of fog begins to overtake the bay. I can feel the hairs on my body spring up from the sudden drop in temperature. I erase the mere thought of fighting the chill and throwing on a jacket or scurrying away in search of shelter if the sky suddenly opened up and poured down rain. All I do is lean back on the wooden bench, take another sip, and soak in the purple overcast sky. I'm learning to simply be still.

I still can't stop myself from smiling. The last few days have been a whirlwind. Even now as I close my eyes, I can recapture only tiny, vibrant, burst-like fragments of a day that was taken from a fairy tale. Hours ago, I had stood with my back facing the Russian River—on the same ground that I had asked Marsha for her hand in marriage. With my son, Stephen, standing beside me as my best man, Marsha strolled down a red velvet runner as if she were an angel walking on water. We stood together beneath a white arch that was practically dripping with an array of vibrant flowers—bright orange lilies, turquoise-blue orchids, and porcelain white gardenias. I caressed

Marsha's trembling hand. My mind wandered as the minister spoke of the wonder of life, love, and commitment. All I could do was gaze out and make eye contact to those who were sharing our private ceremony. Mrs. Woodworth—my fifth-grade English teacher who had told me when I was a child not to worry about my nervous stuttering because I was destined to communicate through writing—wiped the tears from her eyes as I gave her a slight bow. Then looking behind her, I smiled at my childhood friends from foster care, Paul Brazell and Dave Howard, and Dave's lovely wife, Kelly.

When the minister had asked if I would take Marsha's hand, I leaned over and whispered into her ear part of a letter I had written her when we dated on the phone years ago. I then knelt down on one knee and placed the ring on Marsha's delicate finger. Within moments, the minister presented Marsha and me to the world as Mr. and Mrs. Pelzer.

Now opening my eyes, I can still feel my heart pound from the excitement, not only because I am committed to sharing my life with Marsha, but also with how everything has unfolded in my life. I am now happy, healthy, and no longer terrified of what the future may hold. My son is an outstanding, caring young man who has his entire life before him. I want for nothing. I have a terrific career, a small band of close friends, and a personal relationship with my God.

With all the mistakes I've made, I am now my own person. One of the only links to my dark past is my father's badge, which I keep to honor him. I flew with it on every mission while serving in the United States Air Force, and I carried it in my back pocket when I had the honor of meeting President Reagan. When I was selected as a torchbearer for the centennial Olympic games, I carried the badge. And as I stated, "I most certainly do!" when asked if I would take Marsha as my wife, Father's sacred badge was in my tuxedo pocket.

As a responsible adult, I am now old enough and wise enough to understand that no one's life is perfect or even normal. Everyone has a past, everyone has issues. *Life is what we make of it.* I am only concerned about being a kind, humble person, a caring, guiding father, and a loving husband. With each and every day, I simply apply myself as best as I can.

Above me, streaks of maroon and purple begin to spread across the horizon. A cold breeze strikes my face as my fingers find a piece of paper in my shirt pocket. Unfolding the paper, I replay every word in my mind before my eyes scan the letter, that I had in part whispered to Marsha only hours before:

Flying at 28,000 feet westbound, somewhere over Nevada, thinking of you. It is at times extremely difficult for me to open up and talk to a woman like you. Until recently, I never had.

Getting close to someone, anyone is *very, very* hard for me.

It is easier, safer for me to watch from a distance. Sometimes I feel so lost. I've never been able to experience things like normal people; like being held as the sun goes down or feeling safe and "carefree" with a woman. A sensation I have yet to experience. So, I watch others and smile for their joy. Sometimes that's enough. I'll make eye contact, bow my head in respect, and stroll off feeling a little warmer inside, thinking I would *never* be able to share moments in time like other couples.

Somehow lately I believe this is the springtime of my life. I've worked hard, planted many things, and soon they will blossom and grow before my eyes. I'm still scared, but no longer terrified. I can live with that. In an odd sense, being on the constant mental defensive is a comfort zone of its own. But one day I would like to be a *real* person. A person who is able to let down his guard and let someone in. Before I die I would like to experience that. I want to shelve my former life's mistakes. I would like to live in total peace, in every sense of the word.

If I have to remain alone, I will. Above all I know not only can I survive, but I can *trust* myself. And I feel secure with that premise, as well as knowing I will not cause anyone else anguish.

I still dream of a home—my home: clean and fresh and open. The scent of flowers while Pat Metheny plays on the stereo. As always, I dream. I always will. I'm trying to give up control, but it's hard because for so long I was controlled by so many. But maybe if I surrender, I'll find my answer. I'll find peace.

Maybe, one day, I'll have a home. Then maybe one day I can come home . . . home to you.

After replacing Marsha's letter, I wipe away a tear, while staring outward where the swirl of water collides against the beach. I realize how far I've come.

"Here's to my husband," my wife, who was silently sitting beside me, suddenly announces. "And here's to you, princess," I reply, wrapping my arm around Marsha's shoulders, while an elderly couple strolls by, smiles, and nods at the newlyweds.

Within the recesses of my heart, I know with hope, effort, and a little luck that anything is possible.

I am living a fantastic life.

PERSPECTIVES

DAVE PELZER
HUSBAND, FATHER, AUTHOR, AND ADVOCATE

As I enter midlife, even to this day it is difficult for me to fully understand the magnitude of what happened to me as a child. Because of the life I am able to live today, it is as if my past experiences never happened. Every one of us has situations from their past. On a daily basis all of us are faced with dilemmas. I am no different, then or now. As a child I believed with all of my heart that if I could survive my ordeal, then not only could I accomplish what I set my mind to, but anything else I would encounter had to be easier. This is why my story is *not* about my being a victim of child abuse, but of the indomitable human spirit within us all.

I lived through an extraordinary experience, yet I was fortunate enough to learn from it and walk away a better person. I can't change my past, and it does not grant me the right to use it as a crutch, nor am I destined to become a prisoner because of it. For years I have lived by the philosophy: that which does not kill you can only make you stronger. I simply had to learn to pick myself up at an earlier age.

It seems all of my life I have been put down, taken advantage of, and at times fallen flat on my face. But, by the grace of God, I have somehow found myself being able to stand up, repair any damage, and forge ahead.

Years ago, a dear friend once told me a great deal of people mature in their thirties. As much as I have been through in my life, I am now a believer. With every day I soak in something previously unknown to me the day before. Like any adult I carry regrets, one of which is Patsy. With time, hindsight, and maturity, no matter what others may say, I realize we were simply two different people and that she in fact applied herself to our union more than I. That is why I call Patsy my former wife rather than my "ex." I know what it's like to be a non-person, and I refuse to treat anyone as such. I can only pray my mistakes as a parent do not reverberate to my son. Strangely, because of my failed relationship, I have committed myself to be a better husband to Marsha, and this makes me appreciate her all the more. I am now fortunate enough to share my life with a person who truly makes me whole.

But as I look back, I fully realize I made a fair amount of mistakes. Like many individuals who suffer from low self-esteem, I, too, allowed myself to become associated with others who mistook my kindness or generosity as a sign of weakness and attempted to exploit that for their own agenda. At the time, part of me felt as though I were a schoolboy willing to do anything just to gain acceptance so others would approve or believe in me. I never even thought about protecting my interests, or maintaining my standards I had fought so hard for—even though I had fully realized how grave my situations were—because of fear of rejection and being all alone. But now time, experience, and maturity have become valuable allies for me.

Because of all that was stacked against me, I should have never made it. Not a single day passes that, no matter how strenuous, hair-pulling, or defeating the day may have been, I do not thank my lucky stars. I appreciate everything—from a soggy, cold hamburger that has been sitting in the car for hours as I make my way to the airport in the middle of the night, to struggling to find the precise answer to someone's problem even after speaking nonstop for the entire day. I cherish every breath, spend hours staring at the delicate, vibrantly colored petals of flowers, become excited at the touch of my lover's fingers, or love to hear the sound of my son's laugh. Perhaps because of my past, the most important things for me are still the simplest—feeling the sun's warm rays upon my back or gazing up at the clear blue sky. Even to this day, I would not change one moment of my life. If it all ends now, I have lived, I have learned, and I have been loved. The greatest lesson is the gift of life, and no matter what, tomorrow is always another day.

There are still times when I am overwhelmed by immense feelings of hollowness, guilt, and fear of anyone becoming too close to me. It is something I will have to stand up to on a daily basis. All I can do is maintain my vow that I took years ago when I was eight years old, immediately after my mother had burned my arm on the gas stove. From this day forward I will never give up. From this day forward I will give everything my all. As an adult I expect nothing less from myself.

When my time comes, I would like to know that I have repaid my debt to those who have made a difference in my life. And to be at peace knowing that I stopped the cancer from spreading to those I love.

PERSPECTIVES

CLAIRE FRAZIER-YZAGUIRRE,
M. DIV., MFCC
MARRIAGE AND FAMILY THERAPIST

As a full-time marriage and family therapist, I have been involved for many years with people who've suffered childhood trauma and its tremendous impact in their lives as adults. Together with my husband, Dr. John Yzaguirre, we are passionate about empowering people to overcome this cycle of hurting themselves and others, and create dynamic and healthy families. We believe that relationships, where priority is given to cooperation and unity, are at the very heart of not only preventing the hurt, but will create in us the ability to become a *culture of caring* that will renew our society from the devastating effects of the indifference, domination, and submission that characterize toxic relationships.

I love reading and sharing stories about people who've experienced triumph over tragedy. And the *best part,* for me always, is how someone can reclaim their power through pain and inspire others with hope and healing. It was on just such a day of story gathering in a nearby bookstore that I came across Dave Pelzer's poignant and heartbreaking story. As I devoured his incredible story in *A Child Called "It"* and *The Lost Boy,* I knew I had to talk with Dave about how he was able to transform his immense suffering into a life of helping others.

As I read *A Man Named Dave,* I found myself reading from all my own experiential perspectives—as a woman, wife, mother, daughter, friend, minister, and therapist—and wept most during his tender and so-long-awaited reunion with his father, his excruciating confrontation with his mother, his joyous discovery of Marsha as his life mate, and later his heart-to-heart talk with his precious son, Stephen. At long last I, along with countless of you reading, could understand how Dave answered the many questions of his life. How he came to forgive his brutal mother for the years of torture through the life-restoring skill of empathy. How he came to forgive his passive father, who died in his arms, for not stopping the abuse, finding a way of giving up hateful lies that bind, and commending each of these wounded and incompetent parents to God. And ultimately how he, equipped with empathy, forgiveness, and the love of supportive relationships, could help others find the way too.

It is exciting to witness Dave's triumph over tragedy through the power of forgiveness and love! Dave's whole story can be seen as a testament to the endurance of the human spirit. I rejoice with and for him, and for all who will be touched by this tender yet powerful trilogy. I am also sobered and motivated (you, too?) by the fact that there is much for all of us to do to help others and ourselves.

We've come a long way in understanding the dynamics of pain, survival, and healing. Some of the best research about the effects of trauma on the human psyche comes, not surprisingly, from war victims and victims of domestic violence. Children and adults *who do survive* use creative and powerful defenses of denial, dissociation, repression, and fantasy, which keep them alive (and for many, sane) until they can escape and hopefully find the necessary support and resources to heal. The lucky ones are not only those who get out, but those who heal, while others fall into a private hell, an abyss of mental illness, die, or propagate their horrific legacy by hurting others.

Survival, yes, but there is a huge cost to the soul and mind as important parts of one's self are buried. These survival skills provide the needed road map for healing later, tracing, as it

were, the path to the *buried treasure* that all survivors, along
with their skilled helpers, must find to heal—encountering
and conquering the dreaded monsters of their past and liber-
ating all the *precious bits of self*—innocence, the capacity to
play, laugh, trust, love, and belief in one's intrinsic value—
that were buried in the time of war.

It is not enough to survive. We can see, as in Dave's life,
that when people are left unprotected at length, as he was, the
situation can become frightfully ritualistic, as it did between
him and his mother. Fueling this dynamic, often, is addiction,
poor self-esteem and -worth, secret keeping, denial, fear, or
indifference by those who can make a difference (Dave's
father, relatives, neighbors, even society at this time in the
seventies). The powerful "shame rules"—don't feel, talk
about, or stop the shameful and abusive behavior—that exist
in these families, and to an alarming degree still in our society,
leave members, especially children, vulnerable to attack. It's
as if the alarm system in a house has been disconnected,
allowing any intruder easy access to burglarize.

And we can see this in Dave's life, as his attachment disor-
der was his "protective barrier" that kept him from being
hurt, but also kept him from getting close to anyone—even
more so to people he felt he couldn't trust. His very low self-
esteem made him the perfect target to be taken advantage of.
And what is very common to many people, Dave ended up
having a relationship with someone from a similar background. In fact, individuals with problematic pasts seem to be
magnetized to each other. But these two negatives did not
equal a positive, but rather created and fueled more problems,
barriers, and isolations. Ultimately Dave's misery was endured
only because of the absolute love and devotion he had for his
son. He felt an obligation to make the marriage last.

The good news is how many people are now mobilizing and
joining hands from across many fields to create a world where
not only intervention occurs, as in Dave's life, but *prevention*
as well. How do we create such a world? By creating relation-

ships where the first priority is mutual love and concern for all, we overcome the indifference, domination, and submission that create problems in the first place. Dave and others like him are saved when people care and take action.

When we see how the consistent love of several people in Dave's life helped to transform his great suffering into even greater loving service to others, we witness a miracle. We see then how love can redeem every suffering, and how embracing another's suffering can work a miracle of unity in all of our relationships. When we forgive, we free ourselves from the bitter ties that bind us to the one who hurt us.

I will always remember the questions that prompted my call to Dave: "How long does it take to forgive?" "Can suffering be transformed into love?" And I will remember that the answers to these questions are largely determined by how well and how long we love and are loved. Through healing and forgiveness we get better, not bitter. Dave, thanks so much for your inspiring and courageous role-modeling to grow and help others to help themselves. We, along with all who are forever touched by your story, join you in this mighty work of hope and healing!

PERSPECTIVES

STEPHEN PELZER
SON

Over the past thirteen years my dad has done so much for me and for many other people. I still do not totally understand what happened to my father, but I know that it made him see that he never wanted that to happen to anybody else. During the times I have watched him help people, I decided that when I become an adult and have children, I will try to be as good of a father as my dad.

One of my first memories of my dad was when he was in the air force and was sent off to the "war in the Gulf" the day of my fourth birthday. I don't exactly know what was going on, but when he returned, I remember going to the base and seeing the SR-71 Blackbird land right before his plane landed. It was such a happy feeling to finally see my father again.

Now when I see him, my eyes light up. He has taught me great manners, morals, and so many other things that they can't all be named. I hope that someday I can somehow make it up to him. I really and truly love my dad. He is a very great father and person. So, I guess what I am trying to say is that my father will always be in my heart.

PERSPECTIVES

MARSHA PELZER
WIFE AND EXECUTIVE DIRECTOR

This man named Dave, where do I begin? There's so much to say about him. There is so much I feel for him. He's a man of virtue, an individual of countless accomplishments, and has a heart of gold. A man so dedicated, energetic, and adorably wholesome. Yet he's the most haunted person I know, constantly swimming upstream. What I admire most about him is he's the most genuine of souls and gives his *all* to everything he does. Whether he's working in his garden perfecting his impatiens, or living his life of "Planes, Trains, and Automobiles" while performing programs back-to-back, Dave gives it his all. When writing a letter to uplift the defeated spirit of a young fan, or driving over eight hours on weekends to see his son play baseball, Dave gives every ounce of himself. While giving a soul-stirring interview on TV, or holding me at night as we drift off to sleep, Dave never holds back. In everything he does, Dave willingly offers his heart and soul. He maps out every detail, predicts every scenario, and handles everything gracefully. He does because he is. No ulterior motives. No disguises. Nothing is expected in return. To give it his all with every fiber of his being is for Dave to be Dave. Nothing else will do.

Dave has a gift—and a curse, for that matter—of making things look effortless. The passerby sees Dave ease into his daily routine of traveling, speaking, writing, and being a loving father and husband. They interpret his life as exciting, enterprising, and predestined. People feed off Dave's energy and outlook, and some expect him to solve their problems with his magic wand. His label as a *New York Times* best-selling author usually implies an overnight success and the lap of luxury lifestyle. But only a small handful knows how grueling, disturbing, belittling, and erratic Dave's life truly can be. How his sacrifices are far greater than the rewards. And only those behind the scenes of his world can understand the consequences of his struggles. Dave's life is indicative of the fact that you can't have roses without thorns. And he welcomes both without reservation. So why does he do it? Where does he muster up the fortitude? How does he sustain the dedication to what he considers responsibility? To relive his horrific past every day in his quest to help others, and do it with such passion, humor, and honesty? As close as I am to the fire, I don't completely know. Sharing a life with him, inside and outside of his heart, I catch glimpses of what inspires him. I can tell you that the indebtedness he has for those who saved his life and the compassion he has for helping others is his cause, while the love he has for Stephen and me fuels the fire. He most certainly is a man on a mission. Dave is Batman, Indiana Jones, and James Bond all rolled into one. Like these characters, Dave possesses a dark side, a haunted past, a life on the run, only to expose the light; and he will do whatever it takes to bring peace to a dying world.

Dave is such an admirable human being. I know and understand him more than anyone who's ever been honored to know him, and I consider myself blessed because of it. But it's so difficult to know of the sacrifices required—past and present—just to be Dave Pelzer. God love 'im, he's been through so much and has always been the "bigger person" in spite of the wrong done to him. Concerning Dave's mother and father, his distorted nine-year marriage, the deceptions from his former speaking firm, not to mention his inept business relations in his career, I can simply say: Dave was way too kind! I do not mean to sound harsh and don't intend to encourage hatred and resentment, but please understand that based on what I know and what I personally have witnessed, I feel these individuals were not worthy of his understanding, much less his kindness and patience for them. To Dave, the worst thing you can do is to break his trust. He feels that is the ultimate dishonor. And that's exactly what these people did. Although I consider myself a very kind, well-grounded, and compassionate individual, I could have never endured a fraction of what Dave did in these relationships. No offense to anyone, but I would have kicked their butts (really hard), then run as fast and as far away from them as I could! I can testify that the events that have happened in Dave's life he has given to the readers in bite-sized pieces; although the reality was and is much more crude. But if it was revealed to people in full strength, it would blow their minds and the message Dave is trying so desperately to convey. This is why God has bestowed on him all the well-deserved blessings: because Dave did the right thing; he was the bigger person; he turned the other cheek. Dave has endured and accomplished things that neither I nor a lot of other people ever could. I liken him to Job in the Bible. He lived a good life only after he lived a hell on earth and remained steadfast amidst it all. And I'm sure the story told of Job cannot justly describe his reality. The same for Dave's life.

Dave is simply precious. In fact, this is the nickname I gave him years ago, and I don't hesitate to call him Precious whenever I can (much to his embarrassment!). And Dave is *very* modest! If you think he is a great individual, then you don't know how great he really is. Dave is—without ego—the most compassionate, level-headed, unselfish, and devoted individual I've ever known. He is one of the Ten Outstanding Young Americans, the Outstanding Young Persons of the World, and a torchbearer for the centennial Olympic games, just to name a few. They don't grant awards like these every day or for just any reason. These are distinguished commendations for unparalleled individuals who've made a difference in this world. But Dave would rather have you think it's no big deal!

And even when his first two books were officially published and only a few believed in their potential, while many folks predicted them as "fillers" in a book catalog and some went out of their way to sabotage the books and even laugh at Dave in the process, the books wouldn't die. They not only became *New York Times* best-sellers, but Dave is the first author to have two books simultaneously on the trade paperback list. (Of course, this was when those doubting Thomases gave him the old "we were behind you all the way" routine!) Again, Dave remained humble and appreciative amidst such a great feat.

As his wife, I want the world to know how adorable, loving, and dependable he is. How strong yet fragile his heart is. How brave yet vulnerable. How wonderful a provider and friend. My ally. My greatest fan and my biggest critic. Dave spoils me rotten. He says I'm his best friend, his princess, and his kryptonite. He jokes that on my good days I'm Bambi, on bad days I'm the Terminator. He's the only one who can make me laugh or cry just by looking at me, and makes me feel like I can conquer the world. His unyielding persistence and impatience wears me out, but he's my knight in shining armor, my soul mate, the most handsome man I know. I always feel the need to stick up for him, protect him, and defeat the enemy for him—when all the while he's protecting and defending me.

The greatest day in my life, besides being born into a wonderful family, and my beautiful Cinderella wedding, was picking up the phone years ago and introducing myself to a man named Dave. When I was assigned as his editor for *A Child Called "It,"* my life was forever changed. Soon I would ride the most frightening and blissful roller coaster of all time. From swimming in the depths of despair to dropping to my knees every day thanking God for the air in my lungs, my life with Dave Pelzer was destined to be. Because of Dave I have learned to appreciate *life*—with all its ups and downs. I've learned to love flowers, the Russian River, and the color of the sky. The smell of jasmine and the softness of silk. Because of Dave I've learned to forgive and to forget. To see the brighter side of life.

He has shown me how important it is to walk the talk and to be an example to others. And most important, he has helped me to see how broken lives can mend from hearts and hands that care.

My precious Dave, I love you so. I'm proud to know you, blessed to love you, unworthy to be loved by you. And to be your wife and friend . . . no words under heaven could ever describe.

HELP YOURSELF

*Finding Hope,
Courage, and
Happiness*

This book is dedicated to my lovely wife, Marsha, and my incredible son, Stephen, who both guide and inspire me in ways that only God knows.

This book is also dedicated to you, the reader, in the sincere hope that you, too, can live a more fulfilling, productive life that you truly deserve.

Acknowledgments

I wish to take a moment and give thanks to those who contributed to this endeavor. First and foremost my wife—and editor for the fourth time—Marsha, for her fine eye for the written word.

To my research assistant, Rey Thayne, for his endless hours of reverifying "the reverifications" and hunting down the smallest of details to help ensure the validity of the stories.

A special thank you to my personal assistant, Ray Worthington, for keeping chaos in order so as to allow me to scribe at any hour of the day, night, weekends, holidays. . . .

To my agent, Laurie Liss, for her time and tenacity.

To the entire family of professionals at Dutton Plume, especially to Brian Tart, editor in chief, for his time, patience, and genuine friendship. Besides the editing process, it's always a pleasure.

The Standard

I know something about resilience. For the first twelve years of my life I was subjected to practically every form of continuous physical and psychological torture you could imagine. I should have died. After I was rescued from my alcoholic mother and was fortunate enough to be placed in the care of others, there were a few who boasted that because of my extreme situation I would end up either dead or in prison—the odds against me were insurmountable.

I never saw it that way.

As a child, when my mother stabbed me in the chest, days later I literally crawled on my hands and knees hunting for a wet rag so I could clean my infected wound. At the time I simply applied what I had learned from a first aid class. When my mother refused to feed me for more than ten days, I survived by sneaking water. I did this by swallowing as much as I could from the silver metal ice cube trays whenever I had filled them;

another trick I learned was to suck water from the water basin in the garage. I had to be careful not to turn on the faucet too fast or too slow, for fear that the water pipe might vibrate and alert Mother. When I was thrown in a bathroom with a bucketful of a deadly mixture of ammonia and Clorox that can kill a person in a matter of minutes, I had enough sense to understand that gas rises. All I had to do was stay close to the floor with a wet cloth wrapped around my mouth and nose, praying that the heating vent would come on to circulate fresh air. My relationship with my mother became one of extreme survival. All I had to do was think ahead, believe in myself, and never give up . . . in order to remain alive.

If I learned anything from my unfortunate childhood it is that there is nothing that can dominate or conquer the human spirit. How can you expect to be a good parent, an astute businessperson, or achieve your greatness if you do not focus and harness your inner potential? This is the essence of the message I wish to present to you.

Please understand, this book is not about child abuse. For years I have been mislabeled as "that child abuse guy." I admit I have and I will continue to assist those in the child care fields of awareness and prevention, as well as doing what I can to praise those who give their all to help others in need. After what others have graciously done for me, I feel it is the least I can do. Yet, ever since I was a boy, living at times minute by minute, from the depths of my soul I believed that if I were to live, if I could overcome all that I had suffered, then anything else had to be better. In other words, I learned the value of personal responsibility, resilience, and gratitude. Only, I had to learn at a younger age than most.

When I was a child, Mother did not *allow* me to speak in her house. Period. So at school I would stutter or tremble so badly that kids would tease me, as if I were somehow mentally deficient. Now as an adult, I make a living speaking and I even do comedic storytelling, to the point that I have often been often dubbed "the Robin Williams with Glasses." As a child, because I lived in a garage and never played sports, I had limited coordination. When I was placed in foster care, because of my lack of developmental skills I could not play a simple game of catch, let alone toss a football. Yet years later as a young adult, after a great deal of self-determination, I was fortunate enough to serve my country as an elite aircrew member, entrusted to fly highly classified missions for the United States Air Force. (Can you imagine me passing the psychological examination?) Days after I turned eighteen, I discovered my childhood case had been identified as one of the most severe instances of child abuse in the state of California. And nearly twenty years from the day that I was rescued, I was privileged enough to be selected as one of the Ten Outstanding Young Americans. Other recipients have been President John F. Kennedy, Orson Welles, Anne Bancroft, and my childhood heroes Chuck Yeager and Christopher Reeve.

Please understand, I am not revealing my former experiences to extract sympathy or mentioning my accomplishments for the purpose of feeding my ego. My lovely wife, teenage son, and my higher power keep me grounded. I only offer these examples because, if you are going to spend your precious time and hard-earned money on this book, you should at least be given the decency to know your author's qualifications.

If you want to know the truth, even with all that I've experienced, I still have much to learn. Just like you, I am not perfect. I have problems that I have to address on a daily basis—my self-esteem, being a good husband and father, issues pertaining to my health and my demanding business—which at times can be overwhelming. I simply try to deal with things as best I can. I am not special in any way. I do not possess some magic crystal that contains the secrets of the cosmos. The truth be told: no one has all the answers. There is no such thing as a perfect life. I am simply a regular person who wants to relate to you what I have learned and how you may apply my experiences in your professional and private life. This is my goal.

I mean no disrespect to others in this self-help field who have greater intellect than me, but while there are those who are genuinely sincere in assisting others, there are so many "experts" I know who are full of hot air. I am not a professional "motivational" person. (In fact I hate being called or labeled a "speaker.") I am not a motivational guru, psychic, or New Age "life coach." While I do not have a degree in psychology, I have studied a great deal in this field and have encouraged individuals for over fifteen years with practical, commonsense advice—

ranging from gentle guidance to a psychological kick in the pants.

This book is basically simple and straightforward. I will not attempt to fool you with New Age psycho-babble. Yet as simplistic as this book may be, it will be deep rooted on addressing and changing your attitude and behavior. While I pray that this book helps you through the bumps of life, I know it will not solve every problem that suddenly arises. (I wish it could.) For life is ever changing.

Help Yourself is broken down into three separate yet interconnecting sections: 1) Get Rid of the Garbage in Your Life; 2) Know What You Want out of Your Life; and 3) Celebrate Who You Are and What You Have. In their own way, as each chapter deals with specific areas, the underlying meaning will be your own determination to make whatever adjustments you believe necessary as well as a calming sense of appreciation of who you are as a unique individual and what you have accomplished thus far. However, the premise of resilience and gratitude will be more evident in the last two sections. At the end of each chapter I will recap with a few sentences in bold print to help you for future reference.

As you've probably already noticed, I will be speaking directly to you—as if you and I were sitting directly across from each other having a dialogue together. After years assisting others, this is the best way I know how to get my point across. In addition to using some of my experiences as examples throughout this book, I will also provide illustrations from other peoples' lives—some well known to you, others not, but all of whom overcame seemingly impossible odds.

Those who know me know that I loathe writing. I have limited mechanics and it takes me hours to construct a single paragraph. I'd rather visit a dentist to have my teeth extracted without the aid of Novocaine, than spend countless hours on my laptop computer. I am doing this to make a difference. I strongly believe that as a society we some time ago crossed a threshold at which a great number of individuals give up on themselves too easily. We have raised generations who not only look for others to rescue them on virtually every matter concerning their lives, but demand that others—whether parents, friends, employers, or the government—immediately solve their problems to their liking. I learned as a child, shivering in my mother's garage, the value of personal responsibility and opportunity. Where else but America could I be fortunate enough to turn my life around and, more importantly, provide my son with a chance of living a productive, fulfilling life?

In the final analysis, it's up to you. You can read this book or other self-help tomes, watch all the high-energy, all-promising videos, or attend paradise-like weekend retreats, but at the end of the day it is you and you alone who have to make things happen. The cold, hard truth is that outside influences can only propel you so far. The drive has to come from within you. Whether it's this book or anything else you may come in contact with, *you* have to apply what you have learned on a daily basis.

294

HELP YOURSELF

———

With all of my heart I pray the time we spend together helps you now and for the time to come. I promise you this: I will do my absolute best to provide you with all that I have learned to enable you to live a happier, productive life. This is my standard to you.

Dave Pelzer

Part One

Get Rid of the Garbage in Your Life

1

The Need to Free Yourself

I was too young to know any better. It began between my mother and me around the age of four. By that time, mainly when my father was at work, it was normal for me to walk up to Mother, stand exactly three feet in front of her with my head bent towards the floor, and wait for her to grant me permission to speak, so I could then ask her permission to use the bathroom. I found it strange that my two brothers were permitted to go to the bathroom and do other things that for some reason I was not allowed to do.

I thought the way Mother treated me was completely normal, until one Sunday afternoon, when I was four years old, while father was away, Mother burst into the bedroom, forcing my brothers to scurry for cover, while she proceeded to beat me. By Mother's reddened eyes and foul breath, I knew she was drunk. But because of her intoxicated state, while continuing to hit me Mother slipped, grabbed my left arm to stabilize herself, and fell backward, pulling my arm out of its socket.

When I saw Mother's eyes blink, I knew she, too, had heard and felt the jerk of my arm separating from my shoulder. Yet Mother simply stood up, wiped her hands, shot me a look, then turned and walked away. The next day, the moment Father arrived home from his twenty-four-hour shift at work, Mother suddenly burst into tears, explaining how I had mysteriously fallen from the top bunk. My father, a fireman with medical training, didn't even bat an eye. Neither my brothers nor I ever thought of speaking up.

Hours later, when I received medical attention for the first time since the incident, I knew by the look in the doctor's eyes never to disclose what had really happened. Especially since he rattled on about how kind and sweet my mother was to him and his staff. I remember sitting on a metal swivel chair gazing up at the man in the white jacket, thinking that if everyone likes my mom so much and no one seems concerned about the truth, then *I* must be the problem.

I returned home with my arm in a green sling and a handful of tongue depressors, ready to show off to Father. But I somehow became invisible to him as Mother retold her story again and again. After the drama had reached its peak, I found myself completely alone with Mother. While continuing to cradle me in her arms, she swiveled her head to make sure we were alone. Bending down to look at me, she tightened her grip around me, and the color of her face seemed to darken. Without the need for words the message was clear: *Keep your mouth shut. You tell anyone and next time it will be worse. This will be our little secret.*

It was then, as a four-year-old child raised in the 1960s, that I knew *I was the problem*. I knew I deserved whatever treatment Mother gave me. It was at this age that I learned to push down my feelings of fear and self-worth. It was then that I knew I was alone. Above all, I knew exactly what had happened between Mother and me, but I did not, I could not, do anything to change it.

The Dilemma of Unresolved Issues

Every one of us has a past. All of us have had our share of problems. No one has a perfect life. Loved ones pass away. Parents divorce. Others who don't strive as hard and don't deserve the prized promotion receive it. We've all suffered broken hearts and some, like myself, may have had an unfortunate childhood.

The single most critical element I have found that prevents individuals from achieving their greatness is unresolved issues. It doesn't matter who you are—CEO, single parent, teen, a celebrity, or any other everyday folk—you can never reach your full potential unless you deal with and rid yourself of whatever may be troubling you.

A great number of people who don't deal with problematic situations in their lives develop a tendency to bury their emotions. They may truly believe they've not only addressed the problem but totally dealt with it as well—a short-term solution that may be the answer for some, but in reality rarely solves anything. What they're really doing is developing a bad habit. What's worse is they're still not dealing with the heart of the complication and over time the "quick fix" solution can manifest trouble of its own.

If you find yourself *automatically* reacting, over the simplest thing, in a frustrated, angry, defensive, distant manner, or find yourself trying to escape life by indulging more in your vices than you normally do, it's most likely due to an event linked to a past situation. After years or even weeks of becoming conditioned by the predicament, you may be so used to it that you may not even be aware of *why* you are reacting a particular way. Your mind has become so conditioned, it unconsciously responds as it was taught.

While serving on active duty flying for the air force, I became heavily involved working as a volunteer throughout the state of California with anything having to do with "youth at risk" and those who worked with them. When I received an offer to work part-time at a local juvenile hall, I instantly jumped at the opportunity. Because I was a foster child and had been placed in juvenile hall, I knew what it like for some teens. Yet as many books as I have read and courses I have taken in psychology and human development, I've learned more from the teenagers in juvenile hall than anywhere else.

One young woman, Nancy, had a mouth that would embarrass the most seasoned sailor and at times would spontaneously erupt and assault any boy who might have looked at her the wrong way. One particular time when she exploded, out of fear of her harming herself or others around her, it took three of us adults to restrain this wiry teenager until she finally calmed down. It was because of Nancy's constant negative behavior that she landed in the juvenile detention center. At first, as I'm sure a lot of scared teens do in her condition, Nancy felt she had to *act* a certain way, even more so because of her placement, in order to protect herself and her pride. After a few weeks, Nancy's attitude and behavior worsened to the point that she was facing the possibility of being placed in a psychiatric center.

I, and other staff members with far more experience and education than me, knew Nancy was not as bad as she appeared to be. Without sounding too judgmental, and only after she got to know me, I sincerely asked Nancy, "Why do you act that way?"

"You know why." She shrugged.

Getting to the point I stated, "No, I don't. Why are you *acting* the way you do?"

Nancy's response was so pure it almost knocked me over: "It's all I know."

I was lucky. After other counselors had worked with Nancy for months, she opened up to me, telling me that as a young girl she had constantly been tormented by her brothers and always felt she had to defend herself. As we continued to casually talk back and forth, I chided Nancy by saying, "I don't think anyone's going to even think of messing with you *now*." I emphasized the last word, helping Nancy realize she had yet to break her habit that she had acquired from years ago. "Besides," I added, "if you *act* a certain way, how will others not only judge you, but treat you?"

The staff continued to work with Nancy, helping her to recognize her habitual behavior and replace negative responses with more positive ones. So, when Nancy felt threatened, instead of beating up the boys, she would place her hands on her hips and give them a cold, long stare. Some of the male teens became frightened, unsure what Nancy might do to them; but she was simply controlling herself by counting to ten. Instead of spewing obscenities, Nancy would use her quick wit to fire off a thought-provoking anecdote.

As basic as it sounds, Nancy simply did not wish to be hurt. She felt this way because of a past issue that had taken root. She had *acted tough* for so long that over time she had forgotten why she was acting that *particular* way. In the end, once Nancy became aware, she and she alone had to make the change.

When I think about Nancy's initial statement, "It's all I know," it reminds me of something Oprah Winfrey once said on her show when she consoled a young lady with low self-esteem who found herself in trouble as well: "Now that you know better, do better."

A lot of folks harbor portions of their past in their hearts until it hardens and develops as a "reflex" type of response, until the behavior and/or attitude becomes normal for them.

Letting Go

All of us tend to suppress problems rather than deal with them as soon as they unexpectedly "pop up." And it doesn't have to be from some traumatic experience either. Teens and adults, especially those with low esteem, who crave independence and have the tremendous desire to belong, will do anything to fit in. Do you know anyone who's felt slightly intimidated attending college or being the "new guy" at work, and has kept his opinions to himself for fear of making a statement that might appear stupid or antagonistic? There are some of us, including myself, who have been in turbulent relationships and stayed in them, and would rather just go along than to risk being abandoned or face the possibility of a confrontation.

All of us at one time or another have found ourselves in uncomfortable conditions that we did not deal with. Again, it may be because of a habit from our past. I believe if we learn to deal with the everyday problems of life, it helps us all the more when something more arduous comes along.

Let's say you're at work, counting the minutes before you can bolt from the office. You've been looking forward to the weekend—to be with your family or have some quiet time by yourself—ever since Monday when you first rolled out of that warm, comfortable bed. You've been swamped this entire week and because you are so dedicated to your job, you've put off your personal needs. But now, seconds before you grab your things and flee, in strolls your boss. He's a huge, overbearing blowhard with the breath of an ox. With sweat trickling down his brow, he dumps a stack of reports that require your instant attention. With a wave of his hand he apologizes, for he would have gotten them to you sooner but he was out playing a round of golf. "Either way," he demands, "you've got to take care of this."

"But I'm about to leave; I've got plans!" you plead.

"That's okay," your boss replies as he leaves your cubicle, "I don't mind. Just make sure it's all done and ready for me first thing Monday morning."

You're fuming. Your heart rate quickens, your body becomes tense. You want to give your boss a piece of your mind, a spray can of deodorant, and a case of Altoids. On the drive home all you can think about is that man. Suddenly, you're stuck in traffic. The air conditioner is on the fritz. You miss your exit. Then you run out of gas because you were thinking about work when you passed the gas station. You're the poster child for Murphy's Law: If it can get worse, it will.

While I mean no disrespect to those in management and while the preceding is simply an illustration, I've known people who have had that type of experience. But answer this: With all that frustration, what kind of weekend are you going to have? Probably not a good one. In the preceding story, unless you quit, the only way out is to complete the task as best as you can and as quickly as possible so as to spend the remainder of your time on your terms.

In reality, have you ever had a similar overbearing problem that stemmed from work, a different kind of situation at home, or a more personal matter that, not dealt with, became so overwhelming that you became consumed by the situation, to the point it affected your attitude and every aspect of your day? I have. Have your problems affected your sleep, to the point that you could not get the rest you needed because of your bad day, then got up feeling groggy, unfocused, and still consumed by that troubling issue?

The Need to Rest Your Mind

So why is it that you can't get your mind to let go? The basic answer is your brain is simply trying to find the precise solution to that particular problem. If the problem is overwhelming, your mind will not function to its full capacity because it is being drawn to the dilemma it is focused on. If you find yourself constantly losing sleep, this is a serious predicament. If the brain is not allowed to rest it can, psychologically speaking, crash.

When it comes to the importance of resting one's mind, I recall a time years ago while I was serving in the military. I had the rare opportunity to observe one of the army's elite organizations, the Rangers, during the last phase of their training. Having been a graduate of the army's paratrooper jump school, I appreciate and respect how grueling and rigorous their qualifications are. These razor-sharp commandos working in small units are hardened to accomplish their objective at all costs and against all odds. Since the last part of the Rangers' training is under constant, intense conditions of simulated combat, the trainees are required to complete their various tasks while being physically and psychologically pushed and pulled in every direction, with only one hour's sleep a day.

Imagine yourself wearing the same set of clothes for over a week, chilled to the bone, past exhaustion, muscles aching from being weighed down by your weapon, ammunition, and forty-pound backpack, and all the while you're crawling, hiking, rappelling, or rafting with not only simulated mortars exploding wherever you step and gunfire rattling off, but a mock force that wishes you harm. Yet, as physically tired as these men were, their reflexes remained razor sharp and their morale was extremely high. To answer the question how in the world these men were able to do it, a veteran instructor smiled, stating, "These men are in top physical and, more importantly, psychological condition. The brain only needs thirty to forty minutes of sound sleep a day to recharge itself. It's like resetting a circuit breaker. We bombard these men with ever-changing, life-threatening scenarios, so when they sleep, they sleep well. By the time they wake up, their brains are rested and ready to go.

"They have to adjust quickly, effectually. They cannot allow anything to get into their minds that may bog them down. This entire course is more psychological than physical. If your mind's not rested, focused, or if you tell yourself you ain't gonna make it, you're history, you're washed out of the program. The body can endure practically anything—pain, fatigue, you name it—*but it's the mind that matters.*"

I think of my experience with the Rangers as a hardcore business-management course. Those professionals are able to work through a multitude of situations and are able to do so, in part because they allow their minds to rest. The main lesson I learned, which I use to this day, is no matter the situation anyone may be facing, the brain has to shut down or "reset" itself every day, in order to deal with the challenges of the next day.

I'm in no way saying you have to be some he-man Rambo commando in order to sort through your issues. Truth be told, I'm a wimp compared to those in uniform. I'm middle aged, too lazy, and no longer do three hundred sit-ups a day. But I know this: With all that every one of us does in a single day, with all the problems that bombard us, if we do not learn to deal with these issues and turn off "the switch," we will run ourselves into the ground.

The reason why you may not be able to get a good night's sleep is your mind is desperately searching for an answer to your problem. Look at it this way: Your brain is like a CD-ROM—it is constantly spinning at extreme speeds in its function to keep the machine, your body, operating. The brain not only processes information but stores data faster and better than any computer chip mankind can devise. If you have "programmed" your brain not to address a situation, your "computer" in a way will store your problems in its "To be solved at a later date" file; but over time when that file becomes full, the CD-ROM becomes task saturated, continuing to spin as it searches for a solution to its function. So what can eventually happen? The computer crashes.

This is why I cannot stress enough the value of a good night's sleep. With a recharged battery you are all the better when it comes to tackling whatever comes your way. When it comes to dealing with issues, think of it as removing data from your computer disk that you need to do on a daily basis, so your file does not become too full, forcing your computer to crash.

You need to reprogram how you deal with troubling issues, just as Nancy did when she became upset, by replacing a bad program with a more positive one. Imagine being the president of the United States. Every single day the president is bombarded by countless situations, up to life-threatening crises, that can have repercussions around the world. How does the president do it? The president does not have superhero powers with Einsteinian intelligence, but is a human being just like you and me. And like any good manager, the president deals with any situation by confronting it. After collecting all the information, the president considers all the options and consequences of each scenario, makes a decision, and moves on to the next problem. Not to downplay the magnitude of the office of the president, but it is basically what most of us do on a daily basis—from single parents balancing their budget, those who apply themselves every day at work, to students trying to remain focused when studying for final exams.

So, when a situation arises, address *your problem*, consider *your options*, then accept the repercussions of *your decision*. If you believe in spiritual guidance, meditate or pray about it, *then* make *your decision* and let the situation go. After you've made your decision it is vital that you relax, just as the president plays a round of golf in the middle of a crisis so that his mind can unwind and can focus on the next series of situations. And you, just like the president, will find that once a problem is solved another one quickly replaces it. But over time as you learn to continually deal with problems, however frustrating or disgusting they may be, you'll discover that not only will your esteem grow because now you're in charge of your life—and not some ghost from your past keeping you down—but more important, psychologically you will be all the healthier.

Controlled Eruptions

Please understand: you will never be able to solve all your problems to your liking. And at times you will feel overwhelmed and frustrated. That's life. Remember that story about the pompous boss with the bad breath? You know you can't tell him off, and you will most likely have to give up another weekend to ensure the job is done. Yet, inside of you this enormous pressure is building up like a volcano. What can you do? Two words: *controlled eruptions.*

We now realize how damaging it is to keep everything bottled up, so we have to relieve that pressure. Years ago my son, Stephen, was playing Little League baseball. As much as he tried, he simply was not playing one of his best games. Inning after inning I could tell by his body language that the strain was building up inside of him. On the drive home Stephen was like a statue; he refused to talk and barely moved. As a parent I believe in being a positive role model and instilling manners. However, Stephen and I have always had an agreement that when a situation dictated I would, for just a few minutes, not grade him as my son but as his friend. This was one of those times. I told Stephen that for the next five minutes he could kick, yell, swear, or basically do whatever he had to, to get the tension out of his system. After a few seconds of hesitation, Stephen purged. Five minutes later he collected himself, then we talked a bit more and within a few miles he felt better. Keep in mind it didn't change the outcome of his game. But by opening up, Stephen was able to think about what to do *the next time* he might be in that same position, and by relieving that pressure he felt different than he had immediately after his game.

Stephen basically addressed the situation, made a decision on what to do next time, and moved on.

Opening up not only helps you relieve that pent-up

anxiety, but sometimes can be just enough to get you through.

You can do the same thing Stephen did. Having a bad day at work? Or on your way to work or school after a problem at home? And, to make matters worse, is it a big day for you and you only have little time between where you've been and where you're going? If you have to, and if you have no other way of relieving the strain, during the drive to your destination allot yourself a specific amount of time to vent a little and shout in the car. Smack that steering wheel a few times. Screech at that radio talk-show host. Imagine that your supervisor or that person who made you upset is beside you and give that person a piece of your mind. Within reason, alleviate some of that pressure to clear your mind and enable it to focus on the events of your day.

Do not get so upset that you cause an accident. Again, I stress the term *controlled eruptions. You are in control* as you *vent that pressure.* Sometimes when I'm driving, I bark at the radio for a few minutes until I feel better. When I'm alone, looking at photos of my wife and son, realizing they are the reason I do what I do is enough to pull me through. Before or after a big day I work out at the gym. At home I'll walk for hours among the redwood trees. No matter my hectic schedule, *every day* I try to do something that will alleviate the stress of my day. My wife, Marsha: she shops. She has a weakness for makeup, shoes, and anything within the confines of a mall. But at least Marsha comes home happier than when she left, and proudly proclaims her mantra "I feel much better!"

On a more serious note, by leaving the office Marsha gets away from her pressure-filled environment. In her car Marsha applies that time to decompress as she sings out loud. In a psychological sense, walking the length of the mall several times at a brisk pace helps Marsha diminish her stress all the more. The point I'm trying to make is: within reason do what you have to in order to relieve your daily stress. Take some form of control—get away from that confrontation, write a scathing letter that you never mail, take a stroll anywhere you feel at peace. Once a day, three times a day, a hundred times a day, whatever it takes, make a sincere effort to deal with life's unpleasantries as best as you can.

Once, when I was speaking for a business and after hearing how the morale was low and production was down, I recommended that the organization dispose of office rank and have a productive gripe session. Without the fear of reprisal, anyone would be allowed to speak her mind, not only on what was wrong, but she had to have a recommendation to make things better. In this way, those who were preoccupied not only addressed their problems once and for all, but became proactive in the process. The only stipulations I made were that the discussion not be a onetime quick fix, but should at least be a quarterly conference or when the situation warranted; and secondly, it was not an opportunity to be used as a perpetual whine fest. As time went on, morale and productivity rose while stress, apprehensiveness, and needless complaining declined.

This is basically the same method that Stephen and I used after his troublesome ball game, as well as do a lot of families. Every so often dispense with the protocol, speak your mind freely, openly or to yourself, and do something about the complication. By addressing and relieving pressure you are helping to ensure that the circuit breaker in your head can be reset, so you can live your life better.

Cleansing Your Soul

However, on the other side of the coin, I cannot tell you how many people I have met who have become helpless victims or jaded souls. Why? They either became too frightened of opening up or allowed their unresolved issues to get the best of them. Even though some of these individuals fully realized, through their own choice, they were destined to live a joyless life, the prospect of dealing with their problematic situation became too much for them. The sad reality is that if some of these people could have confronted the problem they would have seen the situation for *what it was*, rather than *what they thought it was*, and they might have turned the tide.

To use my son as another example, when Stephen was about five years old I could tell something was troubling him. Whenever I had tried to get him to talk about it, he simply blushed with embarrassment, saying I wouldn't understand. Finally, for whatever reason, I was able to get

Stephen to talk. At first he was a little apprehensive. He even stopped before he got to the core of the issue and wanted to run off. Thankfully, as he plowed through, his eyes suddenly widened with the discovery that his problem was not as bad as he had thought it was. The second Stephen finished, he sat amazed at his own breakthrough of simply opening up and telling me everything, and before I could give him any fatherly advice he kissed me and ran off to spend the rest of his day playing outside.

When I listen to folks who tell me their predicaments, I try to get them to open up, to tell me everything, rather than scratch the surface. For the most part, when we get to the core of the issue, we realize the situation that we held on to for so long, that caused us so much pain, is not as bad as it seems or seemed at the time.

For lack of a better word, it's what I call *purging*. When you have stomach troubles, and if they're bad enough, your body will physically reject whatever it is that is making you sick. Often when I have been sick, I did not physically regurgitate everything I should have, so I remained in great pain until I purged whatever it was that made me feel ill. Then, like a lot of people, within a short time I actually felt better. The reason: There was nothing left within me to make me sick.

I am not trying to sound tasteless, but I cannot tell you how important, how imperative, it is for you to *psychologically purge* yourself of whatever is ailing you. After everything you have read thus far, if you still have situations that seem to pull you down or if you seem tied to something in your past, if you do not "vomit" from the recesses of your soul, you are most likely destined to be a slave of your experience.

Have you ever known someone who has been in therapy for years? Now, I am not taking a jab at those in the field of psychology, but one of the reasons a person may feel she needs that much help may be because she is still skating around the edges, rather than getting to the core of the issue that required her to be in therapy in the first place.

* * *

I have had the privilege of meeting hundreds of thousands of people, and I have seen so many lives that were crushed because some kept issues locked away deep in their hearts. But once they purged, and I mean released everything, at the very least they felt a little alleviated, cleaner. Their lives' perspective changed for the better. Overall they became more self-reliant and independent. Over time they became whole. Like everyone else, these folks still had to deal with everyday situations, but having freed themselves from their shackled past they were able to do so now with a little more relative ease.

To reiterate, I am not talking about a troubled childhood. Divorce, losing a love, a career that might have been, violated trust . . . you name it, all of us have endured the deepest of pain. But are you a prisoner to your past or stronger and wiser because of it?

317

Yes, purging yourself can be painful, embarrassing, and at times disgusting. What other options do you have? Ask yourself this: *If what I've been doing so far isn't working, isn't it about time I did something different?*

Years ago Bob, a dear friend of mine, lost his father to cancer. Three years after the death of his father, Bob still grieved over his loss. Over time he became reclusive, overweight, and miserable. It affected Bob's marriage, the relationship with his children, his promising career, his sleep, and ultimately his health. On one visit, because he had known me for years, Bob allowed me to take him out for a drive. Without his knowing our destination, I drove him to the cemetery. Once there, I had to pry him from the car and lead him to his father's tombstone, where he sheepishly stood until suddenly his body shook, then he exploded with a surge of tears. While a grown man weeping on his hands and knees in the middle of the day might prove unmasculine and embarrassing to some, Bob later confessed not only how cleansed he felt, but how an invisible weight—that had held him down for years—lifted from his soul.

For years Bob had carried in his heart the regret that he'd never had the opportunity to say good-bye to his father. Bob also lived with the guilty sense that he could have been a better son. That evening back at home Bob finally fell into a deep, sound sleep. With every day afterward he made progress. While he informed me he would never be the *same,* he has now dedicated himself to being a *better* person and a more loving father to his children.

It had taken Bob three years and an endless amount of

suffering for him to finally come face to face with his issue. His upbeat outlook didn't come overnight, and it took him several more "talks" with his father until he felt strong enough to shed himself of guilt and of whatever baggage he had carried with him for so long.

Bob's situation changed when he achieved a sense of closure with his father. He was able to open up at his father's grave site. For others, I recommend talking to someone, anyone. Sometimes it just takes that one person whom you know to make the difference—a parent, spouse, lover, friend, someone at work. As long as you feel comfortable and trust that person, I recommend you take the chance. For folks with more serious issues, I recommend professional help—counselor, therapist, psychologist, someone who specializes in that particular field—which can help guide you along the path to becoming a more wholesome, fulfilled, happy person.

Again—if what you are doing so far isn't working, isn't it about time you did something different? Make the change to free yourself!

HELP YOURSELF REMINDERS

* SETTLE YOUR PROBLEMS AS PROMPTLY AND AS THOROUGHLY AS YOU ARE ABLE.

* LET GO OF A PAST YOU CANNOT CHANGE.

* IN THE MIDST OF FIGHTING LIFE'S BATTLES, RELAX.

* VENT YOUR FRUSTRATIONS IN A CONTROLLED YET CLEANSING MANNER.

* HAVE THE COURAGE TO PURIFY YOURSELF OF WHAT-EVER MAY BE HOLDING YOU BACK.

———

2

Surviving a Negative Environment

Recently I read an article about a confessed killer's defense attorney who pleaded for the court's mercy. The attorney claimed that his defendant, "Mr. Smith," was simply a victim of society. Since Mr. Smith had no father figure, his mother became an unwilling slave to drugs, and as a teenager Mr. Smith could not adapt to the stringent guidelines of school, so he fell in with the wrong crowd. His only role models were from television, violent movies, and graphic video games. If there was an injustice, the attorney ranted, it was against Mr. Smith. The attorney was then reported to have lowered his voice and, dipping his head toward the jury that would decide on his client's fate, sighed, "My client is simply a product of a negative environment."

With all due respect to the Mr. Smiths of the world, being exposed to a negative setting *does not* mean you are either destined for a life of crime or doomed to an unfulfilled life. Former chairman of the Joint Chiefs of Staff

General Colin Powell, the first African American to hold such office, was raised in a rat-infested ghetto in Harlem, New York. His parents—immigrants from Jamaica—did all they could for their son, yet it was Colin who had to decide his fate. Some may say it would have been understandable for young Colin to have been swallowed up by the gritty streets of New York or fallen through the cracks of society, but he, wanting something more for himself, enlisted in the army, immersed himself in college, and eventually came up through the ranks to lead America's armed forces in operations Desert Shield and Desert Storm.

As previously addressed in the last chapter, all of us have had unpleasant experiences and situations that we have had to deal with on a daily basis. And, many of us have been subjected to bad surroundings. Again, it comes down to awareness. While both Mr. Smith and General Powell experienced unfortunate conditions, in my estimation both individuals made vastly different choices that drastically affected their futures. No matter the environment, there comes a time when the choice is ours.

When I was removed from my mother's custody and became a ward of the court through the foster-care system, I was required to meet with a psychiatrist. One time the doctor had a private meeting with my foster mother and informed her that, in his professional opinion, because of my extended exposure to a violent and desperate world, there was little hope of my becoming "normally adjusted." And he believed that since the law of averages was against me, I would most likely end up in prison or would commit suicide.

But what if we, like Colin Powell, used our negative environment to make us strive for something better?

Because of my childhood experience, all I desired was a better life for myself. From generations ago to this very day, countless individuals who have lived under oppressive conditions have made the journey to America, to have an opportunity to make a life for themselves and their children. These individuals took a gamble and faced whatever obstacles were in their way and paid whatever price they had to pay in order to change their setting. And once they arrived, things did not get better overnight. The bottom line: Our country's bedrock is one man or woman with a resilient, self-reliant attitude. While adverse surroundings play an important role in our lives, if we are willing we do not have to be dominated by them.

That is why when I hear or read a story of a Mr. Smith and how his dismal surroundings *forced* him to harm others, I become slightly agitated. Through a choice of his own, Mr. Smith used his past environment as a crutch. And no matter one's environment, that does not give a person the excuse to promote chaos and inflict harm on others.

To be fair, I must say I have been told that by the time children reach ten years of age, their environment does have a significant bearing on their lives—their esteem, prejudices, limitations, how they view the world, and how they fit into it. However, from all the reports I have read and the specialists I know in the field of human behavior, I strongly believe: if people have a basic understanding of right from wrong, possess a strong desire to better themselves and persist in their cause, they can break the chain of a negative environment.

A Matter of Choice

But even with the best of surroundings, *it is the individual who decides his or her own fate.* Years ago as a foster child, I had a close friend who came from the epitome of the perfect family. My friend Joe had two loving parents, who both worked hard and were active in church, and their neighborhood resembled something out of *Leave It to Beaver.* Joe seemingly had everything. With Joe's passion for science fiction and space exploration, we all knew he was destined to work with NASA. But some anomaly happened to Joe during his teenage years—an issue he refused to address with even his closet friends and family—and to this day Joe, even with the support that I would have killed for when I was a kid, has a fraction of the ambition he once had and his dreams are a thing of the past. As sad as it is for me to say, Joe, even with a positive environment and guidance, lost his desire, and the loss affects him still.

When it comes to dealing with negative surroundings, I believe it boils down to three options: We become a product of a negative environment; we find a way out of the environment; or adjust to it as best we can.

Mr. Smith is the perfect example of a person's becoming the product of a negative environment. I believe that all of us carry portions of our past throughout our lives. But even a bad experience doesn't have to be detrimental. My mother, before she began treating me so inhumanely, would always decorate the entire house with Christmas ornaments the day after Thanksgiving. Now, every year, the day following Thanksgiving, my family and I break open the boxes of ornaments, hang the bright lights, and adorn our home as my mother once did. With all that Mother did to me, remembering some of the good times helps me to let go of the bad ones.

When You Can't Let Go of Your Past

But some people who can't seem to let go of their negative past may find themselves doomed because of it. A woman whom I have known for years, Nora, had a tough childhood and was constantly berated by her mother, who either lied to Nora over the smallest things or made reflexive excuses, blaming her problems on her daughter. One day, as a teenager, Nora ran away, so no one could "control her" or "tell her what to do" any longer. That was over twenty-five years ago, and to this day whenever a serious or everyday situation needs to be addressed, Nora psychologically runs away. She either brushes off the predicament, instantaneously fires off a veil-thin lie, or blames her woes on someone else. As an adult she has become a carbon copy of her mother, to the point that Nora, who still loathes her mother's behavior toward her, has moved away several times to begin anew, but within weeks has always returned to be near her. And Nora, who hates her mother's meddling in her everyday affairs, calls her mother several times a day seeking her approval. At times Nora, who has the tremendous capacity for kindness and could achieve her greatness, lacks the resolve to break away from her environment.

I have the highest respect for anyone who gives her all to better herself, for I know from personal experience how arduous it can be to break away from a controlling situation. That's why it's hard for me to tell Nora's story. I saw so much within her; if she could only have dealt with her issues and "broken away" once and for all, I believe with all my heart that Nora would have been a happier more fulfilled person.

When it comes to breaking away from a negative environment, sometimes we have to do just that, and as hard and as emotional as it may be, we have to make a clean break. When folks tell me that they absolutely cannot, for whatever reason, get along with that one person, to the point that the relationship consists of yelling or tempers constantly erupting like a volcano, then my advice is: Stay away. There is practically no reason why someone has to expose himself to that setting. Maintain your distance from that family member, lover, friend, or those at work. If things are that bad, for now, at least, there's no need to complicate or ignite the situation further, for it can only pull you in deeper. And if you have to attend those family reunions, social events, or meetings at work, keep your cool and limit your exposure. On behavioral matters, if you find yourself saying things or acting in ways you normally never did before, it may be because of your negative surroundings. Sure, that one person or that group may supposedly accept you or be nice to you, but ask yourself this: Do you really like the person you are becoming? If not, then break away and stay away.

Maybe for Nora and others like her, the "pull" from her environment was too much for them to deal with. I'm not sure if we can even appreciate how much our everyday environment may have an affect on us. Have you known anyone who has tried to quit smoking but had friends who constantly smoked? It's nearly impossible unless he makes a drastic change. The same goes for those who are addicted to drugs or alcohol, or fight to keep their emotions under control. While serving in the air force and volunteering to work with those in prison and juvenile hall, I found that as much as the inmates wanted to change their lives, without hesitation nearly all of them, when finally released, went back to the same setting and eventually "cycled" by reacting as they had before . . . and were returned to be incarcerated again.

The refusal either to stay away or break away once and for all from such a detrimental setting could possibly—just as with those who "cycle" in and out of institutions—lead to serious consequences. One can never tell if suddenly one day they will find themselves "sucked in" and by the time they realize their situation discover it is too late to escape. For some folks who are already neck deep in their environment, over time it becomes part of their psychological makeup. Are you familiar with the fable about the coyote and the scorpion? Being stranded on one side of the river and wanting to cross, the scorpion tried to convince the coyote to carry him across the water. "But if I do, surely you will sting me with your deadly tail," stated the coyote. "No, I promise, I will not," guaranteed the scorpion. So the coyote allowed the scorpion to crawl on his back and began to make his way across the river. All went well until they reached the middle of the stream when suddenly the coyote felt a sharp sting behind his head. "Why did you do that?" the coyote cried. "By doing so you realize both of us are now doomed to die!" "Yes," replied the deadly creature, "I am fully aware. But I could not help myself. It's in my nature!"

My point is be extremely careful of where you "tread" and the types of people you may "pick up along the way" during the course of your life.

The Baggage of Guilt

From what I know, those who try to break away from a negative environment may carry with them either guilt or a form of appeasement or combination of both, making it all the harder to break free. Even with the fantastic life I am able to live today, at times I feel a wall of shame crash over me like a wave. There are instances when my hands shake, I stutter, and parts of my body lock up. When I was rescued, my brothers still had to endure my

mother's insanity, while I was being nurtured and protected by my foster parents. Today, I focus on applying
myself to help others so they will not have to suffer the
same treatment as my brothers and I did.

I'm not the only one who has to deal with the burden
of guilt. A few years ago I had the honor of meeting a
woman named Michelle, who is a survivor of the Holo-
caust. When she was a child, toward the end of World
War II in Europe, the Nazis put Michelle and her mother
on a train that was to be sent to a death camp. Michelle's
mother gave her life to save her young daughter Michelle.
When I had the opportunity to speak with Michelle, she
revealed a crushing force that had weighed upon her all
of her life. "Why was I spared when so many others
died?" After she poured out her feelings, I held her and
asked her the question "Was there anything you could
have done to prevent what had happened?" Michelle
shook her head no. "Then you can do no more."

I think all of us in one way or another carry a regret
that's connected to our circumstances. As stressed in the
last chapter: In order to move forward one has to let go.
When I was being consoled as a teenager in foster care
for the immense guilt and shame I felt at the time, as I
was desperately trying the find the precise answers to
the conflict between Mother and me, the therapist asked
a bold question: "Is there anything you can do to change
the past?" I sobbed, shaking my head no. "Then you can
do no more!" My therapist instructed, "Learn from it and
move forward."

As simplistically obvious as this may sound, none of

us has the capability to step into a time machine and transport ourselves to the past and change the one single event or element in our lives that would have made things right. Even if you could, I believe—as in the case with my mother and me—that it was in fact a *small series of events* that led to our situation. If I were sitting with you right now I would simply say, "Learn from your past! Don't become a prisoner of it!"

If you feel guilty because you were the cause of what may have happened, again learn from the situation, and resolve not to repeat the same mistake. Unfortunately, there are a great number of people who make the same errors over and over again, in part because of their environment. Just over a year ago I remarried. Because my first marriage failed, I am now more determined to work daily on my relationship with my wife. All of us have regrets and I'm sure we have said and done things we are not proud of. If you find yourself unable to move forward or feel "pulled in" because of your past environment, ask yourself: *Was there anything I could have done to prevent the situation?* If the answer is yes, then *do* something different now and become a better person because of it. If your response is no, then you have your answer. Next, ask yourself: *Did I do the best I could at the time?* If the answer is yes, then let the past go. If the response is no, again, learn something from it and *do* something positive about the situation the next time.

When it comes to breaking the chains of a negative environment, I think of my eldest brother, Ron, who has been a police officer for nearly twenty-five years. Ron, like countless others, including Mr. Smith and Nora, could have been pulled down because of his negative environment. However, as if in response to it Ron has applied himself to serving and protecting others. I have found that a great number of those who work in the law-enforcement, social-services, and foster-care fields do so because of their unfortunate environment. Part of the reason I do what I do is so I can assist others to break free as well.

Pop star legend and super diva Tina Turner is another example. After surviving years of an abusive marriage to a controlling, drug-addicted husband, Ms. Turner summoned the strength and guts needed to literally crawl away from her environment. Afterward, and with over-whelming odds, this lady gave everything she had—physically, emotionally, and spiritually—for the mere chance of recapturing the career she so desperately loved. But because Ms. Turner did what she had to in order to free herself, she was able to achieve the phenomenal career that she maintains to this day.

Those Who Appease

Making sure you don't become a prisoner to a negative environment also means being careful that you don't become a "please-aholic." So many folks, myself included, who are or were exposed to a negative setting, with or without knowing may find themselves overcompensating by trying to obtain other people's approval—parents, relatives, friends, spouses, coworkers, etc.—especially those who make them feel inferior. As a child, when my mother constantly berated me for being stupid, I tried to compensate for her affection. Without the aid of glasses I would read mammoth-sized books in a dark garage. Months later, when I brought home good grades on my report card, Mother would beat me because she claimed she was still disappointed with me. But even after the next report card, when I proudly displayed to Mother the highest marks, she still wasn't satisfied. No matter how many chores I flawlessly accomplished, no matter how hard I strove as a child to be perfect for her, nothing I did made Mother love me.

Years later as a teenager in foster care, because I was so desperate to make friends at school I made myself into the class goof and soon became the butt of everyone's jokes. When I was approached by a group of kids who were *thinking* about being my friends, craving their approval I began stealing candy bars, then toys and records, for my newfound "friends." As you can guess, sad to say in the end, after I gave all of myself, no one liked me or wanted anything to do with me.

As an adult I realized I was still trying to please others too much when it came to business matters. At times I was fully aware that I was getting walked on, taken advantage of, or was doing more and going to more extremes than others. When I discovered that as an author and speaker I was "mismanaged," I asked, "Why? After all I've done, why? Why me?" The responses were that I was such a nice guy, no one ever thought I would say anything. My overwhelming need to please kept me from standing up for myself.

Just a few years ago, out of habit I found myself practically begging one of my relatives to attend a prestigious award ceremony in which I had been selected as one of the Ten Outstanding Young Americans. Because my esteem was so low, not only did I not feel worthy of the recognition, but with every word that spilled from my mouth I found myself promising my relative the moon, while inside I knew I was making a complete jerk out of myself. Even as I hung up the phone, I thought if I could only do this *one thing* or maybe if I did or said *something else*, then I might be worthy of the attention and respect of a family member who had never truly cared about me in the first place! For most of my life, my desire to please others was so powerful that I instantly did so without a second thought for myself.

Please don't get me wrong: I think it's important for all of us to apply ourselves, with everything we have, every day, but we need to channel our efforts for the right cause. And while I believe it's vital for all of us to be kind and display manners while being humble, I have learned the valuable lesson of doing so *without* giving myself away in the process. Because of my initial environment, grappling for others' approval was all I knew. For people like my mother, my fair-weather friends, or the inconsiderate people I worked with as an adult, I could have discovered the cure for cancer, AIDS, *and* the common cold, but, alas, it would not have been enough to make anyone like me for who I was.

I'm only suggesting that you be careful of being a please-aholic. The truth is, no matter what you do for the sole purpose of having others admire you, your efforts, as mine were, will most likely be in vain. And no matter how much you do for others—those so-called "friends"—it can never be enough. You may be liked by others for a while, but only as long as you have something they want from you. How many stories have you read about movie stars or rock stars who are suddenly surrounded by so many so-called "friends," right up until the moment their fame or money runs out?

Remember that, as much as Nora detested her mother, she would still desperately crave her approval? It seems to me that there are people who feed, in a sense, off of others. These people are not happy in their lives, for whatever reason (most likely an unresolved issue from their past) and keep drawing from the well of others to fill whatever ails them. No matter how much they suck off of others, no matter how miserable they can make others in order to elevate their own self-worth . . . it is never enough!

Resolve to Take a Stand

There can be endless reasons why folks may not like us, no matter what we do. Without any feelings of revenge or animosity, I truly believe my mother basically hated herself, *then* the world around her. Unfortunately, Mother took her frustrations out on me, my brothers, and anyone else she believed got in her way. As a teenager in foster care, my "friends" at school never liked me, but fed off my desperation for companionship, that enabled them to lead me on. Those I worked with may have thought I was too naive or lacked the guts to stand up for myself. As for my relative whom I pleaded with to attend the ceremony with me, his refusal may have been the result either of resentment that I was to receive an accolade or of shame at what had happened to me as a child. In the final analysis, does it really matter? I cannot tell you how many hours I have wasted dissecting the hows or whys and what I could have done for the sole result of appeasing others. In the end, you must have the will to simply be yourself.

My pivotal moment came minutes after my father's funeral. Just days before, my father had passed away in my arms, as a lonely broken man who could not even say good-bye with mere words or a blink of his eyes due to the severity of his cancer. In the months that Father lay in the hospital bed, Mother never made the ten-mile drive to see him. Immediately after the service, beside the church, in a fit of rage Mother exploded at me, slapping me on the side of my face so that a trickle of blood fell to the pavement. As she raised her hand to strike me again, I surprised myself by saying, "Don't even think about it! All those years you tried to break me and I'm still here. I'm a good person. I try my best in everything I set out to do. I make mistakes, I screw up, but I learn. I don't blame others for my problems. I stand on my own. I won't waste my life away. If you taught me *anything*, you taught me that."

That was a crucial juncture for me. I never planned it, and I never meant to be arrogant, but as I spoke those words I could feel a giant weight lift from my shoulders. Those few moments in time set my life on a different course. I didn't have to repeat the cycle of hate and self-destruction that I had been exposed to. And no matter my past, I had just made my declaration to break away from a sickening environment.

Now, after a few hard knocks, I stand up for myself. I ask the hard questions. Without being arrogant or rude, I'll speak my piece. Every day I do my best and if there are those who disagree with me, it's not the end of the world. I no longer beat myself up in the vain hope of others' consent. At times it's a hard balancing act, but I keep myself in constant check. I can do no more.

My recommendation is not to waste your time and energy. There are far more important things in life. When you please others in the hopes of being accepted, you lose your self-worth in the process. As elementary as this sounds: To help yourself, you have to be yourself. Be the best person you can possibly be. When you make a mistake or feel beaten down, learn from the situation and pick yourself up. The folks you may be trying to impress, if they like what they see, will most likely come to you. And instead, you can apply your time and efforts in a different direction, in favor of others in need who could benefit from your unique qualities and sincerity.

By being more self-assured, you're not only taking a

stand but you will actually learn more quickly to adapt to a negative environment.

It's Not All Bad

Basically, we all know what to do when it comes to our environment, and if the world were perfect we wouldn't have to give it a second thought. The reality is that the world we live in isn't perfect and we are only human, prey to our emotions; even though at times we know what we may be doing isn't the best thing for us, especially when it comes to matters of the heart. And since there is so much that can pull us down and because we are constantly bombarded by negativity, all I am trying to suggest is for you to lessen your exposure to a negative environment. Even though parents continually remind their children and teenagers of the importance of this admonition—ranging anywhere from whom they hang out with, whom they date, and whom to stay away from—a large number of adults I have met believe that *they* are impervious to their environment.

Have you noticed at work that the smallest amount of negativity can erode or even paralyze someone's home or business? Personality conflicts, political agendas, or feelings of revenge become the main focus. The negativity takes your mind off your objective, your everyday activities, your studies, or your work, and you become caught up in something that doesn't really matter. On the personal side, I'm sure we all know someone who hates the idea of family reunions or being with friends of friends who are so strange that they must be from another planet. At work, have you ever seen or heard those at the "water cooler club"? A small band of whiners, conspirators, gossipers, whose work output is marginal at best, who know who's been doing what to whom and for how long.

What do you do? Since we will never be able to change everything in our world to our liking, we have to learn to adjust and make the most of what we have. The one thing I have been told is that the key to a good marriage, whether it is one of business or a personal union, is *compromise*. When it comes to surviving a negative environment you can at least begin by limiting your exposure. Think of it as radiation: a sudden burst of exposure can instantly vaporize you, but what a lot of people forget is that small continual doses of radiation can be just as deadly. So, limit your *exposure* to a negative environment. If possible stay the heck away from those water cooler gossipers, the folks craving your appeasement, or anyone or group that you don't *have to* put up with. And whenever you come into contact with those people or situations that drive you up the wall, be the better person and make the best of things. Grit your teeth, and smile, smile, smile.

For my second deployment to Saudi Arabia, I left behind my four-year-old son days before Christmas of 1990. I was fully aware of the high probability of fighting a war against Saddam Hussein and all the elements that went with it. I could have complained how unfair the situation was, whined about lack of creature comforts that I and the other five hundred thousand men and women did not have due to our location in the desert, but the only thing it would have accomplished would be to take my mind off my assigned mission. There was not one thing I could have done to change my environment, so to make things a little bit better I brought with me several freshly cut Christmas trees that were so huge I could barely fit them into the airplane, stockings with candies, and a few cases of apple cider. Others brought small CD players with Christmas music. On Christmas day the celebration only lasted a few minutes. And it didn't change the stress and anxiety we were dealing with daily, but it did make matters just a little bit better. I believe that sometimes these small things might be just enough to get you through.

So many folks complain about things without dealing with their circumstances, and sooner or later these same folks find themselves part of the same setting they complained about in the first place. Is there anything *you* can do to *change* things at home or work that can alter the environment? I have found for some, things weren't quite as bad as they thought they were. Another question: Are you willing to *compromise* in your current situation that troubles you, or can you *put up with* how things are? If you are willing to change something in order to make things better, then do it, but do so on a continual basis— whether it's your attitude, staying away from others who pull you down—whatever the case, *do* something. If you can put up with the situation, I recommend making the most of it. Family members don't always get along; even with the best of jobs one or two folks can bring down morale and productivity. With everything, some days, some situations are better than others.

But if you are adamant that, after everything, you cannot survive your current environment, then the only thing I can recommend is for you to get out. If you have tried everything you can and after exhausting all options, and if you wish for something better, then you have to be willing to change your environment. Again, so many folks complain how bad things are for them, but few are willing to *follow through* and do something about it. If your job is too stressful and you cannot be with your family as much as you want, then you may have to change jobs, work part-time, or find an alternate source of income. Now, the trade-off is you may not have the income you were accustomed to but are willing to give that up for better peace of mind. I have consoled countless mothers and fathers who confided in me how miserable their relationships were, even to the point of extreme domestic violence, and even though most of these individuals knew that after everything they had tried in the past their situation only became worse, they still would not leave. I would stress to them, "That's no way to live." The answer I nearly always received was something like "Well, who's gonna take care of my kids?" Or "I'll never be able to be with someone else. No one else wants me." The statements went on and on. I truly feel so bad for these folks who hate their situations, but as uncompassionate as this may sound: If *they* got themselves into their predicament, then *they*—if their environment is that bad—have to get themselves out of it.

Once again there are so many people who, when all else fails them, look for others to solve their problems. This is why I have the highest respect for single parents, like a friend of my wife's named Susan. Here's a lady who is self-employed, working seven days a week, raising her two children totally on her own, providing them a natural, caring, loving, and safe environment. When asked, "You refuse child support from your ex?" Susan smiles and says, "Yes. I broke away on my terms and didn't want anything to tie me down. It was hard. But in the end that atmosphere was killing me and my girls. I had to make a clean break. We all love each other very much and have a very happy home."

The Choice Is Yours

For many of us bad relationships, situations, or environments are extremely hard to walk away from. All of us for the most part know what we need to do, but *doing* it is something of its own. In the end for Susan, like countless others from a bad situation, it's that inner peace that truly matters.

Again, that is one of the reasons I respect those dedicated single parents so much. For the most part they work their tails off, sometimes in menial jobs, come home to a Spartan setting, and do whatever they have to in order to provide for their children and lastly themselves. In life, mistakes are made, and even with the best of intentions things don't always work out. Most of the single parents I've had the privilege of meeting, have had the courage to make the most of the situation and quite frankly don't waste their time on what could have been or how life isn't fair. Unlike the Mr. Smiths of the world, they do not blame their problems on their environment. Many single parents, no matter how despairing or ugly their environment may have been, are committed—by every ounce of themselves—to making things better for their future. They carry on. They deal with the situation, make the most of their past, and strive to carry little or no animosity from the garbage in their lives.

As always, the choice is yours.

HELP YOURSELF REMINDERS

* DON'T USE YOUR ENVIRONMENT AS A CRUTCH. IF YOU DO, YOU'LL ONLY LIMIT YOURSELF.

* IF YOU FEEL GUILTY ABOUT WHAT HAS TRANSPIRED, MAKE AMENDS AS BEST AS YOU CAN, AND IF POSSIBLE TURN IT AROUND AND USE IT AS A STEPPING-STONE TO MAKE THINGS BETTER.

* DON'T GIVE YOURSELF AWAY IN THE VAIN HOPE OF APPEASING OTHERS.

Help Yourself

* Make and maintain the commitment of being your own person.

* Limit your exposure to negative circumstances and, if possible, make the best of it.

* Above all, it's your life and your choice.

3

Learning to Forgive

It took all the reserve and discipline I had to stop myself from killing her. On a warm day during the summer of 1987, I sat in front of Mother, as an adult, while she explained in ice-cold deliberate detail the time she had stabbed me as a child. It was simply an accident, she calmly stated—as if she had spilled some milk at the breakfast table. One of "those things." When I failed to anoint her with instant forgiveness, *she* became upset, giving me a look of displeasure. She went on to justify her treatment against me further by stating, "Well, David, 'the Boy' was always in trouble. 'The Boy' deserved to be punished. 'It' was always stealing food, David. I would have fed 'It' if 'It' wasn't stealing so much. . . ." The more Mother sneered while playing another one of her sick games, the more I began to slowly feel myself consumed with an overwhelming sensation of absolute rage. As she continued her diatribe, my blood raced and I began to imagine myself throwing away my "goody-goody," "that-a-boy" lifestyle of helping others, and for once making someone pay for all the years of torture, mind games, and loneliness; transferring everything onto . . . Mother—the source of all my hatred.

I could now crystallize in my mind's eye my exact plan of kidnapping "her," stripping "her" of every normal sense of existence . . . as she had me. But now I would do it with even more relish. Since I had lived in a garage and had slept on an army cot with no blanket, I'd have her subsist in a run-down motel out in the middle of nowhere, with no heat, clothing, food, or even electricity. She would survive in total darkness. She would be without any form of human contact, just as I had been as a child when Mother had forbidden me to have any contact with my brothers. As she had used food as a weapon against me, I would only offer her bread and water, which I might or might not give her depending upon *my* mood. And not one hour of any day would pass that she would not think of me. I wouldn't kill her, but rather I'd let her mind kill her for me. I wouldn't want her to die instantly—not after all the those years when, as a child, I had existed solely as the object of her sick pleasure—no, I imagined to myself. I wanted her to feel the magnitude of what she had done to me.

Then afterward looking at Mother as she rambled on, full force, about how I had been such a burden to her and how I'd had to be put in my place, it struck me that I could simply . . . tell the authorities that . . . I had freaked out . . . from some sort of childhood posttraumatic stress. If that line worked for all the other scumbags of the universe, why shouldn't I be entitled to it? My body, which had turned ice cold before I had entered Mother's house, now seemed warm. *I could do it*, I stated to myself. *I'd have my revenge! I could become—become like* her!

The Need to Listen Better

All of us have said and have had wrongful thoughts during the heat of the moment. We've lashed out at our parents, our loved ones, and those at work. And I'm sure most of us regret what we may have said and the pain our actions and words may have caused. With the exception of those who are truly mentally ill, I don't believe any of us want to hurt others or carry feelings of animosity, but for some of us, particularly those who have experienced difficulty, especially if we feel we have been wronged, these feelings of bitterness may be hard to reconcile with. The truth of the matter is, those who do not deal with these feelings are almost destined to become what they detest.

For some of us these feelings of hostility may begin with something as simple as a disagreement or misunderstanding. Years ago in college the professor of my communication course taught something that sticks with me to this day—the four basic elements of communication: 1) the Messenger, 2) the Message, 3) the Receiver, and 4) the Feedback. Within these four distinctive elements is the opportunity to become confused or frustrated, especially if you put into the equation of communication that seventy percent of all communication is nonverbal, primarily referring to body language, and that twenty-three percent of all communication is pitch, tone, and the rate of the message's delivery; which only leaves about seven percent of what is actually being said. Seven percent! The biggest problem facing us as individuals, whether dealing with the opposite sex, one on one, with groups, organizations, or other nations or cultures, is *miscommunication*! Think about it: How many times have you been with a loved one, or with a coworker, or on a date, and everything seemed fine, right up until the moment you may have said or communicated the wrong message at the wrong time? You're not the only one! To this day I cannot tell you how many millions of times I have done just that. (Just ask my family.) Then, you desperately try to undo what you have already done, only to bury yourself further. Because of the miscommunication, now add the frustration we may be feeling until we're not sure what to say or do next. We doubt ourselves. Or we may not trust the actual message we are in receipt of—the messenger or the feedback we had anticipated. The biggest single component in miscommunication is we simply do not listen! Whether it's the messenger, the message, or the feedback, we do not consider what is being stressed to us. This statement rings particularly true for those we are the closest to. At times we brush off those we know and who understand us the most for reasons of complacency. At times we will take in information provided by others whom we do not know as well, even though both elements of the information are the same. We simply choose not to listen.

As the world around us continues to accelerate and as America has become more ensconced as the information capital of the world, it's easy to misinterpret the exact context of everything being thrown our way.

Lowering Your Defenses

When it comes to miscommunication, I have found that for some people the frustration stems from something simple—someone may have looked at us the wrong way or said the wrong thing to us. Again, the key words are *may have*. (Keep in mind those four elements and how we neglect to listen.) Over time this unresolved apprehension builds. I have personally been in situations in which I have met individuals who are highly agitated, yet they do not remember the reason why. All that these people know is they are upset; and for them that's all that matters. Once I joked with a person who was upset with someone by asking that person, "How long have you been mad at so-and-so?" "I've been pissed at so-and-so for over thirty-five years!" came the reply. "Well," I said, nodding my head, "that's amazing. So-and-so is only twenty-eight!" "Don't matter!" my companion countered. "That's how mad I am!"

We've all done it. All of us have judged others in the blink of an eye and processed that information before storing it into our "CD-ROM" for future reference. Then, every time we see that person or think of that particular element, like eating that one vegetable we've hated ever since we were a kid, we reopen that file that's been stored away in our brain, basing our attitude on our former judgment. (Remember the old saying about how others judge us based upon the first impression?) In other words, we have a tendency to misjudge. Have you ever met someone, then a split second later you knew you didn't like that person *until* you processed the information being presented to you differently, *then* you lowered your defenses by either relaxing or dropping your guard? Over time, if you do not change your attitude, if you keep your defenses up at maximum guard, you may find yourself continually becoming upset for really no justifiable reason—all from a simple misunderstanding.

Another example is: Have you been so upset that the words seemed to fly out of your mouth? Words you didn't truly mean? And as they spilled out, you wished you could have swallowed those words? But for some reason you kept your guard up; for above all you did not want to appear weak. Part of you knows that if you had apologized or explained yourself better, the matter could have been resolved, but seconds pass, then minutes, until a disagreement or misunderstanding goes unresolved and turns into revenge or defensiveness.

Most of us, myself included, always seem to hurt the ones we love, or the ones close to us—our significant others, our children, parents, family members, those at work, or our best friends. A psychologist I know once told me, "We take out our aggressions on those we know because we believe we can." Has this ever happened to you? I'm in a heated disagreement with my wife—the one person I am closest to, the one person on this planet whom I adore, who knows every aspect of my complex nature, my lover, my best friend, the only person I trust with all my heart—but in a disagreement I want nothing more than to prove *how wrong she is*! We banter back and forth, not listening to what either of us is trying to convey, but rather focus our efforts on wanting the other to hear our opinion. Time passes, frustration builds, hurtful things are said, and the issue goes unresolved. Neither one of us lowers our guard. I persist, determined to show my wife, my lover, my best friend, the only person I trust, the one person I wish to spend the rest of my life with, how tough I am, how hurt I have become. "Hell," I say to myself, "I'm so mad at her, I'm—I'm not gonna breathe for a week. I'm—I'm not gonna talk to her for the rest of the day . . . and night! I'm never going to talk to that woman again! Yeah, I might lose a good night's sleep, but every time I see her, I'll fire off some wisecracks just so she knows how much she's hurt me. I'm going to show her!"

Now, apply that same example toward your children— the ones who made your eyes light up when they took their first steps or made you feel such pride when you saw them in the school play. Think about your parents or guardians, those adult figures whom you felt inspired by, or that one mentor you ran to when you felt the world was going to end. Do you remember that single defining moment when that person in front of you became your best friend, your lifelong soulmate whom you shared everything with and had the best of times with by simply being together? But now you feel, for whatever reason, those people who had such a profound effect on your life, you are no longer as close as you once were. Maybe you grew in different directions, maybe you saw things differently, maybe that one disagreement became the straw that broke the camel's back, and now, with time, pride, ego, shame, resentment, or defensiveness, it keeps you from resolving the matter.

In the example of my wife and me, because we did not listen, coupled with our charged emotions, we allowed our disagreement to get the better of us. Eventually we both felt embittered and hurt. Finally, with cooler heads, when my wife and I both sat down, when we *listened*, we discovered that the issue that had made us both upset was not as bad as it had seemed during the heat of our disagreement. After making up we both forgot what it was exactly that had upset us in the first place. The element that matters is both Marsha and I do our best to resolve our issues as soon as possible, before time or an embroiled attitude can amplify the situation. Working together as a couple, like my son and me, like countless others, we try our best not to allow the sun to set without trying to find some form of resolution to whatever may be troubling us. I may not solve all the problems with my son who, let's say, is adamant about dying his hair orange, but I will still hug him good-night and tell him how much I love him. My reference is almost like the one

I read some time ago that stated: A couple should never bring their argument into the sanctuary of their bedroom. As stressed in Chapter One, if we have an unresolved issue, over time those feelings may not only consume us but may even give rise to further problems.

Even with the "best of friends," the "perfect parents," the "perfect marriage," the "greatest job," or the "greatest clients" in the world, if there were two people stranded on a deserted island they would eventually get on each others' nerves. As long as there is more than one person in the world, there will always be trouble in paradise. I am only trying to stress the importance of solving an issue before it comes to a head; before it leads to anger, outrage, or brews into feelings of hatred.

Not to get on my soapbox, but I cannot begin to tell you how many people I have met, how many folks I have known over the course of my life, who have wasted, and I do mean *wasted*, a large part of their time, energy, and life force proving to *that* person, *that* parent, *that* boss, or *whoever* else, how wrong *they* were. Can you imagine being on your deathbed when you finally forgave *that* person or brought closure to *that* issue that had dominated your life for so long? With all due respect to you: that in itself would be a tragedy.

In May of 1991, while in Salt Lake City visiting a relative, out of the blue I received a distressing phone call from Mother. The next day I rushed over and saw a person I could barely recognize. Slumped in the same worn-out recliner chair in which I'd seen her in the summer of

1987 was the person who had tried to take out her revenge on me, but had now become a victim of her own hate. Her halfhearted smile only exposed Mother's darkened yellow teeth. Her face was puffy and dark red and her once shiny, perfume-scented hair was now greasy and matted against the sides of her face. Mother claimed she would cry out in pain whenever she tried to walk because her feet were so swollen. Unless Mother clasped her hands, they would constantly shake.

Mother's hygiene reflected the appearance of her home. After surveying her unkept living room, I sensed Mother knew she didn't have much time left. After a few hollow pleasantries, with glee Mother quickly launched into her never-ending rants about how her mother had done this to her, that to her, how hard, cruel, and unfair life was for Mother. Building on her own tempo, Mother went on to boast, "I'll tell you what! I showed your grandmother. I showed her! She can't control me! No one, no one's gonna tell me what to do. Not now, not ever!"

Whatever feelings of shame or anger that had bubbled to the surface before I came face to face with Mother once again, slowly washed away. All I could do was nod my head at the end of Mother's diatribes. I was in no way agreeing with what she said, but rather educating myself that this was a complete waste of Mother's time, energy, and life. A majority of her life, from what I had seen for over twenty-five years, was built on revenge and hate. Finally, after expelling her frustrations, for a rare fleeting moment Mother dropped her defenses and I was able to see through her facade and how absolutely broken and completely lonely Mother had become. All I could say to myself was *what a waste*. More than ever, I renewed my vow to not travel down the same path as Mother had.

Never Go to Bed Upset

This is why when I work with teenagers, whom I address as "young adults," I often joke with them, stressing, "Never never go to bed upset! If you're that annoyed with your parents, if you feel the need, burst through their bedroom door, march up to them, and state, 'Mother, Father, I know you may be concerned about my spiky green hairdo, outrageous loud music, and my neurotic friends. But it's gonna be okay. I love you. I know right from wrong; I just want to be my own person. Not to worry, it's gonna be fine!'" If you're a teenager and you act like a child, you will be treated as a child. If, however, you wish to be treated as a young adult, take some accountability, and understand that in life when dealing with others—no matter who it is you're dealing with or how old you are—it's a matter of give and take: in order to have "this" you have to be willing to give up "that." So, when talking to your parents or guardians, don't beat around the bush, but get right to it; whether it's about dating, insecurity, sex, peer pressure, school, whatever. Lower your defenses and open up your heart. Even if you or your parents say something in the heat of the moment, I implore you not to develop the *attitude* and shut them out. Don't use your frustration as a way of getting back at them—*I'm gonna show them a thing or two; I'm gonna date him/her 'cause I know it's going to drive my parents crazy! I'm gonna do whatever I please, whenever I please!* If you begin to act in such a way, it may become a habit, which can become a lifestyle of self-destruction, and don't you deserve better than that? And, *who* are you really hurting? All I'm trying to say is as a young adult, before you develop *that* kind of attitude, think long and hard about the consequences of your decisions and where they can lead you to in the future.

Think of my mother! Here's a person who somehow got caught up in her own unresolved issues, developed that I'm-gonna-show-her! attitude that led to a destructive rampage, until she wasted her life by all the hell she put everyone and herself through right up until the moment she finally died.

After assisting others for over sixteen years, I have found that most parents/guardians are just plain scared when it comes to raising you. They simply don't want you to repeat the same mistakes they have made and desire for you to have the opportunity to live a better life. That's it! They want you to succeed! Some are even scared to death with all the temptation "out there." Those who've raised you are terrified of something bad happening to you. Think about it from their position: You are in the most important stage of your life, transitioning into adulthood or what others call "breaking away." For a lot of parents and guardians it's an impossible balancing act of trying to protect you from the atrocities of the

world, while trying to prepare you for what's on the outside as well. My advice: Use your head, keep your cool,
give them respect, and act accordingly. You *will* make a
lot of mistakes (that's how you learn in life), and your
parents or guardians know this. But don't lose yourself
in the process. At the end of the day, when you go to bed
upset or feeling vengeful, ask yourself this: *Who am I
really hurting?*

Parents/guardians, if you find you are having a hard
time getting through to your teenager, even when things
seem grim keep the channels of communication open.
Break down any barrier you can. Maintain your standard
while relating with these young adults *at their level.* I
have found that, as much as teens crave independence,
they still desire nurturing guidance. Even when things
seem volatile, as best as you can lower your defenses and
speak from your heart. If possible, relate to them on a
personal, not parental, level. Reveal your feelings of
anxiety, elements of *your past,* and anything that can help
alleviate any tension. Such as the type of clothes you
wore at their age, the kind of music your parents thought
was either smutty, ear shattering, or "satanic," or how
strange your friends were at the time. As upset as they
may be, and as much as you may disagree with your
teenager, explain to them the importance of their choices,
where their decisions can lead them, and most importantly end your discussion on a positive note.

You can use the same approach when dealing with
those at work. I know of so many who dedicate their

time and energy on either getting even or the I'll-show-them! attitude, to the point of sabotaging the business and themselves in the process. So, when a disagreement or problem arises, rather than brushing it aside and hoping for the best, take a stand and set a standard as a leader by addressing the situation as expeditiously as possible. Investigate all options that may be available to find a solution to the dilemma while trying to maintain the morale of those around you. I believe team members do not mind a serious critique, so long as they are treated with respect. A great deal of productivity can be saved when issues are solved before feelings of animosity take root.

Compromise

Rather than hold a grudge and waste your time hashing over who did what to whom, get to the core of the frustration. If necessary, be the bigger person—compromise and give a little. Don't shut that person down. Don't let powerful, negative emotions get the best of you. Open your heart and make an effort to resolve the situation as best as you can. Even if the issue is not totally resolved, at least you'll have less gnawing at you, you'll feel a little bit cleansed by trying to work through it, *and* you will be less likely to harbor ill feelings. Again, life is not perfect. Not all situations are black and white, to be solved like they are at the end of a sitcom television show. Next time when you find yourself in the middle of a disagreement, instead of proving yourself give a little. When dealing with those close to me, I have learned that sometimes the smallest things—a touch, hug, or a kind word—can make a world of difference. Resolve the matter before it envelopes you. Before your feelings become ensconced . . . and perhaps lead to hate.

The Cancer of Hate

Of all the lessons I have been fortunate enough to learn, the single most powerful, most important one is: Hate no one! If you get nothing else from this book, please, I beg of you, take this advice with you. As a child, I saw firsthand *how much* my mother hated everyone and everything. I can only assume her hatred began with some unresolved issue from her past. She then turned her anger against her mother, her husband, my brothers, her brother and his family, her dearest and closest friends, and, for whatever reason, her hatred nearly killed me, her own son. As a young boy I saw how quickly Mother's feelings of animosity went from one person to another, then another, until it spread to everything connected in her life.

I believe hate is like cancer: it can spread and kill a person, one "life cell," one day, at a time. If hatred goes unchecked it can take over one's life, as it did to my mother and others like her. If you hate today, it's easier for you to hate tomorrow, then the next day and the next, until you've wasted your entire life by becoming dominated by what you detested in the first place. The only cure for the cancer of hatred is dealing with the problem as best as you can, while releasing any animosity you may have. My question to you is: How can you live a productive life and all that goes with it, if you are controlled by intense feelings such as hate? Personally, I don't call that much of a life.

I recently read an article in a national magazine that addressed the issue of letting go of hate. The article made reference to Mitchell Wright, the widower of Shannon Wright, a teacher who was killed at the school shooting in Jonesboro, Arkansas. Before Shannon died she said to Mitchell, "Take care of Zane," their baby boy. While there may be some who would probably say Mitchell has every reason to hate those who have caused such great pain and loss in his life and his son's life, it is Mitchell who said, "If you let the hate and anger build in you, that's a very strong sin. I need to be able to totally forgive. Well, if I lose it, then I can't take care of Zane."

The same article also discussed a study at the Templeton Foundation Campaign for Forgiveness Research where psychotherapists stated that the psychological effects of forgiveness help dissipate anger, improve personal relationships, and help banish depression. The feature then quoted Charlotte Witvliet, a professor in psychology at Hope College, who suggests, through her extensive studies, that we may hold grudges ". . . because that makes us feel like we are more in control and we are less sad." Like others in her field who believe in empathy, Ms. Witvliet continues, "If you are willing to exert the effort it takes to be forgiving, there are benefits both emotionally and physically."

With all the animosity that seems to resonate within our society, I cannot overemphasize the power of forgiveness. In all the years I have assisted others, I have *never* met anyone who woke up with the sole intention of overdosing on drugs or alcohol, killing themselves, or hurting others. Something led them to it. While there are some who adamantly made excuses, I've found that most of these people believe that a series of events, coupled with deep frustration, led them to their course of action. Unresolved issues, bad situations, and feelings of animosity over time became a habitual lifestyle. These individuals, like my mother, became consumed with their own hate.

I think of my mother's life as a tragedy. Before things became very bad between us, I remember her as a beautiful, caring woman who wanted nothing more than to live for her children. As a child I used to pray for my *mommy* to wake up from her drunken state and take me in her arms so we could live happily ever after. Yet, as the years passed, I knew something had a hold over my mother's goodness. She pushed down whatever feelings troubled her, became addicted to alcohol, and ultimately treated me as she did. A lot of people are quick to state that it was because she was simply an alcoholic. I think Mother drank, like others who abuse drugs or alcohol, largely to mask whatever was gnawing at her.

At the time when Mother was raised, America was far more restricted than it is today, especially for women.

During my mother's time there was little help or professional guidance available for her.

I am not making excuses or defending my mother's actions, but what can you take with you, what can you learn from my mother's calamity and others like her? Right now, YOU have a choice. In this informational age that we live in there are infinite resources to help you work through practically any issues that seem to be pulling you down. And because our society is becoming more open, we can talk about things—AIDS, cancer, child abuse, spousal abuse, sexual preferences, just to name a few—that we would not only never have uttered in public, but deliberately kept in the closet just a short time ago. As an individual you have the power to choose. You can either work through your anxieties or become a slave to them, like my mother. Like a lot of things in life, dealing with frustration or feelings of animosity is not going to be easy. But you deserve a life of happiness and the opportunity to do whatever you want, rather than dread and sorrow that you will have to live with the rest of your days.

When I worked in juvenile hall, I would see teenagers who would often hurt others in the exact manner in which they had been harmed, but with far more cruelty and relish. When I asked them why, the reply I usually received was "I want them to feel what I felt and then some, so I won't be hurt again!" *When does it end?* How much does it take? How tough do we have to act, how much pain do we have to inflict on others, how much of ourselves do we have to lose in order to prove ourselves to others? After mankind has been on this planet for thousands of years, fighting endless wars, and with the millions upon millions who have died, the world is not enough. For some, all the hatred they keep locked away in their hearts will never satisfy whatever ails them. As tough as they may act, as much pain as they may inflict on themselves and others, as much as they may lose themselves in denial, drugs, booze, or instant-gratification relationships, the frustration and anger will always dominate their lives. I believe *you* deserve better than that!

Do not become trapped by your hatred. My mother died a very lonely person. When I was very young, I thought Mother was the epitome of regal—the way she smiled when she strolled into a room, the sound of her soothing voice—she was my princess mommy. The most outgoing, caring person with a perfect house, prized flower garden, and model family. Yet, her anger toward herself, then directed toward others, made her into an unkempt, overweight alcoholic, living in a house that I can only describe as vile. Alone, the only contact she had with the outside world was basically whatever she saw on television. As lonely as Mother became, she would, at least when I saw her, instantly recite how she had been wronged in her life. Her body would shake and her face would turn crimson as she would recite how much she detested everyone and everything in her life. Think of it: a lifetime wasted. Minute after minute, day after day, year after year . . . wasted. A person with unresolved issues, who became trapped by her own hate.

Forgiveness

I am always asked if I hate my mother. Without hesitation I respond with a resounding *no*! I saw firsthand, through the eyes of a bewildered child, the changes within Mother and the damage they inflicted on my brothers, my father, others, and me. As a child, the time I spent sitting on top of my hands at the base of the staircase in the dark garage gave me time to think. During one of those lonely hours, I came to realize that if Mother's hate had made her as she was, then I would be different. . . . *I had to be different.* At times when she would beat me to the point I could not even crawl away, I vowed to be nothing like her. While in foster care, some of my teenage friends would either cop out or quit on themselves at any kind of minor obstacle that was in their path or immediately flare up and act tough. Some of them tried to drown the pain and animosity by picking on others, or with drugs and alcohol. Eventually some of them became slaves to their outlets and found themselves being controlled all over again.

Even now, as an adult, I come in contact with so many people who are still tied to their past partly because of their unpleasant emotions. I have a dear friend, Barbara, who years ago was happily married. But after ten years the union ended in divorce. That was nearly twenty years ago, and whenever I spoke to her, after we would exchange initial salutations, I could sense her breathing accelerating and the slight change in her voice as she exploded into the phone, ranting about how her ex-

husband had done this or did that, until she became so
worked up that I feared she might have passed out from
hyperventilation. Barbara would become so upset and
lost in her berating that she'd forget she'd been complaining to me about the exact same things for almost
two decades! She would "loop"; her mind would just run
in circles. For Barbara it seemed to never end. Over the
years Barbara had spent more time and energy putting
down her former husband than she had spent being married to him.

Once, after Barbara calmed down, I gently reminded
her that, as a couple, they had spent *some* good times together, at least enough to have stayed married for ten
years and had two beautiful children whom they both
adore. Yet I think Barbara, without knowing, as most of
us do when intimate feelings are involved, got caught up
in taking a stroll down vengeance lane for so long that it
became a habitual response whenever she thought of her
former husband. Unlike my mother, Barbara is a caring,
functional, responsible person who, once she became
aware of her vindictive emotional state, began to forgive
her former husband and move on with her life.

When I stress *forgiveness*, I do so mainly to encourage freeing yourself. To me, forgiveness does not mean
forgetting what may have happened to or against
you. And, like grieving, forgiveness takes time just like
any emotion. Forgiveness doesn't happen overnight. But
with time, maturity, and a different perspective we can
free ourselves of emotions that can only lead to great
suffering.

Noted psychologist Bernie Zilbergeld echoes my thoughts. Mr. Zilbergeld states: "Holding a grudge is one of the most self-destructive things you can do. If you want to have a happy life, you have to move on and let go."

Today my mother, I believe with all my heart, is in heaven and finally resting in peace. Not a day passes that I do not think of her. I believe she was a person who carried so much pain within the deepest recesses of her heart. Maybe I had to learn from Mother's unfortunate lifestyle how *not* to live my life.

In forgiving my perpetrator, I feel cleaner. It frees me to not only live a more fulfilled life, but, more importantly, to rid myself of any animosity. I am able to love my wife, my son, and life all the more. When we elect to hate, we not only lose our compassion for others but we lose ourselves in the process. Keep in mind that for someone to hurt you, someone must have hurt them too.

Hate no one. Get closure with the person you need to forgive. Pick up that phone, talk to that person, write that letter even if you never mail it. Hug that person. Lower your defenses. Listen with your heart and an objective mind. Just do whatever you have to do to expel those bad feelings from your system. Every day, wipe your slate clean.

* * *

To me, getting rid of the garbage in our lives is like taking out the daily trash. Every day we toss out rotten food, used newspapers, and, for some, those soiled diapers we don't want to touch with a ten-foot pole. But, once we do, we wash our hands and never give it a second thought. Yet, somehow we allow the psychological garbage from our lives to rot away our esteem . . . day after day after day. To keep ourselves from deteriorating, we need to look at our situations for what they were, take some form of action now, and let the past go.

If you harbor ill feelings, if you stay in a negative environment and do not deal with troubling situations, you can only go so far in life. You may have the world in the palm of your hand, but at the cost of running away from yourself. Every day when you get up and look at yourself in the mirror, you will see yourself as who you truly are and the baggage and disparity you carry—*every day* for the rest of your life. You will be so busy with all the troubles of your world, you will lose sight of what truly matters in your life. Again, I ask you: With all that you have experienced and as unhappy as you may be, don't you deserve better than that? *I believe you do!*

HELP YOURSELF REMINDERS

* LISTEN NOT ONLY TO WHAT IS BEING SAID, BUT TO THE MESSAGE BEHIND THE WORDS.

* LOWER YOUR GUARD.

———

* CONSTANTLY DO YOUR BEST TO RESOLVE WHATEVER PROBLEMS YOU HAVE.

* COMPROMISE, AT LEAST JUST ENOUGH TO MAKE THINGS BETTER.

* HATE, JUST LIKE CANCER, IF NOT DEALT WITH EARLY ON, KILLS ONE DAY AT A TIME.

* FORGIVENESS ALLOWS YOU TO BE CLEANSED AND HELPS TO EASE YOUR PAIN.

———

Part Two

Know What You Want out of Your Life

4

The One Thing

O ver and over I had kept thinking, *This is it*. My knees were shaking, not because I was eight years old and had been embarrassed standing in front of Mother wearing only my underwear briefs, but because by the look in her eyes I truly believed Mother was going to kill me. Of all the "games" Mother played against me, she had never acted as she did that day when my father was away at work and my two brothers, Ron and Stan, were at their Boy Scout meeting. That afternoon as Mother screeched, my mind raced to find a way out. "Today," Mother had bellowed, "I saw—I saw 'the Boy' playing on the school grass!"

As I had for years, I simply stood in front of Mother dumbfounded. Since the age of four I had done my best to keep our secret between Mother and me. But by the time I was eight, I had felt the games were getting out of control. One day Mother had taken a drastic turn exposing our secret further by announcing to my brothers that

I was no longer a member of the family; that I was to be addressed as "the Boy." She then threatened my two brothers Ron and Stan; they were not allowed to talk to or even look at the Boy, otherwise they'd receive the same treatment as I did. As always I remained docile, retreating further inside my shell. Back then, no matter what Mother did to me, I kept my mouth shut. I buried my feelings of fear, frustration, and the sense of shame deep inside. From the bottom of my heart I truly believed everything was my fault—if Mother had a bad hair day; if she stubbed her toe; somehow, some way, it was my fault and there would be hell to pay. I had replayed in my mind the countless times I was punished and knew it had to be me because I never did anything to stop her. Part of me so desperately wanted to believe things weren't as bad as they were between Mother and me. I remembered how years ago Mommy, after kissing Ron and Stan good-night, would sometimes bend down whispering how sorry she was, that things had simply just got out of hand, or that she had had a bad day. As always I prayed, aching with all of my heart, that things between Mother and me would get better.

Yet that afternoon, although my knees were shaking, I remained motionless. My mind tried to understand Mother's statement of "the Boy playing on the school grass." But it did not make any sense to me. For years I had allowed Mother to control me—to the point that I never did anything without first asking for her approval. I knew the Boy was absolutely forbidden to play, stand on, or even touch the school grass. *"But how?"* I had thought to myself. *"How could this be?"* Finding no answer, I believed it was simply a mix-up. At times Mother had claimed she would drive to the school during lunch to watch her *two* children play. That day, I had figured, Mother must have mistaken me for another kid.

My analysis was interrupted as Mother again thundered how I not only had played on the school grass, but how she caught me rolling around, flailing like a madman. The more Mother ranted, the better I felt. I knew it was a mistake. A simple mistake. Mother's claims were completely unfounded, and I thought to myself that as soon as I tell Mother the truth, as soon as she looks down at my unmarked, pressed pants, she'll let it go. Just as soon as I tell her.

But my dilemma was that I was not allowed to speak unless granted permission to do so. I was not even allowed to gaze at Mother's face without her approval. Even though I had known this entire matter could have been resolved within the blink of an eye, I deliberately did not do a thing. I did not move my finger to point to my unstained pants; I did not utter a syllable; but I did lift my head to have Mother search within my heart. I had been more terrified of what she would do to me if I violated her rules than of whatever she had in store for me. Even though I had felt trapped between two separate worlds, I remained docile and once again provided Mother with another opportunity to punish me for a crime I had not committed.

That day at that moment, when I refused to do anything, I despised myself. I never did anything to stop

Mother. I never uttered a response to her accusation, I never defended myself, and I never walked out the door. I never stood up for myself and stopped Mother dead in her tracks with a single word: I never said no. So I thought that maybe I somehow deserved or even wanted to be treated as I had been. Either way, I had known Mother was out of control, and my only response had been to stand in front of her, with my head bent down, eyes fixed on the multicolored spotted kitchen floor, with my mouth tightly shut, waiting to endure the brunt of Mother's madness.

"Look at me!" Mother exploded, with a finger thrust toward my face. "For years you, you've made my life a living hell! You're the reason your father and I argue, you're the reason why I drink, why I feel so bad! You've made my life a living hell, so now I'm going to show you what hell is all about!" With that Mother stepped over and flipped on the burners to the gas stove. Even as my mind screamed for me to flee, yell at the top of my lungs, wish myself to become invisible, to do something, anything, I remained immobile. In a flash Mother seized the tips of my fingers of my right hand, dragging me over to the stove before holding my exposed forearm to the flames. As I yelled, emptying my lungs, I could not believe what was happening to me.

The instant Mother released her grip, I fell to the floor licking my arm. Through my tears I saw her standing above me with her hands on her hips, when she announced, "Now, I want the Boy to lay down on the stove and burn for me!" Part of me became numb. I had some-

how thought that Mother would bend down and scoop
me into her arms before racing me off to the hospital. Yet
at the time, over and over my mind repeated, *I still can't
believe it! This can't be happening!*

At the snap of Mother's fingers, while cradling my
arm I stood with my head bent down, exactly three feet
in front of her in my "position of address." Even though
my arm began to throb, I gave it little attention. I blocked
out the pain thinking of what I could do next. With tears
in my eyes, I took a chance and stole a glance at Mother,
in the veiled hope that she would see I had somehow
learned my lesson, that I would never do again whatever
she claimed I had done. Surely, I believed, Mother had
taken her game as far as she dared.

"I said," Mother bellowed, "I want you to lay down
on this stove and burn for me." With no more tears to cry,
and my muscles feeling like Jell-O, I stared at the stove
until I imagined myself on top of it. I gave up. I knew
there was nothing I could do. Mother was always right: I
was the Boy who deserved to be punished.

Without thinking, I looked up at Mother. While clutching a glass in her hand, she cocked her head to one side
smiling. *She really wants me to do it,* I told myself, *She
really wants me to lay down on the stove and burn, burn for
her!* This wasn't another game, I thought. She knew: if I
obeyed her command, I was going to die.

At that moment I became so scared, so terrified of dying, I had to do something, anything, to stop Mother. At
that precise time in my life, nothing else mattered. Yet, I
didn't budge. I didn't flee or scream out how sick she

was. For some reason I had transfixed my attention on the kitchen clock that was stained with grease and dust and hung just above the doorway beside a set of copper-colored baking molds.

Everything seemed to slow down. As I focused my attention at the red second hand that swept past the black numbers of the clock, my fear and even my throbbing arm seemed almost distant. It was then I had noticed that the two other hands to the clock read ten minutes to four. *Ten minutes to four!* Suddenly it hit me: my brothers Ron and Stan . . . they would be home from Boy Scouts at four o'clock. . . . So, if I could slow her down . . . if *I* could steal ten minutes' worth of time, *maybe today I won't die!*

The answer was that simple. I would do whatever I had to in order to stay away from the gas stove. Mother could beat me, spit at me, berate me, or break every bone in my body; just as long as she didn't kill me, I did not care. Since Mother's games had been a closely guarded secret for years, she would never think of acting as she just had in front of Ron and Stan—who were closer to exposing Mother's latest game and saving me with every passing second. By focusing my entire being on stealing ten minutes' worth of time, I did so one second at a time. I had stepped out of my obedient servant mode and, without knowing, applied a form of passive resistance.

As Mother continued to screech at me, without permission I slowly ran my eyes up her body until I met hers. Without permission I spoke. By automatic reflex Mother raised her hand. I then lay crumpled on the kitchen floor. While Mother bellowed on and on, between taking gulps from her glass, I counted: *Forty-eight, forty-seven, forty-six. . . .* Then, with a snap of Mother's fingers I was required to stand in front of her within one second. *I took three.* Since before kindergarten, I had been conditioned to stand in the position of address: exactly three feet in front of Mother, within striking distance. That afternoon when I stood in front of her, I deliberately took a half step backward, extending my distance a few extra inches. I did so knowing full well when Mother would hit me, *she* would have to adjust and take a step closer to strike me; thus, wasting more time.

My strategy worked. Mother had no idea *I was working her.* The pattern repeated itself every few seconds until I extended my ploy further by stuttering. Amazingly Mother tilted her head, waiting for me to complete my sentence before berating me, then hitting me until I landed on the floor. Mother again snapped her fingers, commanding me to assume the position of address. Counting backward, I took a couple of deep breaths before wobbling in front of her. While I carefully slid one foot at a time backward, until the cycle had replayed itself again, again, and again. Every time the side of my face struck the kitchen floor and tiny silver stars filled my vision, I smiled. As Mother lashed out at me, I wiped the blood from my nose and squinted at the clock's red hand making its way closer to my goal.

By sheer luck my oldest brother, Ron, came home five minutes early. Stealing another glance at Mother, I saw the blood instantly drain from her face—she had not expected Ron to come home so soon either. The second after Mother heard the front door open, she grabbed my clothes and threw them and me down the staircase to the garage. At the bottom of the stairs I dressed in the dark. I began to shiver. So many emotions began to take over. At the time I desperately wanted to convince Mother, to prove to her beyond any doubt, that I had not played on the school grass. I began yelling at myself, saying if only I were better—if only I brought home better grades; did my chores faster, better. If only I'd stop screwing up and making Mother so furious—then maybe, just maybe, I would be worthy of her love.

Without knowing, I found myself purging every emotion I had kept buried deep within my heart for the last four years. What began as a trickle became a waterfall of tears. I knew that "big boys don't cry," but I didn't care. I let everything out. The more I opened up to myself, the more I came to realize: no matter what I did—if I brought home the best grades on my report card; if I completed the dinner dishes in fifteen minutes rather than thirty; if by some chance I had one, just one day in which I was absolutely perfect for her—Mother would hate me just the same. As my mind replayed everything that had just happened, I suddenly realized *I* was not forcing Mother to drink; I was not solely responsible for the arguments between my parents. I kept thinking over and over again, *I* was not putting a gun to my mother's head and having her pull the trigger. Yes, I was slow and it took me forever to do anything; I was stupid, and somehow I had always landed myself in some sort of hot water, but *Mother*, not *I*, was responsible for her actions against me.

When I understood that I was not solely accountable for Mother's rage, I felt a trembling sensation that ran from my legs to my arms. In the blackness of the garage, where I believed giant snakes and other swamplike creatures lived that could snatch me away at any second, I looked down at my right arm, which I had forgotten about during my moments of purging, but which now seemed to throb with pain. I had focused so much energy on manipulating Mother by stealing time, that I had somehow suppressed my burn. After I had gently brushed off the tiny burnt hairs, I could see blisters beginning to form. Holding my arm and feeling the sensation of cool air when I blew on it had meant only one thing: *I was alive!* If I could feel my arm throb, then it meant I wasn't dead. If I wasn't dead, it meant that Mother hadn't killed me. I was alive! I had won! I gave it everything I had. I had come up with an instantaneous plan, focused on every move, every breath I took; paid the price to steal a few seconds of precious time, and I beat a drunken adult. I won. Lowering my arm, I shook off my fear of the imaginary serpents and stood just a little taller. I thought to myself, *If I could accomplish what I just did* against Mother and survive, *what could I not possibly do?*

While my knees had vibrated from a rush of emotions and shock beginning to take hold, I made a vow. As I had raised my arm, I could feel the blisters rub against my bicep. Not caring if anyone heard me, I stated, "No matter what happens from this moment on, I am going to give everything my best shot. No matter what happens . . . from this moment on, I will never, ever quit."

The one thing I wanted, the one thing I craved more than anything, was to remain alive.

Your Defining Moment

I realize the preceding may seem harsh or even brutal, but as terrifying as it was for me, that one incident became the turning point of my life. For the first time in my life, I found myself in what I believed was a deadly situation that forced me not only to concentrate on what truly mattered but to take some form of action for myself. Above all, because of that one situation I was fortunate enough to take something with me that I'm still able to apply each and every day.

And again, my example is not a gruesome illustration for the purpose of exploitation or to extract sympathy. Think of it this way: If that *child*—whether it was me or anyone else, for that matter—could endure, alter, and survive that situation without any help, without any professional training, coaching, or college degree, let alone a great deal of practical experience, what is stopping *you* from achieving your desires?

My intention is to help you realize the indomitable human spirit within us all. Many predicaments in our lives are unexpected and we may not be up to the initial challenge. It may even seem overwhelming. But, as explained in the first section of this book, as individuals we can either run from our situations, bury them, or face our problems and deal with them accordingly.

When negative situations arise, it is mainly up to you as an individual to address them and take some form of action in order to deal with them. It comes down to choice: you can let your brain spin like that CD-ROM we posited earlier, telling yourself life isn't fair, that you're a victim, or get so scared that you become immobile; *or* you can at least try to do something, anything, about the problem at hand. At that time, I would rather have had Mother do anything she damn well pleased, just as long as she didn't burn me—I simply did what I had to do.

As naive as I was, my first form of defense was to become aware of the gravity of my situation. Being aware and fearful of any possible outcome, I had to think for myself, then take some form of action, which happened to be passive resistance. I blocked out the pain from my arm and focused on stealing whatever precious time I could. Afterward, at the bottom of the stairs, I purged my emotions, understanding for the first time the extent of my situation that for years I had denied. I felt utterly helpless, but decided I had to do something *for* myself. Coming to realize what I had just accomplished by manipulating Mother, I used that as a mental platform to build upon. Making a declaration to myself—in a child's viewpoint seeing things as black and white, right or wrong, with no room for ambiguity—from that moment on I had to think ahead and plan for any event or situation before it happened. Doing so not only relieved some of the pain and loneliness, but kept my mind sharp and on the offensive.

You Do Not Need to Be a Victim

Just because bad things happen to you, or unexpected situations arise, doesn't mean you are destined to be a victim. Years ago when I flew for the air force, before any of the crew stepped aboard the aircraft we would address various possible in-flight emergencies that might occur, then step by step go over the exact sequence we would initiate in order to counter the event. Because of the dangers inherent in flying, when something unforeseen did arise, we had thought ahead and our responses were calm and automatic; we didn't stop and whine, getting ourselves into an emotional state that would take our focus away from what needed to be accomplished. None of us was a robot or an Einstein, but simply an individual determined not to succumb to a negative situation. After every in-flight event I always walked away a better, wiser person. Ask yourself this: When you faced a situation and did your absolute best, even if it wasn't the exact outcome you desired, weren't you able to use that as a catalyst to change other parts of your life? A milestone to look back on to draw strength from? Again, if you can do that by yourself, without a great deal of help or professional guidance or training, what can you not possibly achieve?

When you know what you want and either physical or

emotional pain is involved, think of women giving birth and the hours of labor they endure. Some mothers have told me that during labor, rather than focusing on their anguish, they detach themselves and think how soon they will be able to hold their babies. In a sense the same goes for those who play sports. When a slight injury occurs, the players get right back up and focus on the task at hand. To achieve what you want, you do what you have to do!

All of us have had and will continue to face issues in our lives for the rest of our lives. Nothing and no one on this planet can stop it. It's a fact of life. Someone once said that it is not one's external but his internal environment that truly counts. So, *your* attitude is everything.

Prisoners of war, who have endured years of extreme torture and solitude, have applied the same techniques of detaching from their negative circumstances and concentrated instead on what truly mattered to them: survival with a sense of honor. Not willing to give up, many of them harnessed their internal environment, using their solitude to solve mathematical equations. I have studied one American officer who built a house in his head. This person began by formulating a blueprint in his mind. Next, he laid the foundation, built the frame, and visualized every beam, every window, and didn't stop until he had imagined himself placing every room with the exact furniture. Years later the officer stated, "I knew how grave my situation was. I alone had to do something about it. Accepting the hand I was dealt, I knew I couldn't escape and knowing the enemy's sole intention was to break us and get inside our heads, I kept my sanity by changing how and what I thought about." This same man now claims that because he had survived what he had, when he now faces a situation he taps back into what got him through before, "when it really mattered."

Whenever I'm asked, "Dave, when did your life turn around for you? When did things get better?" by habit I rub my right arm and tell the story of my being burned and what I had to do at the time. I wasn't courageous, not all that bright, but I—like countless others forced to confront a dilemma—did what I had to at the time. Taking some form of responsibility over that *one* situation allowed me to open a door and steer my mind in a completely different direction. With one sentence: *If I could survive Mother trying to kill me, what can I not possibly achieve?* my entire attitude, my entire life, changed for the better.

Creating Better Options

After making my vow, rather than feeling dejected, I was able to shed years of feeling stupid and worthless. Deep inside I knew better. It didn't happen overnight, but day by day I began to believe in myself. All I did was maintain my focus. I accepted my situation for what it was and took some form of action to make my circumstance just a little bit better. As a child alone at the bottom of the stairs, I spent countless hours imagining with perfect clarity what I would do *before* anything happened to me. For instance, when Mother would walk down the hallway, if I was in her way I was required, no matter what chore I was doing, to stop and stand erect in the position of address with my back against the wall. Before, Mother would hit me and I'd instantly collapse on the floor in pain. But since making my vow and knowing there was nothing I could do to change Mother's behavior, when the same situation occurred I was able to initiate my plan—which I had analyzed to the smallest detail. Because I was not allowed to look at Mother as she came near me and was not allowed to wear my glasses, I'd focus instead on listening to the speed of her approach. Then, before Mother would raise her hand to strike, I'd turn my head down and in the opposite direction of her. Knowing that she usually hit me on the upper part of my chest, by making a slight adjustment in my stance I'd expose and tighten that part of my chest so it didn't hurt as much as before. Later on I would even tighten the upper part of my arms, forcing my upper chest to harden all the more. This was years before I learned of the word *kinesiology*, the movement of muscles. And, this in no way prevented my mother from attacking me. My detailed plan wasn't foolproof. But at least I was a little better off than I had been before. And at the time that was enough to get me through.

Mother would refuse to feed me for whatever reason she'd choose. If I looked at her without permission, breathed in front of her, or if I did not clear the dinner table and wash, dry, and put the dishes away in ten minutes or less, my punishment was starvation. Realizing whatever I did or didn't do was futile, I resolved to come up with a plan to feed myself. I was fully aware that stealing was wrong, but at the time I believed it was my only way to survive. I began by snatching bits of food from the refrigerator. When I was caught, I later stole food from the downstairs pantry. When I was discovered there, I scrounged food from the garbage can in the garage.

When I could no longer find enough food at home, I began stealing lunches from my classmates before school would start. Thinking ahead, I'd drop to one knee so I could shield what I was doing as I rummaged through the brown paper bags and metal lunch boxes. Not wanting the other kids to go hungry, I'd snatch a sandwich wrapped in wax paper, take half of it, then replace the other half. Other times I'd grab an apple and take a few bites before putting the fruit back exactly where I'd found it. Over the course of a few weeks everyone realized someone was taking food from the lunches, so the staff kept them locked up in the classroom closets. When that option expired, my next plan was sneaking into the cafeteria, until someone found me stealing frozen hot dogs and Tater Tots.

One day during lunchtime recess, not having eaten for more than a day, I became envious of the other kids who had just had lunch, and were playing and laughing without a care in the world. I turned ice cold to everything I was seeing. I threw my hands up in disgust, yelling to myself how unfair life was. How *they* had more than me, a better life than me, and didn't have to live like I did. They had better clothes than me, nicer parents, ate food whenever they pleased, were able to sleep in a real bed. . . . The list became endless. Inside my head, I threw a temper tantrum, screaming, *"Life isn't fair! Life isn't fair!"* over and over, until I became filled with hate and jealousy.

I was completely right and completely wrong. I realize this may be hard to swallow, but the cold reality is: *Life is not now nor ever will be fair*. Period. Someone else always appears to have more, live better, or achieve whatever they want without the slightest effort. It seems that *they* will have better clothes, nicer parents, more fulfilled relationships, perfect, obedient children, superior health, nicer bodies, and surround themselves with fancier lifestyles. It seems that others who do not apply or dedicate themselves as much as you, will drive around in that new car, live in a bigger house, receive that promotion, have a corner office with windows . . . blah, blah, blah, blah. And there is little you can do about it. As I emphasized before, it's important to recognize your situation for what it is, let out feelings of frustration, deal with it, then let it go. But you need to be careful not to find yourself trapped in a vicious circle of complaining or of letting your emotions get the best of you about things you have absolutely no control over. In that sense, I was completely wrong when I yelled "Life isn't fair!" It is very disheartening to know there are scores of people who rant endlessly, jump up and down, or go down that endless hallway about something from their past, about how unfair such and such was or how they got ripped off, *rather than* taking stock in themselves, being realistic about the dilemma, and doing something positive about it for themselves!

Maybe it's a good thing that life isn't fair. When you're behind a little, that's when you're focused on what's important. When you're hungry for that one thing, that single element, whatever it is, it's astounding what you can achieve! And when you dedicate yourself to your cause, no matter the outcome, you can be proud that no one, no one on this planet, did what you did. You earned it. Against all odds, you did what you had to do.

I believe those who have faced situations entirely alone, without assistance, with nothing more than absolute determination, not only dealt with those particular issues, but they became better off *for themselves* and used the specific situations as stepping-stones to achieve what mattered most to them. I recommend that if needed, if possible, get help and guidance. Receive consolation. Think about the issue. Look at all of your options. Get a good night's sleep before making a decision. However, in the end it is *you* and you alone who have to *do* whatever it takes to accomplish your goal. Not your teacher, your parents, those at work, your spiritual leader, close friends, spouse, master motivator, guru, or psychic advisors. It's you!

Resolve to Make Things Happen for You

I mean no disrespect to anyone, but I have known many people who seemingly wake up with the idea of what they want and throw up their hands demanding that others do it for them in a right-now attitude. Maybe it's a learned behavior from years ago. That would explain why there are so many who seem so unable or unwilling to do for themselves. When I work with tough teenagers who feel that, for whatever reason, they cannot climb out of their situation, I ask them a series of questions: "If you are capable of getting dressed, going to the bathroom, and nuking something to eat in the microwave, then aren't you are old enough and capable enough to *do for yourself*?"

Years ago when my son, Stephen, turned ten, as we were talking about how proud I was of him and how far he had come, I said something that seemed to resonate within him. "Stephen," I stated, "you're ten years old now. You know right from wrong, good from evil, and the repercussions of your actions. I will always help you as best as I can. But realize this: From this moment on, you are a young man. And as a young man, understand that I can only help you so far."

Make this sentence your daily axiom, stating it aloud: "Whatever/whoever can only help me so far, can only do so much for me." It's like the old proverb, It is better to teach someone how to fish than to fish for them. As individuals, as a generation, as a society, and as a nation, I believe we need to be more responsible and rely more on ourselves. *At the end of the day those in our lives can only help us so far.*

Yes, it *may* seem impossible or hard to do, but when there is something that you want, that one thing you crave, ask yourself this: *How badly do I want it?* If your desire is that great, if it burns deep inside of you, day in and day out, then *you* will most likely find a way to make it happen.

This in no way means that you need some insurmountable challenge in your life to know what you want. Some have always known their desires; others one day out of the blue get that little idea that sprouts up within them. I am not saying you have to endure a gargantuan calamity to achieve success; yet I have found that when situations happen, whether big or small, *that's* when folks become more focused on what truly matters to them. When situations suddenly arise—whether problems with health, marriage, finances, work, college studies—in those everyday things that we take for granted, *that's* when we harness our motivation not only to overcome that one situation, but to ensure we are not likely to be in that dilemma ever again.

Years ago I read an article about the Air Florida plane crash and how some of the passengers were dying of hypothermia because they were unable to swim across the Potomac River. Because of the extreme conditions, the rescue team was limited as to what they could do to save those clinging for their lives. One such man who was freezing to death told himself he had two options: stay where he was and die, or at least try to swim across that river filled with large chunks of frozen ice. With every stroke this man imagined his wife and children. This brave individual not only overcame while focusing on what mattered most to him, but was able to save the lives of others who were either too terrified or unable to save themselves. This man, who before the event was criticized by his wife for being overly stoic and for not spending a great deal of time with his children, because of that event now beams with pride whenever he's at a family gathering and adores his wife, treating her like a princess. In a statement he later said that the plane crash was his wake-up call. With every day he knows he's living on borrowed time and intends to make the most of it.

Another story of overcoming is that of a young lady who ran for the track team in high school. She told me she knew that she wasn't the fastest person on the course and always felt defeated when others sprinted past her. One afternoon she exploded with a burst of energy and finished far ahead of the others. Afterward she confessed, "Even though I finished every race, in my mind I knew it was over whenever the other runners passed me. I just went through the motions. Today, I kept saying: one more kick, one more step, just one more. I wanted first place like never before. I gave it all I had and left nothing in reserve."

When there is something you long for, give it everything you have. How do you know what you are capable of unless you give it your all? Not halfway, but all the way. Not half speed, but full speed. You have a choice: you can freeze in that river or swim across and live life. You can halfheartedly run that race knowing all along that you will probably lose, or you can give it your all! Don't you quit on what's important to you. Don't give up on yourself! Again, I ask the question: Don't you deserve better?

Self-Respect

You may not even realize or may have forgotten that you already have accomplished a great deal in your life. Again, the smallest things can make a world of difference. And a little bit of struggle is not a bad thing. Take a moment. Ask yourself, without emotion, without a sulking attitude, what have you accomplished? Now, if your instantaneous reply is "Nothing!" you're not being fair to yourself, and you wouldn't be reading this book unless you took yourself seriously. So, what have you accomplished? Now, how did you do it? Whatever the situation, you most likely didn't have someone like a coach on the sidelines giving you the play-by-play game plan. It's not like you can throw up your hand and yell, "Hey, Ref, time out!" The truth of the matter is *you* simply did what you had to do. To meet that objective, short term or long term, whatever it was, *you* addressed that situation, took some responsibility, some action, a little bit of moxie, and gave it your best. If you didn't give it your all, next time do better. And you may have had butterflies in your stomach or you might have been a little scared, but *you* did it.

Give yourself some credit. Be grateful for yourself. Because of what you experienced and the challenges you addressed, are you not at least a little bit better off than before? A little stronger inside? A wee bit wiser? Do you find that when push comes to shove, you're a little more focused? A little more determined? Overall, because of what you've been through, do you realize what your true desires are? Then, stay on track and keep applying yourself. Even if you answer yes to only one of these questions, give yourself the credit you deserve, and instead of contaminating yourself by saying what you can't do, ask yourself *what* can you not accomplish when you truly commit to that one thing?

This is why I have the highest respect for hardworking single parents—both moms and dads—who bust their tails not only to provide for their kids, but to ensure that their children have at least a chance at a better life. And those with disabilities who—without any thought of being down-in-the-mouth or wasting their time and energy worrying how unfair life is—are far more upbeat and do far more than those who are so-called "without disabilities." I have the highest respect for anybody who, win or lose, feast or famine, knows what she wants and at least tries, even if it's against all odds, to better herself. As a country we root for the underdog, the Rocky Balboas, who step into the ring only to get beaten senseless by that overwhelming opponent, but yet the Rocky Balboas somehow find that inner strength to get up for the next round and give it their all. That's life. Win or lose, you take a few hits, you fall down, but when you get up from the mat, battered and bruised, you brush yourself off, tap into that inner drive, and give it what you've got. *That's* what counts.

In America all of us, every single one of us, from all walks of life, under the best and the worst of circumstances, has at least a chance of achieving, of fulfilling his or her desires. When you have a passion for that one thing, at times you have to go beyond the pain, the loneliness, frustration, even humiliation. You just do what you have to do.

As morbid as this may sound, not a single day passes that I do not look back at the time I was burned on the gas stove, starved for days, or anything else that happened to me, and have an odd sense of appreciation for at least having tried to learn something from the experience to better myself, to do something positive for myself. If I had the opportunity I would not change one moment of one day of my life. Not one! My experiences enabled me to become stronger inside, independent, and determined to make something out of myself. My challenges gave me a different perspective on life and made me want it more. To quote the international best-selling author of *The Christmas Box* and one of the most compassionate people I know, Richard Paul Evans, "It is in the darkest skies that the stars are best seen."

Discovering Your One Thing

So now that we are well versed on challenge, sacrifice, and resilience, let's get to the core of the issue: What do *you* want? I am not talking short-term goals or long-range, five-to-ten-year master plans; rather what is that singular thing that you desire? Now if you find yourself stumped, don't get discouraged; a majority of folks have no idea of what they want out of life. In fact, I have read several periodicals that claim as many as seventy percent of Americans haven't given it much thought, that most folks just live day by day, with few hopes or ambitions. Personally I think that's sad. Especially when we think of immigrants who have, even to this day, gone to great lengths, to the point of risking their own lives, just to *live* in America. Did you know that they have four to five times a better chance of reaching their goals, of achieving financial success, of fulfilling their dreams, for the simple fact that they have always known what they wanted and were determined to make it happen? How many people do you know who roll out of bed, go through the motions, drag themselves to school, or make their living doing "whatever," day in and day out, thinking to themselves that this is as good as life gets? I am not implying that everyone jump up and plan every aspect of their lives down to the second, but shouldn't we at least apply ourselves and utilize our gifts to our fullest potential?

Sometimes when I address an audience, I ask the question: "What do you want?" I then recommend for them—whether they are business professionals or everyday private citizens—to spend time and "purge" on paper everything they desire. Everything! This alone would take hours. Because of this, I advise folks to list specific categories their "wants" would fall into: health, family, spirituality, education, business, finances, interpersonal relationships, personal desires; whatever it is that may be important to that person. Next, I have the person pick a category, find the first item in that category, and compare it to their next and without hesitation check off what they want out of the two. Then, compare the first item to the third item and instantly place a check mark next to the choice made, followed by the first item to the fourth, and so on, until all the items have been ranked against the first one. Next, I have the audience compare the second item on their list with the third item, then the second item with the fourth and so on. All the items on the list will be ranked against the others and value-graded accordingly by that person's desires, with a check mark.

If you do this exercise, I ask you to do it exactly as just explained, and without apprehension or pretense. Lower your defenses and invest some absolute quality time in yourself and you will discover something amazing. The things you thought were *so* important—that new car, office promotion, acing that test, losing a few pounds, "getting" that "new thing" for your home—are way, way down on your list of priorities of what you really, truly want.

As highly as I recommend this exercise, and as imperative as it is for you to bare your soul to yourself, if you wish to cut to the chase I can save you a great deal of time. I have found over the years the unequivocal "thing" that folks want out of life is: TO BE HAPPY!! That's it! Feast or famine, rain or shine, good days or bad, happiness is what nearly all of us want out of life. When we're happy does it truly matter how much we have, what people think of us, or what we look like? When you are happy with who you are and what you have in your life right now, isn't everything else a bonus? How many weddings have you attended where you see that look of love in the bride's and groom's eyes but know they have a long road ahead of them? That they may live in a hole-in-the-wall rundown apartment, with limited furnishings, and both working full-time jobs just to make ends meet? And yet, when they're together, the world stops for them. Being with each other is all they need.

In just about every situation I have been exposed to—whether flying combat support missions during the War in the Gulf or working nonstop for days on end while not seeing my family for weeks at a time—I've tried my best to maintain a positive attitude. Maybe all that I have endured in the past has made it easier for me to find something optimistic about either my surroundings or whatever I had to deal with at that particular time. During the War in the Gulf, while thousands of service members lived in tents and ate food from a tube, I was fortunate enough to receive one hot meal a day and take a shower with hot water. I was happy and appreciative. As a presenter, at times when I've pushed myself beyond my normal boundaries, I've become energized about the opportunity of "just one more program"—then afterward I will reward myself and relax with a simple cup of coffee. I grab or sometimes "steal" a few moments alone outside, a few hours reading a book—just a little bit of happiness anywhere, anytime, I can. It's not easy and I may rant and complain as much as the next person; however, as much as I apply myself in whatever I do, I now apply that same amount of energy and focus in doing *something* for myself that enables me to feel from deep within just a little bit better.

So, if being happy ranks number one, did you know that the second most important thing is love and/or acceptance? As you know, once we feel secure in ourselves and among others, this not only enables us to face all the better the challenges that may be in store for us, but being accepted is one of the main needs we have as human beings. When I worked in juvenile hall, I had the chance to work with teens who would join gangs. The main reasons they did so were for "love" and a "family"-like acceptance.

Next on the list, immediately after love and/or acceptance, is their children's prosperity, or for those who do not have children it's health for themselves and others they care for. After happiness, love/acceptance, health/prosperity, this "List of Life" varies. But in my years of assisting others and the stories I have read or people I have had the privilege to meet, these are what truly resonate within just about all of us on a continual basis.

I've found "the things" that folks thought were so important, so imperative—fame, fortune, weight loss, hair gain—were way, way, way down the list. I'm not surprised. I cannot tell you how many people I know who *have* fame, fortune, stellar careers, immaculate bodies, *and* every, and I mean every, materialistic item the world can offer, and yet some of these folks are unfulfilled, insecure, and absolutely miserable. While I believe one shouldn't judge those who live in a fishbowl world—as none of us truly knows what these people have been through or what they gave up in order to achieve their status—I'd rather be grounded and appreciative of the everyday "little things" in life. How many movies have you seen in which the main characters crave escaping small-town USA to make something of themselves in search of fame and fortune? The characters push themselves past normal limits, take a few hard knocks, then finally break through and receive everything they longed for and have the world in the palm of their hand, yet still feel so hollow, so incomplete. In the end they discover they have lost themselves in the process of their quest and would give up everything just to live a "normal life."

Invest in Yourself

Sit down, spend some quality time with yourself, and discover from the deepest recesses of your heart *what is truly important to you.* Find it. Hold on to it. Live it. No matter how hard it may be, keep a positive attitude. Don't take setbacks personally. Look at them as opportunities to see what you're truly made of. Never lose sight of your objective. But *please* don't lose yourself in the process. Don't be too hard on yourself, for you will fall down; yet it is getting up that truly matters. Find something, do something, every single day that brings you one step closer to your goal and reward yourself for your valiant efforts, no matter how insignificant they may seem. *Be happy within yourself and what you have right now, every single day.* Find that solace within yourself, for anything else can only make things better.

HELP YOURSELF REMINDERS

* DEFINING MOMENTS OR SITUATIONS CAN BE A POSITIVE CATALYST AS *THE* TURNING POINT IN YOUR LIFE.

* BEFORE YOU QUIT ON YOURSELF WHEN LIFE ISN'T FAIR, EXHAUST ALL YOUR OPTIONS FOR MAKING THINGS HAPPEN.

* IF YOU WANT IT, YOU HAVE TO MAKE IT POSSIBLE.

* WHEN FIGHTING TO MAKE YOUR LIFE BETTER, GIVE YOURSELF THE CREDIT YOU DESERVE.

* TAKE THE TIME AND ENERGY TO TRULY INVEST IN YOUR MOST IMPORTANT ASSET: YOURSELF.

5

The Price You Pay

Knowing what you want out of life is critical, but it's not enough to make your dreams come true. As you know, just because you long for something or even have a dying passion for that one thing does not mean you will automatically obtain it. I believe when it comes to fulfilling your dreams there is always a price you must pay.

In the preceding chapter I deliberately went into specific detail about how I had feared for my life. The price I paid to stay alive was being attacked by my mother. That day I lost a lot of blood and my face felt like a punching bag, but the expense was not only worth it to me but it became my foundation for survival. In the end it always comes down to how badly you really, truly want it.

While there are a great many folks who *think* they know what they want, many are unwilling to apply even the smallest amount of effort to obtain their goals.

For years our country has become a culture of "quick fix." Words like *sacrifice*, *diligence*, and *honor* no longer matter and have been replaced with *I want it all and I want it now!* Relationships flourish and dissolve faster than paint can dry. Some see that flashy sports car and they want it. They cannot afford it but it doesn't matter, for they have to have it now! With a quick scribble on a check, the car they have been dreaming of for ten minutes is suddenly theirs. But when the payment comes due, suddenly that thing they wanted isn't all that appealing as it was a few months ago. Emotions become involved, egos get bruised, and it's always the other guy's fault when the car is repossessed. I've seen the same in the job market. With only a few weeks of experience under their belts, some people tell others how the task should be performed, that they don't *have* to do such and such, and are the first to complain about every single thing, while the entire time they barely apply themselves to the job; and yet they are the ones who become extremely agitated when they are not promoted to a management position after being with the company for an earth-shattering six weeks.

Another approach society has is: if things don't turn out, we can always sue. In this day and age we can file lawsuits for mental duress, loss of sleep, coffee being too hot or too cold, and even air turbulence when flying. Years ago I read where a prison inmate sued the state because the mattress hurt his back, and another inmate sued because he slipped and fell on the wet floor. And when folks complain how justice is slower than a snail, part of the reason for that is today's courts spend a great deal of time tied up in frivolous lawsuits. I have the staunchest belief in justice. I believe in equal treatment for one and all, yet every day we can pick up the paper and read how Mr. So-and-So is attempting to collect millions over something that seems entirely ridiculous.

It Doesn't Happen Overnight

Maybe it's me, but as a society haven't we become just a bit too cynical? While some folks spend a great deal of time and energy plotting the next quick-fix, get-rich, have-it-all-right-now scheme, the reality is they would be better off applying their time and energy in more proven conventional areas—studying hard, applying themselves at their craft, sacrificing a little, praying they get lucky—for there are no quick fixes. Unless you hit Lotto, and that's only after you called one of the psychic hotlines to receive the exact numbers, there is no such thing as an overnight success. Remember the old saying If it sounds to good to be true it probably is? If you doubt me, turn on your television any time after 2:00 A.M., flip to the infomercials, and find the so-called expert who is so excited that he is on the verge of exploding into your home because, "Now, right now, I've got something so incredible, so earth shattering, that—that . . . I can't put it into words! But I can tell *you*! I just discovered something that will change your life. . . . But you have to act now! For a limited time only, I am making *you* a one-time offer. . . ."

This person implores you to listen to his patented, fool-proof, instant results, super-duper, hundred-percent-guaranteed secret, "... just so you, *my dear friend,* can have it all, *right now,* at the amazing low low price of ..." And it's gotta be true, for you see the endless testimonials of couples who were on the brink of oblivion and are now living the good life. And in the early-morning hours everything makes sense and looks good—the fleet of fancy cars, the breathtaking mansion, the streamlined race boats, the helicopters, the luscious bikini-clad smiling models who somehow can't keep their hands off of our newfound savior. With only a few hours of sleep under my belt this makes perfect sense to me. If it works for the host and *all* those people, and if I can see all that stuff with my own eyes, then it's gotta be true!

I know of many professionals who are truly sincere in helping others, but, hello! Reality check! Not to sound selfish or stoic, but think of it this way: If you had a secret that you had recently discovered, would *you* hawk your discovery on late-night TV for the entire world? In the same vein, I know many who have confessed to me that they fear so many people coming after them if they ever came into a great deal of money, that aside from their spouse and maybe their children, they wouldn't tell a soul.

The funny thing is after all these years and the countless overnight experts who have promised the world and in the end have had their businesses shut down, some indicted, and some of them jailed, there are still those who are desperately looking for "the next big thing."

I am not trying to limit your options or discourage you from exploring your boundaries; for if you truly believe in something that strongly, then by all means go for it. However, the cold hard truth is if you make it overnight—if you get the girl, the boy, the money, the car, the whatever—you can lose it just as fast. When you give it a great deal of thought with a clear head and discover your one desire, the truth is there: it's not going to happen overnight.

Absolute Devotion

Just a few years ago, immediately after Tiger Woods won the Masters in Augusta, Georgia, everyone bombarded him. I read how one person asked Tiger, "Son, what's it like to pick up a golf club and start whacking those balls as well as you do?" Tiger, who I believe is one of America's positive role models for all ages, smiled and replied, "Sir, I've been hitting balls for about nineteen years." "Nineteen years?!" the older man exclaimed, "Son, how old are you?" Again smiling, Tiger answers, "Twenty-one, sir."

Think about it: when Tiger was a toddler, his father, Earl, would teach him how to hold a putter, swing a club, address the ball, and sink a putt. Every day, Tiger played golf. Every day. I've read about how, when Tiger was still in elementary school, he would memorize golf courses, plotting every hit with specific clubs. Tiger devoted his time and efforts to his art. He sacrificed a lot in the process, but paid the price to achieve his greatness.

To get a little, you have to be willing to give up a lot.

The Tonight Show talk show host Jay Leno took a lot of flack when he received the slot as the host for the television show. Countless people wrote the network claiming that since they didn't know who this "new" comedian was, obviously Jay didn't deserve the coveted job; that Jay was simply a product of being recently discovered. Now, even though I am a huge David Letterman fan, I must give Mr. Leno his due. After reading Leno's book, *Leading with My Chin,* I learned that it took Jay fifteen years to become an overnight success. Day in and day out, Jay worked in strip bars, condemned rooms, practically every college campus, every day for years. What made him different from other comics was that Jay's approach was humble, straightforward, and clean, while relating to his audience on everyday experiences. At the time, he had racked up so many air miles that he was considered to have more frequent flier miles than anyone else in the United States!

Work hard, study your craft, get lucky.

Years ago, I knew a young woman named Mary who as an ice skater was yearning to make the Olympics. She would get up at three-thirty in the morning, have her father drive her to the ice rink at four, skate nonstop for over two and a half hours, shower, grab a quick bite, attend a full day of school, and work part-time. *Then* after eight in the evening, Mary would again skate for another two hours, only to return home exhausted, but feeling fulfilled that she had given it her all. Astonished, years later I asked Mary how in the world was she even able to do half of all she did. "I never saw it that way. I knew if I were to stand a chance [of making the Olympics], I was going to have to give it my all and dig deep. Seeing all those beautiful princesses gliding on the ice was so inspiring to a young girl. Every day and every night I wanted to be like one of them! My room was covered with posters of Peggy Fleming and Dorothy Hamill. They were the first thing I saw in the morning and the last thing I saw at night. And even though I didn't make the cut, it was one of the most fulfilling times of my life. No one took anything away from me because I gave it my all. To this day whenever I tackle something, all I do is reach back to where I was back then as a teenager."

Now, there's a person who has earned the right to complain that all her time, efforts, and sacrifices didn't pay off. But Mary, like most of us, realized even with the best of intentions, even if you pay the price, there are no guarantees to achievement. You can give it your all, climb that mountain against all odds, and *still* come up just short of your well-deserved goal. With all my heart I do wish I could tell you differently. Yet as for Mary's endeavor, she was able to take something away from her experiences that no one could give her: humility and self-fulfillment.

While a lot of people see someone like Mr. Leno deliver a hilarious monologue that *seems* so off the cuff or a skater like Mary give a flawless performance on ice, they have little idea of the resolve it took, the sacrifices made, or how many times both people fell flat on their faces, just for Jay and Mary to reach the bottom rung of the ladder of success. Most of us only see the finished product, forgetting entirely the immense work involved.

Tiger, Jay, and Mary all applied themselves, but *not* for the sole quest of glory, but rather for the glimmer of hope of achieving their desires. Again, just for the chance of achieving success. The lesson is, whether staying home an extra half hour studying for a test, doing additional research for a project at work, or just being there for that one person you love, somehow make your venture an everyday part of your life so it won't seem as much a monumental effort on your part.

The Boundless Optimist

When I think of one person who paid the price of hard work with constant enthusiasm as an everyday lifestyle, the name Arnold Schwarzenegger comes to mind. After years of extensive planning and barely out of his teens Arnold broke the status quo by not only moving away from his small village of Thal, but leaving his country of Austria with the sole objective of making it in America. Totally out of his element and with nothing more than a few dollars in his pockets, Arnold arrived in America seeing only the vast opportunities that lay before him. While most of America *discovered* Arnold in his earlier B films, he had *already* conquered the world of body building by winning an unprecedented seven Mr. Olympia titles. It is said that Arnold would work out four hours in the morning, then another four hours in the afternoon. While some of us gripe about putting in eight hours a day for our jobs, Arnold would make his workouts his vocation, lifting, curling, pressing tons of weights, eight hours a day! During the same time period, struggling to understand and comprehend the English language, he attended college six hours a day, working on two different degrees at the same time. If that weren't enough, in order to feed himself and maintain his sparse apartment, Arnold, with his friend Franco Columbo, worked late into the evening until the early morning hours as masons at their own business called Pumping Bricks, six hours a day. When you add the time involved, that's twenty hours a day, every day, for years on end.

When researching articles written about Mr. Schwarzenegger, I discovered how baffled folks were by his drive. How in the world could someone like Arnold accomplish so much, so fast, when folks like you and me, who have lived in America all of our lives, become so pessimistic? Answer: unyielding determination. While others badmouthed every situation they were in, how tough or unfair life was, how all the opportunities were used up, Arnold pressed forward with nothing more than pure optimism. He actually enjoyed every challenge that came his way.

Arnold's phenomenal success was not without enormous setbacks. Knowing full well a career as a body builder was limited, as a child Arnold had already set his eyes on acting; but when he arrived in America some agents and producers went out of their way to belittle Arnold, that as a body builder he obviously lacked intelligence, his body was too big for the screen, his German accent too thick, and even his name too long for the marquee. Arnold not only deflected every obstacle with his charming quick wit, but he applied himself even more. Becoming a relentless self-promoter, Arnold would *inform* practically anyone he met that he was destined to succeed, thus becoming one of the biggest draws in the film business and one of the most recognized names in the world. Today, Arnold lends his limited free time traveling throughout the nation at his own expense to some of the country's toughest inner-city schools, promoting health, physical fitness, and more importantly, challenging the younger generation to strive to better themselves.

Constant Application

Again, there is no such thing as an overnight success. Period. If there is one key to success, one key to obtaining your desires, then it's one word: Work. Work, work, work, work, work. In everything you do, apply yourself. Like all these individuals we've discussed, or anyone else for that matter, harness your ambitions, be enthusiastic, and dedicate yourself to your cause.

Don't be alarmed. I'm not looking to frighten anyone and I'm not endorsing a workaholic mentality. Absolutely not. But, what if your mind-set was to accomplish your objective with seemingly little effort, and it merely became a part of your everyday routine? How do you do something that seems so overwhelming? You do a little here and a little there until your overwhelming, arduous, impossible challenges become your everyday routine. In a nutshell, that's it.

Think of it as a baby learning to walk. As simple as it may seem for most of us, to me the act of walking, or anything else that involves motor function, is nothing short of extraordinary. The brain has to think it, and relay to the body where to go and the speed of the stride; all within a fraction of a millisecond. So how do most of us learn to walk? First and foremost we have to process a desire to do so. We stand up, we wobble a few times because we're unsure of the new experience. Maybe we have a little apprehension, but that's okay, for our ambition kicks in. We take a step, maybe two, then unexpectedly we fall down. Sometimes on our padded behind, sometimes flat on our face. It hurts, it's not fair, sometimes we cry, but we get up; we still have that drive to move forward. For some babies, you can see that pure excitement in their eyes with each foot placed in front of the other, until suddenly, without thinking, these kids are tearing up the house running away from frantic parents who are trying to put them in the bathtub! Wow!

And yet, the act of walking was performed without government assistance, with no one to prosecute when the toddlers fell down, or no one to complain to if Mommy, Daddy, or any other person tricked the young tyke by taking a step or two backward so baby could walk just a few more steps on her own, before being caught in the arms of the one who helped her along the way.

When we are willing to pay the price, when we carry that desire deep within our heart that no one or any situation can take away from us, are there truly any excuses? In every article I have read, among people I have been privileged to interview, the ones who accomplished something significant to themselves, against enormous odds, all, one way or another, have had the same philosophy: *They wanted it more and were willing to pay the price it took to achieve their desires.*

When San Francisco Giants pitcher Dave Dravecky discovered he had cancer in his pitching arm, through tremendous pain, and placing his health at extreme risk, he fought back to pitch yet again before the disease got the best of his arm, which eventually was amputated. Because of his belief that all races are equal, Nelson Mandela was a political prisoner for over twenty-five years, subjected to torture, mock executions, and isolation. Willing to lay down his life for a better nation, Mr. Mandela not only survived but became the president of South Africa. As a teenager Michael Jordan didn't make the cut for his high-school basketball team, so he resolved to practice for hours on end every single day. Years later, in 1997 during a critical playoff game and while suffering from the stomach flu, through sheer intensity and fighting off overwhelming coverage from the opposing team, Mr. Jordan tapped back into the time when he'd wanted nothing more than to play basketball. That day Michael's commitment was so great that immediately after the closing buzzer of the game, he physically collapsed into the arms of his teammate Scottie Pippen. When U.S. Air Force F-16 pilot Captain Scott O'Grady was shot down while flying a mission over Bosnia, desperate to avoid capture by those searching for him literally inches away, he not only survived by eating bugs for over six days, but was even careful of how he breathed so his would-be captors could not hear him or see the cold white mist escape from his mouth.

In all instances these brave individuals longed for that *one thing* and were more than willing to forfeit whatever it took to reach their goals. You and I are no different. We simply have to make that commitment to make it happen.

Don't Give Your Best Away

We all have desires. On any given day in our lives. And I believe all of us have the best of intentions. Especially young minds. I *know* you do, otherwise you would not be spending your valuable time and brain cells digesting this book. But the reality is that we give our best away. No one takes it from us; we give it away. *We* do— not the government, our parents, our past, our boss, our spouse, the floods, hurricanes, tornadoes, high tide, solar eclipse . . . whatever. We quit. We have wants, needs, we *try* to make a go of it, or maybe we do just enough to get by. We allow time, situations, or whatever else to erode our dreams. We quit on ourselves. We carry regret, regret turns into frustration, frustration into anger, anger into sorrow. And all the while life has slipped away from us . . . one day, one grain of sand, at a time. In the end, we look into the mirror and we can't even recognize that person staring back at us. We've lost one of life's most precious gifts: the excitement, the fear, the heart-pounding sensation of taking a step outside our protective womb. Just a step, or two, into the unknown. Sometimes in the blink of an eye to get that quick fix, or in a moment of frustration, anger, self-doubt, or weakness we give up our desire to do *something* to better ourselves.

And all you have to do is *apply yourself*.

As I confessed before, I despise writing. It takes me forever to write a halfway decent, semi-intelligent sentence. I lack patience, my brain goes a million miles a minute, I have limited mechanics, and cannot type to save my life. Years ago I was inspired by something that famed author of over 150 Western novels, Louis L'Amour, once said—something like "At times, when I can't think of a thing to write, I commit myself to writing just one sentence a day. One sentence. Sometimes that one sentence will lead to two, and soon I'm on a roll."

Work, work, work, work. Whether it's your marriage, interpersonal relationships, raising kids, your health, schooling, or your career, apply yourself. When it comes to relationships, I think a lot of us unknowingly take the other person for granted. Remember when "that person" was all you thought about, almost as if you were possessed? No matter how bad your day was, when you thought of him/her, your day was just a little bit better.

But now that you've been together all this time, you may feel like "Yeah, we're still in love, I guess, but, uh . . ." I don't care how long you've been together, or how many struggles you've endured, how deep, secure, head over heels you *think* your love is, don't take your institution for granted. When was the last time you applied yourself to your relationship? When was the last time you just held hands as you sat outside alone together, gave that person a ten-second kiss or a thirty-second hug? Before you answer, just stop for a moment, close your eyes, and think. Think about it. *The person I'm with today can leave me tomorrow.*

When it comes to children, all of us just ogle over every little thing babies do—the things they try to stick in their mouths, the way they drool on themselves, even the first time they fill their Pampers. But, after the first ten to fourteen years, the kids . . . well, they lose that "cuteseyness." Totally. Especially those teenagers who come home with a body tattoo that reads "All access here." So how did we lose that "ogleness"? Complacency, overriding priorities, or it may be that as parents we believe we've already raised them to know right from wrong, how to make decisions for themselves, and we grant them independence, as they start to push for it. A couple of years ago I read a report from the American Medical Association, on the subject of child psychology, that stressed preteens and teenagers require just as much time, attention, and guidance as babies. All of us know the importance of a proper diet and exercise to maintain our health. Regarding education, don't rest too much on your past—it doesn't matter how good a grade you received on that test yesterday, but what you can discern and be graded upon today. There is so much to learn. Continue to apply yourself. Remember: knowledge is power. The same goes for sports: you're only as good as your last game. In the corporate world I've seen those who get so pumped up about that new job opportunity and how they've poured everything they had into the interview; what they wore, how they walked, sat, how they responded to each and every question, but after a while the exuberance erodes and the output slackens, therefore lessening their chances of climbing that career ladder of success.

All I'm trying to stress in all these illustrations is the importance of not becoming too complacent, that's all. With all that you are able to do, apply a little extra, just an extra nudge, every day, and see the difference it makes in your attitude and the outcome of your achievements.

Again, it will take some effort on your part *and* your world will not change overnight, but think of it in this light: with that additional push you're giving, things can only get better. I think a lot of us rush into some things without having the faintest idea of what in the hell we're doing, why we're so intent on doing it, let alone the sacrifices it will take to get us there. Not to be too judgmental, but an example that stands out is that of the been-there-done-that corporate individual I once read about who joined an expedition to climb Mount Everest. Without all the necessary training and self-reliance required, this individual nearly died by stupidly pushing too hard, not listening to experienced guides when needed, and packing so many needless items—such as gourmet food, a portable TV with video player, hoards of computer equipment including a satellite phone—that it took four expert Sherpas to carry them. All this just to boast of filing dispatches via the Internet from the top of Mount Everest. For all this person's lofty goals, such as they may have been, others had to expend their precious energy while placing their own well-being at risk, and had to *assist* this person down from the summit.

Practical, Obtainable Objectives

Some of us take on too much or attempt to tackle our objectives too fast. I think part of the problem stems from our setting outrageous, unattainable goals, thus setting ourselves up for failure, which can leave us feeling more defeated than we were beforehand. That's why I become so irritated when I hear of individuals who are taken advantage of by some of these late-night infomercial saviors of the universe.

I recommend small, bite-sized, just-beyond-reach kinds of goals that can be fulfilled on a daily basis. Years ago, before serving in the air force, I sold cars for a living. Because there were over forty salespeople scrambling over each other in every which way they could for a possible sale, I quickly learned not only what to do, but more importantly, what *not* to do. While a majority of the sales force would thrust their business cards at every customer who drove onto the lot before sprinting off to give another card to another person, I would spend time with each and every potential client. I freely admit that most of the time I did not sell a lot of vehicles. However, there were many times when I was fortunate enough to be the only salesman at the dealership that day to sell not just one but two cars.

Whenever I speak at sales conferences, I stress the same ideology. In this hypersonic, information-runs-the-universe, *press-one-for-further-options*-just-so-you-can-speak-to-a-machine type of virtual world, I think we are losing that authentic face-to-face personal service. So many people are so busy chasing their tails, they forget that these things man invented were to make our lives easier. I see so many brilliant businesspeople, particularly in the sales force, wasting their time and energy, and at the end of the day they've accomplished little to nothing that improved their overall position. Case in point: For a few days I shadowed a salesman who would literally give you a card, e-mail address, and pager number if you, whatever your name is, have any questions, before racing off to meet another "client," before dashing to attend a meeting, then another, then another, until he saw one more "client." At the end of the day I asked this salesman, "What did you accomplish?" "Look," he proudly showed me, "I got all these business leads!" Thinking to myself, I calculated that he spent about three minutes per "client." He was so busy rushing to rush that I didn't think it was worth the energy he expended. "No, you don't," I replied to the salesman. "You've got cards with names, addresses, and phone numbers." "Aha!" laughed the salesman, "That's where you're wrong. These are great leads. You watch when I follow up on them. . . ." This gentleman that I had spent the day with was truly a nice fellow, and he was so proud that I almost didn't have the heart, but I felt I had to do it. He chuckled at me about his "leads" right up until the moment I opened his glove box, which literally spilled with "leads" accumulated over the past few months.

My friend somehow got so caught up grabbing every lead he could as his short-term goal, he forgot about spending some time on his customers' needs in order to sell his product. All I advised was for him to pay the price of spending his time and focusing his entire attention on one client at a time. Build that relationship. Fill that pipeline. In business or even in more personal matters, if you made a good contact in the morning, hey, you're on a roll; go for another one that afternoon. Don't worry about what you might be missing; focus on what you may have right now. When dealing with a mass market, that's the price you pay. In a sense, you have to kiss a lot of frogs until you come across that prince.

The same goes for those I know who battle with weight. They want to lose all those unsightly pounds and have that beautiful body . . . right now! First of all, that's not going to happen. No one gains weight overnight and I don't believe we can lose it overnight either. Secondly, you don't want to *lose* weight, you want to *get rid* of it.

Think of it in these terms: When you lose your keys, you find them. When you ditch that bad date, you hope he/she doesn't turn up. You don't want to wake up one day to discover that the weight you "lost" found your thighs or abdominal area, do you? Now, you could pay the price and take a chance at trying every "just-discovered-from-the-far-reaches-of-an-ancient-society," "herbal," "organic," "safe-for-all-ages," "fun-for-the-whole-family" diet. Or, you can even literally exercise yourself to death. Another option: You can watch and weigh every gram of fat, analyze protein versus carbohydrates all you want, but do you really want to live that type of life, *every single day*? Certain athletes and models certainly do, and it's not all that it's cracked up to be. But again that's the price they pay. I'm sure Mr. Schwarzenegger every so often indulges in a piece of strudel; or supermodel X probably sneaks a slice of pizza every once in a while. But to do all that, to put yourself through so much in the hopes that *you'll like yourself* more or *others will notice you*, is it worth it? Especially for women who battle with issues of low esteem that are placed upon them in part by society. Like my friend, who I swear looks like a skeleton but has brainwashed herself into thinking she is overweight and fears her husband will leave her if she wears anything more than a size two. Knowing this lady as I do, I think it is more about an unresolved issue of self-esteem and fear of abandonment, than her physical appearance.

From what I know, human beings have several different body structures and there is only so much you can do with any specific form. And if you're basically happy with the one you have and are in good health, I would hate for you or someone you may know to go through all the time and anguish of trying to change it, if it's really not going to make all that much of a difference. I know so many folks who do lose a great deal of weight, but those yo-yo diets mean just that—they will gain back what they lost, if not more, when the yo-yo comes back up. The sad part is those extreme diets can actually do more harm than good, not only on that person's esteem but it places a tremendous amount of stress on that person's heart. So, is it truly worth the cost?

Believe me, I'm one for physical fitness. I watch what I eat and have a set exercise routine so I can live a long productive life. However, I'm not going to have my life dictated with worry of trying to have this imaginary chiseled body that in reality I can never have. That doesn't mean that I'm some couch potato. Nobody enjoys a slice of chocolate cheesecake and a frothy mocha more than me! But those who know me know that if I splurge, the next morning I start my day with an extra few sets with the weights and run an extra mile or two on the treadmill. I'm never going to have a rippling chest, twenty-inch arms, or washboard stomach. As I approach midlife, I'm content. I'm always looking for ways to improve my body so I can look good in that one shirt, but it's not the end of the world if I rarely wear shorts because I feel I have the legs of a chicken. I'm only human.

Keep Plugging Away

Even when people pay the price, a fair number of them expect instantaneous results and become upset that they didn't receive all they wanted. It's like anyone who's self-employed: there is a tremendous amount of sweat equity involved. Some folks say it takes a good business three to five years of scraping by just to build a good foundation. But there are many who become upset and throw up their hands because they are still, day in and day out, paying the price. I've known a few people in the music business who actually believed in their hearts that they would "make it overnight," but even after being given the opportunity they cut their music video, became disgruntled, and soon enough tempers flared until the band with the latest breakthrough sound finally broke up.

Renowned ice climber Yvon Chouinard became a blacksmith to invent the perfect ice ax for his fellow climbers. But even as Mr. Chouinard's reputation grew throughout the nation and parts of the globe as the only person at the time making unique equipment for climbers, Yvon had to sell his wares from the trunk of his dilapidated car, while surviving on game hunted in the nearby forest or on cans of cat food that he purchased by the case. With time, diligence, and immense sacrifice, Yvon Chouinard now has a fifty-million-dollar business selling what many consider the premier outdoor equipment in the world.

Some folks quit on themselves even though they're so close to achieving their goals. I had a friend, Don, who wanted to get rid of a hundred pounds. After taking control and persisting in his lifelong battle, Don, God bless him, got rid of sixty pounds, but after a run of bad luck at work and some problems at home, he felt like a loser and wanted to throw in the towel. "I'm never going to make it. I'm destined to be a loser. Look at me!" he cried.

"That's right!" I fired back. "Look at you. You're looking good, feeling better. This time last year you couldn't even walk around the block once, and now you're riding your mountain bike eight, ten miles a day. Maybe you've got a way to go, but *look at how much you've done!*"

When Don replied that getting rid of sixty pounds wasn't that much and complained how far he was from his goal, I gave him a pair of thirty-pound dumbbells. "Here," I said, "hold these for a while. Or better yet, tie them around your neck. Heavy, eh?" I smiled. "Now, *that's* how far you've come!"

Peaks and Valleys

Life is not now nor ever will be black and white. In Don's case, life pulled him a little off course. Just as with an airplane, sometimes a crosswind may blow us off course or we hit an unexpected air pocket and lose our altitude. Yet all we have to do is check our direction and make a slight adjustment to get where we want to go. To quote a friend of mine, Del Mearse, who knows about diligence and staying on course, and who is also in the top one percent of all chartered financial consultants in the United States: "Life is like walking up the stairs while playing yo-yo." Even when you're progressing, every once in a while you will hit some peaks and valleys. Every day you're working, you're studying, you're scrimping, you're saving, paying your dues, and *bam*: life just slaps you down on the mat. Again, it's not fair, it's not right, but what are you going to do about it? After all that you've done, all you've been through and now sacrificed for, don't you deserve better? My advice: brush yourself off, get up, and *go the distance*.

Pardon my language, but sometimes life just sucks. And even if you try to stay away from all those mud puddles, life's pool of muck will find you, no matter what you do. Some days you're on top of your game and can do no wrong, and other days, well, you would have been better off if you'd stayed in bed. And let's say you had a bad day and had a few bites of "Chunky Monkey" ice cream, or in a moment of weakness at the mall this pair of shoes or that power tool that you know you're never going to use screamed to you, "Take me home!" Big deal: so you spent a few bucks, you gained a whopping half a pound. It's not the end of the world.

Here's an exercise: Before you throw in the towel, before you become your own worst enemy ask yourself this: "Am I better off today than I was yesterday, last week, last month, or last year?" If the answer's yes, well then, keep on keeping on. Part of the thrill of success is the journey of the struggle. If it were easy, everyone would be doing it. The truth is you're probably on the downstroke of that yo-yo. Again, every day you're climbing that ladder of success, but you just hit some unexpected turbulence and lost a little bit of altitude. Don't cave in at the first sign of trouble. Before you even think about it, take a good sound look at where you were, where you're at now, and how close you are to achieving that one thing you've hungered for so long. The reality is you will fall down, but as always it's getting up that counts. That's the making of a successful person—someone who takes a few hits but is willing to accept them and more in order to pay the price. And if you quit now, all that you've fought for and forfeited would have been in vain. Personally, I can think of nothing sadder than a person who quits on herself.

So give yourself a little bit of credit for even attempting to accomplish something others wouldn't even consider. Every day, keep paying your dues and make a stride or two to bring yourself closer to your goal. Just be mindful of the road apples in your path. And when you step in one, scrape it off and continue your journey. Remember, everyone has setbacks. Half of Jay Leno's jokes are so bad, they should be flushed. As phenomenal as Tiger Woods is, he does not win every tournament. I once saw Michael Jordan on his last shot of his last game of his career, with only seconds left in the game, make the basket that won the Chicago Bulls their NBA championship. Afterward, as everyone praised Mr. Jordan for his concentration and for pulling through in the clutch, he smiled and said something like "Yeah, I got lucky. But do you know how many times I've blown the game because

I missed that exact same shot?" You're not going to succeed unless you try. And you will fail more than you succeed.

Even with the perfect master plan there is only so much under your control. But you will not get anywhere unless you know where you're going. And, in order to get there you have to be willing to give up something in return. The test of mettle is what you have endured that made the impossible possible. Before you quit, get a good night's sleep. Situations have a tendency to look different when you have all your perceptions in your corner. See how you feel. Regroup. Take a time out. Realize you may never get the golden ring. But are you better off now than you were just a little bit ago? For there are so many people pushing, striving for that one thing. *And having that one thing is great, but if you're not enough with it, you'll never be enough without it.*

HELP YOURSELF REMINDERS

* If you can obtain it overnight, you can lose it just as quickly.

* Devote yourself every day to your cause.

* Apply yourself with enthusiasm for what you will accomplish.

* Attempt the so-called "impossible" until it becomes an everyday part of your life.

HELP YOURSELF

---

* NO ONE TAKES ANYTHING AWAY FROM US, UNLESS WE GIVE UP ON OURSELVES FIRST.

* WHEN YOU HIT THAT EXPECTED BUMP IN THE ROAD, IT'S ONLY A BUMP IN THE ROAD.

Part Three

CELEBRATE WHO YOU ARE AND WHAT YOU HAVE

6

If It All Ended Tomorrow

As a kid, I had to make the most of my situation. Since I was about six, Mother had decided, for whatever reason, that I was no longer allowed the privilege of being a member of "the family," and was therefore banished to live in the garage. At first, surrounded by darkness, I was terrified of every little sound above and around me. I had thought for sure that some huge, hairy, five-eyed, demonic swamp monster or gigantic orange-red snake would emerge from underneath the car, an overhead water pipe, or from some water drain and either eat me alive or squeeze me to death. At first, if my imagination didn't get the best of me, the chilling dampness and the hard reality of exclusion depressed me all the more. The winters were the hardest, especially during the holiday season. As "the family" trimmed the tree, listened to Christmas records, or watched television specials, I stood at the base of the garage stairs, leaning my shoulders and the

431

back of my neck against a beam of wood, with my eyes clamped shut, fantasizing I was somewhere else.

My days started and ended in the garage. Sleeping on an army cot that I used as my bed, I'd awake with a shred of hope of being fed breakfast. I'd push myself with lightning speed trying to complete my morning chores before sprinting off to school. Then, the moment school was dismissed, as conditioned I'd run home to perform Mother's endless list of afternoon chores, then either stand at the base of the garage stairs or sit on top of my hands on a bed of rocks in the backyard. Even if it rained or a gray blanket of fog rolled in from the nearby ocean, I was not allowed back inside until Mother summoned me to clear the table, wash the dinner dishes, clean the cat's litter box with my fingers, and anything else she could conjure. Afterward in the garage and feeling exhausted, I'd do my best to remain perfectly straight, trying not to fall whenever my head fell forward. I'd stay in that position until Mother granted me permission to assemble my army cot bed in the dark. Before drifting off I'd say my prayers, thankful I could escape through my dreams.

I had no television, no neighborhood baseball games, no playing at a friend's house, or even a warm meal. No hugs or sitting on someone's lap, no sharing a laugh, or "that one magical childhood moment" that I would forever cherish. No wonderment or sense of discovery, no self-worth. My home was the darkness of the garage and the disposition I brought with it.

But in some sense living in the garage at least provided a barrier of protection. As I became self-aware, especially after being burned on the gas stove and taking my vow of survival, the garage became a world of its own for me. The garage was far better than shivering outside in the backyard where my hands and shoulders would become numb from sitting on the rocks. And after learning to distinguish the different sounds from above and knowing Mother's television habits, I was able to take down my guard just a notch. Only when I felt it was absolutely safe would I sit down, lower my head, and steal a few minutes of sleep. On some afternoons I was lucky enough to sneak two quick naps before I was required to do the evening chores.

During the summer months I didn't have to worry about the cold, and sometimes I'd smile inside whenever I'd hear the neighborhood kids scream with joy as they rode their bikes down the block. It took me forever to understand that the "clicking" sounds were baseball cards hitting the spokes of their wheels.

I quickly learned that feeling sorry for myself only got me so far, so I vowed to make the most of my time. If I wasn't imagining myself flying away as one of my superheroes, I'd read encyclopedia-sized books that I brought home from school. For years Mother had berated me on how stupid I was, so I tricked her into thinking that I was indeed incompetent and needed to complete extra homework in order to keep up. I knew full well how closely Mother wished to guard our relationship, so our "attention time" became a little shorter than before, as she believed the teachers would question why my homework was not completed. So, between my chores and Mother beating me, I'd strain my eyes in the darkness and race through every page of my books, absorbing every picture in detail and every word of every sentence. Besides school, my favorite part of the day was expanding my imagination by reading books about reptiles or volcanology, or adventure stories like *Robinson Crusoe* or *The Count of Monte Cristo*. Sometimes I would rush through my chores or stand impatiently waiting for Mother to finish doing whatever she did to me, so I could finish another page in one of my books.

On rare occasions, late into the night Mother would turn off the television and play a Bill Cosby record. For me there was no greater treat. Knowing she would soon be going to bed, I felt safe enough to shut my eyes, and while standing I'd imagine Mr. Cosby's words spilling like water. Since Mother played the same record over and over again, I'd study the rhythm of the stories, the timing of the punch lines, how Mr. Cosby spoke with perfect clarity, and his ability to make his characters seem so real. Over time, in my mind I'd lip-sync certain parts of the stories and even though I'd become terrified and stuttered whenever at school or in front of Mother, after hearing Cosby's voice I knew I wanted to become a storyteller. Listening to Bill Cosby was like celebrating Christmas and a birthday rolled into one. Sometimes I'd still shiver in the garage, but whenever I heard, "Hey, Hey, Hey . . . Fat Albert . . ." I'd laugh and all my troubles would melt away.

Being alone gave me the opportunity to educate myself and to plot every move of any situation Mother might dream up. Whenever I felt depressed or self-pity, I'd remember one of Bill Cosby's stories or a passage from one of my adventure books. The darkness became my home. I only had to make it through—one morning, one afternoon, and one evening at a time.

* * *

One winter afternoon I came close to losing it. I hated my life—how unfair everything was and how other people, like my brothers and every kid at school, had more and were treated better than me. That January of 1973 after Father moved out of the house, I felt betrayed. Even though he did little to stop Mother, I always felt safer with his presence upstairs. Somehow I knew with Father gone Mother was going to kill me. The beatings became more intense and far more bizarre. Food became nonexistent.

That Saturday, after not eating for several days, I took the chance of being caught and risked stealing food from the refrigerator just a few feet from me in the garage. I was that desperate: to attempt moving a single inch in the middle of the afternoon—the prime time when Mother might either suddenly open the door to check on me or summon me upstairs to do with me as she pleased. Knowing every inch of the garage and praying my worn-out sneakers didn't make any noise or the hinges to the refrigerator door didn't squeak, I stood on my toes while sliding a frozen pie tin into my hand. I could feel the drool in my mouth while I gazed down at one of Mother's prized homemade pumpkin pies. I knew I could never eat the entire dessert or even take a piece of it. Mother counted every piece of every item of food she kept in the house. Even if eating the pie was my only refuge between life and death, I feared Mother's retributions more. My terror and the rush of cold air escaping from the freezer, coupled with the risk of being caught, made my hands shake so much that I nearly dropped the pie. Caught between survival and fear, I took my chance. With my free hand I pinched a loosened piece of frozen crust, then another and another, until I had a small pile in my hand. Being careful to replace the pie precisely as I had found it, I felt Mother would never know. I had lost track of time, and fearing Mother might get up at any second if a television commercial came on, I scurried back over to my position. Alone in the dark, I blinked my eyes at the prize I cupped in my hand. As my body temperature warmed the frozen crust, I rolled the pieces into a ball. Before popping it into my mouth, I realized how incredibly fortunate I was. Not only did Mother not catch me, but I now held in my hand more food than I had been given in the last few days. I was alive, and I had a keen mind to think with. At least I had a roof over my head, I kept telling myself, and if Mother didn't freak out and kill me, I stood a chance of staying alive. I knew in my heart if I could survive all that I had up till then, anything else had to be a little easier, a little better.

At the bottom of the stairs, the pie crust seemed as if it

was melting in my mouth . . . as if I were eating a grand meal. Even after swallowing I could still taste my bountiful feast. I shivered, but not from the cold, my self-imposed fear, or anxiety. I trembled with the pleasure of fulfillment. I had risked everything to accomplish my task. Alone in the dark I smiled at my good fortune. For a rare moment in my life, I was happy with myself.

*   *   *

I never forget how lucky I am, no matter what I'm doing in life. When giving a presentation I am almost always asked, "Dave, if you had the chance, what would you change about your past?" And I always give the question serious thought: Would I run away, defend myself from Mother, or maybe have the opportunity to be born to a different set of parents? But for me the answer is always the same: Nothing! I wouldn't change a single element of my former life. As previously stated, and as weird as it may sound, my past experiences—every one of them—as grim and at times terrifying as they were, made me appreciate everything, and I mean *everything*, in my life today. After the experiences I have had, *what* do I really have to complain about?

If there's one thing that drives me crazy it is people who, after living through an unfortunate, extraordinary experience, by their own choice wallow in self-pity or are absolutely miserable for the rest of their lives. Why in the world would someone go through all that pain, suffering, and despair just to be so unhappy? In my case, the first twelve years of my life were not good ones, so I'm going to live the remainder of my sixty to seventy years as best I can.

Why is it a lot of folks are so unhappy? Why are there great numbers of people who, no matter what they have or whatever they strive to achieve, seem so unfulfilled? I'm guessing unresolved issues would play a major role, but part of the solution could be that maybe the older we get, the more complacent, hopeless, and despondent we become. I don't think we mean to; however, some of us may forget that we try to resolve issues, deal with the everyday situations, work hard, sacrifice, and push ourselves for the simple purpose of obtaining some form of satisfaction. And over time we forget what we're fighting for. For one reason or another we believe life burns us out and we forget to *be* happy.

The Race to Grow Up and Get Ahead

Being a film buff, there is one film that I highly recommend, and it's about getting caught up in the daily grind of life: *Hook,* the Steven Spielberg film starring Robin Williams and Dustin Hoffman. The film is an account of what happens to Peter Pan once he's grown up. Mr. Williams plays the role of Peter Banning, who's forgotten he used to be the carefree, adventurous Peter Pan. As an adult, Peter's life consists of high-powered corporate business dealings. In Peter's pursuit of wealth he not only neglects his wife and children, and drinks too much, while griping about every little thing, but he has become the New Age version of a cutthroat pirate. In the course of the film Peter's children are kidnapped by his old nemesis, Captain Hook, and before Peter can rescue his children by doing battle with his adversary, he must relearn what was so critically important to him as a child: the love and security of being part of a family. In other words, Peter Banning must rediscover his happy thoughts. After doing so and defeating Captain Hook in a duel, Peter triumphantly returns home with his children. In the glow of the family reunion Peter is asked, "Are you done with all of your adventures?" Peter, with a childlike grin and a sparkle in his eyes, replies, "To live; now, that would be an adventure!"

Again, it's sad to say, but for so many folks it seems the older they become in the race of "get ahead and have it all," even if they achieve their desires, in the end they lose themselves and that exhilarated innocence. They lose that prime motivating element that made it all possible in the first place. They lose their happy thoughts. When you were younger, what did you aspire to be? What did you wish to do? Are you truly doing what you want today? Overall, are you a fulfilled person?

Naturally, at any given time any of us would answer, "Well, I really don't like what I'm doing now," or "No, at the moment I'm not happy at all." That's the reality of life: we all can't do what we want at every given moment of every day. Now, I'm not saying you should walk through life grinning from ear to ear like your facial muscles are frozen, but I am saying to at least be happy in your quests and the world you live in right now, today. Don't wait to get that job, pass that exam, marry that person, buy that car, or survive some immense crisis for you to be appreciative. Because while you think you are truly happy, you are only basing your happiness on your surroundings or the situation and not yourself as a person. And don't you deserve better than that?

At one time in all of our lives, being happy was the overriding thing on our minds. But, like Peter Banning, as we grew older we lost our happy thoughts. Here's something: From ages two until about fifteen, what do kids think about? Answer: PLAYING! Being happy and exploring everything to its fullest capacity is basically all that's on kids' minds. The younger they are, the more they believe that anything is possible. And they're happy with things that really don't cost a lot or amount to a great deal—holding their hands, reading to them in bed, or giving them praise for something they accomplish. And if they're having a bad day, their world is suddenly brighter when you mention "ice cream." When it comes to gifts, babies and toddlers seem more euphoric over tearing open a box than in discovering what's inside. They spend more time popping the bubble wrap that protected the gift that you broke your back and blitzed through countless malls and waited in line for hours to buy, than they do in playing with it. For some kids, no matter the age, you can't get them to stay in bed even if you put lead weights on them, for the simple reason that they want to play and *play right now*.

Between the ages of fifteen and twenty as they become more mature, these young adults craving independence still wish to play, but do so primarily when adult supervision is nowhere to be found. The older teenagers get, the less they can wait to move out and be on their own, so no one can tell them what to do or how to do it. *Then* life will be grand and they can do whatever they want, at any given moment of any day. Their lives will be completely filled with carefree ecstasy.

Around the ages of twenty to twenty-five, the carefree priorities take a slight shift because of one word from Dr. Abraham Maslow, a gentleman considered the father of modern psychology, who created the pyramid theory of human needs: *Survival*. For the most part, if these twenty-somethings do not have gainful employment, they have difficulty purchasing food and having a place to rest their heads. Amusing themselves and doing all those "adults things" they've dreamt of for so many years is still on their minds, yet college, trade school, and/or landing a job ebbs away at their youthful ambitions.

By the ages of twenty-five to thirty-five, we've pretty much settled into our careers, and saving for our own home and other materialistic things takes precedence. Usually at this age, out of the blue we see that person from across the way, then Cupid shoots his arrow and we fall victim to this crazy emotion called love. We marry, become a little bit pregnant, and soon *the* number-one priority in our lives is to ensure we have an arsenal of Pampers within our reach.

From thirty-five to forty-five, after a few medical examinations, we discover we're not immortal. We can't believe that we not only subjected our bodies to the things we did in our youth—stunts that would surely have gotten us arrested in these days—but that we actually lived to tell about it. We have become our generation's biggest foe: we are now part of the establishment. One day we woke up and became our father, mother, uncle, aunt, or anyone else we despised in our childhood. We join health clubs. We pay exorbitant sums in order to sweat out built-up toxins (in public) and watch, weigh, and worry about every gram of fat that enters our bodies just so we can pay more taxes by living longer. We frantically purchase every piece of workout contraption or video we see on television, and after a few weeks we find ourselves running out of spaces for the "easy-to-use, easy-to-store" revolutionary equipment, so we begin to think about the idea of purchasing a bigger home, just so we can have a bigger garage and more closet space— so we can cram it with more stuff from our lives.

With the greatest of anticipation we try every diet, buy gallons of Rogaine, and in our limited time off we go to the "fake and bake" for that Saint-Tropez tan. Looking young is now the foremost goal in our lives. Stability is important too. The average American has car insurance for her 2.5 cars—that she'll be paying for right up until the warranty expires or the engine blows up in the middle of rush-hour traffic, while she's driving a herd of children in her minivan (that years ago she swore she wouldn't be caught dead in) to soccer practice. We have house insurance, health insurance (including dental), and another policy to take care of whatever the other insurance policies were supposed to. There's insurance for the boat, Wave Rider, and any other toy that makes us happy. After a big scare we purchase tornado, hurricane, flood, earthquake, and "dust bowl" insurance as a package deal—just in case ol' Mother Nature decides to promote chaos. We have insurance protection for not only every credit card we need, but practically every piece of appliance we're still making payments on—the television, DVD player, and Nintendo; the washer, dryer, and refrigerator, to the puree blender that we use for our high-energy, high-carb, high-protein, low-fat, no-taste protein shakes ... so we can live longer, pay more taxes, and purchase more insurance polices.

We plan ahead, we think about retirement and escaping the rat race once and for all. We invest in the market. We have expanded portfolios that include a carefully analyzed quantity of mutual funds and numerous shares of Starbucks, Worldwide Wrestling Federation Entertainment, and Victoria's Secret. We are waiting for the next Amazon.com or Yahoo.com IPOs, so we can get in, clean up, and dump the stock at a huge profit so Uncle Sam can take his share from our successes. We have heated debates about the virtues and drawbacks of 401Ks and IRAs. We count the days until our lovely children, who were once precious babies but in the last few years have acted as if they've been possessed by demons, move out on their own so we can finally buy that motor home, see the world, and wear pants with the elastic waists.

Around the ages forty-five to fifty-five, for some of us our better days are behind us. We're amazed to find ourselves far more conservative about life in general than we were in our twenties. We find ourselves grumbling more. At the corner café we publicly denounce all politicians as crooks. While reminiscing about the good ol' days of President John F. Kennedy who inspired our nation to journey to the moon and how Richard Nixon made us all eye the office of the president with more suspicion, some *kid* with a double shot of espresso and dash of raspberry syrup looks at you with a who-in-the-hell-are-you-talking-about? expression. At home our relaxation is according to what's scheduled on the television. A bad day for us is not some crisis at work or at the home front, but rather when the television cable craps out or when we temporarily lose the remote control. We "armchair-quarterback" every play of every sport, we screech at our soap-opera stars for sleeping with their best friend's bother's uncle who just woke from a ten-year coma, and we are amazingly surprised at every episode of the *Jerry Springer Show*.

We complain more about how unfair life is to us. We make more excuses of *what could have been*: "If it wasn't for my bad knee from high school, I could have gone on and played pro football." "If I hadn't married you, I could have gone to Hollywood and become a star." We're depressed about the fact that whenever we lose our hair we find it growing in our noses, ears, and other areas that we're too ashamed to discuss in public. But, hey, we tell ourselves, retirement is just around the corner. Then I'll have fun!

From ages fifty-five and beyond, we're just too damn tired to do anything. Late-night television shows like Jay Leno or David Letterman seem so juvenile, and besides it's way past our bedtimes. We complain so much about everything that no one will have anything to do with us, except for those "unknowing hostages" known as *babies*— who, with drool spilling from the side of their mouths, are in giggling awe of the old person sitting in front of them with all that white hair sticking out of both ears.

Since they don't make good shows like they used to, we abandon the television and spend our day spouting wisdom that no one in the world wants to hear: "Back in my day, we didn't have those fancy 'Rybook' or 'Neeke' shoes. And, another thing: we didn't have a school bus or some fancy beau pick us up in their parents' fancy SUV. I tell ya, back in my day we walked three miles to school, up and over the hill, barefoot in the snow every day! And we never complained! Not once, not one iota, not one word! We had it hard and we loved it. Oy, you kids today have it too easy! All you want to do is play, play, play. I tell you what—you better learn to grown up and act your age. Life's not all fun and games. Wait till you're my age, then you'll see. Then you'll know something about something. And another thing—let me tell you about the value of a dollar. Back in my day, that's when a dollar meant something. . . ."

The older generation worries that the younger generation either doesn't work hard enough or doesn't appreciate all of the work and sacrifice of others. The older generation seems to believe that the world *is* going to hell in a handbasket and the *young kids* are the ones wearing the UPS uniforms delivering the goods.

Whatever happened to being happy?

A Cheerful Disposition

In a twisted comical sense, a lot of the above rings true. If we take ourselves too seriously in the pursuit of our endeavors all of our good nature could be used up by the time we achieve what we've wanted. For instance, did you know the average child laughs more than four hundred times a day? For the average adult that number dwindles down to less than forty. So many of us work hard, provide for our families, and sacrifice ourselves to the hilt, so much so that we can easily surrender our inner passions and happiness in the process. All we end up doing is feeding the machine. Get up, to go to work, to pay for the car that gets you to work and provides a means to sustain the home and feed the family, so you can bring home more work, then finally go to bed, only to repeat the process the next day. The hard truth is there are dues to be paid, and efforts and forfeits are facts of life. But as you deal with life's complications and strive to achieve your desires, are you happy? Do you feel proud of yourself or get a tiny rush of excitement that you applied yourself in the right direction? *You should.*

In the midst of applying yourself, dealing with whatever issue life throws your way, are you able to relax? Do you clear your head and take a breather? Or do you find yourself constantly getting wrapped around the axle over the most insignificant petty things that take up a majority of your time, energy, and focus? Are you losing sleep, feeling drained and unsatisfied? Do you find yourself always defending your actions, or does your emotional state seem to be just below the boiling point? The answer could entail an endless number of elements. Again, I'm no psychologist, but I'm guessing that if you answered yes to two or more of these questions you, my dear friend, are not relaxing enough! You need a more cheerful disposition. As we discussed in the first section of this book, you need to empty that CD-ROM in your head. You may need to decompress *from* home *before* you arrive at work or school, *so* you have a clear head and are therefore able to tackle your objectives. Continually take little mental breaks whenever and however you can. *Whatever you do, do something positive.*

By force of habit, whenever I say or think something negative, before it becomes ingrained in my mind, I instantly try to replace it with something positive. While in the vortex of hysteria and confusion I silently tell myself, *Well, it could be worse.* Another line I recommend is from the movie *Point of No Return*: "I never did mind the *little* things." The same attitude is the concept of best-selling

447

author Richard Carlson in his book, *Don't Sweat the Small Stuff . . . and It's All Small Stuff.*

Vent when you need to, but don't allow life's twists and turns and bumps on the road to drain your happiness. The more you take control of your attitude, the more cheerful you will be and the more you'll be able take on and complete any task.

A lot of folks take happiness for granted, as if we as individuals had no say-so over this emotion. But we do. Think about it: all of our lives we've been taught to watch what we say, keep that attitude in check, or don't fly off the handle. By coincidence and through years of conditioning a lot of us neglect to work on a positive attitude. So what do you do? I advise that in all of your efforts as you apply yourself in areas of health, in saving for the future, studying for that test, or in working hard for that new car, each and every day do the same on your positive, upbeat attitude. As always, continue to better yourself but do so *now* by being aware of your emotional state. Replace negative attitudes with positive ones. As you are well aware: as bad as things are, they could be a lot worse. And griping and complaining will not get you out of it, but a simple optimistic attitude can turn things around. Again, in the final analysis it is up to you.

Years ago, before the comedian actress Gilda Radner passed away from her battle with cancer, she formed groups with others who, like her, were fighting the disease, and together they found a sense of happiness and reprieve from their situations. It didn't change the fact that these brave people had to deal with their life-threatening

———

disease every day, but spreading a bit of cheer among themselves made their circumstances the more tolerable. In one interview I heard Ms. Radner say, "I look at it this way: as I'm fighting cancer, I think of all the money I'm saving on shampoo." To this day Gilda's disposition has touched countless others who are surviving cancer with dignity and feeling more fulfilled.

The Power of a Positive State of Mind

Happiness is a state of mind—*your mind*—so you take the control. With everything else you're committing to, in order to better yourself don't take this one vital item for granted. Whenever you step out of a certain comfort zone to enhance the person you wish to be, make sure you have a sense of contentment with each and every step you take. If you're doing all that you can without a sense of joy or even satisfaction, there's a strong chance you may not get to where you want to go. Don't throw this important element into the wind; if you do (and if you have the kind of luck I have) it will end up in the hands of Murphy's Law.

Don't leave your happiness to fate. Even with the best of luck, destiny can only take you so far. Years ago, when I flew in the air force, I had an offbeat friend named George who convinced himself his sole path to happiness was to marry. George never went out. He never mingled. He never dated. Yet every Friday night, he would put on his best imitation polo shirt that he had

449

purchased overseas for five dollars, run a comb through his oily hair, and wait. And wait. And wait. After a year of frustration George expressed his concerns, and although I and others offered suggestions he remained ensconced in his faith for happiness. George believed without a doubt that someday, some woman would show up, knock on his door, and make him a happy man. As romantic as this story may sound, *George* never put forth the effort, any effort, needed to obtain the happiness he believed he so desperately craved.

Why would you waste a day of your life waiting for happiness to find you? Do *something* to manage your own destiny. Don't postpone your elation until after your final exams, completion of that one project, or wait until you take *that* vacation. And don't even think about saying, "I'll be happy *once* I get that car, that promotion, lose that weight, or find that one person I'll spend the rest of my life with." If I may say: Make your own happiness. Be happy with who you are and what you have in your life *right now*!

It wasn't too long ago that I lived in an ice-cold, rundown cabinlike summer home in the middle of winter with no insulation and no heater, sleeping on a leaky air mattress, while literally scraping pennies together. I discovered within hours following my return from Japan after receiving the award and being celebrated as one of the Ten Outstanding Young Persons of the World, that my fortunes had suddenly turned upside down. I had been "mismanaged" by the speaking firm that represented me. After collecting myself, with a strong belief in my own cause, scared to death, and not knowing what lay ahead of me, I decided to start my own business. I paid the price for my ambition, put in twenty-hour days while maintaining a high standard, and even worked a few odds jobs in order to get by. Like anybody else in my position, I took a few hard knocks and there were days that the only meal I could afford was a single serving of Cup-a-Soup. And yet, as hard as it was, as many sacrifices as I made, and at times with so much against me, I loved every minute of it! For me, living in that freezing cabin, in the middle of winter, with wrapping my hands around my soup meal as the only way of warming myself, was one of the greatest, most fulfilling times of my life.

Beyond my health, youth, and a few close friends, I was on the threshold of a new life and I made the most of what I had. I appreciated everything—a place to call my own, the sound of the rain hitting the roof, the smell of the redwood trees after a storm, the hours I spent alone reading a book or listening to music.

Some days I'd splurge by having a piece of three-day-old French bread. With every bite I'd smile, thinking that I had nothing to complain about, for the bread was more than I'd had before. No matter how hectic my day or desperate my situation was, I'd try to find something positive in it. I'd decompress by stepping outside on the wooden deck, sometimes in the chilling rain, looking straight up at the majesty of the trees against the darkened sky. I was optimistic. I was living the American dream, and with every day I was closer to living in a real home, chockful of food and with a fireplace to keep me warm. With hope and opportunity, what more could I *really* ask for?

Maybe it's me, but because of all I endured as a child there is literally not a single day that I wake up and don't appreciate the fact that I am alive, not a day that I'm not optimistic of what is before me. Because of my past I was extremely fortunate to learn as a child how much bitterness my mother held in her heart and how unhappy she was. I vowed not to repeat the mistakes she made—if Mother was so unhappy about her past, I decided to deal with my issues as best as I could, before they would overwhelm me as they had her. Since Mother hated everyone and everything, I've learned, through her destructive lifestyle, to hate no one, especially my own perpetrator. And because I had virtually no life as a kid, I've done my best to ensure that my son can live a life full of wonderment and opportunity, but above all that he will never have to be subjected to what I had to endure as a child. And finally, on a deep personal level, maybe I had to suffer what I did, almost dying several times in the process, in order to cherish the value and sanctity of the life I have today.

Everywhere you go, you take yourself. Never forget: *your* attitude *is* everything. And with all that there is to life, don't leave your happiness to destiny; for your lack of effort and ignorance will only result in a hollow, joyless life.

The primary reason why I'm hammering away at you to be content with who you are and what you have in your life right now is there are no guarantees when you go to sleep at night that you are going to wake up tomorrow morning. None! *This* is why I stressed getting closure on our issues. Don't allow every little thing to get to you, drag you down, and consume your life. There may not be a tomorrow to count on, so live the best life that you can today. As stated in the final scene of the movie *Hook*: "Seize the day!"

No Guarantees for Tomorrow

Years ago I read a poem that to this day has had a profound affect on my life. "If I had my life to live over . . . I'd relax, I would limber up. . . . I would take fewer things seriously. . . . I would climb more mountains and swim more rivers. . . . I would eat more ice cream. . . . I would pick more daisies." This poem was written by Nadine Stair, an eighty-five-year-old woman whose words encouraged many to see and live life through new eyes.

If you had only ten days to live, what would you do? Seriously, if your doctor informed you that you had just a few days to live, what would you do with the time you had left? Now, you might say, "Hell, I'd just see another doctor and get a second opinion." Go ahead; make an appointment, take all the time you need. But your time is slipping away with every wasted hour.

I'd tell you what I'd do: I'd pick up the phone and call anyone that came to mind. I'd make the most of my time and have a blast. I'd surround myself with the sounds of my favorite music and fill every room with the scent and vibrant colors of fresh-cut flowers. I would definitely go on a spending binge. I would surprise family and friends with gifts, in the hopes of showing my appreciation and to make their lives just a little brighter. And even though I'm an introvert, I'd host a few parties so I could hold, hug, and just be with those who were important to me during the course of my life. I'd fight for every minute of my life and try to not to squander my time. I wouldn't sleep, but I'd take naps outside. I would watch every sunrise and every sunset. I would make peace with my God and be appreciative of the time I had on this planet and how fortunate I was.

What does your world of happiness mean to you? What does it truly, absolutely take to make you feel fulfilled? How much does it cost to watch a sunset, to feel the rays of the sun on your face, or to hear the surf crash against a sandy beach? What price can you put on holding the hand of another or the warm embrace of that one person who means the world to you? How much effort does it take to change your pessimistic attitude and do something to brighten someone else's life?

In all my travels I've learned the things that make all of us happy are right in front of us, each and every day. Our happiness is readily available to everyone of us *regardless* of our age, sex, nationality, education, religion, our past, our desires, or how much we have or don't have!

Some time ago I ran into a dear friend who had just returned from vacation. Ray had a perfect tan, a bright smile, and a lively spring in his step. I couldn't stop him from telling me about his recent cruise. "I tell ya, my wife and I, all we did was eat and drink. We spent all day at the pool and danced all night. We watched every sunset. We made love every night. We talked for hours on end, we laughed out loud in front of everybody, and played like kids. I tell ya, that was the best money I ever spent!"

When Ray told me the amount, I nearly swallowed my tongue. "Well," I replied, "you and your wife could have done all that at my house for half the price!"

Of course, I was kidding. Ray is one of the hardest workers I know. He is one of the few people who do for others before thinking of themselves, and that one cruise was a lifetime goal for him and his lovely wife. I just find it odd that some people have to "get away" in order to be happy, or lose—or almost lose—that someone or something that's so special to them in order to truly appreciate what they have in their everyday life; like the saying You don't know what you have till it's gone.

Every Thanksgiving and every holiday season all of us take a moment, bow our heads, and reflect on our blessings. I'm sure nearly all of us, no matter what situation we're currently working on or what we've already been put through, realize how lucky we are. With all the troubles in the world, what if we could carry some of that appreciation and sense of joy with us every day?

Take a step back and look at all that you've accomplished and the opportunities before you. Now ask yourself: What does it take for me to *truly* be happy? The answer has been right in front of you all this time.

HELP YOURSELF REMINDERS

* WE WORK AND SACRIFICE FOR THE CAUSE OF FULFILLMENT.

* A CONSISTENT, POSITIVE ATTITUDE MAKES A WORLD OF DIFFERENCE.

* DON'T LEAVE YOUR HAPPINESS TO FATE.

* THERE ARE NO GUARANTEES FOR TOMORROW, SO APPRECIATE ALL THAT YOU HAVE AND DO ALL THAT YOU CAN TODAY!

7

What Do You Say When You Talk to Yourself?

For once I was actually happy to run home. Since my parents' separation just a few weeks ago, I finally had something to smile about. After years of trying to prove to Mother that I wasn't stupid or worthless, I clinched my verification in the palm of my hand.

Just days before the school's winter break, my homeroom teacher, Mr. Ziegler, had come up with an idea of having the students name the school paper. Everyone entered and I, too, came up with a catchy phrase. I never gave it much thought partly because I knew if the kids found out that "Pelzer-Smelzer" had reached the finals, they would all vote against me. But as the numbers to the selections were broadcast over the loudspeaker, my phrase had captured nearly every vote. Before dismissing the class for the weekend, Mr. Ziegler announced to the students that the idea was mine, and to my surprise everyone clapped and howled with applause. I swelled with pride. As my teacher gave me an envelope to present to Mother, he assured me that Mother, too, would be proud.

Before closing the front door to Mother's house, I gazed up at the gray clouds beginning to take form. Seconds later, I stood in front of Mother with my chin to my chest, but this time I extended my arm, revealing the crumpled envelope I held out for her.

After Mother leaned from the couch to snatch the letter, I stole a quick glance. As she tore open the envelope and her eyes swept through Mr. Ziegler's writing, my pulse raced with anticipation. I swallowed hard, waiting for her reaction. I kept thinking, *This is it. Someone has publicly stated that I, David Pelzer, am okay.* For years Mother had fought to justify her "treatment" of me because I was either troubled, pathetic, or simply a slow child. But now, I thought to myself, for someone to write a letter by hand, signing his name to it—it is now official! Mother couldn't brush it off as she always did when I brought home good grades on my report card, claiming I had somehow changed the D's to B's. That I couldn't be that bright. That I had somehow cheated. Now, in Mother's hands, was the confirmation I had wished for for years: *I am a good kid.*

"Well," Mother huffed after pausing to wipe the side of her face, "it says here, your teacher claims you were the student to name the school paper." She stopped for a moment, nodding her head ever so slightly as if taking everything in. "Aren't you the special one?"

I stood in front of Mother almost revealing my grin

as she again read through the letter. Without thinking I raised my head to look up at Mother, searching for the smallest reaction. In a sudden flash Mother erupted, with her pointed finger almost striking my face. "Get one thing straight. There is nothing, nothing, you can do to impress me, not now, not ever! Do you understand? You are nothing to me. Nothing, a nobody, an 'It.' You don't even exist. I hate you and wish you were dead. Do you hear me? Dead!"

I was too numb to say anything as Mother stood up and ripped Mr. Ziegler's letter into pieces. All I could do was stare up as the letter that I had placed all of my hope upon rained down on me like snowflakes from a winter storm. Kneeling to the floor, I tried to somehow put the letter together. I thought if I did, then maybe something would turn out, as if that one piece of paper would help me through all of my problems. But I couldn't fix it. There were too many pieces, and in my heart I held the truth I had always known. So I, too, repeated Mother's words: that I did not exist and wished I was dead.

With Mother standing in her slippers just inches in front of me, I scooped the flakes of my prized paper before dumping them into the kitchen trash can. After completing my series of afternoon chores, I stood perfectly still in the garage. I stared straight ahead at the worn red-colored stairs with the black matting that Mother herself had painted and tacked on years ago. While on the outside I seemed almost robotic, on the inside I had completely lost it. During all the years and thousands of times Mother went out of her way to call me names or put me down, I had somehow brushed everything off. I had always believed, I had always felt from the recesses of my soul, that it was the booze talking or something else that took over Mother that made her treat me as she did. In my years of desperation, every day I had anticipated that tomorrow might be the day—the one day that she would wake up from her stupor and we would reunite as a normal mother and son. But while staring into my world that darkened as the night began to fall, there was no escaping my reality. I knew by the tone of her voice, by the cold, sickening gleam of pure pleasure pouring from her eyes, that Mother had meant every syllable. *I was a nobody.* A nonexistent thing. To Mother I would always be known as the child called "It."

*   *   *

To this day I can still hear Mother's words ringing in my ears and, at times, in my heart. But I am no different from anyone else. All of us have heard such words, if not worse ones, during the course of our lives. It has been said by many in the field of psychology that as individuals it's not the physical pain that we carry with us, but the psychological trauma that hurts us the most. I'm sure you, too, can remember not only what that particular person said to you, but also the look on his face, the time of day, and what was going on in the background. When I work with those who still seem affected by such an event, I recommend for them to look at where that finger of defeat is connected. The individual saying those things or jabbing that finger in your face is not a happy person. In my mother's case she was, for whatever reason, miserable with herself, and she simply took it out on me. She projected her frustration, guilt, shame, and everything else she kept bottled up inside over the years, onto her husband, children, her mother, other family members, and anyone else until her animosity spread to everyone and anything she came in contact with.

This is why it is so critical to address and resolve your issues. No one's perfect, all of us have said and done things we regret. And if you have said some hurtful things, as I've already recommended make amends as best as you can. That doesn't mean you surrender or that you were wrong. But if you still carry some psychological scar, imagine how others, especially those close to you, feel when they hear such words.

Even though what we hear can have a tremendous impact on our lives, that doesn't mean we're doomed. Every day all of us are subjected to tremendous amounts of negativity ranging from home, work, our community, portions of the news, and especially from those we're close to. We are bombarded by so much negativity that part of us may become immune. It's hard to process it all, let alone remain optimistic. If you feel frayed at times, trust me, it's normal. Did you know that the average person from the moment she wakes up to the time she goes to sleep and loses consciousness, has between forty thousand and fifty thousand thoughts a day? That's on the average. Imagine how many thoughts Albert Einstein or

Carl Sagan had, or Stephen Hawking contemplates. Now, if a person is awake eighteen hours a day, that's over twenty-two hundred thoughts an hour, which equates to over thirty-six separate thoughts a minute; which means every other second, you and I have a single concept racing through our heads. And that's every other second of every day for the rest of our lives. No wonder we're so frustrated and tired!

Now, take into account that the average person who, again, has at least forty thousand thoughts every day swimming around in her head, spends nearly ninety percent of her energy talking to herself. Ninety percent! We see folks we don't know, size them up, and decide within seconds whether we like them or not. Without warning we find ourselves in a situation and rather than hear what's being said about the matter at hand, our brains scream "Oh, my God!" Or at a social occasion, when three or more people are gathered around you it always seems that there's one idiot who drones on, and on, and on. Inside you're itching to jump in. You're looking for a pause, as if you're in a "tag team" wrestling match waiting for your turn . . . then *you'll* be able to get in your two cents, so *you* can spout your ideas and impress others, while someone beside you is looking for a sign of momentary lull so he, too, can pounce on the conversation.

And as if all of this weren't confusing enough, out of those forty thousand thoughts, in which ninety percent of your time is spent talking to yourself, at least seventy-five percent are *negative*. With everything we hear from others about ourselves, whatever news we see or hear, or no matter what's going on in our lives, no one, and I mean no one, can put us down as we ourselves can: *I'm not good enough, smart enough, or pretty enough. I'm too fat, too thin, too old, or not old enough. No one likes me. I'm not worthy. I hate myself. I wish I were dead.*

At one time or another *all* of us have had dejected thoughts. Hopefully they have been fleeting ones. None of us lives in a "happy land" animated world filled with lollipops and ginger snaps. In the course of my life I've learned this: Every single one of us is worthy. All of us have unique gifts that no one else can duplicate. Bad things happen to us and against us. How can you accomplish your objective if you don't believe, and I do mean *truly believe* in yourself first and foremost? So, if you find yourself being constantly dominated by unhappy thoughts about yourself, I highly advise you to seek and receive professional guidance and support. Don't waste another moment of your precious life. Better yourself, by getting some help for yourself.

I'm sure no one grows up with the intention of being exposed to so much negativity or having all these pessimistic thoughts running around in her head. But in an awkward sense, negativity has been enforced into all of our lives. Think about it this way: What is the first word from a baby's mouth? Now, some might say *Mama* or maybe *Dada*. There are some adults, particularly grandparents, who boast that their four-month-old prodigy has articulated *Gaga*. Yet, for the most part, the first words from the mouths of babies is *NO*.

As babies begin to discover their world, they are into

everything all at once, all the time. When my son was a toddler, whenever he was put in his little walker he was, for lack of better words, hell on wheels. There was no way I could keep up with him; but I stupidly attempted to do just that. I found myself sprinting after him fast and furiously for the sole purpose of assuring his safety. Whenever Stephen would make a sudden turn around a corner, I'd run after him at warp speed keeping my eyes right on him, fearing what he might get into, and I would literally smash headfirst into the wall at the end of the hallway. I soon found myself barking, "No, no, no"—a hundred, thousand, million, billion times a day. "Stephen! Don't go so fast! Don't pry off the cover and stick your finger in the electrical socket! Don't eat that plant! No, the kitty's tail doesn't come off! And, no, Stephen, do not lift up your aunt's skirt and use it as a tent in front of company. No, no, no!"

During childhood all of us are bombarded with reasonable, protective instructions like: *Don't take candy from strangers; Make sure you look both ways before you cross the street; Never get into a car with someone you don't know;* to the bizarre directives like: *Now, make sure you always wear clean socks and underwear, just in case you get into a car accident, then you won't embarrass yourself with holes in your socks or soiled underpants.* As kids grow older, adults are tired of explaining why, so they simply badger commands: *Wet paint. Don't touch. Off limits. Stay out. You're too young to watch that. Don't say that. You can't listen to that kind of music. Don't you even think about that! Just say no to drugs. You're not wearing that thing in public!* No, No, No, No!

Now, don't get me wrong. I'm a firm believer in boundaries. But what began as genuine concern for our safety and well-being from those who cared for us, without conscious intent became infused by negativity.

Initial Input

So, is there anything we can do about it? Yes: *Watch what you say when you talk to yourself.* Now, while some folks claim that whatever thoughts run through their heads or whatever words fly out of their mouths about any given situation are not a problem for them, with all due respect I beg to differ. Some time ago I asked seven people—of both sexes and of different ages and levels of education, and various backgrounds—to be a part of a onetime experiment. From the moment they opened their eyes when they woke up, all they had to do was record the first five to ten minutes of their day. Every one of them had the same basic reaction: they got out of bed, gazed at the bedroom clock feeling okay, continued to wake up as they wobbled their way to the bathroom, did their business, washed up, and felt relieved without a care in the world . . . right up until they saw themselves in the mirror. That quickly, in the blink of an eye, they either felt apprehension, a sense of numbness, or were in complete shock. The responses were: *Crap, it's Monday!; I better get the kids up and ready for school; I gotta clean the house and go to the grocery store; I knew I should have studied for that test; I hate going to work and fighting that traffic; I hate my hair; I'm so fat; Oh, my God . . . I'm going to be late!*

Every one of these folks was perfectly fine, completely content with their lives the first two minutes or so of their new day, until they told themselves *how* to react. In every case, they didn't have a care in the world for the simple reason that *they did not have a care in the world.* But as they woke up, the more that CD-ROM in their brain spun to life, a random thought or two triggered an emotional response forcing these folks to react a certain way. Does this sound familiar? Have you ever had the same experience? I have. For me, everything's fine and dandy for the first couple of minutes, then one thought instantly connects with another, which can send my heart racing with all the things I have to accomplish on that given day or that one unresolved problem that's been weighing on my mind. At times in the past, I've allowed myself to get so wrapped up in a small band of negative thoughts that has had an adverse effect on my day, *until* I either replaced the negative perceptions with something positive or simply dealt with whatever the issue was and let it go.

Did you know when you conceive just one solitary thought, that message, with the speed of light, sends out thousands of impulses throughout your entire body telling it how to react? Before you can snap your fingers, your body has complied with whatever command initiated from the supercomputer chip within your head. *Wham!* It's that fast. You see that person from across the room and *wham*: you know you don't like him. You catch a whiff of that appetizer you are allergic to and *bing*: you're going to be sick. The pulsating sound of that music is going to give you a splitting headache. You cringe because that person has the coldest hands. Of all the things we taste, touch, see, smell, and hear, our responses are directly related to our initial, internal conceptions.

Have you ever said out loud or to yourself, "I don't feel so good"? Then slowly but surely your senses seem to amplify themselves, reinforcing that one single idea until soon enough you're sick as a dog.

Another example of negative reinforcement is, what do most of us think about after three o'clock on Sunday afternoon? *Arrgghh! Tomorrow's Monday! I gotta go to work. I gotta do all that crap. I'm gonna be buried underneath paperwork or in endless stupid meetings. Man, where did the weekend go?* There are still hours left in our afternoon and we have the entire evening at our disposal but, for most of us, once we see that clock read after four in the afternoon, our minds are a million miles away. The same can be said for those in their last days of vacation time. Even though folks are a thousand miles away from the daily grind, they've allowed their negative thoughts to *ruin* the time they have left.

Positive Input

On the other side of the coin, what do most of us think about on *Thursday* afternoon after three o'clock? "Oh, yeah, Friday! Can't wait. One more day and I'm outta here!" Whether it's work, school, or just getting away from it all for a while, you're completely jazzed because you've just told yourself what's around the corner. The funny thing is, when Friday rolls around you *still* have the same amount of work, still have to go to school to take that test, or get the house together, or do all the things that you detested not even a day ago, but *now* you don't mind. *The only thing different is what you said to yourself.* It's that plain and that simple! Again, your attitude *is* everything!

All you need to do is reprogram what you say when you talk to yourself. It may not be easy, and like anything in life, it didn't happen overnight, so don't expect it to go away overnight. And as we discussed before, when you want something bad enough, there's a price you pay. In this case, readjusting your attitude and how you talk to yourself and perceive all that's thrown at you will take a fair amount of focus and practice on your part. But if you don't at least try to get a handle on what you think and say, even with the best of intentions and all the drive in the world, with all due respect, you, my friend, will only go so far. I believe that a headful of negative thoughts is like swimming across the English Channel, against the tide, and with lead weights. How can you reach your greatness, your true potential, if you don't have yourself in your own corner? Now, I'm not saying for your ego to grow so huge that your head can't pass through a doorway; No! At least, at the very least, believe in yourself and give yourself the respect and dignity that *you* deserve.

So, you want a change in attitude? Let me give you

two words: THINK DIFFERENTLY! From now on, when Monday morning arrives, since there's nothing you can do to change your external environment, since you can't change the calendar, say to yourself, "Once I knock out this day, I only have three more days until Friday!" "Yeah, today may be a long one, but I get a break in another hour." "Just five more years and these kids will be out of my hair!" With everything you attempt, with everything you tackle—whether it's studying for a test, working on your body, or trying to relax when those dreaded relatives from another planet drop by for a month's long stay—it is vital for you to maintain an overall positive attitude.

For the sake of this example, let's say I'm a doctor and I have twin patients that I have just examined and I say, "Ladies, I am sorry to tell you this, but . . . both of you have a strange genetic illness."

Immediately one of the twins leaps out of her chair, screaming at the top of her lungs before fleeing the office, and runs into the street and gets hit by a bus.

The other twin takes a deep breath as she dabs away a tear before asking, "How bad is it, Doc?"

"Well, it's not that bad at all. The illness you have is benign. I can give you a local and you'll be back on your feet in no time. By the way, where is that sister of yours?"

If you tell yourself that your world is going to end, guess what—and don't be surprised: sooner or later it will. If you tell yourself you're not worthy or you cannot accomplish something, your body will respond to the brain's command.

I am telling you that you are worthy, that you have a sense of purpose and belonging. If you didn't, you would never have picked up this book, read as much as you have, and still wanted more. As always, it's up to you. Outside influences can only help you so far. And, as always, you have to not only want it, but you have to be willing to pay the price, and maintaining a confident mind-set is part of your dues. Trust me: little by little, hour by hour, it will pay off. Sometimes the smallest things can make a world of difference. Years ago, I read a magazine article based on two extremely competitive athletes. After lifting weights for hours, one athlete turns to the other and mocks, "Hey, let's see if you can squat five hundred pounds."

The other, who's just a tad bit shorter, eyes the bar with the stack of weights on it and shakes his head, "Nope, can't be done."

"Come on," mocks the taller one, "give it a try!"

The other athlete shakes his head before muttering, "All right, I'll give it a try, but I know I can't do it." To no one's surprise the man levels the bar with the enormous weights on his shoulders, bends slightly to squat the weight, but quickly rises before he reaches the appropriate level of the exercise. After replacing the bar on the rack, the man shakes his head, panting to his antagonistic friend, "See, I told you I couldn't do it!"

The other man rubs his chin. "I bet you one hundred dollars, cash money, right now, that you can squat that weight."

Suddenly the tired athlete's eyes light up. The entire

look on his face changes. And, as you can probably guess, the weary athlete takes a few deep breaths, channeling his attention solely on the bar before he lifts the weight and executes a perfect squat.

So, what was difference between his first, futile attempt and his triumphant second one? After his failure the odds were overwhelmingly against him. He had expended all his energy with his first try, making it almost impossible for him to accomplish a second effort. And, during all this time, the muscles around his legs were beginning to tighten. To top it all off, he had already spent hours working out different muscle groups throughout his body.

The only thing that changed was this professional's attitude. His mind transformed his entire being and became motivated to win the monetary prize. He shifted his inner focus from what he couldn't do, to what he must and would do, in order to obtain that one singular goal.

Maybe you don't know—or maybe you forgot—but you, too, have accomplished the same thing. Okay, maybe you haven't squatted five hundred pounds, but you've overcome something in your life that was far more vital than forming your quadriceps. Maybe you became mad. Maybe you were scared, or tired of hearing or experiencing the same ol' thing. Whatever the circumstance, in the blink of an eye you changed *how* you thought about something and because of that *you changed your outcome.*

The *F* Word

If you look at our country's history, it was founded upon these two words: *optimistic determination.* Imagine, if you will, the thoughts of those who suddenly found themselves on Plymouth Rock. What about those who trekked across the vast open plains? Or the impression of those who awoke one Sunday morning and found themselves in the middle of a world war? As an individual, you could say, "Well, I don't know; we may sink if we sail across that there ocean." Or "Maybe it's best to stay where we are; why would we wanna go that far west anyway?" Or "Well, heck. We're licked. They got the jump on us. What's the use anyhow?" If you or someone you know has that defeatist attitude, he might as well screech in public, run around like a madman, only to get hit by a bus, just because someone uttered something he didn't want to hear.

As parents, what is the primary reason to have kids engage in sports? So they can learn a sense of fair play and to have them discover for themselves what they're made of.

When Stephen first joined the swim team, to be honest he had no right being in the pool. He could barely keep his head above water and as much as he tried, whenever he became tired I believe Stephen expected to have someone jump in at the last second and take care of him. During one of his first swim meets, Stephen gave it his best, but, alas, could not swim the laps required, so he hung on to the flotation dividers, panting, with all of his energy spent, until he realized no one could or would jump in to help him. So one day, out in the middle of a swimming pool, my son, like millions of other children, when faced with a situation he couldn't deny, kept his cool, and drove away whatever defeating thoughts permeated his mind, so he could extend one stroke, then another, then another, until he reached his goal. As a parent, what mattered most to me was that Stephen kept his head above water and didn't quit.

The *only* way to keep your head above water is to convince yourself *you are* going to make it. There's no other way around it. That's life. At times you will find yourself out in the middle of nowhere, bobbing, all alone, surrounded by an overwhelming vastness, with no one to throw you a life ring, while fighting a wall of water that keeps hitting you and hitting you, wave after wave after wave. It can only take a tablespoon of water to do you in. So, what keeps you afloat? What keeps you going? It's whatever you have stored in your noggin. This is what separates those who succeed from those who sit on the sidelines. Not only do you have to want it more, you have to know in your head and in your heart, without a shred of doubt, that you will—not can, but will—accomplish your task.

The key word is *focus*. When you channel your energies on what you can accomplish it replaces your self-inflicted apprehension. You simply replace your negativity, your fear, your whatever, with something indisputable. Forward or reverse. Sink or swim. In the end, as always, it's up to you.

Take baseball legend Mark McGwire: his focus is so intense during a game that he does not make eye contact with anyone or anything that might break his concentration. The day Mark smashed the all-time seasonal home run record, during the postgame interview he stated, "I believe I can accomplish anything I set my mind to. I've said for the last four or five years that the mind's the strongest thing on your body. It will overtake anything you want to overtake."

Focus.

Focus is my *F* word. I'm not trying to sound racy, but I believe every one of us should think about this *F* word and act on it—every hour of every day of our lives. Focus, focus, focus. In everything you do and say, ask yourself the three important questions, just as motivational personality Roger Crawford teaches. And he is a person who truly knows the powerful influence of what you say when you talk to yourself. *Where* are you at? *What* are you doing? And *Where* are you going? As simplistic as these questions sound, they have resonated within me since I was a child.

Back then, not a single day or even an hour slipped by that I did not evaluate my circumstances and harness whatever I could to better myself. When I say to you, *sometimes the smallest things can make a world of difference,* I swear to you that I truly do mean it. It was not just being aware of my dire situation that enabled me to survive, but more so my centralized concentration. It got me through the torrid hell that my mother subjected me to, propelled me through foster care, allowed me to enlist in the air force and become an aircrew member, and enabled me, against a fair number of obstacles, to have a capable career as an author and presenter. But what matters most, what carries me through the seemingly tumultuous times, is what I was able to acquire, learn, build upon, and harness over the course of many years: a quiet sense of inner determination.

Because of my unfortunate past, I value not what hangs on my wall, the accolades I have displayed in the hallway, the car I drive, whatever clothes hang in the closet, or the arsenal of food in my cupboards. But I value that one thing, that constant drive playing in the back of my head that keeps me on track, ensuring that I will *not* repeat a senseless tragedy of living the rest of my days full of hate and destructiveness. That at any given time, any given situation, I can tap into my secret weapon enabling me to become a fulfilled person and a loving husband. As a parent my sole focus has been and will continue to be ensuring that whatever ill I had experienced will not be passed on to my son.

Focus, focus, focus. Ask yourself, where are you at, right now in your life? What are you truly doing to better yourself or your situation? And where on earth are you going? If you lack a central bearing in your life, replace your doubts, your fears, your whatever, with a positive sense of direction. As in the previous section, be consistent every day, but do so now by fixating on the positive.

When I give credit to Mr. Crawford for his positive self-attitude, I do so with the utmost respect. Roger was born without hands or one leg, and he could easily have obsessed on life's unfairness or on the amount of hardship in his everyday life. Instead, with the aid of prosthetics for his leg and after receiving surgery on his left hand, and a lot of personal determination, Mr. Crawford not only played football in high school, but became the first physically handicapped tennis player to be certified as a teaching professional by the United States Professional Tennis Association. As a teenager he became so secure in himself, as one of his high-school coaches told me, that he showed up for a match with his foot deliberately turned backward. To this day Mr. Crawford is happily married, a father, and inspires others to look past their self-induced limitations.

Brad Van Liew, who sailed around the world alone—a voyage that took him over twenty-seven thousand miles—claims being focused literally kept him alive. "There's no question that the 'Around Alone' is a mental as well as a physical battle. If you're going to handle it, you've got to be tough when it counts." During the course of Brad's grueling nine-month adventure, he dealt with loneliness, sleep deprivation that allowed him a mere three hours of rest a night, and physical endurance in which he had to change the ship's sails thirty to forty times a day. Then, of course, there was Mother Nature. Mr. Van Liew fought to keep his fifty-foot ship afloat amid the thirty-foot waves that capsized his fellow competitors, and another storm that nearly put Brad out of the race by destroying his seventy-five-foot mast. In the end, pitted against tremendous odds and the world's greatest sailors, Mr. Van Liew finished third. So how did he do it? In his own words, Brad states, "You can fulfill your own dreams if you really want to. If there's something you really want to do, something you want to remember on your deathbed, make sure you do it. First, make a plan: start with small steps and work your way up to it. You can set out to do the hugest task in the world, but what you need to focus on is the next little task on your way to reaching it. That way it isn't overwhelming."

Final words of encouragement from Brad conclude with, "People who want to push themselves, to discover what they're capable of physically and mentally, will probably discover that it's easier than they think. It *is* hard to tell yourself to do something that doesn't make sense in your head, like sailing alone around the world. But it certainly isn't impossible."

In the final analysis Mr. Van Liew's positive attitude in the middle of nowhere pulled him through, after fighting to remain afloat during those storms, and then on the last leg of his journey when he lost his carbon fiber mast.

Imagine the endless heated debates inspired by the mere *idea* of sailing a ship beyond the *edge of the world*. "Why, that's blasphemous! Everyone knows the world's flat!" The same can be said of fighting the spread of infection before the advent of penicillin. Or the outlandish boldness of having mankind walk on the moon. "No way, absolutely not. It's just way beyond our reach." A lot of nos, a lot of negativity in the air, but the tide turned when that one person said to himself, "But what if . . . ?"

DAVE PELZER

Turning Adversity to Your Advantage

Yet there are times and situations when even the word *no* itself isn't all that detrimental. As I've stated before, because of my past I was fortunate enough to make something positive from it. Just as did John Walsh from *America's Most Wanted*, Gilda Radner for those fighting cancer, and Marc Klaas, the father of the late Polly Klaas and president of the Polly Klaas Foundation. In most matters it takes an unpleasant or even a critical situation to cause something good.

Personally, in some instances I like the word *no*. If there's something I'm set on, or something I may have taken for granted, and now suddenly there's an obstacle in my path, it makes me all the more focused. I become more dedicated if I truly believe in what I'm attempting. Especially when it comes to others who may deliberately go out of their way to obstruct my goals, I think, I pray, I constantly reevaluate my position and dedication. Throughout the process I try to remain calm and not take things so personally. If I do, it takes away from my *F* word: my focus. And I don't push myself and fight as hard as I do for the purposes of revenge or to put others down. I do so for me; to discover for myself if whatever I'm striving for is what I really desire. But I mainly exert myself to see what I'm made of. I never mind paying the price. At times, in the middle of my crusade, when the odds are against me, I go into overdrive. In the end, no matter the results, I'm more appreciative. I can be proud that I at least gave it my all. When I see that "finger of de-

478

feat" pointed in my direction, I take a breath and from deep within my heart, I smile.

Sometimes negative words or situations can literally force us to "step up to the plate." All of us have had to cram for that test, muster up more strength during a sporting event, or work smarter at the workplace. And as you well know, our results were far better than we expected. Years ago a friend of mine, Tina, was in the middle of an emotionally trying divorce and had committed herself to losing some weight—against her former husband's expectations. She informed me that during their relationship, Tina's husband constantly berated her about her size. In the beginning my friend wanted to lose weight, mainly out of spite. Tina's goal was to step into their favorite restaurant, wearing a black spaghetti-strap dress, with all eyes—especially her ex's—on her. As motivation can be a valuable tool, Tina was able to *rid* herself of the weight quicker, when I convinced her to do it for herself and not just for revenge.

And, yes, Tina waltzed into the restaurant. And, yes, all eyes were on her. Her former husband's mouth had to be scraped up from the floor, and everyone was astounded when Tina, who once had been shy and soft-spoken, now waved her freshly manicured red fingernail at this man and uttered, "Big mistake! Huge!"

Another friend of mine, Helen, one of my former air force superiors, told me about how she turned things around for herself. "In my day, because I was a girl I always heard no. Girls don't play sports. Women can't have a professional career. And it's not like the air force

479

exactly welcomed me with open arms. I always had to work harder and faster just to make par with my male counterparts. But inside I knew. I knew my capabilities and my self-worth." Helen not only obtained one of the highest ranks in the air force, but also became the squadron's first sergeant in charge of the 350-plus personnel. When not on call twenty-four hours a day, the person who couldn't achieve because of her gender not only had a stellar career, but raised two teenage girls, completely on her own while pursuing a master's degree.

I asked Helen how she felt after having swum against the tide for so many years. "Wouldn't change a thing. I earned it. Respect, dignity, you name it. I earned it all. I held my head high and pressed on!" "And what about all those folks who put you down?" I asked her. "I never did mind much. I got used to it. I turned it around to my advantage. Folks who put you down aren't willing to work as hard. They're so busy discouraging everyone else, they lose their edge. All I did was say to myself, 'Watch out, don't count me out.'" Smiling at me, Helen concluded, "If I teach my girls anything, it's they're going to be exposed to a lot of negativity and no one can change that. It's how they discern and process that information that counts. It's all in the head. Mind over matter. *I don't mind and the trivial rubbish doesn't matter.*"

On the extreme side of the scale, when it comes to telling someone what he can't do, is one of the country's greatest track stars, Steve Prefontaine. Just hours before an important track meet, Steve severely injured his foot. Now, imagine the excruciating pain of setting a record, running for miles with a swollen foot with stitches between your toes. "Doc said no, coach said don't do it. But being stupid and getting my foot mangled brought me back to reality and made me want it more."

Do you remember the 1984 Summer Olympics when Greg Louganis struck the edge of the diving board with his head? Imagine the force of all that weight coupled with the momentum. Imagine slicing your head in front of millions of people watching you from all over the world. Yet this professional had the inner determination to climb back up the ladder, stand on the edge of the diving board, spring up, and execute a perfect dive, capturing the gold medal. When asked how did he make such an incredible comeback, Mr. Louganis basically stated, "I was definitely scared. I had a fair amount of doubt. I just pushed it away. I worked hard my entire life for this one moment. I couldn't just walk away."

As a teenager, when Michael Jordan was told he was not *good enough* to make the cut for his high-school basketball team, I can only guess how determined that made Michael, forcing him to practice far more than his peers, and with far more intense enthusiasm.

Oprah Winfrey, Arnold Schwarzenegger, Nelson Mandela, Gilda Radner, Michael Jordan, Colin Powell, along with countless others brushed aside whatever negativity faced them and instead decided for themselves, focusing on something better. You and I are no different.

DAVE PELZER

What You Make of Your Internal World

None of us can escape negativity; it's only how we deal with it that truly matters. When it comes to maintaining an optimistic attitude, there is no way in the world that any of us can or ever will evade the word *no* or the traces it has on us all. In fact, you will be subjected to million upon millions of *no*s, along with a host of other skeptical words and phrases. But it takes only one single *yes* to turn things around. And that solitary word has to first resonate from within you.

When it comes to no and all of its connotations, plain and simple: we are immersed in it. Given that fact, the only option we have is to learn to adapt. As I said before, I don't mind the word no. Besides my upbringing and all the negativity that went with it, I have had so many people in my life who have gone out of their way to put me down, trip me up, or make me feel as if I were completely moronic or not worthy enough. I've also known some who have worked themselves into a vicious frenzy to ensure they either kept me in my place or would never allow me to reach my goal. And many of you have had your own negative experiences with others. Again that's a fact of life. Nothing's free. And if everything in life were that easy, everyone would be doing it.

Because of my former situation, I was able to learn how extremely vital it was to influence and control whatever I said to myself. Once, during one of my afternoon kitchen beatings, I found myself unable to crawl away. I simply lay sprawled out on the floor with blood pouring from my mouth and nose. Between kicks, Mother would rant the same words that I had heard all of my life. And yet through the pain and even a sense of numbness, I remember turning my head, making eye contact with Mother, and, out of nowhere I smiled at her. I pierced deep into her eyes and vowed to myself, *I'm going to make it. You'll see, one day I'm going to make it. You're not going to break me. I'm better than that.*

At that time I didn't feel vengefulness against Mother or pity for myself, but rather a secure sense of pride and self-worth. I knew on the outside that Mother thought I was stupid. To her I was worthless, weak, only useful as a thing to vent her problems on. I stuttered; I smelled. In a word: I was pathetic. But I heard a tiny, quiet voice within me that persisted in the midst of the madness saying I would somehow, someday, become the person on the outside that I was from within.

It worked. Once I was rescued and placed in foster care, and as teenager desperately trying to be normal and fit in—so someone might, maybe, just maybe, like me—I quickly saw how many teens *acted* and how fast they got themselves in extreme detrimental situations. Yes, I was a geek, nerd, wacko, weirdo, ash-white, pimple-faced, skinny rat with glasses . . . on the outside. But I kept telling myself every single day and sometimes many times during the day, if needed, "I didn't survive all that crap just to throw everything away." Even though I wasn't cool, didn't have a girlfriend or drive a car, or even have the latest shoes, I knew I was okay. In the end, when it mattered most, I would stand on top of any mountain that I chose.

If I may, for my young adults reading this now—and this is after seeing and experiencing all that I have and working with young adults as long as my son's been alive—my advice to you is: Stick to your guns. Don't throw your best away. *You are better than that.* With all the frustration and immense temptation out there, not now but one day soon *you will* have the things you want and be able *to do as you please.* And when you do, I guarantee you that you'll appreciate the life *you made for yourself* all the more. Why? Because you did it. You held your head high. You showed some resolve, some discipline, and didn't plunge after every quick fix that came your way. Now, my dear friend, that is the makings of a mature person, or in other words: a responsible adult.

On every major thing I've attempted, I've always had to crawl my way to success. As a foster kid in a new neighborhood, there was one lady who exclaimed, "Oh, my Gawd! You're one of those—those *foster children!* I don't know what you did to become what you are, but let me give you a piece of advice: Stick to your own kind. If you try to make it, you'll only end up disappointing yourself. But I can see that you're quite used to that, aren't you?" Even though I felt like a worthless tiny ant in front of her, I kept my cool, clutching my hands behind me while smiling back.

When the air force said they didn't want me, I smiled inside, developed a plan, and showed up every day for over six months at the recruiter's office until I wore them down. It took me another three years and endless hurdles and disappointments until I received one yes to have the chance of becoming an aircrew member. I have had obese, disheveled, clip-on-suspenders types of "professional motivational speakers" dribble to me that I wasn't "cookie cutter" enough, and because I was *abused* that I didn't stand a chance of possibly inspiring others. I won't even begin to go into my journey of becoming a bona fide author and eventually working with a New York–based publisher—finally having professionals on my side. For years upon years I've stood up to my ears in insults and negativity. Yet because of what I learned that one day sprawled out on the kitchen floor, I've remained focused on my prize, made an effort every day to improve my position, and kept a clear head while all the time smiling inside, saying, "Don't count me out. I've fought hard before and will do so again. In the end, righteousness will prevail."

You are no different. You've fought battles and you've overcome struggles; so tell me, tell yourself: what got you through it all? What was the one thing that carried you over the hump? That made you take all those hits and remain standing tall? YOUR INNER ATTITUDE. It was *what you said to yourself* when push came to shove. At that one fraction of that one second, out of those fifty thousand thoughts you had swimming around in your head, you said, "Thanks, but no thanks. I'd like to, but I have other obligations. I'm better than that. I'm not much now, but watch out: I'll be back! I am somebody and I'm worth it!" "Sail across the world, you're right: that's never been done before . . . but what if . . . ?" *People who want to push themselves, to discover what they're capable of physically and mentally, will probably discover that it's easier than they think. . . . It certainly isn't impossible.*

One, just one, positive thought can change your attitude, tell your body how to react, can lead you to that one tiny action that can change the course of your life and the world around you; can help you fulfill not only your dreams but your destiny. Just one thought!

You need to take this into your heart when I say to you that in the beginning, middle, and in the end it's what you say to yourself from deep within that truly matters. Do you even realize how strong that is? If you don't love yourself, how can you expect others to care about you? If you don't believe in yourself, how can you gain the trust and respect of others? How can you get through every day of the rest of your life? Again, you are a person of worth. A person of substance. You have unique abilities and qualities that no one else can match. And, like everybody else, you survived all that you have up to this point because of a little voice, that one thought inside your head. So, think different. Think different, act different, live different. Live better. If what you're doing isn't working, then *do* something different.

America was founded by an impossible dream of a better life for one and all. We didn't even have capable rockets, yet we stretched ourselves with the belief that as a nation we could and would land a man on the moon. *America's Most Wanted* exists thanks to the incredible strength and courage of John Walsh, whose son was murdered. When Martin Luther King stood in front of a mass of people and cried, "I have a dream . . ." he changed the course of history. Because one parent had the guts to make a stand after her child died after being struck down by a drunk driver with known repeated offenses, we now have MADD—Mothers Against Drunk Drivers.

Everything around you—from the water in your home, the paper that you write on, the music from your CD player, to the medicine you take—owes its existence to *someone* taking a no and turning it into a yes. It didn't happen right away, but the smallest amount of optimism can make the world of difference. And if not a difference in the world as a whole, then in you as a person.

So, how do you survive all this negativity? I don't mean to sound crude—as I know of no other way to tip-toe around this matter—but when you hear crap, when you become exposed to filth, or when others go out of their way to fling mud in your direction, you've got to wipe it off and flush everything away, as soon as you can, before it contaminates your brain. Don't allow any crap to get under your skin and into your head! Disinfect yourself, scrape it off, and move on. Replace negativity with something positive. Immediately! Instead of telling yourself no, say maybe, then build up to yes. It's not im-possible—hard, yes, but it *is* possible. When disaster be-falls you, is there anything you take from it to make yourself better, wiser, more appreciative?

Tell yourself, "I've been through worse before, so I can certainly do this." "I never did mind the *little* things." Take a step back, collect yourself, and calmly state, "It's okay." "It's not that bad." "I'm going to be fine." When you've been thrown on the mat, battered and bruised, vow to yourself, "Righteousness will prevail!" "I know in my heart what is true!" Get into the habit. Deflect the negative. As you would a pestering bug, swat it away.

So, out with crap. If it doesn't do you any good, dump it. Take some action, push that lever, flush it away, and don't look back. Take small steps, every single day of your life, and start taking control of what you say when you talk to yourself.

HELP YOURSELF REMINDERS

* YOUR DAY STARTS WITH *WHAT* YOU SAY TO YOURSELF.

* IMMERSE YOURSELF IN POSITIVE INPUTS.

* FOCUS, FOCUS FOCUS: WHERE ARE YOU AT IN YOUR LIFE? WHAT ARE YOU DOING TO MAKE THINGS BETTER? AND WHERE ARE YOU GOING?

* A LITTLE BIT OF ADVERSITY CAN HELP TO REALIGN YOU, MAKE YOU HUMBLE, AND MAKE YOU WANT IT MORE.

* IT'S MIND OVER MATTER—YOU DON'T MIND ALL THE CRAP "OUT THERE" BECAUSE NONE OF IT MATTERS!

8

Creating Your Own Positive Environment

Now that we know the importance of what we say to ourselves, I want to emphasize another way of deflecting negativity by surrounding yourself with a positive environment that *you create*. As we all know how detrimental a negative setting can be, most of us forget the extreme importance of an affirmative one. When facing the every-day sludge that life can throw at us, I think of a positive environment as a protective shield. Family, friends, loved ones, that close-knit group at work and at church, and other specialized organizations are the perfect outlet to draw inspiration, become motivated, and even gain a shoulder to lean on.

I cannot stress enough the importance of having *some-one* not only to talk to or to listen to your fears and dreams, but *someone* who has the same qualities and holds the same set of values as you. As cute as *opposites attract* sounds, I recommend you use more discernment and look at the character of the individual.

As you know, you can't go through life all alone. All of us need assistance and inspiration from time to time. While out in the middle of the ocean, Brad Van Liew drew strength from his wife and a small band of friends constantly pulling for him and, as Mr. Van Liew put it, in some cases giving him a kick in the pants.

We've all heard those seemingly insignificant words *I'm proud of you, Don't give up, You can do it*, but isn't it amazing the absolute power of those words coming from someone you know and trust? To me *that's* the heart of a positive environment. Being with those you feel safe and secure with, enough to open up to, to expose your inner self, for the purpose of empowering you to become a better person. *That's* the value of a positive environment!

If anyone knows about the benefits of receiving help from a realistic, nurturing environment among close family and friends, it's Toni Braxton. Even though Ms. Braxton had two top-selling, multiplatinum albums and was the recipient of five Grammys, there was a time when she wasn't sure she would ever record another album. When Ms. Braxton found herself in the middle of a bitter contract dispute with her record label, which in turn led her to file for bankruptcy, she was humiliated to the point that even her Grammy awards were stickered with price tags. Yet it was her friends and family who helped Toni with that little encouragement when she needed it. Record producer and ally Kenny "Babyface" Edmonds said to her, "You know how to produce yourself. Go do it." For Toni to have someone like Babyface, whom she looked up to as a big brother in the business, "that made me feel real good." With a little inspiration Ms. Braxton is now a stronger, wiser person and after four years has another top-selling album.

But a positive environment isn't all candy canes, soda pops, and warm cuddles. As much as we use it to draw encouragement from, it can also be a hard dose of reality for us when needed. After years of living an internal hell, Oprah Winfrey's life turned for the better when she moved in with her father, a caring but "no-nonsense" individual. Through the many interviews I've seen and read about Ms. Winfrey, she credits her father's tough love for helping make her the woman she is today. While surrounding her with encouragement and praise, it is said that Ms. Winfrey's father also made sure that Oprah read anything she could lay her hands on, and above all expected nothing but the best from her.

What's great about a positive environment is surrounding yourself with those whom you trust, but is not about being told only what you want to hear. It's the reality of the truth. As my lovely bride likes to point out, this is one of the many benefits of the institution called marriage. As much as I do as an author, presenter, and comedic storyteller, my wife is always happy to inform me when I have floundered; when I've stepped or am about to step past the edge. Why? Because she knows my capabilities and expects nothing less. And because we trust each other, I not only can open up to her all the more, but can value the sometimes-hard-to-swallow critiques that in the end keep me grounded, more focused, and a better person as a whole.

Real-Life Resources

But in today's world there are a great number of folks who aren't content with the invaluable everyday resources that are so readily available to them. Rather than take advice from people who actually, truly know them, these folks prefer to wait for the next motivational, all-knowing, quasi-immortal guru to sweep them off their feet and have them live in some distant paradise where they can dedicate themselves to their "conduit of peace." Now, with all due respect, if that's what adults unequivocally wish to do with their lives and they truly believe in that certain cause, and if it makes them happy, well, then, more power to them. I am only trying to emphasize how many times over the years I have seen seemingly lost people throw their lives and worldly possessions away in the vain hope of finding their way through to some divinelike environment. Why travel across the desert if your well is right in front of you?

As mentioned in the very beginning of this book, no one has all the answers. And I highly advise you to stay clear of those who righteously claim they do. The truth is, those seemingly mundane words like, "Come on, don't quit," "Everything's gonna be great," "I believe in you," are the ones that have an extraordinary impact on our lives!

Off the top of your head, how many teachers can you name? Now, how many of those close friends can you recall for every class you had in school, or those select few you were just dying to have a date with? I may be wrong here, but you probably came up with more teachers than those friends whom at the time you couldn't live without. Why? Because *they* were the ones who truly had a genuine influence on your life. As much as we habitually draw from bad experiences, I think it's time we turned that around and tapped—if not *drilled*—into those positive former experiences as well. You'll find those experiences from everyday folks who know you, who don't have all the answers or even the responses you wish to hear, but are definitely the folks making a world of difference in your life today!

So don't wait for the next guru messiah to provide you with divine guidance for every one of life's encounters. That's not going to happen. For me, what I've found that does in fact work every single time is drawing strength and encouragement from myself and a close group of folks that I have a relationship with. Those folks whom I trust and whose opinions I value.

In all my years of helping others I've met so many who said, "I gotta meet Oprah, so *she* can help me!" Or "When I see Arnold, *he'll* become my workout coach!" I realize this may sound obvious, and not to burst anyone's bubble, but it ain't gonna happen! Even with the slightest of chances of bumping into Ms. Winfrey, Mr. Schwarzenegger, Colin Powell, or even someone else who may have had similar experiences to yours, they can only give you a fraction of their time. And even if they throw you a piece of advice such as "Keep a good spirit," "Maintain a healthy body for a healthy mind," "Pursue a solid education," or "I'm sorry you went through that situation, too," there is no way you can have an ongoing affiliation with folks such as these. Again, too many individuals put *their faith in others* rather than in themselves or what's in front of them and readily available. I freely admit that every one of those folks deserves respect, has an incredible message to share with the world, and can *help* inspire us to better ourselves, but that's as far as it goes. Do you have Oprah's cell phone number and can you call her anytime you wish? Can you page Colin Powell whenever you feel the need? No, you can't. *But* you can turn to a family member, someone at work, or that one close friend of yours, for advice. A twelve-step sponsor is only a phone call away. A hug of encouragement is just an arm's reach away. But believing in yourself is the first step.

After all I've just said, if folks still only place little value on the ordinary positive surroundings, then I ask how was I—after the extreme negative environment I've been subjected to—able to become a kind and loving husband and father, and a decent member of our society? With years of enduring psychological and physical torture from my deranged mother, and even while in foster care when certain individuals went out of their way to brag openly about my limited chances of any "normal social adjustment" (while being kind enough to bestow their own credit on my inner determination), it was in fact my foster parents who took me into their homes— when no one else would have me—and who not only made me a part of their family, but gave me a strong sense of values that I could draw from. As a teenager,

when I stepped out of line, my hard-nosed social workers would scold me by asking, "Aren't you better than
that?" While in the air force, when I had to take a pre-
algebra class for the third time, there was this one instructor with the patience of a saint who said the one
thing that enabled me to understand the workings of
numbers, even though he had stated the same thing to
me a hundred plus times before. It has been and always
will be true that the resources of a positive environment
are what are in and around you. If you can pick and
choose who and what to stay away from when it comes
to staying clear of a negative setting, you can certainly
take advantage of selecting from a positive one.

I believe that for every single negative you hear about
yourself, it takes dozens of positives to counter that one
appalling spoken word or that singular bad experience.
In my case, I was able to absorb, to draw from every single seemingly ordinary constructive event, which in turn
propelled me to become the person I am today. That is
the honest-to-God truth! It wasn't meeting some Hollywood celebrity, pretentious radio talk-show host, or that
onetime weekend walking on coals that left such an extraordinary effect on my life. All of those may have
somehow affected our lives, but fleetingly at best. And
you deserve better than that.

I fully realize that not all things work for or apply to all
people. I'm sure, though in my heart I hope it's not true,
that there are some who feel they have no one to turn to
for support that *all* of us need. For that I am truly sorry.
There have been many, many times in my life, just as in

everyone's, when I have felt dejected and completely isolated. As crazy as this sounds, with all the 900 adult entertainment and psychic telephone services there are, I wish
there were a 1-900-*Have-a-Nice-Day* line. Wouldn't it be
great to pick up the line, get something off your chest,
and feel just a little bit better afterward, knowing you're
not alone, the world's not going to end, and tomorrow is
indeed another day? (This is one of the reasons I would
love to have my own radio show!) Heck, in our hypersonic telecommunication age it might be a good thing!
And yet, if one looks hard enough, there are in fact many
outreach services readily available within one's community. Help is there for those who seek it.

And, after all of this, if some folks still feel they do not
have any positive elements in their lives, still feel alone
and worthless, then with all due respect I say: "Get off
your butt and help out others who are worse off than
you!" For folks who think they don't have enough, I recommend spending a few hours a week helping out at a
homeless shelter. For those who believe they're all alone,
I advise manning the phones at suicide prevention or
runaway hotlines. Once I had a person so wrapped up in
his own despair that I took him to visit children diag-
nosed with cancer, AIDS, and other terminal diseases.
Thankfully, afterward this gentleman sobbed, "What do *I*
have to complain about?"

Indeed.

You and I are not alone. We are not the only ones with
insurmountable troubles, for there is always someone
somewhere who's worse off than ourselves. Not to

sound hard nosed, but I highly recommend the film *Saving Private Ryan*. After watching the first thirty minutes, I realized—even after all I have been put through—that I have nothing, and I mean nothing, to complain about. I don't mean to confuse anyone, for it's great and necessary to get things off our chests. And I highly recommend doing just that; however, I only wish to make the point that as individuals we have to make the most of what we have, and when you reach out to assist others, when *you* become that mentor to others, you are in fact creating your own positive environment!

Look at Oprah! She had serious issues, received everyday, commonsense guidance, and is now helping millions! Colin Powell, raised in the ghetto, worked incredibly hard to receive his education, and is now in charge of "America's Promise, The Alliance for Youth" giving his all for other children to better themselves. Nelson Mandela was imprisoned for many years because of his race and his political views, yet became the president of the country that had persecuted him! It all began with the courage to make that change.

Creating your positive environment begins with the little things, so, as I have already advised, take consistent small daily steps. I again recommend the same for your own setting. Once a day, do at least three nice things for others. Just three little seemingly insignificant things every day for the rest of your life. Open the door for that person. When someone cuts you off in traffic, spare your energy by not giving him the bird. If you see someone who can use some spare change, buy her a Happy Meal.

Feeling bad about your own esteem? Then compliment others: "And good morning to you, Denise. Love your hair!" "Hi, Bob, now that's a sharp tie!" "Hey, girlfriend, where did you get those shoes?" "Hello, Matt. Nice toupee!"

That positive environment always has and always will begin with you! And it's what you say to yourself that leads you either to victory or defeat; happiness or despair; mind over matter.

Self-Evaluation

When you watch what you say when you talk to yourself, *listen* to what is being said. Again I know it sounds a little foolish, but do just that. Since listening is the most neglected of all communications skills and we now know the extreme importance of our initial internal thoughts, take it to the next step and improve your own position.

Start with this: Next Monday morning when you go to work, off to school, or do whatever you do, *listen* to what *others say* when they talk about *themselves*. Do they complain much about every single insignificant thing in their lives? Are they constantly making excuses? Are they happy? Do they seem fulfilled or content in any way? What about their body language? Watch their breathing. Is it strained or labored? Are their shoulders hunched over? Do they have bags under their eyes from lack of a sound sleep? Observe how these folks react with others and how productive they actually are. Given, on Mondays, for a fair amount of us, it's hard to get back into the swing of things. And everybody has bad days and even a run of hard times, but over time folks like these are so despondent with themselves, they can barely accomplish anything outside of their problematic realm.

On the other hand, have you seen those people who are constantly chipper? Nothing gets them that down. When push comes to shove these individuals hunker down and do whatever it takes to accomplish their tasks. At times these folks seem so overly optimistic that you're not quite sure if they're on some unlicensed medication. They have dreams and wide-eyed ambitions, and even when bad luck or negative situations befall them, these people seemingly brush it off as if it weren't a big deal. They have the eyes that always seem to be smiling. For them the glass is half full. They create their own environment from within. Their enthusiasm is infectious. And those are the folks whom you want to watch. They are the ones going places!

Now for some, these folks might seem downright odd. But ask yourself: out of the two examples, whom would your rather surround yourself with?

As you know, the brain thinks in pictures rather than words and as you visualize something good or bad, the brain in a sense leads you in that direction. This is why it is imperative for you to control how and what you think! And to stay positive is to do exactly that. Taking control of the everyday turmoil, not allowing things to get you down, destroy you, or take away your passion for a fulfilled life!

When I think of one person who is the master of hard work, envisioning his own destiny years ahead himself, I think of Arnold Schwarzenegger. If you want to see someone with a confident attitude, watch this man whenever he's on the television talk-show circuit.

Years ago, when I didn't even know Arnold's name, I happened to catch him on an afternoon talk show that went something like this: "So, Arnold, tell us about your latest film." "You know I'm so excited to be here. I tell you, for years I worked hard on my body, chiseling every inch to perfection, knowing all the time that I would use it as a tool to get me into movies in America. For me that was my big dream. That's why I'm a success. I see nothing in front of me but endless opportunity. In this film I push myself, I work hard to ensure I have the best body, for my fans expect nothing less. You will also see so much action, you'll feel as if you're in the movie yourself. I've never seen or been a part of anything like it. It's just incredible. And now that I've established myself as an actor, I plan to explore new boundaries, different character dimensions, the works. In fact, in my next film . . ."

Wow! As shamelessly "pluggish" as Mr. Schwarzenegger may be, listen carefully. He tells you where he was, what he has just accomplished, and what he plans on accomplishing next. "When I see it in my mind, it becomes crystallized, and I take whatever steps necessary to make it happen. I follow through!" The intensity of his eyes and his body language match his enthusiasm, not neces-

sarily for the film he's promoting, but more so on his attitude about his life in general. When he talks about his
past, one of his hands is about knee level. Then when
Arnold discusses what he has just accomplished, his hand
rises to his chest. But by the time he tells the audience his
goals for the future, his hand is just above his eyes and all
the time his smile widens with each and every incline.
Besides his lovely wife and children, Arnold claims his
biggest asset is his limitless positive internal environment.

So what's your internal environment like? When you
observe others, what can you learn about yourself in the
process? Do you needlessly rant and complain? Do you
make infinite excuses? Do you find yourself too defensive? Or are you optimistic? When the going gets tough
do you tell yourself that you will do whatever it takes to
make things happen?

When you're feeling blue, do you allow that to pull
you down, or do you make the most of it? Do you go out
of your way to brighten other people's day, rather than
wallow in your own abyss of doom and gloom? Again,
it's up to you. It's all a matter of weeding out the bad and
cultivating more productive thoughts. And just like
pulling weeds, you have to get to the root of the problem;
otherwise that weed, that self-doubt, that negative pro-
gramming, will spring back up and choke off the flower
that can blossom for you in the future. Be consistent. Apply that "weed off" whenever you feel the need. Every
day see the brighter side of things. Continually tell your-

self how lucky you are, how good your life is right now, and how things can only get better.

Don't wait! Now, starting NOW—not tomorrow, next week, next month, or even next year—THINK DIFFER-ENTLY! Deflect all that exterior crap that you probably have little control over in the first place and begin by in-structing yourself that things aren't that bad. When oth-ers put you down, smile inside while telling yourself you are better than that. When others laugh at your delusions of grandeur, tell yourself you will give it all you have, you don't mind paying the price, and how much you will enjoy the journey.

I promise you this: If you carry a bad attitude, you have no chance of being happy, let alone living up to your full potential and achieving your greatness. With a positive mind and a nurturing environment, what can you not truly accomplish? You keep a clear head and an optimistic attitude—day in and day out—and you *will* see a miraculous difference! This I guarantee!

The truth: You may not get the "brass ring," but you will live a better life! Remember, it takes about twenty-seven separate facial muscles to frown and about nine-teen to smile. So reach down deep inside. No matter how hard life hits you, no matter how long it takes, do what-ever it takes. And smile, smile, smile!

I beg of you to take this with you always: Help Your-self . . . to a life you are not only capable of living, but are worthy of living. *It's all in your mind . . . that's where every-thing matters.*

HELP YOURSELF REMINDERS

* DRAW SUPPORT FROM THOSE YOU KNOW AND TRUST.

* CONSISTENTLY KEEP YOURSELF IN CHECK WITH THE ENVIRONMENT THAT YOU CREATE.

EPILOGUE

One Final Note

Congratulations. *You* did it. You stuck it out, you took the time, dedication, and the energy to enhance your life and I am proud of you! You made a commitment to read the material and you followed through. In this day and age, with so much happening to us all at such tremendous speed, I fully realize and appreciate how precious your time is. Of the endless number of self-help books out there, you were willing to invest some of your hard-earned money and take a chance on this one, and that means the world to me. I only hope you are willing to extract and implement parts of this book that apply to your life now and to come, so as to make a significant difference in you. That is my sole desire.

In the first section we learned that all of us, every single person on this planet, face difficult situations of one degree or another, and that we cannot move forward unless we free ourselves from the shackles of our past. We know that unless we have the knowledge, courage, and

constant discipline to maintain our distance from negative settings, there is a chance—but not the excuse—that
we can become a carbon copy of that environment. That
above all, bad things happen to decent folks every single
day, and feelings of animosity or revenge, at any level, do
no one any good and can either take away our whole-
someness or kill us a little bit each and every day ...
until we become what we once detested.

We realized that if we have no goals or even the slightest amount of ambition, we will end up going nowhere.
That what truly matters for nearly all of us is actually the
everyday simple things that are so readily available. That
for everything in life we desire, we have to be willing
to forfeit something for our cause. And we know that
achieving enormous goals requires unyielding dedication and patience, coupled with a fair amount of luck.

That in the end, the sincere appreciation of who we are
and what we have thus far should suffice, and that anything extra that comes into our lives is a bonus, which
can only make our lives the more enjoyable. That diligent
labor is important, yet making the most of our days by
doing things that make us feel fulfilled is just as vital.
That a sustained, proactive environment not only nur-
tures, but can be used as a shield so we can live with less
turmoil and fewer distractions. How a slight amount of
negativity is not only inescapable, but in fact can be used
as a catalyst to better ourselves. That a steadfast, strong,
positive attitude inside ourselves or when we deal with
the world around us makes all the difference.

We see that America is truly the land where God has

shed His grace on thee. Yet perhaps the extraordinary thing about America is not solely its boundless opportunities for one and all, but the guaranteed, undisputable right of the pursuit of happiness. It by no means implies the absolute right for an auspicious life, but rather to simply live a life as we choose. If one wishes to fulfill this promise and be happy, America is a phenomenal place to be.

Every single one of us knows something about resilience. As you were reading, did you tell yourself, "Hey, I've been through worse than that," or "If that person can do it, then I certainly can too!"? Did you find that *you* in fact have some of the same persevering traits as those who were used as examples? Did you rediscover that even in the midst of adversity you are not counted out unless *you* say so? That no matter the past or present situation, you in fact have ownership to your life and deserve to live your life on your own terms?

However, if there was one theme that I want to shine throughout this book, the singular thread that I hope you will weave into your life is the fact that nothing can dominate the hunger, the unstoppable drive, of the human spirit. *Nothing.* Not the test of time, any technology mankind can devise, or any form of oppression—no matter how monumental. Nothing comes close to matching the determination from within you! If you walk away with nothing else, please take that knowledge with you. The only element stopping you is you.

But now that our time together is through, I must emphasize that now it's up to you. Now is the time to follow through, to go the distance, to activate yourself on what you have now acquired. As I have previously stated, this book, myself, or others you know can only propel you so far. If you feel excited, ready to jump up and tackle the world, understand that that stimulation will soon fade. Don't get me wrong; being enthusiastic is great, but don't get so wound up that you use up all your energy ahead of time. Or if you hit a few bumps in life, or run into a roadblock, you turn away, flee, and give up. Personally, I think you've come too far to do that.

My advice: Stay on course. Take a stand and implement a change. Just be consistent in your endeavors. Want it, crave it, do it . . . on a daily basis. Like brushing your teeth whenever you get up each day and before going to bed: take the time required to hit those "hard-to-reach places," then walk away with something to smile about. Dedicate yourself to your changes, so they become a part of your life.

Again the changes may seem small and even insignificant. When we brush our teeth, we don't always walk away with a blinding radiant smile, but imagine not only how our smile would look but the overall condition of our mouths and gums if we did not consistently brush? Trust me, overall you will be so much better off by stepping out of that comfort zone and applying yourself in a positive direction. I'm not going to sugarcoat this: You will teeter and even fall, but simply stand up, brush yourself off, and be all the wiser next time.

I fully realize *Help Yourself* has dealt with some fairly serious topics. My intention was to show you that life, even with all its fury, *does not* have to be so arduous. That even in the midst of chaos, the world is not going to end. With positive perseverance, things do get better. And how can you be an astute businessperson, a loving, guiding parent, an intimate partner, a good student, or live your life as an everyday productive person if you do not take care of your most important asset: yourself?! The answer is you can't. So as much as you apply yourself, don't forget to stop and pick more daisies along the way. Enjoy! Go out and have an ice cream, and hold the hand of someone you love. Do it today!

I only ask one more thing from you: Please don't let it end here. Digest what you can and skim through the parts when you need more clarification or that extra shot in the arm. Just don't quit on yourself. Remember that all of us are worthy and we all deserve to be happy. All you have to do now is do what has to be done. As the beloved Ms. Winfrey once stated, "Now that you know better, do better."

As I close, please permit me to say that it has been an honor for me. I pray the time we spent together will enable you to live your life with a little more dignity, honor, and sense of conviction. If you ever think you are unworthy, that you're reaching too far, that you will never be happy, do me this favor as you read these words:

Imagine a small boy who lives in the bottom of a cold, dark basement. A lonely, terrified child with yellowish skin, wounds and bruises all over his body. A child with no one and nothing to turn to, who is either doomed to die or destined to spend the rest of his life in a living hell. This was the life for a child called "It."

After everything, against all odds, if that little boy can now live a happy, fulfilled, productive life, with all due respect, what is stopping you? In the end there is little that is insurmountable if you are simply willing to help yourself.

With all of my heart I wish you Godspeed on all your journeys and God's blessings on your endeavors. I wish you my very best. Live a good life. Be happy.

Dave Pelzer

About the Author

A retired air force aircrew member, Dave played a major role in Operations Just Cause, Desert Shield, and Desert Storm. Dave was selected for the unique task of mid-air refueling of the once highly secretive SR-71 Blackbird and the F-117 Stealth Fighter. While serving in the air force, Dave worked in juvenile hall and other programs involving "youth at risk" throughout California.

Dave's exceptional accomplishments include commendations from Presidents Reagan, Bush, and Clinton, as well as other heads of state. While maintaining an international active-duty flight schedule, Dave was the recipient of the 1990 J. C. Penney Golden Rule Award, making him the California Volunteer of the Year. In 1993, Dave was honored as one of the Ten Outstanding Young Americans (TOYA), joining a distinguished group of alumni that includes Chuck Yeager, Christopher Reeve, Anne Bancroft, John F. Kennedy, Orson Welles, and Walt

Disney. In 1994, Dave was the *only* American to be selected as one of The Outstanding Young Persons of the World (TOYP), for his efforts involving child-abuse awareness and prevention, as well as for instilling resilience in others. During the centennial Olympic Games, Dave was a torch bearer, carrying the coveted flame.

Dave is one of the only authors to have three books simultaneously on the *New York Times* bestseller list. Dave's first book, *A Child Called "It,"* has been on the *New York Times* bestseller list for over two years. Dave's second book, *The Lost Boy,* has been on the same list for over one year and Dave's third book, *A Man Named Dave,* was an instant *New York Times* bestseller.

Dave is currently working on his next book, *The Privilege of Youth.* His future works will then include themes of humor in relationships.

When not on the road or with his wife, Marsha, or son, Stephen, Dave is either traipsing through Carmel or living a quiet life in Southern California, with his box turtle named Chuck.

You can visit Dave's Web site at **www.davepelzer.com** for more on Dave.

Some of the names in this book have been changed in order to protect the dignity and privacy of others.

KEYNOTES

Dave's unique and inspirational outlook on life, coupled with his "Robin Williams" like wit and sense of humor, entertain and encourage business professionals to overcome any obstacle while living life to its fullest. Dave is a living testament of resilience, faith in humanity, and personal responsibility. This is what makes him one of the most exceptional and unequaled personalities in corporate America today.

Dave also provides specific programs to those who work in the human services and educational fields.

For additional information on having Dave for your group, please call us, fax us, or visit our Web site at:

D-ESPRIT
P.O. Box 1846
Rancho Mirage, CA 92270
Phone: 760-321-4452
Fax: 760-321-6842
www.davepelzer.com

And for those who wish to write letters to Dave, please include a SASE and keep in mind that due to the large volume of letters we receive daily, we will not be able to answer every letter. But we sincerely thank you for your time and support.